THE STANDA
COMPLETE PSYCHOLOGICAL WORKS
OF SIGMUND FREUD

VOLUME VII

**19 BERGGASSE, VIENNA**
Freud's home and consulting rooms from 1891 to 1938

# The Standard Edition of the Complete Psychological Works of Sigmund Freud

## Volume VII
## (1901 – 1905)

### A Case of Hysteria
### Three Essays on Sexuality
### *and*
### Other Works

TRANSLATED FROM THE GERMAN UNDER
THE GENERAL EDITORSHIP OF
James Strachey

IN COLLABORATION WITH
Anna Freud

ASSISTED BY
Alix Strachey and Alan Tyson

**VINTAGE BOOKS**
London
THE HOGARTH PRESS
AND THE INSTITUTE OF PSYCHOANALYSIS

Published by Vintage 2001
24

Translation and editorial matter
Copyright © The Institute of Psychoanalysis 1953

First published in Great Britain in 1953 by
The Hogarth Press

Vintage
Random House, 20 Vauxhall Bridge Road,
London SW1V 2SA

www.vintage-books.co.uk

Addresses for companies within The Random House Group Limited
can be found at: www.randomhouse.co.uk/offices.htm

The Random House Group Limited Reg. No. 954009

A CIP catalogue record for this book
is available from the British Library

ISBN 9780099426585

Penguin Random House is committed to a sustainable future for
our business, our readers and our planet. This book is made from
Forest Stewardship Council® certified paper.

Printed and bound in Great Britain by Clays Ltd, Elcograf S.p.A.

# CONTENTS

## VOLUME SEVEN

## FRAGMENT OF AN ANALYSIS OF A CASE OF HYSTERIA (1905 [1901])

## THREE ESSAYS ON THE THEORY OF SEXUALITY (1905)

# FRAGMENT OF AN ANALYSIS
## OF A CASE OF HYSTERIA
### (1905 [1901])

# EDITOR'S NOTE

## BRUCHSTÜCK EINER HYSTERIE-ANALYSE

(a) GERMAN EDITIONS:
(1901 Jan. 24. Completion of first draft under title 'Traum
    und Hysterie' ['Dreams and Hysteria'].)
 1905 *Mschr. Psychiat. Neurol.*, **18** (4 and 5), Oct. and Nov.,
    285–310 and 408–467.
 1909 *S.K.S.N.*, II, 1–110. (1912, 2nd. ed.; 1921, 3rd. ed.)
 1924 *G.S.*, **8**, 3–126.
 1932 *Vier Krankengeschichten*, 5–141.
 1942 *G.W.*, **5**, 163–286.

(b) ENGLISH TRANSLATION:
    'Fragment of an Analysis of a Case of Hysteria'
 1925 *C.P.*, **3**, 13–146. (Tr. Alix and James Strachey.)

The present translation is a corrected version of the one
published in 1925.

Though this case history was not published until October
and November, 1905, the greater part of it was written in
January, 1901. The recovery of Freud's letters to Wilhelm
Fliess (Freud, 1950a) has given us a quantity of contemporary
evidence on the subject.
    On October 14, 1900 (Letter 139), Freud tells Fliess that he
has recently begun work with a new patient, 'an eighteen-
year-old girl'. This girl was evidently 'Dora', and, as we know
from the case history itself (p. 13 *n.* below), her treatment came
to an end some three months later, on December 31. All through
the same autumn he had been engaged on his *Psychopathology of
Everyday Life* (1901b), and on January 10 he writes (in an unpublished letter) that he is now engaged simultaneously on *two*
works: the *Everyday Life* and 'Dreams and Hysteria, a Fragment
of an Analysis', which, as we are told in Freud's preface (p. 10),
was the original title of the present paper. On January 25
(Letter 140) he writes: ' "Dreams and Hysteria" was completed

3

yesterday. It is a fragment of an analysis of a case of hysteria, in which the explanations are grouped round two dreams. So that it is in fact a continuation of the dream book. [*The Interpretation of Dreams* (1900*a*) had been published a year earlier.] It further contains solutions of hysterical symptoms and considerations on the sexual-organic basis of the whole condition. Anyhow, it is the most subtle thing I have yet written and will produce an even more horrifying effect than usual. One does one's duty, however, and what one writes is not for the passing day. The work has already been accepted by Ziehen.' The latter was joint editor, with Wernicke, of the *Monatsschrift für Psychiatrie und Neurologie,* in which the paper ultimately appeared. A few days later, on January 30 (Letter 141), Freud continues: 'I hope you will not be disappointed by "Dreams and Hysteria". Its main concern is still with psychology—an estimation of the importance of dreams and an account of some of the peculiarities of unconscious thinking. There are only glimpses of the organic side—the erotogenic zones and bisexuality. But it [the organic side] is definitely mentioned and recognized and the way is paved for an exhaustive discussion of it another time. The case is a hysteria with *tussis nervosa* and aphonia, which can be traced back to the characteristics of a thumb-sucker; and the principal part in the conflicting mental processes is played by the opposition between an attraction towards men and one towards women.' These extracts show how this paper forms a link between *The Interpretation of Dreams* and the *Three Essays.* It looks back to the one and forward to the other.

On February 15 (Letter 142) he announces to Fliess that *The Psychopathology of Everyday Life* will be finished in a few days and that then the two works will be ready to be corrected and sent off to the publishers. But actually their history was very different. On May 8 (Letter 143) he is already correcting the first proofs of *The Psychopathology of Everyday Life* (which was duly published in the July and August issues of the *Monatsschrift*); but he now says that he has not yet made up his mind about publishing the case history. On June 9, however (in another unpublished letter), he reports that ' "Dreams and Hysteria" has been sent off, and will meet the gaze of an astonished public in the autumn'. We have no information as to how it happened that Freud once more changed his mind and deferred publication for another four years. See p. 322.

There is no means of deciding the extent to which Freud revised the paper before its ultimate publication in 1905. All the internal evidence suggests, however, that he changed it very little. The last section of the 'Postscript' (pp. 120 to 122) was certainly added, as well as some passages at least in the 'Prefatory Remarks' and certain of the footnotes. But apart from these small additions it is fair to regard the paper as representing Freud's technical methods and theoretical views at the period immediately after the publication of *The Interpretation of Dreams*. It may seem surprising that his theory of sexuality had reached such a point of development so many years before the appearance of the *Three Essays* (1905*d*), which were actually published almost simultaneously with this paper. But the footnote on p. 51 explicitly vouches for the fact. Moreover, readers of the Fliess correspondence will be aware that much of this theory was in existence at an even earlier date. To take only a single instance, Freud's dictum about psychoneuroses being the 'negative' of perversions (p. 50) occurs in almost the same words in a letter to Fliess of January 24, 1897 (Letter 57). Even before this the idea is hinted at, in a letter of December 12, 1896 (Letter 52), which also introduces the notion of 'erotogenic zones' and adumbrates the theory of 'component instincts'.

It is curious that three times in his later writings Freud assigns his treatment of 'Dora' to the wrong year—to 1899 instead of 1900. The mistake occurs in the first section of his 'History of the Psycho-Analytic Movement' (1914*d*) and is repeated twice in the footnote which he added to the case history in 1923 (p. 13 *n.*). There can be no question that the autumn of 1900 was the correct date, since, quite apart from the external evidence quoted above, the date is absolutely fixed by the '1902' given at the end of the paper itself (p. 122).

This chronological summary, based on the data given in the case history, may make it easier for the reader to follow the events in the narrative:

1882          Dora born.
1888 (*Aet.*  6) Father ill with T.B. Family move to B——.
1889 (*Aet.*  7) Bed-wetting.
1890 (*Aet.*  8) Dyspnoea.
1892 (*Aet.* 10) Father's detached retina.

1894 (*Aet.* 12) Father's confusional attack. His visit to Freud.
Migraine and tussis nervosa.

1896 (*Aet.* 14) Scene of the kiss.

1898 (*Aet.* 16) (Early summer:) Dora's first visit to Freud. (End
of June:) Scene by the lake. (Winter:) Death
of Aunt. Dora in Vienna.

1899 (*Aet.* 17) (March:) Appendicitis. (Autumn:) Family leave
B—— and move to factory town.

1900 (*Aet.* 18) Family move to Vienna. Suicide threat. (October
to December:) Treatment with Freud.

1901          (January:) Case history written.

1902          (April:) Dora's last visit to Freud.

1905          Case history published.

# FRAGMENT OF AN ANALYSIS
# OF A CASE OF HYSTERIA

## PREFATORY REMARKS

In 1895 and 1896 [1] I put forward certain views upon the pathogenesis of hysterical symptoms and upon the mental processes
occurring in hysteria. Since that time several years have
passed. In now proposing, therefore, to substantiate those views
by giving a detailed report of the history of a case and its treatment, I cannot avoid making a few introductory remarks, for
the purpose partly of justifying from various standpoints the
step I am taking, and partly of diminishing the expectations to
which it will give rise.

No doubt it was awkward that I was obliged to publish the
results of my enquiries without there being any possibility of
other workers in the field testing and checking them, particularly as those results were of a surprising and by no means
gratifying character. But it will be scarcely less awkward now
that I am beginning to bring forward some of the material upon
which my conclusions were based and make it accessible to the
judgement of the world. I shall not escape blame by this means.
Only, whereas before I was accused of giving *no* information
about my patients, now I shall be accused of giving information
about my patients which ought not to be given. I can only hope
that in both cases the critics will be the same, and that they
will merely have shifted the pretext for their reproaches; if so,
I can resign in advance any possibility of ever removing their
objections.

Even if I ignore the ill-will of narrow-minded critics such as
these, the presentation of my case histories remains a problem
which is hard for me to solve. The difficulties are partly of a
technical kind, but are partly due to the nature of the circumstances themselves. If it is true that the causes of hysterical disorders are to be found in the intimacies of the patients' psychosexual life, and that hysterical symptoms are the expression

---

[1] [E.g. in *Studies on Hysteria* (Breuer and Freud, 1895) and 'The
Aetiology of Hysteria' (Freud, 1896c).]

of their most secret and repressed wishes, then the complete elucidation of a case of hysteria is bound to involve the revelation of those intimacies and the betrayal of those secrets. It is certain that the patients would never have spoken if it had occurred to them that their admissions might possibly be put to scientific uses; and it is equally certain that to ask them themselves for leave to publish their case would be quite unavailing. In such circumstances persons of delicacy, as well as those who were merely timid, would give first place to the duty of medical discretion and would declare with regret that the matter was one upon which they could offer science no enlightenment. But in my opinion the physician has taken upon himself duties not only towards the individual patient but towards science as well; and his duties towards science mean ultimately nothing else than his duties towards the many other patients who are suffering or will some day suffer from the same disorder. Thus it becomes the physician's duty to publish what he believes he knows of the causes and structure of hysteria, and it becomes a disgraceful piece of cowardice on his part to neglect doing so, as long as he can avoid causing direct personal injury to the single patient concerned. I think I have taken every precaution to prevent my patient from suffering any such injury. I have picked out a person the scenes of whose life were laid not in Vienna but in a remote provincial town, and whose personal circumstances must therefore be practically unknown in Vienna. I have from the very beginning kept the fact of her being under my treatment such a careful secret that only one other physician—and one in whose discretion I have complete confidence [1]—can be aware that the girl was a patient of mine. I have waited for four whole years since the end of the treatment and have postponed publication till hearing that a change has taken place in the patient's life of such a character as allows me to suppose that her own interest in the occurrences and psychological events which are to be related here may now have grown faint. Needless to say, I have allowed no name to stand which could put a non-medical reader upon the scent; and the publication of the case in a purely scientific and technical periodical should, further, afford a guarantee against unauthorized readers of this sort. I naturally cannot prevent the patient herself from being pained if her own case history

[1] [No doubt Fliess. See p. 3 above.]

should accidentally fall into her hands. But she will learn nothing from it that she does not already know; and she may ask herself who besides her could discover from it that she is the subject of this paper.

I am aware that—in this city, at least—there are many physicians who (revolting though it may seem) choose to read a case history of this kind not as a contribution to the psychopathology of the neuroses, but as a *roman à clef* designed for their private delectation. I can assure readers of this species that every case history which I may have occasion to publish in the future will be secured against their perspicacity by similar guarantees of secrecy, even though this resolution is bound to put quite extraordinary restrictions upon my choice of material.

Now in this case history—the only one which I have hitherto succeeded in forcing through the limitations imposed by medical discretion and unfavourable circumstances—sexual questions will be discussed with all possible frankness, the organs and functions of sexual life will be called by their proper names, and the pure-minded reader can convince himself from my description that I have not hesitated to converse upon such subjects in such language even with a young woman. Am I, then, to defend myself upon this score as well? I will simply claim for myself the rights of the gynaecologist—or rather, much more modest ones—and add that it would be the mark of a singular and perverse prurience to suppose that conversations of this kind are a good means of exciting or of gratifying sexual desires. For the rest, I feel inclined to express my opinion on this subject in a few borrowed words:

'It is deplorable to have to make room for protestations and declarations of this sort in a scientific work; but let no one reproach me on this account but rather accuse the spirit of the age, owing to which we have reached a state of things in which no serious book can any longer be sure of survival.' (Schmidt, 1902, Preface.)

I will now describe the way in which I have overcome the *technical* difficulties of drawing up the report of this case history. The difficulties are very considerable when the physician has to conduct six or eight psychotherapeutic treatments of the sort in a day, and cannot make notes during the actual session with the patient for fear of shaking the patient's confidence and of disturbing his own view of the material under observation.

Indeed, I have not yet succeeded in solving the problem of how to record for publication the history of a treatment of long duration. As regards the present case, two circumstances have come to my assistance. In the first place the treatment did not last for more than three months; and in the second place the material which elucidated the case was grouped around two dreams (one related in the middle of the treatment and one at the end). The wording of these dreams was recorded immediately after the session, and they thus afforded a secure point of attachment for the chain of interpretations and recollections which proceeded from them. The case history itself was only committed to writing from memory after the treatment was at an end, but while my recollection of the case was still fresh and was heightened by my interest in its publication.[1] Thus the record is not absolutely—phonographically—exact, but it can claim to possess a high degree of trustworthiness. Nothing of any importance has been altered in it except in some places the order in which the explanations are given; and this has been done for the sake of presenting the case in a more connected form.

I next proceed to mention more particularly what is to be found in this paper and what is not to be found in it. The title of the work was originally 'Dreams and Hysteria', for it seemed to me peculiarly well-adapted for showing how dream-interpretation is woven into the history of a treatment and how it can become the means of filling in amnesias and elucidating symptoms. It was not without good reasons that in the year 1900 I gave precedence to a laborious and exhaustive study of dreams (*The Interpretation of Dreams*) over the publications upon the psychology of the neuroses which I had in view. And incidentally I was able to judge from its reception with what an inadequate degree of comprehension such efforts are met by other specialists at the present time. In this instance there was no validity in the objection that the material upon which I had based my assertions had been withheld and that it was therefore impossible to become convinced of their truth by testing and checking them. For every one can submit his own dreams to analytic examination, and the technique of interpreting dreams may be easily learnt from the instructions

[1] [Freud had intended to publish it immediately after writing it. (See p. 4.)]

and examples which I have given. I must once more insist, just as I did at that time,[1] that a thorough investigation of the problems of dreams is an indispensable prerequisite for any comprehension of the mental processes in hysteria and the other psychoneuroses, and that no one who wishes to shirk that preparatory labour has the smallest prospect of advancing even a few steps into this region of knowledge. Since, therefore, this case history presupposes a knowledge of the interpretation of dreams, it will seem highly unsatisfactory to any reader to whom this presupposition does not apply. Such a reader will find only bewilderment in these pages instead of the enlightenment he is in search of, and he will certainly be inclined to project the cause of his bewilderment on to the author and to pronounce his views fantastic. But in reality this bewildering character attaches to the phenomena of the neurosis itself; its presence there is only concealed by the physician's familiarity with the facts, and it comes to light again with every attempt at explaining them. It could only be completely banished if we could succeed in tracing back every single element of a neurosis to factors with which we were already familiar. But everything tends to show that, on the contrary, we shall be driven by the study of neuroses to assume the existence of many new things which will later on gradually become the subject of more certain knowledge. What is new has always aroused bewilderment and resistance.

Nevertheless, it would be wrong to suppose that dreams and their interpretation occupy such a prominent position in all psycho-analyses as they do in this example.[2]

While the case history before us seems particularly favoured as regards the utilization of dreams, in other respects it has turned out poorer than I could have wished. But its short-comings are connected with the very circumstances which have made its publication possible. As I have already said, I should not have known how to deal with the material involved in the history of a treatment which had lasted, perhaps, for a whole year. The present history, which covers only three months, could be recollected and reviewed; but its results remain

----

[1] [Preface to the first edition of *The Interpretation of Dreams*, Standard Ed., **4**, xxiii.]

[2] [For a later assessment of the part played by dream-interpretation in analytic procedure see Freud's paper devoted to that subject (1911*e*).]

incomplete in more than one respect. The treatment was not carried through to its appointed end, but was broken off at the patient's own wish when it had reached a certain point. At that time some of the problems of the case had not even been attacked and others had only been imperfectly elucidated; whereas, if the work had been continued, we should no doubt have obtained the fullest possible enlightenment upon every particular of the case. In the following pages, therefore, I can present only a fragment of an analysis.

Readers who are familiar with the technique of analysis as it was expounded in the *Studies on Hysteria* [Breuer and Freud, 1895] will perhaps be surprised that it should not have been possible in three months to find a complete solution at least for those of the symptoms which were taken in hand. This will become intelligible when I explain that since the date of the *Studies* psycho-analytic technique has been completely revolutionized. At that time the work of analysis started out from the symptoms, and aimed at clearing them up one after the other. Since then I have abandoned that technique, because I found it totally inadequate for dealing with the finer structure of a neurosis. I now let the patient himself choose the subject of the day's work, and in that way I start out from whatever surface his unconscious happens to be presenting to his notice at the moment. But on this plan everything that has to do with the clearing-up of a particular symptom emerges piecemeal, woven into various contexts, and distributed over widely separated periods of time. In spite of this apparent disadvantage, the new technique is far superior to the old, and indeed there can be no doubt that it is the only possible one.

In face of the incompleteness of my analytic results, I had no choice but to follow the example of those discoverers whose good fortune it is to bring to the light of day after their long burial the priceless though mutilated relics of antiquity. I have restored what is missing, taking the best models known to me from other analyses; but, like a conscientious archaeologist, I have not omitted to mention in each case where the authentic parts end and my constructions begin.

There is another kind of incompleteness which I myself have intentionally introduced. I have as a rule not reproduced the process of interpretation to which the patient's associations and communications had to be subjected, but only the results of that process. Apart from the dreams, therefore, the technique of the analytic work has been revealed in only a very few places. My object in this case history was to demonstrate the intimate structure of a neurotic disorder and the determination of its symptoms; and it would have led to nothing but hopeless confusion if I had tried to complete the other task at the same time. Before the technical rules, most of which have been arrived at empirically, could be properly laid down, it would be necessary to collect material from the histories of a large number of treatments. Nevertheless, the degree of shortening produced by the omission of the technique is not to be exaggerated in this particular case. Precisely that portion of the technical work which is the most difficult never came into question with the patient; for the factor of 'transference', which is considered at the end of the case history [p. 116 ff.], did not come up for discussion during the short treatment.

For a third kind of incompleteness in this report neither the patient nor the author is responsible. It is, on the contrary, obvious that a single case history, even if it were complete and open to no doubt, cannot provide an answer to *all* the questions arising out of the problem of hysteria. It cannot give an insight into all the types of this disorder, into all the forms of internal structure of the neurosis, into all the possible kinds of relation between the mental and the somatic which are to be found in hysteria. It is not fair to expect from a single case more than it can offer. And any one who has hitherto been unwilling to believe that a psychosexual aetiology holds good generally and without exception for hysteria is scarcely likely to be convinced of the fact by taking stock of a single case history. He would do better to suspend his judgement until his own work has earned him the right to a conviction.[1]

---

[1] [*Footnote added* 1923:] The treatment described in this paper was broken off on December 31st, 1899. [This should be '1900'. See p. 5.] My account of it was written during the two weeks immediately following, but was not published until 1905. It is not to be expected that after more than twenty years of uninterrupted work I should see nothing to alter in my view of such a case and in my presentment of it; but it would obviously be absurd to bring the case history 'up to date' by means of emendations and additions. In all essentials, therefore, I have left it as it was, and in the text I have merely corrected a few oversights and inaccuracies to which my excellent English translators, Mr. and Mrs. James Strachey, have directed my attention. Such critical

remarks as I have thought it permissible to add I have incorporated in these additional notes: so that the reader will be justified in assuming that I still hold to the opinions expressed in the text unless he finds them contradicted in the footnotes. The problem of medical discretion which I have discussed in this preface does not touch the remaining case histories contained in this volume [see below]; for three of them were published with the express assent of the patients (or rather, as regards little Hans, with that of his father), while in the fourth case (that of Schreber) the subject of the analysis was not actually a person but a book produced by him. In Dora's case the secret was kept until this year. I had long been out of touch with her, but a short while ago I heard that she had recently fallen ill again from other causes, and had confided to her physician that she had been analysed by me when she was a girl. This disclosure made it easy for my well-informed colleague to recognize her as the Dora of 1899. [This, again, should be '1900'.] No fair judge of analytic therapy will make it a reproach that the three months' treatment she received at that time effected no more than the relief of her current conflict and was unable to give her protection against subsequent illnesses.—[This footnote first appeared in the eighth volume of Freud's *Gesammelte Schriften* (1924), and, in English, in the third volume of his *Collected Papers* (1925). Each of these volumes contained his five longer case histories—that is, besides the present one, the cases (referred to in this footnote) of Little Hans (1909*b*), the 'Rat Man' (1909*d*), Schreber (1911*c*) and the 'Wolf Man' (1918*b*).]

# I

## THE CLINICAL PICTURE

IN my *Interpretation of Dreams*, published in 1900, I showed that dreams in general can be interpreted, and that after the work of interpretation has been completed they can be replaced by perfectly correctly constructed thoughts which can be assigned a recognizable position in the chain of mental events. I wish to give an example in the following pages of the only practical application of which the art of interpreting dreams seems to admit. I have already mentioned in my book [1] how it was that I came upon the problem of dreams. The problem crossed my path as I was endeavouring to cure psychoneuroses by means of a particular psychotherapeutic method. For, among their other mental experiences, my patients told me their dreams, and these dreams seemed to call for insertion in the long thread of connections which spun itself out between a symptom of the disease and a pathogenic idea. At that time I learnt how to translate the language of dreams into the forms of expression of our own thought-language, which can be understood without further help. And I may add that this knowledge is essential for the psycho-analyst; for the dream is one of the roads along which consciousness can be reached by the psychical material which, on account of the opposition aroused by its content, has been cut off from consciousness and repressed, and has thus become pathogenic. The dream, in short, is one of the *détours by which repression can be evaded*; it is one of the principal means employed by what is known as the indirect method of representation in the mind. The following fragment from the history of the treatment of a hysterical girl is intended to show the way in which the interpretation of dreams plays a part in the work of analysis. It will at the same time give me a first opportunity of publishing at sufficient length to prevent further misunderstanding some of my views upon the psychical processes of hysteria and upon its organic determinants. I need no longer apologize on the score of length, since it is now agreed that the exacting demands which hysteria makes upon physician and investigator

[1] *The Interpretation of Dreams*, Chapter II [Standard Ed., **4**, 100 ff.].

can be met only by the most sympathetic spirit of inquiry and
not by an attitude of superiority and contempt. For,

> Nicht Kunst und Wissenschaft allein,
> Geduld will bei dem Werke sein! [1]

If I were to begin by giving a full and consistent case history,
it would place the reader in a very different situation from that
of the medical observer. The reports of the patient's relatives—
in the present case I was given one by the eighteen-year-old
girl's father—usually afford a very indistinct picture of the
course of the illness. I begin the treatment, indeed, by asking
the patient to give me the whole story of his life and illness,
but even so the information I receive is never enough to let me
see my way about the case. This first account may be compared
to an unnavigable river whose stream is at one moment choked
by masses of rock and at another divided and lost among
shallows and sandbanks. I cannot help wondering how it is that
the authorities can produce such smooth and precise histories
in cases of hysteria. As a matter of fact the patients are incapable
of giving such reports about themselves. They can, indeed, give
the physician plenty of coherent information about this or that
period of their lives; but it is sure to be followed by another
period as to which their communications run dry, leaving gaps
unfilled, and riddles unanswered; and then again will come yet
another period which will remain totally obscure and un-
illuminated by even a single piece of serviceable information.
The connections—even the ostensible ones—are for the most
part incoherent, and the sequence of different events is uncertain. Even during the course of their story patients will
repeatedly correct a particular or a date, and then perhaps,
after wavering for some time, return to their first version. The
patients' inability to give an ordered history of their life in so
far as it coincides with the history of their illness is not merely
characteristic of the neurosis.[2] It also possesses great theoretical

---

[1] [Not Art and Science serve, alone;
Patience must in the work be shown.
Goethe, *Faust*, Part I (Scene 6).
(Bayard Taylor's translation.)]

[2] Another physician once sent his sister to me for psychotherapeutic
treatment, telling me that she had for years been treated without success

significance. For this inability has the following grounds. In the first place, patients consciously and intentionally keep back part of what they ought to tell—things that are perfectly well known to them—because they have not got over their feelings of timidity and shame (or discretion, where what they say concerns other people); this is the share taken by *conscious* disingenuousness. In the second place, part of the anamnestic knowledge, which the patients have at their disposal at other times, disappears while they are actually telling their story, but without their making any deliberate reservations: the share taken by *unconscious* disingenuousness. In the third place, there are invariably true amnesias—gaps in the memory into which not only old recollections but even quite recent ones have fallen—and paramnesias, formed secondarily so as to fill in those gaps.[1] When the events themselves have been kept in mind, the purpose underlying the amnesias can be fulfilled just as surely by destroying a connection, and a connection is most surely broken by altering the chronological order of events. The latter always proves to be the most vulnerable element in the store of memory and the one which is most easily subject to repression. Again, we meet with many recollections that are in what might be described as the first stage of repression, and these we find surrounded with doubts. At a later period the doubts would be replaced by a loss or a falsification of memory.[2]

That this state of affairs should exist in regard to the

for hysteria (pains and defective gait). The short account which he gave me seemed quite consistent with the diagnosis. In my first hour with the patient I got her to tell me her history herself. When the story came out perfectly clearly and connectedly in spite of the remarkable events it dealt with, I told myself that the case could not be one of hysteria, and immediately instituted a careful physical examination. This led to the diagnosis of a not very advanced stage of tabes, which was later on treated with Hg injections (Ol. cinereum) by Professor Lang with markedly beneficial results.

[1] Amnesias and paramnesias stand in a complementary relation to each other. When there are large gaps in the memory there will be few mistakes in it. And conversely, paramnesias can at a first glance completely conceal the presence of amnesias.

[2] If a patient exhibits doubts in the course of his narrative, an empirical rule teaches us to disregard such expressions of his judgement entirely. If the narrative wavers between two versions, we should incline to regard the first one as correct and the second as a product of repression. [Cf. a discussion of doubt in connection with dreams in *The*

memories relating to the history of the illness is *a necessary correlate of the symptoms and one which is theoretically requisite.* In the further course of the treatment the patient supplies the facts which, though he had known them all along, had been kept back by him or had not occurred to his mind. The paramnesias prove untenable, and the gaps in his memory are filled in. It is only towards the end of the treatment that we have before us an intelligible, consistent, and unbroken case history. Whereas the practical aim of the treatment is to remove all possible symptoms and to replace them by conscious thoughts, we may regard it as a second and theoretical aim to repair all the damages to the patient's memory. These two aims are coincident. When one is reached, so is the other; and the same path leads to them both.

It follows from the nature of the facts which form the material of psycho-analysis that we are obliged to pay as much attention in our case histories to the purely human and social circumstances of our patients as to the somatic data and the symptoms of the disorder. Above all, our interest will be directed towards their family circumstances—and not only, as will be seen later, for the purpose of enquiring into their heredity.

The family circle of the eighteen-year-old girl who is the subject of this paper included, besides herself, her two parents and a brother who was one and a half years her senior. Her father was the dominating figure in this circle, owing to his intelligence and his character as much as to the circumstances of his life. It was those circumstances which provided the framework for the history of the patient's childhood and illness. At the time at which I began the girl's treatment her father was in his late forties, a man of rather unusual activity and talents, a large manufacturer in very comfortable circumstances. His daughter was most tenderly attached to him, and for that reason her critical powers, which developed early, took all the more offence at many of his actions and peculiarities.

Her affection for him was still further increased by the many

*Interpretation of Dreams*, 1900a (Chapter VII, Section A; Standard Ed., 5, 515 ff.). For the very different mechanism of doubt in obsessional neurosis, see the case history of the 'Rat Man', 1909d (Part II, Section C).]

severe illnesses which he had been through since her sixth year. At that time he had fallen ill with tuberculosis and the family had consequently moved to a small town in a good climate, situated in one of our southern provinces. There his lung trouble rapidly improved; but, on account of the precautions which were still considered necessary, both parents and children continued for the next ten years or so to reside chiefly in this spot, which I shall call B——. When her father's health was good, he used at times to be away, on visits to his factories. During the hottest part of the summer the family used to move to a health-resort in the hills.

When the girl was about ten years old, her father had to go through a course of treatment in a darkened room on account of a detached retina. As a result of this misfortune his vision was permanently impaired. His gravest illness occurred some two years later. It took the form of a confusional attack, followed by symptoms of paralysis and slight mental disturbances. A friend of his (who plays a part in the story with which we shall be concerned later on [see p. 29, n. 3]) persuaded him, while his condition had scarcely improved, to travel to Vienna with his physician and come to me for advice. I hesitated for some time as to whether I ought not to regard the case as one of tabo-paralysis, but I finally decided upon a diagnosis of a diffuse vascular affection; and since the patient admitted having had a specific infection before his marriage, I prescribed an energetic course of anti-luetic treatment, as a result of which all the remaining disturbances passed off. It is no doubt owing to this fortunate intervention of mine that four years later he brought his daughter, who had meanwhile grown unmistakably neurotic, and introduced her to me, and that after another two years he handed her over to me for psychotherapeutic treatment.

I had in the meantime also made the acquaintance in Vienna of a sister of his, who was a little older than himself. She gave clear evidence of a severe form of psychoneurosis without any characteristically hysterical symptoms. After a life which had been weighed down by an unhappy marriage, she died of a marasmus which made rapid advances and the symptoms of which were, as a matter of fact, never fully cleared up. An elder brother of the girl's father, whom I once happened to meet, was a hypochondriacal bachelor.

The sympathies of the girl herself, who, as I have said,

became my patient at the age of eighteen, had always been with the father's side of the family, and ever since she had fallen ill she had taken as her model the aunt who has just been mentioned. There could be no doubt, too, that it was from her father's family that she had derived not only her natural gifts and her intellectual precocity but also the predisposition to her illness. I never made her mother's acquaintance. From the accounts given me by the girl and her father I was led to imagine her as an uncultivated woman and above all as a foolish one, who had concentrated all her interests upon domestic affairs, especially since her husband's illness and the estrangement to which it led. She presented the picture, in fact, of what might be called the 'housewife's psychosis'. She had no understanding of her children's more active interests, and was occupied all day long in cleaning the house with its furniture and utensils and in keeping them clean—to such an extent as to make it almost impossible to use or enjoy them. This condition, traces of which are to be found often enough in normal housewives, inevitably reminds one of forms of obsessional washing and other kinds of obsessional cleanliness. But such women (and this applied to the patient's mother) are entirely without insight into their illness, so that one essential characteristic of an 'obsessional neurosis' is lacking. The relations between the girl and her mother had been unfriendly for years. The daughter looked down on her mother and used to criticize her mercilessly, and she had withdrawn completely from her influence.[1]

---

[1] I do not, it is true, adopt the position that heredity is the only aetiological factor in hysteria. But, on the other hand—and I say this with particular reference to some of my earlier publications, e.g. 'Heredity and the Aetiology of the Neuroses' (1896a), in which I combated that view—I do not wish to give an impression of underestimating the importance of heredity in the aetiology of hysteria or of asserting that it can be dispensed with. In the case of the present patient the information I have given about her father and his brother and sister indicates a sufficiently heavy taint; and, indeed, if the view is taken that pathological conditions such as her mother's must also imply a hereditary predisposition, the patient's heredity may be regarded as a convergent one. To my mind, however, there is another factor which is of more significance in the girl's hereditary or, properly speaking, constitutional predisposition. I have mentioned that her father had contracted syphilis before his marriage. Now a *strikingly high* percentage of the patients whom I have treated psycho-analytically come of fathers who

During the girl's earlier years, her only brother (her elder by a year and a half) had been the model which her ambitions had striven to follow. But in the last few years the relations between the brother and sister had grown more distant. The young man used to try so far as he could to keep out of the family disputes; but when he was obliged to take sides he would support his mother. So that the usual sexual attraction had drawn together the father and daughter on the one side and the mother and son on the other.

The patient, to whom I shall in future give the name of 'Dora',[1] had even at the age of eight begun to develop neurotic symptoms. She became subject at that time to chronic dyspnoea with occasional accesses in which the symptom was very much aggravated. The first onset occurred after a short expedition in the mountains and was accordingly put down to over-exertion. In the course of six months, during which she was made to rest and was carefully looked after, this condition gradually passed off. The family doctor seems to have had not a moment's hesitation in diagnosing the disorder as purely nervous and in excluding any organic cause for the dyspnoea; but he evidently considered this diagnosis compatible with the aetiology of over-exertion.[2]

The little girl went through the usual infectious diseases of childhood without suffering any lasting damage. As she herself told me—and her words were intended to convey a deeper

have suffered from tabes or general paralysis. In consequence of the novelty of my therapeutic method, I see only the *severest* cases, which have already been under treatment for years without any success. In accordance with the Erb-Fournier theory, tabes or general paralysis in the male parent may be regarded as evidence of an earlier luetic infection; and indeed I was able to obtain direct confirmation of such an infection in a number of cases. In the most recent discussion on the offspring of syphilitic parents (Thirteenth International Medical Congress, held in Paris, August 2nd to 9th, 1900: papers by Finger, Tarnowsky, Jullien, etc.), I find no mention of the conclusion to which I have been driven by my experience as a neuro-pathologist—namely, that syphilis in the male parent is a very relevant factor in the aetiology of the neuropathic constitution of children.

[1] [The determinants of Freud's choice of this pseudonym were discussed by him in Chapter XII, Example A (1), of his *Psychopathology of Everyday Life* (1901b).]

[2] The probable precipitating cause of this first illness will be discussed later on [p. 80].

meaning [see p. 82 *n.*]—her brother was as a rule the first to
start the illness and used to have it very slightly, and she would
then follow suit with a severe form of it. When she was about
twelve she began to suffer from unilateral headaches in the
nature of a migraine, and from attacks of nervous coughing.
At first these two symptoms always appeared together, but they
became separated later on and ran different courses. The
migraine grew rarer, and by the time she was sixteen she had
quite got over it. But attacks of *tussis nervosa*, which had no
doubt been started by a common catarrh, continued to occur
over the whole period. When, at the age of eighteen, she came
to me for treatment, she was again coughing in a characteristic
manner. The number of these attacks could not be determined;
but they lasted from three to five weeks, and on one occasion
for several months. The most troublesome symptom during the
first half of an attack of this kind, at all events in the last few
years, used to be a complete loss of voice. The diagnosis that
this was once more a nervous complaint had been established
long since; but the various methods of treatment which are
usual, including hydrotherapy and the local application of
electricity, had produced no result. It was in such circumstances
as these that the child had developed into a mature young
woman of very independent judgement, who had grown accustomed to laugh at the efforts of doctors, and in the end to
renounce their help entirely. Moreover, she had always been
against calling in medical advice, though she had no personal
objection to her family doctor. Every proposal to consult a new
physician aroused her resistance, and it was only her father's
authority which induced her to come to me at all.

I first saw her when she was sixteen, in the early summer.
She was suffering from a cough and from hoarseness, and even
at that time I proposed giving her psychological treatment.
My proposal was not adopted, since the attack in question, like
the others, passed off spontaneously, though it had lasted un-
usually long. During the next winter she came and stayed in
Vienna with her uncle and his daughters after the death of the
aunt of whom she had been so fond. There she fell ill of a
feverish disorder which was diagnosed at the time as appendicitis.[1] In the following autumn, since her father's health seemed
to justify the step, the family left the health-resort of B—— for

[1] On this point see the analysis of the second dream [p. 101].

good and all. They first moved to the town where her father's factory was situated, and then, scarcely a year later, settled permanently in Vienna.

Dora was by that time in the first bloom of youth—a girl of intelligent and engaging looks. But she was a source of heavy trials for her parents. Low spirits and an alteration in her character had now become the main features of her illness. She was clearly satisfied neither with herself nor with her family; her attitude towards her father was unfriendly, and she was on very bad terms with her mother, who was bent upon drawing her into taking a share in the work of the house. She tried to avoid social intercourse, and employed herself—so far as she was allowed to by the fatigue and lack of concentration of which she complained—with attending lectures for women and with carrying on more or less serious studies. One day her parents were thrown into a state of great alarm by finding on the girl's writing-desk, or inside it, a letter in which she took leave of them because, as she said, she could no longer endure her life.[1] Her father, indeed, being a man of some perspicacity, guessed that the girl had no serious suicidal intentions. But he was none the less very much shaken; and when one day, after a slight passage of words between him and his daughter, she had a first attack of loss of consciousness [2]—an event which was subsequently covered by an amnesia—it was determined, in spite of her reluctance, that she should come to me for treatment.

No doubt this case history, as I have so far outlined it, does not upon the whole seem worth recording. It is merely a case of '*petite hystérie*' with the commonest of all somatic and mental

---

[1] As I have already explained, the treatment of the case, and consequently my insight into the complex of events composing it, remained fragmentary. There are therefore many questions to which I have no solution to offer, or in which I can only rely upon hints and conjectures. This affair of the letter came up in the course of one of our sessions [p. 97 f.], and the girl showed signs of astonishment. 'How on earth', she asked, 'did they find the letter? It was shut up in my desk.' But since she knew that her parents had read this draft of a farewell letter, I conclude that she had herself arranged for it to fall into their hands.

[2] The attack was, I believe, accompanied by convulsions and delirious states. But since this event was not reached by the analysis either, I have no trustworthy recollections on the subject to fall back upon.

symptoms: dyspnoea, *tussis nervosa*, aphonia, and possibly migraines, together with depression, hysterical unsociability, and a *taedium vitae* which was probably not entirely genuine. More interesting cases of hysteria have no doubt been published, and they have very often been more carefully described; for nothing will be found in the following pages on the subject of stigmata of cutaneous sensibility, limitation of the visual field, or similar matters. I may venture to remark, however, that all such collections of the strange and wonderful phenomena of hysteria have but slightly advanced our knowledge of a disease which still remains as great a puzzle as ever. What is wanted is precisely an elucidation of the *commonest* cases and of their most frequent and typical symptoms. I should have been very well satisfied if the circumstances had allowed me to give a complete elucidation of this case of *petite hystérie*. And my experiences with other patients leave me in no doubt that my analytic method would have enabled me to do so.

In 1896, shortly after the appearance of my *Studies on Hysteria* (written in conjunction with Dr. J. Breuer, 1895), I asked an eminent fellow-specialist for his opinion on the psychological theory of hysteria put forward in that work. He bluntly replied that he considered it an unjustifiable generalization of conclusions which might hold good for a few cases. Since then I have seen an abundance of cases of hysteria, and I have been occupied with each case for a number of days, weeks, or years. In not a single one of them have I failed to discover the psychological determinants which were postulated in the *Studies*, namely, a psychical trauma, a conflict of affects, and—an additional factor which I brought forward in later publications—a disturbance in the sphere of sexuality. It is of course not to be expected that the patient will come to meet the physician half-way with material which has become pathogenic for the very reason of its efforts to lie concealed; nor must the enquirer rest content with the first 'No' that crosses his path.[1]

In Dora's case, thanks to her father's shrewdness which I have remarked upon more than once already, there was no

---

[1] Here is an instance of this. Another physician in Vienna, whose conviction of the unimportance of sexual factors in hysteria has probably been very much strengthened by such experiences as this, was consulted in the case of a fourteen-year-old girl who suffered from dangerous

need for me to look about for the points of contact between
the circumstances of the patient's life and her illness, at all
events in its most recent form. Her father told me that he and
his family while they were at B—— had formed an intimate
friendship with a married couple who had been settled there
for several years. Frau K. had nursed him during his long illness,
and had in that way, he said, earned a title to his undying
gratitude. Herr K. had always been most kind to Dora. He had
gone walks with her when he was there, and had made her
small presents; but no one had thought any harm of that. Dora
had taken the greatest care of the K.'s two little children, and
been almost a mother to them. When Dora and her father had
come to see me two years before in the summer, they had been
just on their way to stop with Herr and Frau K., who were
spending the summer on one of our lakes in the Alps. Dora was
to have spent several weeks at the K.'s, while her father had
intended to return home after a few days. During that time
Herr K. had been staying there as well. As her father was preparing for his departure the girl had suddenly declared with
the greatest determination that she was going with him, and she
had in fact put her decision into effect. It was not until some
days later that she had thrown any light upon her strange
behaviour. She had then told her mother—intending that what
she said should be passed on to her father—that Herr K. had
had the audacity to make her a proposal while they were on a
walk after a trip upon the lake. Herr K. had been called to
account by her father and uncle on the next occasion of their

hysterical vomiting. He made up his mind to ask her the painful
question whether by any chance she had ever had a love-affair with a
man. 'No!' answered the child, no doubt with well-affected astonishment; and then repeated to her mother in her irreverent way: 'Only
fancy! the old stupid asked me if I was in love!' She afterwards came to
me for treatment, and proved—though not during our very first conversation, to be sure—to have been a masturbator for many years, with
a considerable leucorrhoeal discharge (which had a close bearing on
her vomiting). She had finally broken herself of the habit, but was tor-
mented in her abstinence by the most acute sense of guilt, so that she
looked upon every misfortune that befell her family as a divine punishment for her transgression. Besides this, she was under the influence of
the romance of an unmarried aunt, whose pregnancy (a second determinant for her vomiting) was supposed to have been happily hidden
from her. The girl was looked upon as a 'mere child,' but she turned
out to be initiated into all the essentials of sexual relations.

meeting, but he had denied in the most emphatic terms having on his side made any advances which could have been open to such a construction. He had then proceeded to throw suspicion upon the girl, saying that he had heard from Frau K. that she took no interest in anything but sexual matters, and that she used to read Mantegazza's *Physiology of Love* and books of that sort in their house on the lake. It was most likely, he had added, that she had been over-excited by such reading and had merely 'fancied' the whole scene she had described.

'I have no doubt', continued her father, 'that this incident is responsible for Dora's depression and irritability and suicidal ideas. She keeps pressing me to break off relations with Herr K. and more particularly with Frau K., whom she used positively to worship formerly. But that I cannot do. For, to begin with, I myself believe that Dora's tale of the man's immoral suggestions is a phantasy that has forced its way into her mind; and besides, I am bound to Frau K. by ties of honourable friendship and I do not wish to cause her pain. The poor woman is most unhappy with her husband, of whom, by the by, I have no very high opinion. She herself has suffered a great deal with her nerves, and I am her only support. With my state of health I need scarcely assure you that there is nothing wrong in our relations. We are just two poor wretches who give one another what comfort we can by an exchange of friendly sympathy. You know already that I get nothing out of my own wife. But Dora, who inherits my obstinacy, cannot be moved from her hatred of the K.'s. She had her last attack after a conversation in which she had again pressed me to break with them. Please try and bring her to reason.'

Her father's words did not always quite tally with this pronouncement; for on other occasions he tried to put the chief blame for Dora's impossible behaviour on her mother— whose peculiarities made the house unbearable for every one. But I had resolved from the first to suspend my judgement of the true state of affairs till I had heard the other side as well.

The experience with Herr K.—his making love to her and the insult to her honour which was involved—seems to provide in Dora's case the psychical trauma which Breuer and I declared long ago [1] to be the indispensable prerequisite for the

[1] [In their 'Preliminary Communication' (Breuer and Freud, 1893a).]

production of a hysterical disorder. But this new case also presents all the difficulties which have since led me to go beyond that theory,[1] besides an additional difficulty of a special kind. For, as so often happens in histories of cases of hysteria, the trauma that we know of as having occurred in the patient's past life is insufficient to explain or to determine the *particular character* of the symptoms; we should understand just as much or just as little of the whole business if the result of the trauma had been symptoms quite other than *tussis nervosa*, aphonia, depression, and *taedium vitae*. But there is the further considera-tion that some of these symptoms (the cough and the loss of voice) had been produced by the patient years before the time of the trauma, and that their earliest appearances belong to her childhood, since they occurred in her eighth year. If, therefore, the trauma theory is not to be abandoned, we must go back to her childhood and look about there for any influences or im-pressions which might have had an effect analogous to that of a trauma. Moreover, it deserves to be remarked that in the investigation even of cases in which the first symptoms had not already set in in childhood I have been driven to trace back the patients' life history to their earliest years.[2]

When the first difficulties of the treatment had been over-come, Dora told me of an earlier episode with Herr K., which was even better calculated to act as a sexual trauma. She was

[1] I have gone beyond that theory, but I have not abandoned it; that is to say, I do not to-day consider the theory incorrect, but incomplete. All that I have abandoned is the emphasis laid upon the so-called 'hypnoid state', which was supposed to be occasioned in the patient by the trauma, and to be the foundation for all the psychologically ab-normal events which followed. If, where a piece of joint work is in question, it is legitimate to make a subsequent division of property, I should like to take this opportunity of stating that the hypothesis of 'hypnoid states'—which many reviewers were inclined to regard as the central portion of our work—sprang entirely from the initiative of Breuer. I regard the use of such a term as superfluous and misleading, because it interrupts the continuity of the problem as to the nature of the psychological process accompanying the formation of hysterical symptoms.—['Hypnoid states' were referred to in the 'Preliminary Com-munication', but they were discussed at greater length by Breuer in his contribution to the *Studies on Hysteria* (1895), Chapter III, Section IV. Freud enters into his theoretical disagreements with Breuer in more detail in the first section of his 'History of the Psycho-Analytic Move-ment' (1914*d*).]

[2] Cf. my paper on 'The Aetiology of Hysteria' (1896*c*).

fourteen years old at the time. Herr K. had made an arrangement with her and his wife that they should meet him one
afternoon at his place of business in the principal square of
B—— so as to have a view of a church festival. He persuaded
his wife, however, to stay at home, and sent away his clerks,
so that he was alone when the girl arrived. When the time for
the procession approached, he asked the girl to wait for him
at the door which opened on to the staircase leading to the
upper story, while he pulled down the outside shutters. He then
came back, and, instead of going out by the open door,
suddenly clasped the girl to him and pressed a kiss upon her
lips. This was surely just the situation to call up a distinct feeling
of sexual excitement in a girl of fourteen who had never before
been approached. But Dora had at that moment a violent feeling of disgust, tore herself free from the man, and hurried past
him to the staircase and from there to the street door. She
nevertheless continued to meet Herr K. Neither of them ever
mentioned the little scene; and according to her account Dora
kept it a secret till her confession during the treatment. For
some time afterwards, however, she avoided being alone with
Herr K. The K.'s had just made plans for an expedition which
was to last for some days and on which Dora was to have
accompanied them. After the scene of the kiss she refused to
join the party, without giving any reason.[1]

In this scene—second in order of mention, but first in order
of time—the behaviour of this child of fourteen was already
entirely and completely hysterical. I should without question
consider a person hysterical in whom an occasion for sexual
excitement elicited feelings that were preponderantly or exclusively unpleasurable; and I should do so whether or no the
person were capable of producing somatic symptoms. The
elucidation of the mechanism of this *reversal of affect* is one of the
most important and at the same time one of the most difficult
problems in the psychology of the neuroses. In my own judgement I am still some way from having achieved this end; and

[1] [In all the editions before 1924 the following footnote appeared at
this point: 'A contributory reason for this refusal will be found on
p. (24).' (This would correspond to pages 30–1 in the present edition.)
As no such reference could be traced either there or elsewhere, the
footnote was omitted, on Freud's instructions, in the English translation
of 1925, and in all the later German editions.]

I may add that within the limits of the present paper I shall be able to bring forward only a part of such knowledge on the subject as I do possess.[1]

In order to particularize Dora's case it is not enough merely to draw attention to the reversal of affect; there has also been a *displacement* of sensation. Instead of the genital sensation which would certainly have been felt by a healthy girl in such circumstances,[2] Dora was overcome by the unpleasurable feeling which is proper to the tract of mucous membrane at the entrance to the alimentary canal—that is by disgust. The stimulation of her lips by the kiss was no doubt of importance in localizing the feeling at that particular place; but I think I can also recognize another factor in operation.[3]

The disgust which Dora felt on that occasion did not become a permanent symptom, and even at the time of the treatment it was only, as it were, potentially present. She was a poor eater and confessed to some disinclination for food. On the other hand, the scene had left another consequence behind it in the shape of a sensory hallucination which occurred from time to time and even made its appearance while she was telling me her story. She declared that she could still feel upon the upper part of her body the pressure of Herr K.'s embrace. In accordance with certain rules of symptom-formation which I have come to know, and at the same time taking into account certain other of the patient's peculiarities, which were otherwise inexplicable,—such as her unwillingness to walk past any man whom she saw engaged in eager or affectionate conversation with a lady,—I have formed in my own mind the following

[1] [This is one of the problems which recurs constantly throughout Freud's writings. He touches upon it, for instance, in considering anxiety-dreams in Chapter VII, Section D, of the *Interpretation of Dreams*, 1900*a* (Standard Ed., 5, 582), in the opening paragraphs of his paper on 'Repression' (1915*d*), at the end of the first chapter of *Beyond the Pleasure Principle* (1920*g*), and again at the beginning of the second chapter of *Inhibitions, Symptoms and Anxiety* (1926*d*), where a fresh solution is proposed.]

[2] Our appreciation of these circumstances will be facilitated when more light has been thrown upon them. [Cf. p. 84 f.]

[3] The causes of Dora's disgust at the kiss were certainly not adventitious, for in that case she could not have failed to remember and mention them. I happen to know Herr K., for he was the same person who had visited me with the patient's father [p. 19], and he was still quite young and of prepossessing appearance.

reconstruction of the scene. I believe that during the man's passionate embrace she felt not merely his kiss upon her lips but also the pressure of his erect member against her body. This perception was revolting to her; it was dismissed from her memory, repressed, and replaced by the innocent sensation of pressure upon her thorax, which in turn derived an excessive intensity from its repressed source. Once more, therefore, we find a displacement from the lower part of the body to the upper.[1] On the other hand, the compulsive piece of behaviour which I have mentioned was formed as though it were derived from the undistorted recollection of the scene: she did not like walking past any man who she thought was in a state of sexual excitement, because she wanted to avoid seeing for a second time the somatic sign which accompanies it.

It is worth remarking that we have here three symptoms—the disgust, the sensation of pressure on the upper part of the body, and the avoidance of men engaged in affectionate conversation—all of them derived from a single experience, and that it is only by taking into account the interrelation of these three phenomena that we can understand the way in which the formation of the symptoms came about. The disgust is the symptom of repression in the erotogenic oral zone,[2] which, as we shall hear [p. 51], had been over-indulged in Dora's infancy by the habit of sensual sucking. The pressure of the erect member probably led to an analogous change in the corresponding female organ, the clitoris; and the excitation of this second erotogenic zone was referred by a process of displacement to the simultaneous pressure against the thorax and became fixed there. Her avoidance of men who might possibly be in a state of sexual excitement follows the mechanism of a

---

[1] The occurrence of displacements of this kind has not been assumed for the purpose of this single explanation; the assumption has proved indispensable for the explanation of a large class of symptoms. [Cf. below, p. 82, n. 2] Since treating Dora I have come across another instance of an embrace (this time without a kiss) causing a fright. It was a case of a young woman who had previously been devotedly fond of the man she was engaged to, but had suddenly begun to feel a coldness towards him, accompanied by severe depression, and on that account came to me for treatment. There was no difficulty in tracing the fright back to an erection on the man's part, which she had perceived but had dismissed from her consciousness.

[2] [See below, p. 52.]

phobia, its purpose being to safeguard her against any revival of the repressed perception.

In order to show that such a supplement to the story was possible, I questioned the patient very cautiously as to whether she knew anything of the physical signs of excitement in a man's body. Her answer, as touching the present, was 'Yes', but, as touching the time of the episode, 'I think not'. From the very beginning I took the greatest pains with this patient not to introduce her to any fresh facts in the region of sexual knowledge; and I did this, not from any conscientious motives, but because I was anxious to subject my assumptions to a rigorous test in this case. Accordingly, I did not call a thing by its name until her allusions to it had become so unambiguous that there seemed very slight risk in translating them into direct speech. Her answer was always prompt and frank: she knew about it already. But the question of *where* her knowledge came from was a riddle which her memories were unable to solve. She had forgotten the source of all her information on this subject.[1]

If I may suppose that the scene of the kiss took place in this way, I can arrive at the following derivation for the feelings of disgust.[2] Such feelings seem originally to be a reaction to the smell (and afterwards also to the sight) of excrement. But the genitals can act as a reminder of the excretory functions; and this applies especially to the male member, for that organ performs the function of micturition as well as the sexual function. Indeed, the function of micturition is the earlier known of the two, and the *only* one known during the pre-sexual period. Thus it happens that disgust becomes one of the means of affective expression in the sphere of sexual life. The Early Christian Father's '*inter urinas et faeces nascimur*' clings to sexual life and cannot be detached from it in spite of every effort at idealization. I should like, however, expressly to emphasize my opinion that the problem is not solved by the mere pointing out of this path of association. The fact that this association *can* be

[1] See the second dream [p. 99.—Cf. also pp. 36 *n.*, 62 and 120 *n.*]

[2] Here, as in all similar cases, the reader must be prepared to be met not by one but by several causes—by *overdetermination*. [Freud had mentioned this characteristic of hysterical symptoms in Section III of his chapter on the psychotherapy of hysteria in Breuer and Freud's *Studies on Hysteria*, 1895. It was also discussed by Breuer (with an acknowledgement to Freud) in Section III of his theoretical contribution to the same work.]

called up does not show that it actually *will* be called up. And indeed in normal circumstances it will not be. A knowledge of the paths does not render less necessary a knowledge of the forces which travel along them.[1]

I did not find it easy, however, to direct the patient's attention to her relations with Herr K. She declared that she had done with him. The uppermost layer of all her associations during the sessions, and everything of which she was easily conscious and of which she remembered having been conscious the day before, was always connected with her father. It was quite true that she could not forgive her father for continuing his relations with Herr K. and more particularly with Frau K. But she viewed those relations in a very different light from that in which her father wished them to appear. In her mind there was no doubt that what bound her father to this young and beautiful woman was a common love-affair. Nothing that could help to confirm this view had escaped her perception, which in this connection was pitilessly sharp; *here there were no gaps to be found in her memory.* Their acquaintance with the K.'s had begun before her father's serious illness; but it had not become intimate until the young woman had officially taken on the position of nurse during that illness, while Dora's mother had kept away from the sick-room. During the first summer holidays after his recovery things had happened which must have opened every one's eyes to the true character of this 'friendship'. The two families had taken a suite of rooms in common at the hotel. One day Frau K. had announced that she could not keep the bedroom which she had up till then shared with one of her children. A few days later Dora's father had given up his bed-

[1] All these discussions contain much that is typical and valid for hysteria in general. The subject of erection solves some of the most interesting hysterical symptoms. The attention that women pay to the outlines of men's genitals as seen through their clothing becomes, when it has been repressed, a source of the very frequent cases of avoiding company and of dreading society.—It is scarcely possible to exaggerate the pathogenic significance of the comprehensive tie uniting the sexual and the excremental, a tie which is at the basis of a very large number of hysterical phobias. [This topic recurs very frequently in Freud's writings. It appears, for instance, as early as 1897 in Draft K in the Fliess correspondence (Freud, 1950a), and as late as 1930 in the long footnote at the end of Chapter IV of *Civilization and its Discontents* (1930a).]

room, and they had both moved into new rooms—the end rooms, which were only separated by the passage, while the rooms they had given up had not offered any such security against interruption. Later on, whenever she had reproached her father about Frau K., he had been in the habit of saying that he could not understand her hostility and that, on the contrary, his children had every reason for being grateful to Frau K. Her mother, whom she had asked for an explanation of this mysterious remark, had told her that her father had been so unhappy at that time that he had made up his mind to go into the wood and kill himself, and that Frau K., suspecting as much, had gone after him and had persuaded him by her entreaties to preserve his life for the sake of his family. Of course, Dora went on, she herself did not believe this story; no doubt the two of them had been seen together in the wood, and her father had thereupon invented this fairy tale of his suicide so as to account for their rendezvous.[1]

When they had returned to B——, her father had visited Frau K. every day at definite hours, while her husband was at his business. Everybody had talked about it and had questioned her about it pointedly. Herr K. himself had often complained bitterly to her mother, though he had spared her herself any allusions to the subject—which she seemed to attribute to delicacy of feeling on his part. When they had all gone for walks together, her father and Frau K. had always known how to manage things so as to be alone with each other. There could be no doubt that she had taken money from him, for she spent more than she could possibly have afforded out of her own purse or her husband's. Dora added that her father had begun to make handsome presents to Frau K., and in order to make these less conspicuous had at the same time become especially liberal towards her mother and herself. And, while previously Frau K. had been an invalid and had even been obliged to spend months in a sanatorium for nervous disorders because she had been unable to walk, she had now become a healthy and lively woman.

Even after they had left B—— for the manufacturing town, these relations, already of many years' standing, had been

---

[1] This is the point of connection with her own pretence at suicide [p. 23], which may thus be regarded as the expression of a longing for a love of the same kind.

continued. From time to time her father used to declare that he could not endure the rawness of the climate, and that he must do something for himself; he would begin to cough and complain, until suddenly he would start off to B——, and from there write the most cheerful letters home. All these illnesses had only been pretexts for seeing his friend again. Then one day it had been decided that they were to move to Vienna and Dora began to suspect a hidden connection. And sure enough, they had scarcely been three weeks in Vienna when she heard that the K.'s had moved there as well. They were in Vienna, so she told me, at that very moment, and she frequently met her father with Frau K. in the street. She also met Herr K. very often, and he always used to turn round and look after her; and once when he had met her out by herself he had followed her for a long way, so as to make sure where she was going and whether she might not have a rendezvous.

On one occasion during the course of the treatment her father again felt worse, and went off to B—— for several weeks; and the sharp-sighted Dora had soon unearthed the fact that Frau K. had started off to the same place on a visit to her relatives there. It was at this time that Dora's criticisms of her father were the most frequent: he was insincere, he had a strain of falseness in his character, he only thought of his own enjoyment, and he had a gift for seeing things in the light which suited him best.

I could not in general dispute Dora's characterization of her father; and there was one particular respect in which it was easy to see that her reproaches were justified. When she was feeling embittered she used to be overcome by the idea that she had been handed over to Herr K. as the price of his tolerating the relations between her father and his wife; and her rage at her father's making such a use of her was visible behind her affection for him. At other times she was quite well aware that she had been guilty of exaggeration in talking like this. The two men had of course never made a formal agreement in which she was treated as an object for barter; her father in particular would have been horrified at any such suggestion. But he was one of those men who know how to evade a dilemma by falsifying their judgement upon one of the conflicting alternatives. If it had been pointed out to him that there might be danger for a growing girl in the constant and unsupervised companionship of a man who had no satisfaction from his own wife, he would have been certain to answer that he could rely upon his daughter, that a man like K. could never be dangerous to her, and that his friend was himself incapable of such intentions, or that Dora was still a child and was treated as a child by K. But as a matter of fact things were in a position in which each of the two men avoided drawing any conclusions from the other's behaviour which would have been awkward for his own plans. It was possible for Herr K. to send Dora flowers every day for a whole year while he was in the neighbourhood, to take every opportunity of giving her valuable presents, and to spend all his spare time in her company, without her parents noticing anything in his behaviour that was characteristic of love-making.

When a patient brings forward a sound and incontestable train of argument during psycho-analytic treatment, the physician is liable to feel a moment's embarrassment, and the patient may take advantage of it by asking: 'This is all perfectly correct and true, isn't it? What do you want to change in now that I've told it you?' But it soon becomes evident that the patient is using thoughts of this kind, which the analysis cannot attack, for the purpose of cloaking others which are anxious to escape from criticism and from consciousness. A string of reproaches against other people leads one to suspect the existence of a string of self-reproaches with the same content. All that need be done is to turn back each particular reproach on to the speaker himself. There is something undeniably automatic about this method of defending oneself against a self-reproach by making the same reproach against some one else. A model of it is to be found in the *tu quoque* arguments of children; if one of them is accused of being a liar, he will reply without an instant's hesitation: 'You're another.' A grown-up person who wanted to throw back abuse would look for some really exposed spot in his antagonist and would not lay the chief stress upon the same content being repeated. In paranoia the projection of a reproach on to another person without any alteration in its content and therefore without any consideration for reality becomes manifest as the process of forming delusions.

Dora's reproaches against her father had a 'lining' or

'backing' of self-reproaches of this kind with a corresponding content in every case, as I shall show in detail. She was right in thinking that her father did not wish to look too closely into Herr K.'s behaviour to his daughter, for fear of being disturbed in his own love-affair with Frau K. But Dora herself had done precisely the same thing. She had made herself an accomplice in the affair, and had dismissed from her mind every sign which tended to show its true character. It was not until after her adventure by the lake p. [25] that her eyes were opened and that she began to apply such a severe standard to her father. During all the previous years she had given every possible assistance to her father's relations with Frau K. She would never go to see her if she thought her father was there; but, knowing that in that case the children would have been sent out, she would turn her steps in a direction where she would be sure to meet them, and would go for a walk with them. There had been some one in the house who had been anxious at an early stage to open her eyes to the nature of her father's relations with Frau K., and to induce her to take sides against her. This was her last governess, an unmarried woman, no longer young, who was well-read and of advanced views.[1] The teacher and her pupil were for a while upon excellent terms, until suddenly Dora became hostile to her and insisted on her dismissal. So long as the governess had any influence she used it for stirring up feeling against Frau K. She explained to Dora's mother that it was incompatible with her dignity to tolerate such an intimacy between her husband and another woman; and she drew Dora's attention to all the obvious features of their relations. But her efforts were vain. Dora remained devoted to Frau K. and would hear of nothing that might make her think ill of her relations with her father. On the other hand she very easily fathomed the motives by which her governess was actuated. She might be blind in one direction, but she was sharp-sighted enough in the other. She saw that the governess was in love with her father. When he was there, she seemed to be quite

[1] This governess used to read every sort of book on sexual life and similar subjects, and talked to the girl about them, at the same time asking her quite frankly not to mention their conversations to her parents, as one could never tell what line they might take about them. For some time I looked upon this woman as the source of all Dora's secret knowledge, and perhaps I was not entirely wrong in this. [See, however, the footnote on p. 120.]

another person: at such times she could be amusing and obliging. While the family were living in the manufacturing town and Frau K. was not on the horizon, her hostility was directed against Dora's mother, who was then her more immediate rival. Up to this point Dora bore her no ill-will. She did not become angry until she observed that she herself was a subject of complete indifference to the governess, whose pretended affection for her was really meant for her father. While her father was away from the manufacturing town the governess had no time to spare for her, would not go for walks with her, and took no interest in her studies. No sooner had her father returned from B—— than she was once more ready with every sort of service and assistance. Thereupon Dora dropped her.

The poor woman had thrown a most unwelcome light on a part of Dora's own behaviour. What the governess had from time to time been to Dora, Dora had been to Herr K.'s children. She had been a mother to them, she had taught them, she had gone for walks with them, she had offered them a complete substitute for the slight interest which their own mother showed in them. Herr K. and his wife had often talked of getting a divorce; but it never took place, because Herr K., who was an affectionate father, would not give up either of the two children. A common interest in the children had from the first been a bond between Herr K. and Dora. Her preoccupation with his children was evidently a cloak for something else that Dora was anxious to hide from herself and from other people.

The same inference was to be drawn both from her behaviour towards the children, regarded in the light of the governess's behaviour towards herself, and from her silent acquiescence in her father's relations with Frau K.—namely, that she had all these years been in love with Herr K. When I informed her of this conclusion she did not assent to it. It is true that she at once told me that other people besides (one of her cousins, for instance—a girl who had stopped with them for some time at B——) had said to her: 'Why you're simply wild about that man!' But she herself could not be got to recollect any feelings of the kind. Later on, when the quantity of material that had come up had made it difficult for her to persist in her denial, she admitted that she might have been in love with Herr K. at B——, but declared that since the scene by the lake it had all been over.[1] In any case it was quite certain that the reproaches which she made against her father of having been deaf to the most imperative calls of duty and of having seen things in the light which was most convenient from the point of view of his own passions—these reproaches recoiled on her own head.[2]

Her other reproach against her father was that his ill-health was only a pretext and that he exploited it for his own purposes. This reproach, too, concealed a whole section of her own secret history. One day she complained of a professedly new symptom, which consisted of piercing gastric pains. 'Whom are you copying now?' I asked her, and found I had hit the mark. The day before she had visited her cousins, the daughters of the aunt who had died. The younger one had become engaged, and this had given occasion to the elder one for falling ill with gastric pains, and she was to be sent off to Semmering.[3] Dora thought it was all just envy on the part of the elder sister; she always got ill when she wanted something, and what she wanted now was to be away from home so as not to have to look on at her sister's happiness.[4] But Dora's own gastric pains proclaimed the fact that she identified herself with her cousin, who, according to her, was a malingerer. Her grounds for this identification were either that she too envied the luckier girl her love, or that she saw her own story reflected in that of the elder sister, who had recently had a love-affair which had ended unhappily.[5] But she had also learned from observing Frau K. what useful things illnesses could become. Herr K. spent part of the year in travelling. Whenever he came back, he used to find his wife in bad health, although, as Dora knew, she had been quite well only the day before. Dora realized that the presence of the husband had the effect of making his wife ill, and that she was glad to

[1] Compare the second dream.

[2] The question then arises: If Dora loved Herr K., what was the reason for her refusing him in the scene by the lake? Or at any rate, why did her refusal take such a brutal form, as though she were embittered against him? And how could a girl who was in love feel insulted by a proposal which was made in a manner neither tactless nor offensive?

[3] [A fashionable health resort in the mountains, about fifty miles south of Vienna.]

[4] An event of everyday occurrence between sisters.

[5] I shall discuss later on what further conclusion I drew from these gastric pains [p. 78].

be ill so as to be able to escape the conjugal duties which she so much detested. At this point in the discussion Dora suddenly brought in an allusion to her own alternations between good and bad health during the first years of her girlhood at B——; and I was thus driven to suspect that her states of health were to be regarded as depending upon something else, in the same way as Frau K.'s. (It is a rule of psycho-analytic technique that an internal connection which is still undisclosed will announce its presence by means of a contiguity—a temporal proximity—of associations; just as in writing, if 'a' and 'b' are put side by side, it means that the syllable 'ab' is to be formed out of them.) Dora had had a very large number of attacks of coughing accompanied by loss of voice. Could it be that the presence or absence of the man she loved had had an influence upon the appearance and disappearance of the symptoms of her illness? If this were so, it must be possible to discover some coincidence or other which would betray the fact. I asked her what the average length of these attacks had been. 'From three to six weeks, perhaps.' How long had Herr K.'s absences lasted? 'Three to six weeks, too', she was obliged to admit. Her illness was therefore a demonstration of her love for K., just as his wife's was a demonstration of her *dislike*. It was only necessary to suppose that her behaviour had been the opposite of Frau K.'s and that she had been ill when he was absent and well when he had come back. And this really seemed to have been so, at least during the first period of the attacks. Later on it no doubt became necessary to obscure the coincidence between her attacks of illness and the absence of the man she secretly loved, lest its regularity should betray her secret. The length of the attacks would then remain as a trace of their original significance.

I remembered that long before, while I was working at Charcot's clinic [1885–6], I had seen and heard how in cases of hysterical mutism writing operated vicariously in the place of speech. Such patients were able to write more fluently, quicker, and better than others did or than they themselves had done previously. The same thing had happened with Dora. In the first days of her attacks of aphonia 'writing had always come specially easy to her'. No psychological elucidation was really required for this peculiarity, which was the expression of a physiological substitutive function enforced by necessity; it was noticeable, however, that such an elucidation was easily to be found. Herr K. used to write to her at length while he was travelling and to send her picture post-cards. It used to happen that she alone was informed as to the date of his return, and that his arrival took his wife by surprise. Moreover, that a person will correspond with an absent friend whom he cannot talk to is scarcely less obvious than that if he has lost his voice he will try to make himself understood in writing. Dora's aphonia, then, allowed of the following symbolic interpretation. When the man she loved was away she gave up speaking; speech had lost its value since she could not speak to *him*. On the other hand, writing gained in importance, as being the only means of communication with him in his absence.

Am I now going on to assert that in every instance in which there are periodical attacks of aphonia we are to diagnose the existence of a loved person who is at times away from the patient? Nothing could be further from my intention. The determination of Dora's symptoms is far too specific for it to be possible to expect a frequent recurrence of the same accidental aetiology. But, if so, what is the value of our elucidation of the aphonia in the present case? Have we not merely allowed ourselves to become the victims of a *jeu d'esprit*? I think not. In this connection we must recall the question which has so often been raised, whether the symptoms of hysteria are of psychical or of somatic origin, or whether, if the former is granted, they are necessarily *all* of them psychically determined. Like so many other questions to which we find investigators returning again and again without success, this question is not adequately framed. The alternatives stated in it do not cover the real essence of the matter. As far as I can see, every hysterical symptom involves the participation of *both* sides. It cannot occur without the presence of a certain degree of *omatic compliance* [1] offered by some normal or pathological process in or connected with one of the bodily organs. And it cannot occur more than once—and the capacity for repeating itself is one of the characteristics of a hysterical symptom—unless it has a psychical significance, a *meaning*. The hysterical symptom does not carry

[1] [This seems to be Freud's earliest use of the term, which scarcely reappears in later works. (See the last words of his paper on psychogenic disturbances of vision, 1910*i*, and the discussion on masturbation, 1912*f*.)]

this meaning with it, but the meaning is lent to it, soldered to it, as it were; and in every instance the meaning can be a different one, according to the nature of the suppressed thoughts which are struggling for expression. However, there are a number of factors at work which tend to make less arbitrary the relations between the unconscious thoughts and the somatic processes that are at their disposal as a means of expression, and which tend to make those relations approximate to a few typical forms. For therapeutic purposes the most important determinants are those given by the fortuitous psychical material; the clearing-up of the symptoms is achieved by looking for their psychical significance. When everything that can be got rid of by psycho-analysis has been cleared away, we are in a position to form all kinds of conjectures, which probably meet the facts, as regards the somatic basis of the symptoms—a basis which is as a rule constitutional and organic. Thus in Dora's case we shall not content ourselves with a psycho-analytic interpretation of her attacks of coughing and aphonia; but we shall also indicate the organic factor which was the source of the 'somatic compliance' that enabled her to express her love for a man who was periodically absent. And if the connection between the symptomatic expression and the unconscious mental content should strike us as being in this case a clever *tour de force*, we shall be relieved to hear that it succeeds in creating the same impression in every other case and in every other instance.

I am prepared to be told at this point that there is no very great advantage in having been taught by psycho-analysis that the clue to the problem of hysteria is to be found not in 'a peculiar instability of the molecules of the nerves' or in a liability to 'hypnoid states'—but in a 'somatic compliance'. But in reply to the objection I may remark that this new view has not only to some extent pushed the problem further back, but has also to some extent diminished it. We have no longer to deal with the *whole* problem, but only with the portion of it involving that particular characteristic of hysteria *which differentiates it* from other psychoneuroses. The mental events in all psychoneuroses proceed for a considerable distance along the same lines before any question arises of the 'somatic compliance' which may afford the unconscious mental processes a physical outlet. When this factor is not forthcoming, something other than a hysterical symptom will arise out of the total situation;

yet it will still be something of an allied nature, a phobia, perhaps, or an obsession—in short, a psychical symptom.

I now return to the reproach of malingering which Dora
brought against her father. It soon became evident that this
reproach corresponded to self-reproaches not only concerning
her earlier states of ill-health but also concerning the present
time. At such points the physician is usually faced by the task
of guessing and filling in what the analysis offers him in the
shape only of hints and allusions. I was obliged to point out to
the patient that her present ill-health was just as much actuated
by motives and was just as tendentious as had been Frau K.'s
illness, which she had understood so well. There could be no
doubt, I said, that she had an aim in view which she hoped to
gain by her illness. That aim could be none other than to
detach her father from Frau K. She had been unable to achieve
this by prayers or arguments; perhaps she hoped to succeed by
frightening her father (there was her farewell letter), or by
awakening his pity (there were her fainting-fits) [p. 23], or if
all this was in vain, at least she would be taking her revenge on
him. She knew very well, I went on, how much he was attached
to her, and that tears used to come into his eyes whenever he
was asked after his daughter's health. I felt quite convinced that
she would recover at once if only her father were to tell her that
he had sacrificed Frau K. for the sake of her health. But, I
added, I hoped he would not let himself be persuaded to do this,
for then she would have learned what a powerful weapon she
had in her hands, and she would certainly not fail on every
future occasion to make use once more of her liability to ill-
health. Yet if her father refused to give way to her, I was quite
sure she would not let herself be deprived of her illness so
easily.

I will pass over the details which showed how entirely correct
all of this was, and I will instead add a few general remarks
upon the part played in hysteria by the *motives of illness*. A
*motive* for being ill is sharply to be distinguished as a concept
from a *liability* to being ill—from the material out of which
symptoms are formed. The motives have no share in the formation of symptoms, and indeed are not present at the beginning
of the illness. They only appear secondarily to it; but it is not

until they have appeared that the disease is fully constituted.[1] Their presence can be reckoned upon in every case in which there is real suffering and which is of fairly long standing. A symptom comes into the patient's mental life at first as an un-welcome guest; it has everything against it; and that is why it may vanish so easily, apparently of its own accord, under the influence of time. To begin with there is no use to which it can be put in the domestic economy of the mind; but very often it succeeds in finding one secondarily. Some psychical current or other finds it convenient to make use of it, and in that way the symptom manages to obtain a *secondary function* and remains, as it were, anchored fast in the patient's mental life. And so it happens that any one who tries to make him well is to his astonishment brought up against a powerful resistance, which teaches him that the patient's intention of getting rid of his

[1] [*Footnote added* 1923:] This is not quite right. The statement that the motives of illness are not present at the beginning of the illness, but only appear secondarily to it, cannot be maintained. In the very next para-graph motives for being ill are mentioned which were in existence before the outbreak of illness, and were partly responsible for that outbreak. I subsequently found a better way of meeting the facts, by introducing a distinction between the *primary* advantage derived from the illness and the *secondary* one. The motive for being ill is, of course, invariably the gaining of some advantage. What follows in the later sentences of this paragraph applies to the secondary gain. But in every neurotic illness a primary gain has also to be recognized. In the first place, falling ill involves a saving of psychical effort; it emerges as being economically the most convenient solution where there is a mental conflict (we speak of a 'flight into illness'), even though in most cases the ineffectiveness of such an escape becomes manifest at a later stage. This element in the primary gain may be described as the *internal* or psychological one, and it is, so to say, a constant one. But beyond this, external factors (such as in the instance given [in the following paragraph in the text] of the situation of a woman subjugated by her husband) may contribute motives for falling ill; and these will constitute the *external* element in the primary gain. [This question was already adumbrated by Freud in a letter to Fliess of November 18, 1897 (Freud, 1950a, Letter 76). The distinc-tion between the primary and secondary gain from illness was fully dis-cussed in Lecture XXIV of his *Introductory Lectures* (1916–17), though it had been indicated earlier, in his paper on hysterical attacks (1909a, Section B) where the term 'flight into illness' was also used. At a much later date he returned to the topic once more (in *Inhibitions, Symptoms and Anxiety*, 1926d, particularly in Chapter III). The terms 'paranosic' and 'epinosic' gain have been used in English to distinguish primary and secondary gain from illness respectively.]

complaint is not so entirely and completely serious as it seemed.[1] Let us imagine a workman, a bricklayer, let us say, who has fallen off a house and been crippled, and now earns his livelihood by begging at the street-corner. Let us then suppose that a miracle-worker comes along and promises him to make his crooked leg straight and capable of walking. It would be unwise, I think, to look forward to seeing an expression of peculiar bliss upon the man's features. No doubt at the time of the accident he felt he was extremely unlucky, when he realized that he would never be able to do any more work and would have to starve or live upon charity. But since then the very thing which in the first instance threw him out of employment has become his source of income: he lives by his disablement. If that is taken from him he may become totally helpless. He has in the meantime forgotten his trade and lost his habits of industry; he has grown accustomed to idleness, and perhaps to drink as well.

The motives for being ill often begin to be active even in childhood. A little girl in her greed for love does not enjoy having to share the affection of her parents with her brothers and sisters; and she notices that the whole of their affection is lavished on her once more whenever she arouses their anxiety by falling ill. She has now discovered a means of enticing out her parents' love, and will make use of that means as soon as she has the necessary psychical material at her disposal for producing an illness. When such a child has grown up to be a woman she may find all the demands she used to make in her childhood countered owing to her marriage with an inconsiderate husband, who may subjugate her will, mercilessly exploit her capacity for work, and lavish neither his affection nor his money upon her. In that case ill-health will be her one weapon for maintaining her position. It will procure her the care she longs for; it will force her husband to make pecuniary sacrifices for her and to show her consideration, as he would never have done while she was well; and it will compel him to treat her with solicitude if she recovers, for otherwise a relapse will threaten. Her state of ill-health will have every appearance of being objective and involuntary—the very doctor who treats

[1] A man of letters, who incidentally is also a physician—Arthur Schnitzler—has expressed this piece of knowledge very correctly in his [play] *Paracelsus*.

her will bear witness to the fact; and for that reason she will not need to feel any conscious self-reproaches at making such successful use of a means which she had found effective in her years of childhood.

And yet illnesses of this kind *are* the result of intention. They are as a rule levelled at a particular person, and consequently vanish with that person's departure. The crudest and most commonplace views on the character of hysterical disorders —such as are to be heard from uneducated relatives or nurses— are in a certain sense right. It is true that the paralysed and bedridden woman would spring to her feet if a fire were to break out in her room, and that the spoiled wife would forget all her sufferings if her child were to fall dangerously ill or if some catastrophe were to threaten the family circumstances. People who speak of the patients in this way are right except upon a single point: they overlook the psychological distinction between what is conscious and what is unconscious. This may be permissible where children are concerned, but with adults it is no longer possible. That is why all these asseverations that it is 'only a question of willing' and all the encouragements and abuse that are addressed to the patient are of no avail. An attempt must first be made by the roundabout methods of analysis to convince the patient herself of the existence in her of an intention to be ill.

It is in combating the motives of illness that the weak point in every kind of therapeutic treatment of hysteria lies. This is quite generally true, and it applies equally to psycho-analysis. Destiny has an easier time of it in this respect: it need not concern itself either with the patient's constitution or with his pathogenic material; it has only to take away a motive for being ill, and the patient is temporarily or perhaps even permanently freed from his illness. How many fewer miraculous cures and spontaneous disappearances of symptoms should we physicians have to register in cases of hysteria, if we were more often given a sight of the human interests which the patient keeps hidden from us! In one case, some stated period of time has elapsed; in a second, consideration for some other person has ceased to operate; in a third, the situation has been fundamentally changed by some external event—and the whole disorder, which up till then had shown the greatest obstinacy, vanishes at a single blow, apparently of its own accord, but really because it has been deprived of its most powerful motive, one of the uses to which it has been put in the patient's life.

Motives that support the patient in being ill are probably to be found in all fully developed cases. But there are some in which the motives are purely internal—such as desire for self-punishment, that is, penitence and remorse. It will be found much easier to solve the therapeutic problem in such cases than in those in which the illness is related to the attainment of some external aim.[1] In Dora's case that aim was clearly to touch her father's heart and to detach him from Frau K.

None of her father's actions seemed to have embittered her so much as his readiness to consider the scene by the lake as a product of her imagination. She was almost beside herself at the idea of its being supposed that she had merely fancied something on that occasion. For a long time I was in perplexity as to what the self-reproach could be which lay behind her passionate repudiation of this explanation of the episode. It was justifiable to suspect that there was something concealed, for a reproach which misses the mark gives no lasting offence. On the other hand, I came to the conclusion that Dora's story must correspond to the facts in every respect. No sooner had she grasped Herr K.'s intention than, without letting him finish what he had to say, she had given him a slap in the face and hurried away. Her behaviour must have seemed as incomprehensible to the man after she had left him as to us, for he must long before have gathered from innumerable small signs that he was secure of the girl's affections. In our discussion of Dora's second dream we shall come upon the solution of this riddle as well as upon the self-reproach which we have hitherto failed to discover [p. 106 ff.].

As she kept on repeating her complaints against her father with a wearisome monotony, and as at the same time her cough continued, I was led to think that this symptom might have some meaning in connection with her father. And apart from this, the explanation of the symptom which I had hitherto obtained was far from fulfilling the requirements which I am accustomed to make of such explanations. According to a rule which I had found confirmed over and over again by experi-

---

[1] [Later, however, Freud took a very different view of the therapeutic difficulties in cases of *unconscious* desire for self-punishment. See, e.g., Chapter V of *The Ego and the Id* (1923b).]

ence, though I had not yet ventured to erect it into a general principle, a symptom signifies the representation—the realization—of a phantasy with a sexual content, that is to say, it signifies a sexual situation. It would be better to say that at least *one* of the meanings of a symptom is the representation of a sexual phantasy, but that no such limitation is imposed upon the content of its other meanings. Any one who takes up psycho-analytic work will quickly discover that a symptom has more than one meaning and serves to represent several unconscious mental processes simultaneously. And I should like to add that in my estimation a single unconscious mental process or phantasy will scarcely ever suffice for the production of a symptom.

An opportunity very soon occurred for interpreting Dora's nervous cough in this way by means of an imagined sexual situation. She had once again been insisting that Frau K. only loved her father because he was '*ein vermögender Mann*' ['a man of means']. Certain details of the way in which she expressed herself (which I pass over here, like most other purely technical parts of the analysis) led me to see that behind this phrase its opposite lay concealed, namely, that her father was '*ein unvermögender Mann*' ['a man without means']. This could only be meant in a sexual sense—that her father, as a man, was without means, was impotent.[1] Dora confirmed this interpretation from her conscious knowledge; whereupon I pointed out the contradiction she was involved in if on the one hand she continued to insist that her father's relation with Frau K. was a common love-affair, and on the other hand maintained that her father was impotent, or in other words incapable of carrying on an affair of such a kind. Her answer showed that she had no need to admit the contradiction. She knew very well, she said, that there was more than one way of obtaining sexual gratification. (The source of this piece of knowledge, however, was once more untraceable.) I questioned her further, whether she referred to the use of organs other than the genitals for the purpose of sexual intercourse, and she replied in the affirmative. I could then go on to say that in that case she must be thinking of precisely those parts of the body which in her case were in a state of irritation,—the throat and the oral cavity. To be sure,

[1] ['*Unvermögend*' means literally 'unable', and is commonly used in the sense of both 'not rich' and 'impotent'.]

she would not hear of going so far as this in recognizing her own thoughts; and indeed, if the occurrence of the symptom was to be made possible at all, it was essential that she should not be completely clear on the subject. But the conclusion was inevitable that with her spasmodic cough, which, as is usual, was referred for its exciting stimulus to a tickling in her throat, she pictured to herself a scene of sexual gratification *per os* between the two people whose love-affair occupied her mind so incessantly. A very short time after she had tacitly accepted this explanation her cough vanished—which fitted in very well with my view; but I do not wish to lay too much stress upon this development, since her cough had so often before disappeared spontaneously.

This short piece of the analysis may perhaps have excited in the medical reader—apart from the scepticism to which he is entitled—feelings of astonishment and horror; and I am prepared at this point to look into these two reactions so as to discover whether they are justifiable. The astonishment is probably caused by my daring to talk about such delicate and unpleasant subjects to a young girl—or, for that matter, to any woman who is sexually active. The horror is aroused, no doubt, by the possibility that an inexperienced girl could know about practices of such a kind and could occupy her imagination with them. I would advise recourse to moderation and reasonableness upon both points. There is no cause for indignation either in the one case or in the other. It is possible for a man to talk to girls and women upon sexual matters of every kind without doing them harm and without bringing suspicion upon himself, so long as, in the first place, he adopts a particular way of doing it, and, in the second place, can make them feel convinced that it is unavoidable. A gynaecologist, after all, under the same conditions, does not hesitate to make them submit to uncovering every possible part of their body. The best way of speaking about such things is to be dry and direct; and that is at the same time the method furthest removed from the prurience with which the same subjects are handled in 'society', and to which girls and women alike are so thoroughly accustomed. I call bodily organs and processes by their technical names, and I tell these to the patient if they—the names, I mean—happen to be unknown to her. *J'appelle un chat un chat.* I have certainly heard of some people—doctors and laymen—who are scan-dalized by a therapeutic method in which conversations of this sort occur, and who appear to envy either me or my patients the titillation which, according to their notions, such a method must afford. But I am too well acquainted with the respecta-bility of these gentry to excite myself over them. I shall avoid the temptation of writing a satire upon them. But there is one thing that I will mention: often, after I have for some time treated a patient who had not at first found it easy to be open about sexual matters, I have had the satisfaction of hearing her exclaim: 'Why, after all, your treatment is far more respectable than Mr. X.'s conversation!'

No one can undertake the treatment of a case of hysteria until he is convinced of the impossibility of avoiding the mention of sexual subjects, or unless he is prepared to allow himself to be convinced by experience. The right attitude is: '*pour faire une omelette il faut casser des œufs.*' The patients themselves are easy to convince; and there are only too many opportunities of doing so in the course of the treatment. There is no necessity for feeling any compunction at discussing the facts of normal or abnormal sexual life with them. With the exercise of a little caution all that is done is to translate into conscious ideas what was already known in the unconscious; and, after all, the whole effectiveness of the treatment is based upon our knowledge that the affect attached to an unconscious idea operates more strongly and, since it cannot be inhibited, more injuriously than the affect attached to a conscious one. There is never any danger of corrupting an inexperienced girl. For where there is no know-ledge of sexual processes even in the unconscious, no hysterical symptom will arise; and where hysteria is found there can no longer be any question of 'innocence of mind' in the sense in which parents and educators use the phrase. With children of ten, of twelve, or of fourteen, with boys and girls alike, I have satisfied myself that the truth of this statement can invariably be relied upon.

As regards the second kind of emotional reaction, which is not directed against me this time, but against my patient—supposing that my view of her is correct—and which regards the perverse nature of her phantasies as horrible, I should like to say emphatically that a medical man has no business to in-dulge in such passionate condemnation. I may also remark in passing that it seems to me superfluous for a physician who is writing upon the aberrations of the sexual instincts to seize every opportunity of inserting into the text expressions of his personal repugnance at such revolting things. We are faced by a fact; and it is to be hoped that we shall grow accustomed to it, when we have put our own tastes on one side. We must learn to speak without indignation of what we call the sexual perversions—instances in which the sexual function has extended its limits in respect either to the part of the body concerned or to the sexual object chosen. The uncertainty in regard to the boundaries of what is to be called normal sexual life, when we take different races and different epochs into account, should in itself be enough to cool the zealot's ardour. We surely ought not to forget that the perversion which is the most repellent to us, the sensual love of a man for a man, was not only tolerated by a people so far our superiors in cultivation as were the Greeks, but was actually entrusted by them with important social functions. The sexual life of each one of us extends to a slight degree—now in this direction, now in that—beyond the narrow lines imposed as the standard of normality. The perversions are neither bestial nor degenerate in the emotional sense of the word. They are a development of germs all of which are contained in the undifferentiated sexual disposition of the child, and which, by being suppressed or by being diverted to higher, asexual aims—by being 'sublimated' [1]—are destined to provide the energy for a great number of our cultural achievements. When, therefore, any one has *become* a gross and manifest pervert, it would be more correct to say that he has *remained* one, for he exhibits a certain stage of *inhibited development*. All psychoneurotics are persons with strongly marked perverse tendencies, which have been repressed in the course of their development and have become unconscious. Consequently their unconscious *phantasies* show precisely the same content as the documentarily recorded *actions* of perverts—even though they have not read Krafft-Ebing's *Psychopathia Sexualis*, to which simple-minded people attribute such a large share of the responsibility for the production of perverse tendencies. Psychoneuroses are, so to speak, the *negative* of perversions. In neurotics their sexual constitution, under which the effects of heredity are included, operates in combination with any accidental influences in their

[1] [Cf. the second of Freud's *Three Essays* (1905d), this volume p. 178.]

life which may disturb the development of normal sexuality. A
stream of water which meets with an obstacle in the river-bed
is dammed up and flows back into old channels which had
formerly seemed fated to run dry. The motive forces leading to
the formation of hysterical symptoms draw their strength not
only from repressed *normal* sexuality but also from unconscious
perverse activities.[1]

The less repellent of the so-called sexual perversions are very
widely diffused among the whole population, as every one
knows except medical writers upon the subject. Or, I should
rather say, they know it too; only they take care to forget it at
the moment when they take up their pens to write about it. So
it is not to be wondered at that this hysterical girl of nearly[2]
nineteen, who had heard of the occurrence of such a method of
sexual intercourse (sucking at the male organ), should have
developed an unconscious phantasy of this sort and should have
given it expression by an irritation in her throat and by coughing. Nor would it have been very extraordinary if she had
arrived at such a phantasy even without having had any enlightenment from external sources—an occurrence which I have
quite certainly observed in other patients. For in her case a
noteworthy fact afforded the necessary somatic prerequisite for
this independent creation of a phantasy which would coincide
with the practices of perverts. She remembered very well that
in her childhood she had been a thumb-sucker. Her father, too,
recollected breaking her of the habit after it had persisted into
her fourth or fifth year. Dora herself had a clear picture of a
scene from her early childhood in which she was sitting on the
floor in a corner sucking her left thumb and at the same time
tugging with her right hand at the lobe of her brother's ear as
he sat quietly beside her. Here we have an instance of the complete form of self-gratification by sucking, as it has also been
described to me by other patients, who had subsequently
become anaesthetic and hysterical.

[1] These remarks upon the sexual perversions had been written some
years before the appearance of Bloch's excellent book (*Beiträge zur
Ätiologie der Psychopathia sexualis*, 1902 and 1903). See also my *Three
Essays on the Theory of Sexuality*, published this year [1905d, particularly
the first essay (this volume pp. 135–72), in which most of the points in
the present paragraph are enlarged upon. For the following paragraph,
see the third section of the second essay (p. 183 ff.)].

[2] [This word was added in 1924.]

One of these patients gave me a piece of information which sheds a clear light on the origin of this curious habit. This young woman had never broken herself of the habit of sucking. She retained a memory of her childhood, dating back, according to her, to the first half of her second year, in which she saw herself sucking at her nurse's breast and at the same time pulling rhythmically at the lobe of her nurse's ear. No one will feel inclined to dispute, I think, that the mucous membrane of the lips and mouth is to be regarded as a primary 'erotogenic zone',[1] since it preserves this earlier significance in the act of kissing, which is looked upon as normal. An intense activity of this erotogenic zone at an early age thus determines the subsequent presence of a somatic compliance on the part of the tract of mucous membrane which begins at the lips. Thus, at a time when the sexual object proper, that is, the male organ, has already become known, circumstances may arise which once more increase the excitation of the oral zone, whose erotogenic character has, as we have seen, been retained. It then needs very little creative power to substitute the sexual object of the moment (the penis) for the original object (the nipple) or for the finger which does duty for it, and to place the current sexual object in the situation in which gratification was originally obtained. So we see that this excessively repulsive and perverted phantasy of sucking at a penis has the most innocent origin. It is a new version of what may be described as a prehistoric impression of sucking at the mother's or nurse's breast —an impression which has usually been revived by contact with children who are being nursed. In most instances a cow's udder has aptly played the part of an image intermediate between a nipple and a penis.[2]

The interpretation we have just been discussing of Dora's throat symptoms may also give rise to a further remark. It may be asked how this sexual situation imagined by her can be compatible with our other explanation of the symptoms. That explanation, it will be remembered, was to the effect that the

[1] [Cf. Section 5 of the first of Freud's *Three Essays* (1905*d*), this volume p. 167 f.]

[2] [See the confirmation of this detail in the case of 'Little Hans', Freud, 1909*b* (near the beginning of Section I).]

coming and going of the symptoms reflected the presence and absence of the man she was in love with, and, as regards his wife's behaviour, expressed the following thought: 'If *I* were his wife, I should love him in quite a different way; I should be ill (from longing, let us say) when he was away, and well (from joy) when he was home again.' To this objection I must reply that my experience in the clearing-up of hysterical symptoms has shown that it is not necessary for the various meanings of a symptom to be compatible with one another, that is, to fit together into a connected whole. It is enough that the unity should be constituted by the subject-matter which has given rise to all the various phantasies. In the present case, moreover, compatibility even of the first kind is not out of the question. One of the two meanings is related more to the cough, and the other to the aphonia and the periodicity of the disorder. A closer analysis would probably have disclosed a far greater number of mental elements in relation to the details of the illness.

We have already learnt that it quite regularly happens that a single symptom corresponds to several meanings *simultaneously*. We may now add that it can express several meanings *in succession*. In the course of years a symptom can change its meaning or its chief meaning, or the leading role can pass from one meaning to another. It is as though there were a conservative trait in the character of neuroses which ensures that a symptom that has once been formed shall if possible be retained, even though the unconscious thought to which it gave expression has lost its meaning. Moreover, there is no difficulty in explaining this tendency towards the retention of a symptom upon a mechanical basis. The production of a symptom of this kind is so difficult, the translation of a purely psychical excitation into physical terms—the process which I have called 'conversion' [1] —depends on the concurrence of so many favourable conditions, the somatic compliance necessary for conversion is so seldom forthcoming, that an impulsion towards the discharge of an unconscious excitation will so far as possible make use of any channel for discharge which may already be in existence. It appears to be far more difficult to create a fresh conversion than to form paths of association between a new thought which

[1] [The term 'conversion' was introduced by Freud in Section 1 of his first paper on the neuro-psychoses of defence (1894*a*).]

is in need of discharge and the old one which is no longer in
need of it. The current flows along these paths from the new
source of excitation to the old point of discharge—pouring into
the symptom, in the words of the Gospel, like new wine into an
old bottle. These remarks would make it seem that the somatic
side of a hysterical symptom is the more stable of the two and
the harder to replace, while the psychical side is a variable
element for which a substitute can more easily be found. Yet
we should not try to infer anything from this comparison as
regards the relative importance of the two elements. From the
point of view of mental therapeutics the mental side must
always be the more significant.

Dora's incessant repetition of the same thoughts about her
father's relations with Frau K. made it possible to derive still
further important material from the analysis.

A train of thought such as this may be described as excessively intense, or better *reinforced*, or 'supervalent' ['*überwertig*']
in Wernicke's [1900, 140] sense. It shows its pathological character in spite of its apparently reasonable content, by the single
peculiarity that no amount of conscious and voluntary effort
of thought on the patient's part is able to dissipate or remove
it. A normal train of thought, however intense it may be, can
eventually be disposed of. Dora felt quite rightly that her
thoughts about her father required to be judged in a special
way. 'I can think of nothing else', she complained again and
again. 'I know my brother says we children have no right to
criticize this behaviour of Father's. He declares that we ought
not to trouble ourselves about it, and ought even to be glad,
perhaps, that he has found a woman he can love, since Mother
understands him so little. I can quite see that, and I should like
to think the same as my brother, but I can't. I can't forgive him
for it.' [1]

Now what is one to do in the face of a supervalent thought
like this, after one has heard what its conscious grounds are and
listened to the ineffectual protests made against it? Reflection
will suggest that *this excessively intense train of thought must owe its*

---

[1] A supervalent thought of this kind is often the only symptom,
beyond deep depression, of a pathological condition which is usually
described as 'melancholia', but which can be cleared up by psycho-
analysis like a hysteria.

*reinforcement to the unconscious.* It cannot be resolved by any effort of thought, either because it itself reaches with its root down into unconscious, repressed material, or because another unconscious thought lies concealed behind it. In the latter case, the concealed thought is usually the direct contrary of the supervalent one. Contrary thoughts are always closely connected with each other and are often paired off in such a way that *the one thought is excessively intensely conscious while its counterpart is repressed and unconscious.* This relation between the two thoughts is an effect of the process of repression. For repression is often achieved by means of an excessive reinforcement of the thought contrary to the one which is to be repressed. This process I call *reactive* reinforcement, and the thought which asserts itself with excessive intensity in consciousness and (in the same way as a prejudice) cannot be removed I call a *reactive thought.* The two thoughts then act towards each other much like the two needles of an astatic galvanometer. The reactive thought keeps the objectionable one under repression by means of a certain surplus of intensity; but for that reason it itself is 'damped' and proof against conscious efforts of thought. So that the way to deprive the excessively intense thought of its reinforcement is by bringing its repressed contrary into consciousness.[1]

We must also be prepared to meet with instances in which the supervalence of a thought is due not to the presence of one only of these two causes but to a concurrence of both of them. Other complications, too, may arise, but they can easily be fitted into the general scheme.

Let us now apply our theory to the instance provided by Dora's case.[2] We will begin with the first hypothesis, namely. that her preoccupation with her father's relations to Frau K,

[1] [The subject of 'excessively intense' ideas had been discussed at some length (and on much the same lines) in the first two sections of Part II of his posthumously published 'Project for a Scientific Psychology' in 1895. (See Freud, 1950a.)]

[2] [Of the two possibilities—viz. that the supervalent thought may be due (a) to *direct* and (b) to *reactive* reinforcement from the unconscious —(a) is discussed in this and the next two paragraphs, while (b) is shown to be present in two forms—the first of which is considered in the three paragraphs that follow, and the second in the remainder of the section.]

owed its obsessive character to the fact that its root was unknown to her and lay in the unconscious. It is not difficult to
divine the nature of that root from her circumstances and her
conduct. Her behaviour obviously went far beyond what would
have been appropriate to filial concern. She felt and acted
more like a jealous wife—in a way which would have been
comprehensible in her mother. By her ultimatum to her father
('either her or me'), by the scenes she used to make, by the
suicidal intentions she allowed to transpire,—by all this she was
clearlyputting herself in her mother's place. If we have rightly
guessed the nature of the imaginary sexual situation which
underlay her cough, in that phantasy she must have been
putting herself in Frau K.'s place. She was therefore identifying
herself both with the woman her father had once loved and
with the woman he loved now. The inference is obvious that her
affection for her father was a much stronger one than she
knew or than she would have cared to admit: in fact, that she
was in love with him.

I have learnt to look upon unconscious love relations like this
(which are marked by their abnormal consequences)—between
a father and a daughter, or between a mother and a son—as a
revival of germs of feeling in infancy. I have shown at length
elsewhere [1] at what an early age sexual attraction makes itself
felt between parents and children, and I have explained that
the legend of Oedipus is probably to be regarded as a poetical
rendering of what is typical in these relations. Distinct traces
are probably to be found in most people of an early partiality
of this kind—on the part of a daughter for her father, or on the
part of a son for his mother; but it must be assumed to be more
intense from the very first in the case of those children whose
constitution marks them down for a neurosis, who develop
prematurely and have a craving for love. At this point certain
other influences, which need not be discussed here, come into
play, and lead to a fixation of this rudimentary feeling of love
or to a reinforcement of it; so that it turns into something
(either while the child is still young or not until it has reached
the age of puberty) which must be put on a par with a sexual
inclination and which, like the latter, has the forces of the libido

[1] In my *Interpretation of Dreams*, 1900a [Chapter V, Section D (β),
Standard Ed., 4, 257 ff.], and in the third of my *Three Essays*, 1905d [this
volume, p. 227].

at its command.[1] The external circumstances of our patient were by no means unfavourable to such an assumption. The nature of her disposition had always drawn her towards her father, and his numerous illnesses were bound to have increased her affection for him. In some of these illnesses he would allow no one but her to discharge the lighter duties of nursing. He had been so proud of the early growth of her intelligence that he had made her his confidante while she was still a child. It was really she and not her mother whom Frau K.'s appearance had driven out of more than one position.

When I told Dora that I could not avoid supposing that her affection for her father must at a very early moment have amounted to her being completely in love with him, she of course gave me her usual reply: 'I don't remember that.' But she immediately went on to tell me something analogous about a seven-year-old girl who was her cousin (on her mother's side) and in whom she often thought she saw a kind of reflection of her own childhood. This little girl had (not for the first time) been the witness of a heated dispute between her parents, and, when Dora happened to come in on a visit soon afterwards, whispered in her ear: 'You can't think how I hate that person!' (pointing to her mother), 'and when she's dead I shall marry Daddy.' I am in the habit of regarding associations such as this, which bring forward something that agrees with the content of an assertion of mine, as a confirmation from the unconscious of what I have said. No other kind of 'Yes' can be extracted from the unconscious; there is no such thing at all as an unconscious 'No'.[2]

For years on end she had given no expression to this passion for her father. On the contrary, she had for a long time been

[1] The decisive factor in this connection is no doubt the early appearance of true genital sensations, either spontaneously or as a result of seduction or masturbation. (See below [p. 78 f.].)

[2] [*Footnote added* 1923:] There is another very remarkable and entirely trustworthy form of confirmation from the unconscious, which I had not recognized at the time this was written: namely, an exclamation on the part of the patient of 'I didn't think that', or 'I didn't think of that'. This can be translated point-blank into: 'Yes, I was unconscious of that.' [See the longer discussions on this subject in Freud's paper on 'Negation' (1925h) and in the first two sections of his 'Constructions in Analysis' (1937d).]

on the closest terms with the woman who had supplanted her with her father, and she had actually, as we know from her self-reproaches, facilitated this woman's relations with her father. Her own love for her father had therefore been recently revived; and, if so, the question arises to what end this had happened. Clearly as a reactive symptom, so as to suppress something else—something, that is, that still exercised power in the unconscious. Considering how things stood, I could not help supposing in the first instance that what was suppressed was her love of Herr K. I could not avoid the assumption that she was still in love with him, but that, for unknown reasons, since the scene by the lake her love had aroused in her violent feelings of opposition, and that the girl had brought forward and reinforced her old affection for her father in order to avoid any further necessity for paying conscious attention to the love which she had felt in the first years of her girlhood and which had now become distressing to her. In this way I gained an insight into a conflict which was well calculated to unhinge the girl's mind. On the one hand she was filled with regret at having rejected the man's proposal, and with longing for his company and all the little signs of his affection; while on the other hand these feelings of tenderness and longing were combated by powerful forces, amongst which her pride was one of the most obvious. Thus she had succeeded in persuading herself that she had done with Herr K.—that was the advantage she derived from this typical process of repression; and yet she was obliged to summon up her infantile affection for her father and to exaggerate it, in order to protect herself against the feelings of love which were constantly pressing forward into consciousness. The further fact that she was almost incessantly a prey to the most embittered jealousy seemed to admit of still another determination.[1]

My expectations were by no means disappointed when this explanation of mine was met by Dora with a most emphatic negative. The 'No' uttered by a patient after a repressed thought has been presented to his conscious perception for the first time does no more than register the existence of a repression and its severity; it acts, as it were, as a gauge of the repression's strength. If this 'No', instead of being regarded as the expression of an impartial judgement (of which, indeed, the patient

[1] We shall come upon this [in a moment].

is incapable), is ignored, and if work is continued, the first evidence soon begins to appear that in such a case 'No' signifies the desired 'Yes'. Dora admitted that she found it impossible to be as angry with Herr K. as he had deserved. She told me that one day she had met Herr K. in the street while she was walking with a cousin of hers who did not know him. The other girl had exclaimed all at once: 'Why, Dora, what's wrong with you? You've gone as white as a sheet!' She herself had felt nothing of this change of colour; but I explained to her that the expression of emotion and the play of features obey the unconscious rather than the conscious, and are a means of betraying the former.[1] Another time Dora came to me in the worst of tempers after having been uniformly cheerful for several days. She could give no explanation of this. She felt so contrary to-day, she said; it was her uncle's birthday, and she could not bring herself to congratulate him, she did not know why. My powers of interpretation were at a low ebb that day; I let her go on talking, and she suddenly recollected that it was Herr K.'s birthday too —a fact which I did not fail to use against her. And it was then no longer hard to explain why the handsome presents she had had on her own birthday a few days before had given her no pleasure. One gift was missing, and that was Herr K.'s, the gift which had plainly once been the most prized of all.

Nevertheless Dora persisted in denying my contention for some time longer, until, towards the end of the analysis, the conclusive proof of its correctness came to light [p. 108].

I must now turn to consider a further complication to which I should certainly give no space if I were a man of letters engaged upon the creation of a mental state like this for a short story, instead of being a medical man engaged upon its dissection. The element to which I must now allude can only serve to obscure and efface the outlines of the fine poetic conflict

[1] Compare the lines:

> Ruhig mag ich Euch erscheinen,
> Ruhig gehen sehn.

> [Quiet can I watch thy coming,
> Quiet watch thee go.

The words (from Schiller's ballad 'Ritter Toggenburg') are addressed to a knight on his departure for the Crusades by his ostensibly indifferent but in fact devoted lady-love.]

which we have been able to ascribe to Dora. This element
would rightly fall a sacrifice to the censorship of a writer, for
he, after all, simplifies and abstracts when he appears in the
character of a psychologist. But in the world of reality, which
I am trying to depict here, a complication of motives, an
accumulation and conjunction of mental activities—in a word,
overdetermination—is the rule. For behind Dora's supervalent
train of thought which was concerned with her father's relations
with Frau K. there lay concealed a feeling of jealousy which had
that lady as its *object*—a feeling, that is, which could only be
based upon an affection on Dora's part for one of her own sex.
It has long been known and often been pointed out that at the
age of puberty boys and girls show clear signs, even in normal
cases, of the existence of an affection for people of their own sex.
A romantic and sentimental friendship with one of her school-
friends, accompanied by vows, kisses, promises of eternal correspondence, and all the sensibility of jealousy, is the common
precursor of a girl's first serious passion for a man. Thenceforward, in favourable circumstances, the homosexual current
of feeling often runs completely dry. But if a girl is not happy in
her love for a man, the current is often set flowing again by the
libido in later years and is increased up to a greater or lesser
degree of intensity. If this much can be established without
difficulty of healthy persons, and if we take into account what
has already been said [p. 50] about the fuller development in
neurotics of the normal germs of perversion, we shall expect to
find in these latter too a fairly strong homosexual predisposition.
It must, indeed, be so; for I have never yet come through a
single psycho-analysis of a man or a woman without having to
take into account a very considerable current of homosexuality.
When, in a hysterical woman or girl, the sexual libido which is
directed towards men has been energetically suppressed, it will
regularly be found that the libido which is directed towards
women has become vicariously reinforced and even to some
extent conscious.

I shall not in this place go any further into this important
subject, which is especially indispensable to an understanding
of hysteria in men, because Dora's analysis came to an end
before it could throw any light on this side of her mental life.
But I should like to recall the governess, whom I have already
mentioned [p. 36 f.], and with whom Dora had at first enjoyed

the closest interchange of thought, until she discovered that she was being admired and fondly treated not for her own sake but for her father's; whereupon she had obliged the governess to leave. She used also to dwell with noticeable frequency and a peculiar emphasis on the story of another estrangement which appeared inexplicable even to herself. She had always been on particularly good terms with the younger of her two cousins— the girl who had later on become engaged [p. 38]—and had shared all sorts of secrets with her. When, for the first time after Dora had broken off her stay by the lake, her father was going back to B——, she had naturally refused to go with him. This cousin had then been asked to travel with him instead, and she had accepted the invitation. From that time forward Dora had felt a coldness towards her, and she herself was surprised to find how indifferent she had become, although, as she admitted, she had very little ground for complaint against her. These instances of sensitiveness led me to inquire what her relations with Frau K. had been up till the time of the breach. I then found that the young woman and the scarcely grown girl had lived for years on a footing of the closest intimacy. When Dora stayed with the K.'s she used to share a bedroom with Frau K., and the husband used to be quartered elsewhere. She had been the wife's confidante and adviser in all the difficulties of her married life. There was nothing they had not talked about. Medea had been quite content that Creusa should make friends with her two children; and she certainly did nothing to interfere with the relations between the girl and the children's father. How Dora managed to fall in love with the man about whom her beloved friend had so many bad things to say is an interesting psychological problem. We shall not be far from solving it when we realize that thoughts in the unconscious live very comfortably side by side, and even contraries get on together without disputes—a state of things which persists often enough even in the conscious.

When Dora talked about Frau K., she used to praise her 'adorable white body' in accents more appropriate to a lover than to a defeated rival. Another time she told me, more in sorrow than in anger, that she was convinced the presents her father had brought her had been chosen by Frau K., for she recognized her taste. Another time, again, she pointed out that, evidently through the agency of Frau K., she had been given a present of some jewellery which was exactly like some that she had seen in Frau K.'s possession and had wished for aloud at the time. Indeed, I can say in general that I never heard her speak a harsh or angry word against the lady, although from the point of view of her supervalent thought she should have regarded her as the prime author of her misfortunes. She seemed to behave inconsequently; but her apparent inconsequence was precisely the manifestation of a complicating current of feeling. For how had this woman to whom Dora was so enthusiastically devoted behaved to her? After Dora had brought forward her accusation against Herr K., and her father had written to him and had asked for an explanation, Herr K. had replied in the first instance by protesting sentiments of the highest esteem for her and by proposing that he should come to the manufacturing town to clear up every misunderstanding. A few weeks later, when her father spoke to him at B——, there was no longer any question of esteem. On the contrary, Herr K. spoke of her with disparagement, and produced as his trump card the reflection that no girl who read such books and was interested in such things could have any title to a man's respect. Frau K., there-fore, had betrayed her and had calumniated her; for it had only been with her that she had read Mantegazza and discussed forbidden topics. It was a repetition of what had happened with the governess: Frau K. had not loved her for her own sake but on account of her father. Frau K. had sacrificed her without a moment's hesitation so that her relations with her father might not be disturbed. This mortification touched her, perhaps, more nearly and had a greater pathogenic effect than the other one, which she tried to use as a screen for it,—the fact that she had been sacrificed by her father. Did not the obstinacy with which she retained the particular amnesia concerning the sources of her forbidden knowledge [p. 31] point directly to the great emotional importance for her of the accusation against her upon that score, and consequently to her betrayal by her friend?

I believe, therefore, that I am not mistaken in supposing that Dora's supervalent train of thought, which was concerned with her father's relations with Frau K., was designed not only for the purpose of suppressing her love for Herr K., which had once been conscious, but also to conceal her love for Frau K., which was in a deeper sense unconscious. The supervalent train of thought was directly contrary to the latter current of feeling. She told herself incessantly that her father had sacrificed her to this woman, and made noisy demonstrations to show that she grudged her the possession of her father; and in this way she concealed from herself the contrary fact, which was that she grudged her father Frau K.'s love, and had not forgiven the woman she loved for the disillusionment she had been caused by her betrayal. The jealous emotions of a woman were linked in the unconscious with a jealousy such as might have been felt by a man. These masculine or, more properly speaking, *gynaeco-philic* currents of feeling are to be regarded as typical of the unconscious erotic life of hysterical girls.[1]

[1] [See the footnote on p. 120.]

# THE FIRST DREAM

Just at a moment when there was a prospect that the material that was coming up for analysis would throw light upon an obscure point in Dora's childhood, she reported that a few nights earlier she had once again had a dream which she had already dreamt in exactly the same way on many previous occasions. A periodically recurrent dream was by its very nature particularly well calculated to arouse my curiosity; and in any case it was justifiable in the interests of the treatment to consider the way in which the dream worked into the analysis as a whole. I therefore determined to make an especially careful investigation of it.

Here is the dream as related by Dora: '*A house was on fire.*[1] *My father was standing beside my bed and woke me up. I dressed quickly. Mother wanted to stop and save her jewel-case; but Father said: "I refuse to let myself and my two children be burnt for the sake of your jewel-case." We hurried downstairs, and as soon as I was outside I woke up.*'

As the dream was a recurrent one, I naturally asked her when she had first dreamt it. She told me she did not know. But she remembered having had the dream three nights in succession at L—— (the place on the lake where the scene with Herr K. had taken place), and it had now come back again a few nights earlier, here in Vienna.[2] My expectations from the clearing-up of the dream were naturally heightened when I heard of its connection with the events at L——. But I wanted to discover first what had been the exciting cause of its recent recurrence, and I therefore asked Dora to take the dream bit by bit and tell me what occurred to her in connection with it. She had already had some training in dream interpretation from having previously analysed a few minor specimens.

'Something occurs to me,' she said, 'but it cannot belong to

[1] In answer to an inquiry Dora told me that there had never really been a fire at their house.

[2] The content of the dream makes it possible to establish that it in fact occurred *for the first time* at L——.

the dream, for it is quite recent, whereas I have certainly had
the dream before.'

'That makes no difference,' I replied. 'Start away! It will
simply turn out to be the most recent thing that fits in with the
dream.'

'Very well, then. Father has been having a dispute with
Mother in the last few days, because she locks the dining-room
door at night. My brother's room, you see, has no separate
entrance, but can only be reached through the dining-room.
Father does not want my brother to be locked in like that at
night. He says it will not do: something might happen in the
night so that it might be necessary to leave the room.'

'And that made you think of the risk of fire?'

'Yes.'

'Now, I should like you to pay close attention to the exact
words you used. We may have to come back to them. You said
that "*something might happen in the night so that it might be necessary
to leave the room.*" ' [1]

But Dora had now discovered the connecting link between
the recent exciting cause of the dream and the original one,
for she continued:

'When we arrived at L—— that time, Father and I, he
openly said he was afraid of fire. We arrived in a violent
thunderstorm, and saw the small wooden house without any
lightning-conductor. So his anxiety was quite natural.'

What I now had to do was to establish the relation between
the events at L—— and the recurrent dreams which she had
had there. I therefore said: 'Did you have the dream during
your first nights at L—— or during your last ones? in other
words, before or after the scene in the wood by the lake of
which we have heard so much?' (I must explain that I knew that
the scene had not occurred on the very first day, and that she
had remained at L—— for a few days after it without giving
any hint of the incident.)

[1] I laid stress on these words because they took me aback. They
seemed to have an ambiguous ring about them. Are not certain physical
needs referred to in the same words? Now, in a line of associations
ambiguous words (or, as we may call them, 'switch-words') act like points
at a junction. If the points are switched across from the position in which
they appear to lie in the dream, then we find ourselves on another set
of rails; and along this second track run the thoughts which we are in
search of but which still lie concealed behind the dream.

Her first reply was that she did not know, but after a while she added: 'Yes. I think it was after the scene.'

So now I knew that the dream was a reaction to that experience. But why had it recurred there three times? I continued my questions: 'How long did you stop on at L—— after the scene?'

'Four more nights. On the following day I went away with Father.'

'Now I am certain that the dream was an immediate effect of your experience with Herr K. It was at L—— that you dreamed it for the first time, and not before. You have only introduced this uncertainty in your memory so as to obliterate the connection in your mind.[1] But the figures do not quite fit in to my satisfaction yet. If you stayed at L—— for four nights longer, the dream might have occurred four times over. Perhaps this was so?'

She no longer disputed my contention; but instead of answering my question she proceeded:[2] 'In the afternoon after our trip on the lake, from which we (Herr K. and I) returned at midday, I had gone to lie down as usual on the sofa in the bedroom to have a short sleep. I suddenly awoke and saw Herr K. standing beside me. . . .'

'In fact, just as you saw your father standing beside your bed in the dream?'

'Yes. I asked him sharply what it was he wanted there. By way of reply he said he was not going to be prevented from coming into his own bedroom when he wanted; besides, there was something he wanted to fetch. This episode put me on my guard, and I asked Frau K. whether there was not a key to the bedroom door. The next morning I locked myself in while I was dressing. That afternoon, when I wanted to lock myself in so as to lie down again on the sofa, the key was gone. I was convinced that Herr K. had removed it.'

'Then here we have the theme of locking or not locking a room which appeared in the first association to the dream[3] and

---

[1] Compare what was said on p. 17 on the subject of doubt accompanying a recollection.

[2] This was because a fresh piece of material had to emerge from her memory before the question I had put could be answered.

[3] [In the editions before 1924 this read: 'which appeared in the dream'.]

also happened to occur in the exciting cause of the recent recurrence of the dream.[1] I wonder whether the phrase "*I dressed
quickly*" may not also belong to this context?'

'It was then that I made up my mind not to stop on with the
K.'s without Father. On the subsequent mornings I could not
help feeling afraid that Herr K. would surprise me while I was
dressing: *so I always dressed very quickly.* You see, Father lived at
the hotel, and Frau K. used always to go out early so as to
go on expeditions with him. But Herr K. did not annoy me
again.'

'I understand. On the afternoon of the day after the scene in
the wood you formed your intention of escaping from his persecution, and during the second, third, and fourth nights you
had time to repeat that intention in your sleep. (You already
knew on the second afternoon—before the dream, therefore—
that you would not have the key on the following morning to
lock yourself in with while you were dressing; and you could
then form the design of dressing as quickly as possible.) But your
dream recurred each night, for the very reason that it corresponded to an intention. An intention remains in existence until
it has been carried out. You said to yourself, as it were: "I shall
have no rest and I can get no quiet sleep until I am out of this
house." In your account of the dream you turned it the other
way and said: "*As soon as I was outside I woke up.*" '

At this point I shall interrupt my report of the analysis in
order to compare this small piece of dream-interpretation with
the general statements I have made upon the mechanism of the
formation of dreams. I argued in my book, *The Interpretation of
Dreams* (1900a), that every dream is a wish which is represented
as fulfilled, that the representation acts as a disguise if the wish
is a repressed one, belonging to the unconscious, and that
except in the case of children's dreams only an unconscious
wish or one which reaches down into the unconscious has the
force necessary for the formation of a dream. I fancy my theory

[1] I suspected, though I did not as yet say so to Dora, that she had
seized upon this element on account of a symbolic meaning which it
possessed. '*Zimmer*' ['room'] in dreams stands very frequently for
'*Frauenzimmer*' [a slightly derogatory word for 'woman'; literally,
'women's apartments']. The question whether a woman is 'open' or
'shut' can naturally not be a matter of indifference. It is well known,
too, what sort of 'key' effects the opening in such a case.

would have been more certain of general acceptance if I had contented myself with maintaining that every dream had a meaning, which could be discovered by means of a certain process of interpretation; and that when the interpretation had been completed the dream could be replaced by thoughts which would fall into place at an easily recognizable point in the waking mental life of the dreamer. I might then have gone on to say that the meaning of a dream turned out to be of as many different sorts as the processes of waking thought; that in one case it would be a fulfilled wish, in another a realized fear, or again a reflection persisting on into sleep, or an intention (as in the instance of Dora's dream), or a piece of creative thought during sleep, and so on. Such a theory would no doubt have proved attractive from its very simplicity, and it might have been supported by a great many examples of dreams that had been satisfactorily interpreted, as for instance by the one which has been analysed in these pages.

But instead of this I formulated a generalization according to which the meaning of dreams is limited to a single form, to the representation of *wishes*, and by so doing I aroused a universal inclination to dissent. I must, however, observe that I did not consider it either my right or my duty to simplify a psychological process so as to make it more acceptable to my readers, when my researches had shown me that it presented a complication which could not be reduced to uniformity until the inquiry had been carried into another field. It is therefore of special importance to me to show that apparent exceptions— such as this dream of Dora's, which has shown itself in the first instance to be the continuation into sleep of an intention formed during the day—nevertheless lend fresh support to the rule which is in dispute. [See p. 85 ff.]

Much of the dream, however, still remained to be interpreted, and I proceeded with my questions: 'What is this about the jewel-case that your mother wanted to save?'

'Mother is very fond of jewellery and had had a lot given her by Father.'

'And you?'

'I used to be very fond of jewellery too, once; but I have not worn any since my illness.—Once, four years ago' (a year before the dream), 'Father and Mother had a great dispute about a

piece of jewellery. Mother wanted to be given a particular thing
—pearl drops to wear in her ears. But Father does not like that
kind of thing, and he brought her a bracelet instead of the drops.
She was furious, and told him that as he had spent so much
money on a present she did not like he had better just give it to
some one else.'

'I dare say you thought to yourself you would accept it with
pleasure.'

'I don't know.[1] I don't in the least know how Mother
comes into the dream; she was not with us at L—— at the
time.'[2]

'I will explain that to you presently. Does nothing else occur
to you in connection with the jewel-case? So far you have
only talked about jewellery and have said nothing about a
case.'

'Yes, Herr K. had made me a present of an expensive jewel-
case a little time before.'

'Then a return-present would have been very appropriate.
Perhaps you do not know that "jewel-case" ["*Schmuckkästchen*"]
is a favourite expression for the same thing that you alluded to
not long ago by means of the reticule you were wearing[3]—for
the female genitals, I mean.'

'I knew you would say that.'[4]

'That is to say, you knew that it *was* so.—The meaning of
the dream is now becoming even clearer. You said to yourself:
"This man is persecuting me; he wants to force his way into
my room. My 'jewel-case' is in danger, and if anything happens
it will be Father's fault." For that reason in the dream you
chose a situation which expresses the opposite—a danger from
which your father is *saving* you. In this part of the dream everything is turned into its opposite; you will soon discover why. As

[1] The regular formula with which she confessed to anything that had
been repressed.

[2] This remark gave evidence of a complete misunderstanding of the
rules of dream-interpretation, though on other occasions Dora was
perfectly familiar with them. This fact, coupled with the hesitancy
and meagreness of her associations with the jewel-case, showed me
that we were here dealing with material which had been very intensely
repressed.

[3] [This reference to the reticule will be explained further on [p. 76].

[4] A very common way of putting aside a piece of knowledge that
emerges from the repressed.

you say, the mystery turns upon your mother. You ask how she comes into the dream? She is, as you know, your former rival in your father's affections. In the incident of the bracelet, you would have been glad to accept what your mother had rejected. Now let us just put "give" instead of "accept" and "withhold" instead of "reject". Then it means that you were ready to give your father what your mother withheld from him; and the thing in question was connected with jewellery.[1] Now bring your mind back to the jewel-case which Herr K. gave you. You have there the starting-point for a parallel line of thoughts, in which Herr K. is to be put in the place of your father just as he was in the matter of standing beside your bed. He gave you a jewel-case; so you are to give him your jewel-case. That was why I spoke just now of a "return-present". In this line of thoughts your mother must be replaced by Frau K. (You will not deny that she, at any rate, was present at the time.) So you are ready to give Herr K. what his wife withholds from him. That is the thought which has had to be repressed with so much energy, and which has made it necessary for every one of its elements to be turned into its opposite. The dream confirms once more what I had already told you before you dreamt it—that you are summoning up your old love for your father in order to protect yourself against your love for Herr K. But what do all these efforts show? Not only that you are afraid of Herr K., but that you are still more afraid of yourself, and of the temptation you feel to yield to him. In short, these efforts prove once more how deeply you loved him.'[2]

Naturally Dora would not follow me in this part of the interpretation. I myself, however, had been able to arrive at a further step in the interpretation, which seemed to me indispensable both for the anamnesis of the case and for the theory

[1] We shall be able later on to interpret even the drops in a way which will fit in with the context [p. 90 ff.].

[2] I added: 'Moreover, the re-appearance of the dream in the last few days forces me to the conclusion that you consider that the same situation has arisen once again, and that you have decided to give up the treatment—to which, after all, it is only your father who makes you come.' The sequel showed how correct my guess had been. At this point my interpretation touches for a moment upon the subject of 'transference'—a theme which is of the highest practical and theoretical importance, but into which I shall not have much further opportunity of entering in the present paper. [See, however, p. 116 ff.]

of dreams. I promised to communicate this to Dora at the next session.

The fact was that I could not forget the hint which seemed to be conveyed by the ambiguous words already noticed—*that it might be necessary to leave the room; that an accident might happen in the night*. Added to this was the fact that the elucidation of the dream seemed to me incomplete so long as a particular requirement remained unsatisfied; for, though I do not wish to insist that this requirement is a universal one, I have a predilection for discovering a means of satisfying it.[1] A regularly formed dream stands, as it were, upon two legs, one of which is in contact with the main and current exciting cause, and the other with some momentous event in the years of childhood. The dream sets up a connection between those two factors—the event during childhood and the event of the present day—and it endeavours to re-shape the present on the model of the remote past.[2] For the wish which creates the dream always springs from the period of childhood; and it is continually trying to summon childhood back into reality and to correct the present day by the measure of childhood. I believed that I could already clearly detect those elements of Dora's dream which could be pieced together into an allusion to an event in childhood.

I opened the discussion of the subject with a little experiment, which was, as usual, successful. There happened to be a large match-stand on the table. I asked Dora to look round and see whether she noticed anything special on the table, something that was not there as a rule. She noticed nothing. I then asked her if she knew why children were forbidden to play with matches.

'Yes; on account of the risk of fire. My uncle's children are very fond of playing with matches.'

'Not only on that account. They are warned not to "play with fire", and a particular belief is associated with the warning.'

She knew nothing about it.—'Very well, then; the fear is that

---

[1] [See *The Interpretation of Dreams* (1900a), end of Section B of Chapter V; Standard Ed., **4**, 218.]

[2] [Cf. the last sentence of *The Interpretation of Dreams* (Standard Ed., **5**, 621).]

if they do they will wet their bed. The antithesis of "water" and
"fire" must be at the bottom of this. Perhaps it is believed that
they will dream of fire and then try and put it out with water.
I cannot say exactly.[1] But I notice that the antithesis of water
and fire has been extremely useful to you in the dream. Your
mother wanted to save the jewel-case so that it should not be
*burnt*; while in the dream-thoughts it is a question of the "jewel-
case" not being *wetted*. But fire is not only used as the contrary
of water, it also serves directly to represent love (as in the phrase
"to be *consumed* with love"). So that from "fire" one set of rails
runs by way of this symbolic meaning to thoughts of love; while
the other set runs by way of the contrary "water", and, after
sending off a branch line which provides another connection
with "love" (for love also makes things wet), leads in a different
direction. And what direction can that be? Think of the expressions you used: that *an accident might happen in the night*, and that
*it might be necessary to leave the room*. Surely the allusion must be
to a physical need? And if you transpose the accident into childhood what can it be but bed-wetting? But what is usually done
to prevent children from wetting their bed? Are they not woken
up in the night out of their sleep, *exactly as your father woke you
up in the dream*? This, then, must be the actual occurrence which
enabled you to substitute your father for Herr K., who really
woke you up out of your sleep. I am accordingly driven to conclude that you were addicted to bed-wetting up to a later age
than is usual with children. The same must also have been true
of your brother; for your father said: "*I refuse to let my two
children* go to their destruction. . . ." Your brother has no other
sort of connection with the real situation at the K.'s; he had not
gone with you to L——. And now, what have your recollections
to say to this?'

'I know nothing about myself,' was her reply, 'but my brother
used to wet his bed up till his sixth or seventh year; and it used
sometimes to happen to him in the daytime too.'

I was on the point of remarking to her how much easier it is
to remember things of that kind about one's brother than about
oneself, when she continued the train of recollections which had
been revived: 'Yes. I used to do it too, for some time, but not
until my seventh or eighth year. It must have been serious,

[1] [Freud returned to this question three or four times—at greatest
length in his paper on the Acquisition of Fire (1932*a*).]

because I remember now that the doctor was called in. It lasted till a short time before my nervous asthma.' [P. 21.]

'And what did the doctor say to it?'

'He explained it as nervous weakness; it would soon pass off, he thought; and he prescribed a tonic.'[1]

The interpretation of the dream now seemed to me to be complete.[2] But Dora brought me an addendum to the dream on the very next day. She had forgotten to relate, she said, that each time after waking up she had smelt smoke. Smoke, of course, fitted in well with fire, but it also showed that the dream had a special relation to myself; for when she used to assert that there was nothing concealed behind this or that, I would often say by way of rejoinder: 'There can be no smoke without fire!' Dora objected, however, to such a purely personal interpretation, saying that Herr K. and her father were passionate smokers —as I am too, for the matter of that. She herself had smoked during her stay by the lake, and Herr K. had rolled a cigarette for her before he began his unlucky proposal. She thought, too, that she clearly remembered having noticed the smell of smoke on the three occasions of the dream's occurrence at L——, and not for the first time at its recent reappearance. As she would give me no further information, it was left to me to determine how this addendum was to be introduced into the texture of the dream-thoughts. One thing which I had to go upon was the fact that the smell of smoke had only come up as an addendum to the dream, and must therefore have had to overcome a particularly strong effort on the part of repression.[3] Accordingly it was probably related to the thoughts which were the most obscurely presented and the most successfully repressed in the dream, to the thoughts, that is, concerned with the temptation to show herself willing to yield to the man. If that were so, the

[1] This physician was the only one in whom she showed any confidence, because this episode showed her that he had not penetrated her secret. She felt afraid of any other doctor about whom she had not yet been able to form a judgement, and we can now see that the motive of her fear was the possibility that he might guess her secret.

[2] The essence of the dream might perhaps be translated into words such as these: 'The temptation is so strong. Dear Father, protect me again as you used to in my childhood, and prevent my bed from being wetted!'

[3] [See below, p. 100, n. 2.]

addendum to the dream could scarcely mean anything else than the longing for a kiss, which, with a smoker, would necessarily smell of smoke. But a kiss had passed between Herr K. and Dora some two years further back [p. 28],[1] and it would certainly have been repeated more than once if she had given way to him. So the thoughts of temptation seemed in this way to have harked back to the earlier scene, and to have revived the memory of the kiss against whose seductive influence the little 'thumb-sucker' had defended herself at the time, by the feeling of disgust. Taking into consideration, finally, the indications which seemed to point to there having been a transference on to me—since I am a smoker too—I came to the conclusion that the idea had probably occurred to her one day during a session that she would like to have a kiss from me. This would have been the exciting cause which led her to repeat the warning dream and to form her intention of stopping the treatment. Everything fits together very satisfactorily upon this view; but owing to the characteristics of 'transference' its validity is not susceptible of definite proof. [Cf. p. 117 n.]

I might at this point hesitate whether I should first consider the light thrown by this dream on the history of the case, or whether I should rather begin by dealing with the objection to my theory of dreams which may be based on it. I shall take the former course.

The significance of enuresis in the early history of neurotics is worth going into thoroughly. For the sake of clearness I will confine myself to remarking that Dora's case of bed-wetting was not the usual one.[2] The disorder was not simply that the habit had persisted beyond what is considered the normal period, but, according to her explicit account, it had begun by disappearing and had then returned at a relatively late age—after her sixth year [p. 72]. Bed-wetting of this kind has, to the best of my knowledge, no more likely cause than masturbation, a habit whose importance in the aetiology of bed-wetting in general is still insufficiently appreciated. In my experience, the children concerned have themselves at one time been very well aware of this connection, and all its psychological consequences follow from it as though they had never forgotten it. Now, at the time when

[1] [In the editions before 1924 this read 'a year further back'.]
[2] [Cf. the second of Freud's *Three Essays* (1905d), this volume p. 190.]

Dora reported the dream, we were engaged upon a line of enquiry which led straight towards an admission that she had masturbated in childhood. A short while before, she had raised the question of why it was that precisely she had fallen ill, and, before I could answer, had put the blame on her father. The justification for this was forthcoming not out of her unconscious thoughts but from her conscious knowledge. It turned out, to my astonishment, that the girl knew what the nature of her father's illness had been. After his return from consulting me [p. 19] she had overheard a conversation in which the name of the disease had been mentioned. At a still earlier period—at the time of the detached retina [p. 19]—an oculist who was called in must have hinted at a luetic aetiology; for the inquisitive and anxious girl overheard an old aunt of hers saying to her mother: 'He was ill before his marriage, you know', and adding something which she could not understand, but which she subsequently connected in her mind with improper subjects.

Her father, then, had fallen ill through leading a loose life, and she assumed that he had handed on his bad health to her by heredity. I was careful not to tell her that, as I have already mentioned [p. 20 *n*.], I too was of opinion that the offspring of luetics were very specially predisposed to severe neuropsychoses. The line of thought in which she brought this accusation against her father was continued in her unconscious material. For several days on end she identified herself with her mother by means of slight symptoms and peculiarities of manner, which gave her an opportunity for some really remarkable achievements in the direction of intolerable behaviour. She then allowed it to transpire that she was thinking of a stay she had made at Franzensbad,[1] which she had visited with her mother —I forget in what year. Her mother was suffering from abdominal pains and from a discharge (a catarrh) which necessitated a cure at Franzensbad. It was Dora's view—and here again she was probably right—that this illness was due to her father, who had thus handed on his venereal disease to her mother. It was quite natural that in drawing this conclusion she should, like the majority of laymen, have confused gonorrhoea and syphilis, as well as what is contagious and what is hereditary. The persistence with which she held to this identification

[1] [The Bohemian Spa.]

with her mother almost forced me to ask her whether she too was suffering from a venereal disease; and I then learnt that she was afflicted with a catarrh (leucorrhoea) whose beginning, she said, she could not remember.

I then understood that behind the train of thought in which she brought these open accusations against her father there lay concealed as usual a *self*-accusation. I met her half-way by assuring her that in my view the occurrence of leucorrhoea in young girls pointed primarily to masturbation, and I considered that all the other causes which were commonly assigned to that complaint were put in the background by masturbation.[1] I added that she was now on the way to finding an answer to her own question of why it was that precisely she had fallen ill—by confessing that she had masturbated, probably in childhood. Dora denied flatly that she could remember any such thing. But a few days later she did something which I could not help regarding as a further step towards the confession. For on that day she wore at her waist—a thing she never did on any other occasion before or after—a small reticule of a shape which had just come into fashion; and, as she lay on the sofa and talked, she kept playing with it—opening it, putting a finger into it, shutting it again, and so on. I looked on for some time, and then explained to her the nature of a 'symptomatic act'.[2] I give the name of symptomatic acts to those acts which people perform, as we say, automatically, unconsciously, without attending to them, or as if in a moment of distraction. They are actions to which people would like to deny any significance, and which, if questioned about them, they would explain as being indifferent and accidental. Closer observation, however, will show that these actions, about which consciousness knows nothing or wishes to know nothing, in fact give expression to unconscious thoughts and impulses, and are therefore most valuable and instructive as being manifestations of the unconscious which have been able to come to the surface. There are .two sorts of conscious attitudes possible towards these symptomatic acts. If we can ascribe inconspicuous motives to them we recognize their existence; but if no such pretext can be found for conscious use we usually fail altogether to notice that

[1] [*Footnote added* 1923:] This is an extreme view which I should no longer maintain to-day.

[2] See my *Psychopathology of Everyday Life*, 1901*b* [Chapter IX].

we have performed them. Dora found no difficulty in producing a motive: 'Why should I not wear a reticule like this, as it is now the fashion to do?' But a justification of this kind does not dismiss the possibility of the action in question having an unconscious origin. Though on the other hand the existence of such an origin and the meaning attributed to the act cannot be conclusively established. We must content ourselves with recording the fact that such a meaning fits in quite extraordinarily well with the situation as a whole and with the programme laid down by the unconscious.

On some other occasion I will publish a collection of these symptomatic acts as they are to be observed in the healthy and in neurotics. They are sometimes very easy to interpret. Dora's reticule, which came apart at the top in the usual way, was nothing but a representation of the genitals, and her playing with it, her opening it and putting her finger in it, was an entirely unembarrassed yet unmistakable pantomimic announcement of what she would like to do with them—namely, to masturbate. A very entertaining episode of a similar kind occurred to me a short time ago. In the middle of a session the patient—a lady who was no longer young—brought out a small ivory box, ostensibly in order to refresh herself with a sweet. She made some efforts to open it, and then handed it to me so that I might convince myself how hard it was to open. I expressed my suspicion that the box must mean something special, for this was the very first time I had seen it, although its owner had been coming to me for more than a year. To this the lady eagerly replied: 'I always have this box about me; I take it with me wherever I go.' She did not calm down until I had pointed out to her with a laugh how well her words were adapted to quite another meaning. The box—[in German] *Dose*, πύξις—, like the reticule and the jewel-case, was once again only a substitute for the shell of Venus, for the female genitals.

There is a great deal of symbolism of this kind in life, but as a rule we pass it by without heeding it. When I set myself the task of bringing to light what human beings keep hidden within them, not by the compelling power of hypnosis, but by observing what they say and what they show, I thought the task was a harder one than it really is. He that has eyes to see and ears to hear may convince himself that no mortal can keep a secret.

If his lips are silent, he chatters with his finger-tips; betrayal oozes out of him at every pore. And thus the task of making conscious the most hidden recesses of the mind is one which it is quite possible to accomplish.

Dora's symptomatic act with the reticule did not immediately precede the dream. She started the session which brought us the narrative of the dream with another symptomatic act. As I came into the room in which she was waiting she hurriedly concealed a letter which she was reading. I naturally asked her whom the letter was from, and at first she refused to tell me. Something then came out which was a matter of complete indifference and had no relation to the treatment. It was a letter from her grandmother, in which she begged Dora to write to her more often. I believe that Dora only wanted to play 'secrets' with me, and to hint that she was on the point of allowing her secret to be torn from her by the doctor. I was then in a position to explain her antipathy to every new doctor. She was afraid lest he might arrive at the foundation of her illness, either by examining her and discovering her catarrh, or by questioning her and eliciting the fact of her addiction to bed-wetting—lest he might guess, in short, that she had masturbated. And afterwards she would speak very contemptuously of the doctor whose perspicacity she had evidently over-estimated beforehand. [Cf. p. 73, n. 1.]

The reproaches against her father for having made her ill, together with the self-reproach underlying them, the leucorrhoea, the playing with the reticule, the bed-wetting after her sixth year, the secret which she would not allow the doctors to tear from her—the circumstantial evidence of her having masturbated in childhood seems to me complete and without a flaw. In the present case I had begun to suspect the masturbation when she had told me of her cousin's gastric pains [p. 38], and had then identified herself with her by complaining for days together of similar painful sensations. It is well known that gastric pains occur especially often in those who masturbate. According to a personal communication made to me by Wilhelm Fliess, it is precisely gastralgias of this character which can be interrupted by an application of cocaine to the 'gastric spot' discovered by him in the nose, and which can be cured by the cauterization of the same spot.[1] In confirmation of my

[1] [Some account of this will be found in Section I of Kris's introduction to Freud's correspondence with Fliess (Freud, 1950a).]

suspicion Dora gave me two facts from her conscious knowledge: she herself had frequently suffered from gastric pains, and she had good reasons for believing that her cousin was a masturbator. It is a very common thing for patients to recognize in other people a connection which, on account of their emotional resistances, they cannot perceive in themselves. And, indeed, Dora no longer denied my supposition, although she still remembered nothing. Even the date which she assigned to the bed-wetting, when she said that it lasted 'till a short time before the appearance of the nervous asthma' [p. 73], appears to me to be of clinical significance. Hysterical symptoms hardly ever appear so long as children are masturbating, but only afterwards, when a period of abstinence has set in;[1] they form a substitute for masturbatory satisfaction, the desire for which continues to persist in the unconscious until another and more normal kind of satisfaction appears—where that is still attainable. For upon whether it is still attainable or not depends the possibility of a hysteria being cured by marriage and normal sexual intercourse. But if the satisfaction afforded in marriage is again removed—as it may be owing to *coitus interruptus*, psychological estrangement, or other causes—then the libido flows back again into its old channel and manifests itself once more in hysterical symptoms.

I should like to be able to add some definite information as to when and under what particular influence Dora gave up masturbating; but owing to the incompleteness of the analysis I have only fragmentary material to present. We have heard that the bed-wetting lasted until shortly before she first fell ill with dyspnoea. Now the only light she was able to throw upon this first attack was that at the time of its occurrence her father was away from home for the first time since his health had improved. In this small recollection there must be a trace of an allusion to the aetiology of the dyspnoea. Dora's symptomatic acts and certain other signs gave me good reasons for supposing that the child, whose bedroom had been next door to her parents', had overheard her father in his wife's room at night and had heard him (for he was always short of breath) breathing

---

[1] This is also true in principle of adults; but in their case a *relative* abstinence, a diminution in the amount of masturbation, is a sufficient cause, so that, if the libido is very strong, hysteria and masturbation may be simultaneously present.

hard while they had intercourse. Children, in such circumstances, divine something sexual in the uncanny sounds that
reach their ears. Indeed, the movements expressive of sexual
excitement lie within them ready to hand, as innate pieces of
mechanism. I maintained years ago that the dyspnoea and
palpitations that occur in hysteria and anxiety neurosis are only
detached fragments of the act of copulation;[1] and in many cases,
as in Dora's, I have been able to trace back the symptom of
dyspnoea or nervous asthma to the same exciting cause—to the
patient's having overheard sexual intercourse taking place between adults. The sympathetic excitement which may be supposed to have occurred in Dora on such an occasion may very
easily have made the child's sexuality veer round and have
replaced her inclination to masturbation by an inclination to
anxiety. A little while later, when her father was away and the
child, devotedly in love with him, was wishing him back, she
must have reproduced in the form of an attack of asthma the
impression she had received. She had preserved in her memory
the event which had occasioned the first onset of the symptom,
and we can conjecture from it the nature of the train of thought,
charged with anxiety, which had accompanied the attack. The
first attack had come on after she had over-exerted herself on
an expedition in the mountains [p. 21], so that she had probably been really a little out of breath. To this was added the
thought that her father was forbidden to climb mountains and
was not allowed to over-exert himself, because he suffered from
shortness of breath; then came the recollection of how much he
had exerted himself with her mother that night, and the question
whether it might not have done him harm; next came concern
whether *she* might not have over-exerted herself in masturbating
—an act which, like the other, led to a sexual orgasm accompanied by slight dyspnoea—and finally came a return of the
dyspnoea in an intensified form as a symptom. Part of this
material I was able to obtain directly from the analysis, but the
rest required supplementing. But the way in which the occurrence of masturbation in Dora's case was verified has already
shown us that material belonging to a single subject can only

[1] [In Section III of Freud's first paper on anxiety neurosis (1895*b*).
Much later he put forward another explanation of the physical accom-
paniments of anxiety, in Chapter VIII of *Inhibitions, Symptoms and Anxiety*
(1926*d*).]

be collected piece by piece at various times and in different connections.[1]

There now arise a whole series of questions of the greatest importance concerning the aetiology of hysteria: is Dora's case to be regarded as aetiologically typical? does it represent the only type of causation? and so on. Nevertheless, I am sure that I am taking the right course in postponing my answer to such questions until a considerable number of other cases have been similarly analysed and published. Moreover, I should have to begin by criticizing the way in which the questions are framed. Instead of answering 'Yes' or 'No' to the question whether the aetiology of this case is to be looked for in masturbation during childhood, I should first have to discuss the concept of aetiology as applied to the psychoneuroses.[2] It would then become evident that the standpoint from which I should be able to answer

---

[1] The proof of infantile masturbation in other cases is established in a precisely similar way. The evidence for it is mostly of a similar nature: indications of the presence of leucorrhoea, bed-wetting, hand-cere-monials (obsessional washing), and such things. It is always possible to discover with certainty from the nature of the symptoms of the case whether the habit was discovered by the person in charge of the child or not, or whether this sexual activity was brought to an end by long efforts on the child's part to break itself of the habit, or by a sudden change. In Dora's case the masturbation had remained undiscovered, and had come to an end at a single blow (cf. her secret, her fear of doctors, and the replacement by dyspnoea). The patients, it is true, invariably dispute the conclusiveness of circumstantial evidence such as this, and they do so even when they have retained a conscious recollection of the catarrh or of their mother's warning (e.g. 'That makes people stupid; it's dangerous'). But some time later the memory, which has been so long repressed, of this piece of infantile sexual life emerges with certainty, and it does so in every instance. I am reminded of the case of a patient of mine suffering from obsessions, which were direct deriva-tives of infantile masturbation. Her peculiarities, such as self-prohibi-tions and self-punishments, the feeling that if she had done this she must not do that, the idea that she must not be interrupted, the introduction of pauses between one procedure (with her hands) and the next, her hand-washing, etc.—all of these turned out to be unaltered fragments of her nurse's efforts to break her of the habit. The only thing which had remained permanently in her memory were the words of warning: 'Ugh! That's dangerous!' Compare also in this connection my *Three Essays on the Theory of Sexuality*, 1905d [the section on 'Masturbatory Sexual Manifestations' in the second essay (this volume p. 185 ff.)].

[2] [The various uses of the term 'aetiology' as applied to the neurose were analysed by Freud in his second paper on anxiety neurosis (1895).]

the question would be very widely removed from the standpoint from which it was put. Let it suffice if we can reach the conviction that in this case the occurrence of masturbation in childhood is established, and that its occurrence cannot be an accidental element nor an immaterial one in the conformation of the clinical picture.[1]

A consideration of the significance of the leucorrhoea to which Dora admitted promises to give us a still better understanding of her symptoms. She had learnt to call her affection a 'catarrh' at the time when her mother had had to visit Franzensbad on account of a similar complaint [p. 75]; and the word 'catarrh' acted once again as a 'switch-word' [p. 65 n.], and enabled the whole set of thoughts upon her father's responsibility for her illness to manifest themselves in the symptom of the cough. The cough, which no doubt originated in the first instance from a slight actual catarrh, was, moreover, an imitation of her father (whose lungs were affected), and could serve as an expression of her sympathy and concern for him. But besides this, it proclaimed aloud, as it were, something of which she may then have been still unconscious: 'I am my father's daughter. I have a catarrh, just as he has. He has made me ill, just as he has made Mother ill. It is from him that I have got my evil passions, which are punished by illness.'[2]

---

[1] Dora's brother must have been concerned in some way with her having acquired the habit of masturbation; for in this connection she told me, with all the emphasis which betrays the presence of a 'screen memory', that her brother used regularly to pass on all his infectious illnesses to her, and that while he used to have them lightly she used, on the contrary, to have them severely [p. 22]. In the dream her brother as well as she was saved from 'destruction' [p. 64]; he, too, had been subject to bed-wetting, but had got over the habit before his sister [p. 72]. Her declaration that she had been able to keep abreast with her brother up to the time of her first illness, but that after that she had fallen behind him in her studies, was in a certain sense also a 'screen memory'. It was as though she had been a boy up till that moment, and had then become girlish for the first time. She had in truth been a wild creature; but after the 'asthma' she became quiet and well-behaved. That illness formed the boundary between two phases of her sexual life, of which the first was masculine in character, and the second feminine.

[2] This word ['catarrh'] played the same part with the fourteen-year-old girl whose case history I have compressed into a few lines on p. 24 n. I had established the child in a pension with an intelligent lady, who took charge of her for me. The lady reported that the little girl could not bear her to be in the room while she was going to bed, and that when

Let us next attempt to put together the various determinants that we have found for Dora's attacks of coughing and hoarseness. In the lowest stratum we must assume the presence of a real and organically determined irritation of the throat—which acted like the grain of sand around which an oyster forms its pearl. This irritation was susceptible to fixation, because it concerned a part of the body which in Dora had to a high degree retained its significance as an erotogenic zone. And the irritation was consequently well fitted to give expression to excited states of the libido. It was brought to fixation by what was probably its first psychical coating—her sympathetic imitation of her father—and by her subsequent self-reproaches on account of her 'catarrh'. The same group of symptoms, moreover, showed itself capable of representing her relations with Herr K.; it could express her regret at his absence and her wish to make him a better wife. After a part of her libido had once more turned towards her father, the symptom obtained what was perhaps its last meaning; it came to represent sexual intercourse with her father by means of Dora's identifying herself with Frau K. I can guarantee that this series is by no means complete. Unfortunately, an incomplete analysis cannot enable us to follow the chronological sequence of the changes in a symptom's meaning, or to display clearly the succession and coexistence of its various meanings. It may legitimately be expected of a complete analysis that it should fulfil these demands.

I must now proceed to touch upon some further relations existing between Dora's genital catarrh and her hysterical symptoms. At a time when any psychological elucidation of hysteria was still very remote, I used to hear experienced fellow-doctors who were my seniors maintain that in the case of hysterical patients suffering from leucorrhoea any increase in the catarrh was regularly followed by an intensification of the hysterical troubles, and especially of loss of appetite and vomiting. No one was very clear about the nature of the connection,

she was in bed she had a marked cough, of which there was no trace in the daytime. When the girl was questioned about these symptoms, the only thing that occurred to her was that her grandmother coughed in the same way, and that she was said to have a catarrh. It was clear from this that the child herself had a catarrh, and that she did not want to be observed while she performed her evening ablutions. This catarrh, which, thanks to its name, had been *displaced from the lower to the upper part of her body* [see p. 30], exhibited a quite unusual degree of intensity.

but I fancy the general inclination was towards the opinion held by gynaecologists. According to their hypothesis, as is well known, disorders of the genitals exercise upon the nervous functions a direct and far-reaching influence in the nature of an organic disturbance—though a therapeutic test of this theory is apt to leave one in the lurch. In the light of our present knowledge we cannot exclude the possibility of the existence of a direct organic influence of this sort; but it is at all events easier to indicate its psychical coating. The pride taken by women in the appearance of their genitals is quite a special feature of their vanity; and disorders of the genitals which they think calculated to inspire feelings of repugnance or even disgust have an incredible power of humiliating them, of lowering their self-esteem, and of making them irritable, sensitive, and distrustful. An abnormal secretion of the mucous membrane of the vagina is looked upon as a source of disgust.

It will be remembered that Dora had a lively feeling of disgust after being kissed by Herr K., and that we saw grounds for completing her story of the scene of the kiss by supposing that, while she was being embraced, she noticed the pressure of the man's erect member against her body [p. 29 ff.]. We now learn further that the same governess whom Dora cast off on account of her faithlessness had, from her own experience of life, propounded to Dora the view that all men were frivolous and untrustworthy. To Dora that must mean that all men were like her father. But she thought her father suffered from venereal disease—for had he not handed it on to her and her mother? She might therefore have imagined to herself that all men suffered from venereal disease, and naturally her conception of venereal disease was modelled on her one experience of it—a personal one at that. To suffer from venereal disease, therefore, meant for her to be afflicted with a disgusting discharge. So may we not have here a further motive for the disgust she felt at the moment of the embrace? Thus the disgust which was transferred on to the contact of the man would be a feeling which had been projected according to the primitive mechanism I have already mentioned (p. 35), and would be related ultimately to her own leucorrhoea.

I suspect that we are here concerned with unconscious processes of thought which are twined around a pre-existing structure of organic connections, much as festoons of flowers are twined around a wire; so that on another occasion one might find other lines of thought inserted between the same points of departure and termination. Yet a knowledge of the thought-connections which have been effective in the individual case is of a value which cannot be exaggerated for clearing up the symptoms. It is only because the analysis was prematurely broken off that we have been obliged in Dora's case to resort to framing conjectures and filling in deficiencies. Whatever I have brought forward for filling up the gaps is based upon other cases which have been more thoroughly analysed.

The dream from the analysis of which we have derived this information corresponded, as we have seen, to an intention which Dora carried with her into her sleep. It was therefore repeated each night until the intention had been carried out; and it reappeared years later when an occasion arose for forming an analogous intention. The intention might have been consciously expressed in some such words as these: 'I must fly from this house, for I see that my virginity is threatened here; I shall go away with my father, and I shall take precautions not to be surprised while I am dressing in the morning.' These thoughts were clearly expressed in the dream; they formed part of a mental current which had achieved consciousness and a dominating position in waking life. Behind them can be discerned obscure traces of a train of thought which formed part of a contrary current and had consequently been suppressed. This other train of thought culminated in the temptation to yield to the man, out of gratitude for the love and tenderness he had shown her during the last few years, and it may perhaps have revived the memory of the only kiss she had so far had from him. But according to the theory which I developed in my *Interpretation of Dreams* such elements as these are not enough for the formation of a dream. On that theory a dream is not an intention represented as having been carried out, but a wish represented as having been fulfilled, and, moreover, in most cases a wish dating from childhood. It is our business now to discover whether this principle may not be contradicted by the present dream.

The dream does in fact contain infantile material, though it is impossible at a first glance to discover any connections between that material and Dora's intention of flying from Herr K.'s house and the temptation of his presence. Why should a recollection have emerged of her bed-wetting when she was a child and of the trouble her father used to take to teach the child clean habits? We may answer this by saying that it was only by the help of this train of thought that it was possible to suppress the other thoughts which were so intensely occupied with the temptation to yield or that it was possible to secure the dominance of the intention which had been formed of combating those other thoughts. The child decided to fly *with* her father; in reality she fled *to* her father because she was afraid of the man who was pursuing her; she summoned up an infantile affection for her father so that it might protect her against her present affection for a stranger. Her father was himself partly responsible for her present danger, for he had handed her over to this strange man in the interests of his own love-affair. And how much better it had been when that same father of hers had loved no one more than her, and had exerted all his strength to save her from the dangers that had then threatened her! The infantile, and now unconscious, wish to put her father in the strange man's place had the potency necessary for the formation of a dream. If there were a past situation similar to a present one, and differing from it only in being concerned with one instead of with the other of the two persons mentioned in the wish, that situation would become the main one in the dream. But there *had* been such a situation. Her father had once stood beside her bed, just as Herr K. had the day before, and had woken her up, with a kiss perhaps, as Herr K. may have meant to do. Thus her intention of flying from the house was not in itself capable of producing a dream; but it became so by being associated with another intention which was founded upon infantile wishes. The wish to replace Herr K. by her father provided the necessary motive power for the dream. Let me recall the interpretation I was led to adopt of Dora's reinforced train of thought about her father's relations with Frau K. My interpretation was that she had at that point summoned up an infantile affection for her father so as to be able to keep her repressed love for Herr K. in its state of repression [p. 57 f.]. This same sudden revulsion in the patient's mental life was reflected in the dream.

I have made one or two observations in my *Interpretation of Dreams*[1] on the relation between the waking thoughts which

[1] [Chapter VII, Section C; Standard Ed., 5, 560 f.]

are continued into sleep (the 'day's residues') and the unconscious wish which forms the dream. I will quote them here as
they stand, for I have nothing to add to them, and the analysis
of this dream of Dora's proves afresh that the facts are as I have
supposed: 'I am ready to admit that there is a whole class of
dreams the *instigation* to which arises principally or even exclusively from the residues of daytime life; and I think that even
my wish that I might at long last become a Professor Extra-
ordinarius [1] might have allowed me to sleep through the night
in peace if my worry over my friend's health had not still persisted from the previous day. But the worry alone could not
have made a dream. The *motive force* which the dream required
had to be provided by a wish; it was the business of the worry
to get hold of a wish to act as the motive force of the dream.

'The position may be explained by an analogy. A daytime
thought may very well play the part of *entrepreneur* for a dream;
but the *entrepreneur*, who, as people say, has the idea and the
initiative to carry it out, can do nothing without capital; he
needs a *capitalist* who can afford the outlay, and the capitalist
who provides the psychical outlay for the dream is invariably
and indisputably, whatever may be the thoughts of the previous
day, a wish from the unconscious.'

Any one who has learnt to appreciate the delicacy of the
fabric of structures such as dreams will not be surprised to find
that Dora's wish that her father might take the place of the man
who was her tempter called up in her memory not merely a
casual collection of material from her childhood, but precisely
such material as was most intimately bound up with the suppression of her temptation. For if Dora felt unable to yield to
her love for the man, if in the end she repressed that love instead
of surrendering to it, there was no factor upon which her
decision depended more directly than upon her premature
sexual enjoyment and its consequence—her bed-wetting, her
catarrh, and her disgust. An early history of this kind can afford
a basis for two kinds of behaviour in response to the demands of
love in maturity—which of the two will depend upon the summation of constitutional determinants in the subject. He will
either exhibit an abandonment to sexuality which is entirely

---

[1] This is a reference to the analysis of a dream quoted in the book as
an example [the dream of 'Otto looking ill', in Chapter V, Section D
(Standard Edition, 4, 269 ff.).]

without resistances and borders upon perversity; or there will be a reaction—he will repudiate sexuality, and will at the same time fall ill of a neurosis. In the case of our present patient, her constitution and the high level of her intellectual and moral upbringing decided in favour of the latter course.

I should like, further, to draw special attention to the fact that the analysis of this dream has given us access to certain details of the pathogenically operative events which had otherwise been inaccessible to memory, or at all events to reproduction. The recollection of the bed-wetting in childhood had, as we have seen, already been repressed. And Dora had never mentioned the details of her persecution by Herr K.; they had never occurred to her mind.

I add a few remarks which may help towards the synthesis of this dream.[1] The dream-work began on the afternoon of the day after the scene in the wood, after Dora had noticed that she was no longer able to lock the door of her room [p. 66]. She then said to herself: 'I am threatened by a serious danger here,' and formed her intention of not stopping on in the house alone but of going off with her father. This intention became capable of forming a dream, because it succeeded in finding a continuation in the unconscious. What corresponded to it there was her summoning up her infantile love for her father as a protection against the present temptation. The change which thus took place in her became fixed and brought her into the attitude shown by her supervalent train of thought—jealousy of Frau K. on her father's account, as though she herself were in love with him. There was a conflict within her between a temptation to yield to the man's proposal and a composite force rebelling against that feeling. This latter force was made up of motives of respectability and good sense, of hostile feelings caused by the governess's disclosures (jealousy and wounded pride, as we shall see later [p. 105 f.]), and of a neurotic element, namely, the tendency to a repudiation of sexuality which was already present in her and was based on her childhood history. Her love for

[1] [The remainder of this section was printed as a footnote in editions earlier than 1924. On the subject of the 'synthesis' of dreams see *The Interpretation of Dreams*, Chap. VI, beginning of Section C (Standard Ed. **4**, 310).]

her father, which she summoned up to protect her against the temptation, had its origin in this same childhood history.

Her intention of flying to her father, which, as we have seen, reached down into the unconscious, was transformed by the dream into a situation which presented as fulfilled the wish that her father should save her from the danger. In this process it was necessary to put on one side a certain thought which stood in the way; for it was her father himself who had brought her into the danger. The hostile feeling against her father (her desire for revenge), which was here suppressed, was, as we shall discover, one of the motive forces of the second dream [p. 97 f.].

According to the necessary conditions of dream-formation the imagined situation must be chosen so as to reproduce a situation in infancy. A special triumph is achieved if a recent situation, perhaps even the very situation which is the exciting cause of the dream, can be transformed into an infantile one. This has actually been achieved in the present case, by a purely chance disposition of the material. Just as Herr K. had stood beside her sofa and woken her up, so her father had often done in her childhood. The whole trend of her thoughts could be most aptly symbolized by her substitution of her father for Herr K. in that situation.

But the reason for which her father used to wake her up long ago had been to prevent her from making her bed wet.

This 'wet' had a decisive influence on the further content of the dream; though it was represented in it only by a distant allusion and by its opposite.

The opposite of 'wet' and 'water' can easily be 'fire' and 'burning'. The chance that, when they arrived at the place [L——], her father had expressed his anxiety at the risk of fire [p. 65], helped to decide that the danger from which her father was to rescue her should be a fire. The situation chosen for the dream-picture was based upon this chance, and upon the opposition to 'wet': 'There was a fire. Her father was standing beside her bed to wake her.' Her father's chance utterance would, no doubt, not have obtained such an important position in the dream if it had not fitted in so excellently with the dominating current of feeling, which was determined to regard him at any cost as a protector and saviour. 'He foresaw the danger from the very moment of our arrival! He was in the right!' (In actual fact, it was he who had brought the girl into danger.)

In consequence of certain connections which can easily be made from it, the word 'wet' served in the dream-thoughts as a nodal point between several groups of ideas. 'Wet' was connected not only with the bed-wetting, but also with the group of ideas relating to sexual temptation which lay suppressed behind the content of the dream. Dora knew that there was a kind of getting wet involved in sexual intercourse, and that during the act of copulation the man presented the woman with something liquid *in the form of drops*. She also knew that the danger lay precisely in that, and that it was her business to protect her genitals from being moistened.

'Wet' and 'drops' at the same time opened the way to the other group of associations—the group relating to the disgusting catarrh, which in her later years had no doubt possessed the same mortifying significance for her as the bed-wetting had in her childhood. 'Wet' in this connection had the same meaning as 'dirtied'. Her genitals, which ought to have been kept clean, had been dirtied already by the catarrh—and this applied to her mother no less than to herself (p. 75). She seemed to understand that her mother's mania for cleanliness was a reaction against this dirtying.

The two groups of ideas met in this one thought: 'Mother got both things from father: the sexual wetness and the dirtying discharge.' Dora's jealousy of her mother was inseparable from the group of thoughts relating to her infantile love for her father which she summoned up for her protection. But this material was not yet capable of representation. If, however, a recollection could be found which was equally closely connected with both the groups related to the word 'wet', but which avoided any offensiveness, then such a recollection would be able to take over the representation in the dream of the material in question.

A recollection of this sort was furnished by the episode of the 'drops'—the jewellery ['*Schmuck*'] that Dora's mother wanted to have [p. 69]. In appearance the connection between this reminiscence and the two groups of thoughts relating to sexual wetness and to being dirtied was a purely external and superficial one, of a verbal character. For 'drops' was used ambiguously as a 'switch-word' [p. 65 *n*.], while 'jewellery' ['*Schmuck*'] was taken as an equivalent to 'clean', and thus as a rather forced contrary of 'dirtied'.[1] But in reality the most substantial connections can be shown to have existed between the things denoted themselves. The recollection originated from the material connected with Dora's jealousy of her mother, which, though its roots were infantile, had persisted far beyond that period. By means of these two verbal bridges it was possible to transfer on to the single reminiscence of the 'jewel-drops' the whole of the significance attaching to the ideas of her parents' sexual intercourse, and of her mother's gonorrhoea and tormenting passion for cleanliness.

But a still further displacement had to be effected before this material appeared in the dream. Though 'drops' is nearer to the original 'wet', it was the more distant 'jewellery' that found a place in the dream. When, therefore, this element had been inserted into the dream-situation which had already been established, the account might have run: 'Mother wanted to stop and save her jewellery.' But a subsequent influence now made itself felt, and led to the further alteration of 'jewellery' into 'jewel-case'. This influence came from elements in the underlying group relating to the temptation offered by Herr K. He had never given her jewellery, but he had given her a 'case' for it [p. 69], which meant for her all the marks of preference and all the tenderness for which she felt she ought now to have been grateful. And the composite word thus formed, 'jewel-case', had beyond this a special claim to be used as a representative element in the dream. Is not 'jewel-case' ['*Schmuckkästchen*'] a term commonly used to describe female genitals that are immaculate and intact? And is it not, on the other hand, an innocent word? Is it not, in short, admirably calculated both to betray and to conceal the sexual thoughts that lie behind the dream?

'Mother's jewel-case' was therefore introduced in two places in the dream; and this element replaced all mention of Dora's infantile jealousy, of the drops (that is, of the sexual wetness),

[1] [The German word '*Schmuck*' has a much wider meaning than the English 'jewellery', though that is the sense in which it occurs in the compound '*Schmuckkästchen*', 'jewel-case'. As a substantive, '*Schmuck*' denotes 'finery' of all kinds, not only personal adornments, but embellishments of objects and decorations in general. In an adjectival sense, it can mean 'smart', 'tidy', or 'neat'.]

of being dirtied by the discharge, and, on the otherhand, of her present thoughts connected with the temptation—the thoughts which were urging her to reciprocate the man's love, and which depicted the sexual situation (alike desirable and menacing) that lay before her. The element of 'jewel-case' was more than any other a product of condensation and displacement, and a compromise between contrary mental currents. The multiplicity of its origin—both from infantile and contemporary sources—is no doubt pointed to by its double appearance in the content of the dream.

The dream was a reaction to a fresh experience of an exciting nature; and this experience must inevitably have revived the memory of the only previous experience which was at all analogous to it. The latter was the scene of the kiss in Herr K.'s place of business, when she had been seized with disgust [p. 28]. But this same scene was associatively accessible from other directions too, namely, from the group of thoughts relating to the catarrh (p. 83), and from her present temptation. The scene therefore brought to the dream a contribution of its own, which had to be made to fit in with the dream situation that had already been laid down: 'There was a fire' . . . no doubt the kiss smelt of smoke; so she smelt smoke in the dream, and the smell persisted till after she was awake [p. 73].

By inadvertence, I unfortunately left a gap in the analysis of the dream. Dora's father was made to say, 'I refuse to let my two children go to their destruction . . .' ('as a result of masturbation' should no doubt be added from the dream-thoughts). Such speeches in dreams are regularly constructed out of pieces of actual speeches which have either been made or heard.[1] I ought to have made enquiries as to the actual source of this speech. The results of my enquiry would no doubt have shown that the structure of the dream was still more complicated, but would at the same time have made it easier to penetrate.

Are we to suppose that when this dream occurred at L——it had precisely the same content as when it recurred during the treatment? It does not seem necessary to do so. Experience shows that people often assert that they have had the same dream, when as a matter of fact the separate appearances of the recurrent dream have differed from one another in numerous

---

[1] [Cf. *The Interpretation of Dreams*, Chapter VI, Section F; Standard Ed., 5, 418 ff.]

details and in other respects that were of no small importance. Thus one of my patients told me that she had had her favourite dream again the night before, and that it always recurred in the same form: she had dreamed of swimming in the blue sea, of joyfully cleaving her way through the waves, and so on. On closer investigation it turned out that upon a common background now one detail and now another was brought out; on one occasion, even, she was swimming in a frozen sea and was surrounded by icebergs. This patient had other dreams, which turned out to be closely connected with the recurrent one, though even she made no attempt to claim that they were identical with it. Once, for instance, she was looking at a view of Heligoland (based on a photograph, but life-size) which showed the upper and lower parts of the island simultaneously; on the sea was a ship, in which were two people whom she had known in her youth, and so on.

What is certain is that in Dora's case the dream which occurred during the treatment had gained a new significance connected with the present time, though perhaps its manifest content had not changed. The dream-thoughts behind it included a reference to my treatment, and it corresponded to a renewal of the old intention of withdrawing from a danger. If her memory was not deceiving her when she declared that even at L—— she had noticed the smoke after she woke up, it must be acknowledged that she had brought my proverb, 'There can be no smoke without fire' [p. 73], very ingeniously into the completed form of the dream, in which it seemed to serve as an overdetermination of the last element. It was undeniably a mere matter of chance that the most recent exciting cause—her mother's locking the dining-room door so that her brother was shut into his bedroom [p. 65]—had provided a connection with her persecution by Herr K. at L——, where her decision had been made when she found she could not lock her bedroom door. It is possible that her brother did not appear in the dream on the earlier occasions, so that the words 'my two children' did not form part of its content until after the occurrence of its latest exciting cause.

# THE SECOND DREAM

A FEW weeks after the first dream the second occurred, and when it had been dealt with the analysis was broken off. It cannot be made as completely intelligible as the first, but it afforded a desirable confirmation of an assumption which had become necessary about the patient's mental state [p. 104], it filled up a gap in her memory [p. 105], and it made it possible to obtain a deep insight into the origin of another of her symptoms [p. 101].

Dora described the dream as follows: '*I was walking about in a town which I did not know. I saw streets and squares which were strange to me.*[1] *Then I came into a house where I lived, went to my room, and found a letter from Mother lying there. She wrote saying that as I had left home without my parents' knowledge she had not wished to write to me to say that Father was ill. "Now he is dead, and if you like*[2] *you can come." I then went to the station ["Bahnhof"] and asked about a hundred times: "Where is the station?" I always got the answer: "Five minutes." I then saw a thick wood before me which I went into, and there I asked a man whom I met. He said to me: "Two and a half hours more."*[3] *He offered to accompany me. But I refused and went alone. I saw the station in front of me and could not reach it. At the same time I had the usual feeling of anxiety that one has in dreams when one cannot move forward. Then I was at home. I must have been travelling in the meantime, but I know nothing about that. I walked into the porter's lodge, and enquired for our flat. The maidservant opened the door to me and replied that Mother and the others were already at the cemetery ["Friedhof"].*'[4]

[1] To this she subsequently made an important addendum: '*I saw a monument in one of the squares.*'

[2] To this came the addendum: '*There was a question-mark after this word, thus: "like?".*'

[3] In repeating the dream she said: '*Two hours.*' [In the 1921 German edition only, this is misprinted 'Three hours'.]

[4] In the next session Dora brought me two addenda to this: '*I saw myself particularly distinctly going up the stairs,*' and '*After she had answered I went to my room, but not the least sadly, and began reading a big book that lay on my writing-table.*'

It was not without some difficulty that the interpretation of this dream proceeded. In consequence of the peculiar circumstances in which the analysis was broken off—circumstances connected with the content of the dream—the whole of it was not cleared up. And for this reason, too, I am not equally certain at every point of the order in which my conclusions were reached. I will begin by mentioning the subject-matter with which the current analysis was dealing at the time when the dream intervened. For some time Dora herself had been raising a number of questions about the connection between some of her actions and the motives which presumably underlay them. One of these questions was: 'Why did I say nothing about the scene by the lake for some days after it had happened?' Her second question was: 'Why did I then suddenly tell my parents about it?' Moreover, her having felt so deeply injured by Herr K.'s proposal seemed to me in general to need explanation, especially as I was beginning to realize that Herr K. himself had not regarded his proposal to Dora as a mere frivolous attempt at seduction. I looked upon her having told her parents of the episode as an action which she had taken when she was already under the influence of a morbid craving for revenge. A normal girl, I am inclined to think, will deal with a situation of this kind by herself.

I shall present the material produced during the analysis of this dream in the somewhat haphazard order in which it recurs to my mind.

*She was wandering about alone in a strange town, and saw streets and squares.* Dora assured me that it was certainly not B——, which I had first hit upon, but a town in which she had never been. It was natural to suggest that she might have seen some pictures or photographs and have taken the dream-pictures from them. After this remark of mine came the addendum about the monument in one of the squares and immediately afterwards her recognition of its source. At Christmas [1] she had been sent an album from a German health-resort, containing views of the town; and the very day before the dream she had looked this out to show it to some relatives who were stopping with them. It had been put in a box for keeping pictures in, and she could not lay her hands on it at once. She had therefore said to her

[1] [The dream occurred a few days after Christmas (see p. 105).]

mother: '*Where is the box?*' [1] One of the pictures was of a square
with a monument in it. The present had been sent to her by a
young engineer, with whom she had once had a passing acquaintance in the manufacturing town. The young man had
accepted a post in Germany, so as to become sooner self-
supporting; and he took every opportunity of reminding Dora
of his existence. It was easy to guess that he intended to come
forward as a suitor one day, when his position had improved.
But that would take time, and it meant waiting.

The wandering about in a strange town was overdetermined.
It led back to one of the exciting causes from the day before. A
young cousin of Dora's had come to stay with them for the
holidays, and Dora had had to show him round Vienna. This
cause was, it is true, a matter of complete indifference to her.
But her cousin's visit reminded her of her own first brief visit to
Dresden. On that occasion she had been a stranger and had
wandered about, not failing, of course, to visit the famous
picture gallery. Another [male] cousin of hers, who was with
them and knew Dresden, had wanted to act as a guide and take
her round the gallery. *But she declined and went alone*, and stopped
in front of the pictures that appealed to her. She remained *two
hours* in front of the Sistine Madonna, rapt in silent admiration.
When I asked her what had pleased her so much about the
picture she could find no clear answer to make. At last she said:
'The Madonna.'

There could be no doubt that these associations really belonged to the material concerned in forming the dream. They
included portions which reappeared in the dream unchanged
('she declined and went alone' and 'two hours'). I may remark
at once that 'pictures' was a nodal point in the network of her
dream-thoughts (the pictures in the album, the pictures at
Dresden). I should also like to single out, with a view to subsequent investigation, the theme of the 'Madonna', of the virgin
mother. But what was most evident was that in this first part of
the dream she was identifying herself with a young man. This
young man was wandering about in a strange place, he was
striving to reach a goal, but he was being kept back, he needed
patience and must wait. If in all this she had been thinking of

[1] In the dream she said: '*Where is the station?*' The resemblance
between the two questions led me to make an inference which I shall go
into presently [p. 97].

the engineer, it would have been appropriate for the goal to have been the possession of a woman, of herself. But instead of this it was—a station. Nevertheless, the relation of the question in the dream to the question which had been put in real life allows us to substitute '*box*' for 'station'.[1] A box and a woman: the notions begin to agree better.

*She asked quite a hundred times.* . . . . This led to another exciting cause of the dream, and this time to one that was less indifferent. On the previous evening they had had company, and afterwards her father had asked her to fetch him the brandy: he could not get to sleep unless he had taken some brandy. She had asked her mother for the key of the sideboard; but the latter had been deep in conversation, and had not answered her, until Dora had exclaimed with the exaggeration of impatience: 'I've asked you *a hundred times* already where the key is.' As a matter of fact, she had of course only repeated the question about *five times*.[2]

'Where is the *key*?' seems to me to be the masculine counterpart to the question 'Where is the *box*?'[3] They are therefore questions referring to—the genitals.

Dora went on to say that during this same family gathering some one had toasted her father and had expressed the hope that he might continue to enjoy the best of health for many years to come, etc. At this a strange quiver passed over her father's tired face, and she had understood what thoughts he was having to keep down. Poor sick man! who could tell what span of life was still to be his?

This brings us to the *contents of the letter* in the dream. Her father was dead, and she had left home by her own choice. In connection with this letter I at once reminded Dora of the farewell letter which she had written to her parents or had at least composed for their benefit [p. 23]. This letter had been intended to give her father a fright, so that he should give up

---

[1] ['*Schachtel*', the word which was used for 'box' by Dora in her question, is a depreciatory term for 'woman'.]

[2] In the dream the number five occurs in the mention of the period of 'five minutes'. In my book on the interpretation of dreams I have given several examples of the way in which numbers occurring in the dream-thoughts are treated by dreams. We frequently find them torn out of their true context and inserted into a new one. [See Freud, 1900*a*, Section F of Chapter VI; Standard Ed., **5**, 414 ff.]

[3] See the first dream, p. 66.

Frau K.; or at any rate to take revenge on him if he could not be induced to do that. We are here concerned with the subject of her death and of her father's death. (Cf. 'cemetery' later on in the dream.) Shall we be going astray if we suppose that the situation which formed the façade of the dream was a phantasy of revenge directed against her father? The feelings of pity for him which she remembered from the day before would be quite in keeping with this. According to the phantasy she had left home and gone among strangers, and her father's heart had broken with grief and with longing for her. Thus she would be revenged. She understood very clearly what it was that her father needed when he could not get to sleep without a drink of brandy.[1] We will make a note of Dora's *craving for revenge* as a new element to be taken into account in any subsequent synthesis of her dream-thoughts.

But the contents of the letter must be capable of further determination. What was the source of the words 'if you like'? It was at this point that the addendum of there having been a question-mark after the word 'like' occurred to Dora, and she then recognized these words as a quotation out of the letter from Frau K. which had contained the invitation to L——, the place by the lake. In that letter there had been a question-mark placed, in a most unusual fashion, in the very middle of a sentence, after the intercalated words 'if you would like to come'.

So here we were back again at the scene by the lake [p. 25] and at the problems connected with it. I asked Dora to describe the scene to me in detail. At first she produced little that was new. Herr K.'s exordium had been somewhat serious; but she had not let him finish what he had to say. No sooner had she grasped the purport of his words than she had slapped him in the face and hurried away. I enquired what his actual words had been. Dora could only remember one of his pleas: 'You know I get nothing out of my wife.'[2] In order to avoid meeting him again she had wanted to get back to L—— on foot, by

---

[1] There can be no doubt that sexual satisfaction is the best soporific, just as sleeplessness is almost always the consequence of lack of satisfaction. Her father could not sleep because he was debarred from sexual intercourse with the woman he loved. (Compare in this connection the phrase discussed just below: 'I get nothing out of my wife.') [Cf. also the words quoted from Dora's father on p. 26.]

[2] These words will enable us to solve one of our problems [p. 106].

walking round the lake, and *she had asked a man whom she met how far it was*. On his replying that it was '*Two and a half hours*', she had given up her intention and had after all gone back to the boat, which left soon afterwards. Herr K. had been there too and had come up to her and begged her to forgive him and not to mention the incident. But she had made no reply.—Yes. The *wood* in the dream had been just like the wood by the shore of the lake, the wood in which the scene she had just described once more had taken place. But she had seen precisely the same thick wood the day before, in a picture at the Secessionist exhibition. In the background of the picture there were *nymphs*.[1]

At this point a certain suspicion of mine became a certainty. The use of '*Bahnhof*' ['station'; literally, 'railway-court']²[2] and '*Friedhof*' ['cemetery'; literally, 'peace-court'] to represent the female genitals was striking enough in itself, but it also served to direct my awakened curiosity to the similarly formed '*Vorhof*' ['vestibulum'; literally, 'fore-court']—an anatomical term for a particular region of the female genitals. This might have been no more than mistaken ingenuity. But now, with the addition of 'nymphs' visible in the background of a 'thick wood', no further doubts could be entertained. Here was a symbolic geography of sex! 'Nymphae',[3] as is known to physicians though not to laymen (and even by the former the term is not very commonly used), is the name given to the labia minora, which lie in the background of the 'thick wood' of the pubic hair. But any one who employed such technical names as 'vestibulum' and 'nymphae' must have derived his knowledge from books, and not from popular ones either, but from anatomical text-books or from an encyclopaedia—the common refuge of youth when it is devoured by sexual curiosity. If this interpretation were correct, therefore, there lay concealed behind the first situation in

---

[1] Here for the third time we come upon 'picture' (views of towns, the Dresden gallery), but in a much more significant connection. Because of what appears in the picture (the wood, the nymphs), the '*Bild*' ['picture'] is turned into a '*Weibsbild*' [literally, 'picture of a woman'—a somewhat derogatory expression for 'woman'].

[2] Moreover, a 'station' is used for purposes of '*Verkehr*' ['traffic', 'intercourse', 'sexual intercourse']: this fact determines the psychical coating in a number of cases of railway phobia.

[3] [In German the same word, '*Nymphen*', represents both 'nymphs' and 'nymphae'.]

the dream a phantasy of defloration, the phantasy of a man seeking to force an entrance into the female genitals.[1]

I informed Dora of the conclusions I had reached. The impression made upon her must have been forcible, for there immediately appeared a piece of the dream which had been forgotten: '*she went calmly to her room, and began reading a big book that lay on her writing-table.*'[2] The emphasis here was upon the two details 'calmly' and 'big' in connection with 'book'. I asked whether the book was in encyclopaedia *format*, and she said it was. Now children never read about forbidden subjects in an encyclopaedia *calmly*. They do it in fear and trembling, with an uneasy look over their shoulder to see if some one may not be coming. Parents are very much in the way while reading of this kind is going on. But this uncomfortable situation had been radically improved, thanks to the dream's power of fulfilling wishes. Dora's father was dead, and the others had already gone to the cemetery. She might calmly read whatever she chose. Did not this mean that one of her motives for revenge was a revolt against her parents' constraint? If her father was dead she could read or love as she pleased.

At first she would not remember ever having read anything in an encyclopaedia; but she then admitted that a recollection

[1] The phantasy of defloration formed the second component of the situation. The emphasis upon the difficulty of getting forward and the anxiety felt in the dream indicated the stress which the dreamer was so ready to lay upon her virginity—a point alluded to in another place by means of the Sistine Madonna. These sexual thoughts gave an unconscious ground-colouring to the wishes (which were perhaps merely kept secret) concerned with the suitor who was waiting for her in Germany. We have already [p. 98] recognized the phantasy of revenge as the first component of the same situation in the dream. The two components do not coincide completely, but only in part. We shall subsequently come upon the traces of a third and still more important train of thought. [See p. 108, *n.* 1.]

[2] On another occasion, instead of 'calmly' she said 'not the least sadly' (p. 94, *n.* 4)—I can quote this dream as fresh evidence for the correctness of an assertion made in my *Interpretation of Dreams* (Chapter VII, Section A; Standard Ed., 5, 518) [see also p. 73 above] to the effect that those pieces of a dream which are at first forgotten and are only subsequently remembered are invariably the most important from the point of view of understanding the dream. In the same place I went on to the conclusion that the forgetting of dreams must also be explained as an effect of endopsychic resistance.—[The first sentence of this footnote was added in 1924.]

of an occasion of the kind did occur to her, though it was of an innocent enough nature. At the time when the aunt she was so fond of had been so seriously ill and it had already been settled that Dora was to go to Vienna, a *letter* had come from another uncle, to say that they could not go to Vienna, as a boy of his, a cousin of Dora's therefore, had fallen dangerously ill with appendicitis. Dora had thereupon looked up in the encyclopaedia to see what the symptoms of appendicitis were. From what she had then read she still recollected the characteristic localization of the abdominal pain.

I then remembered that shortly after her aunt's death Dora had had an attack of what had been alleged to be appendicitis [p. 22]. Up till then I had not ventured to count that illness among her hysterical productions. She told me that during the first few days she had had high fever and had felt the pain in her abdomen that she had read about in the encyclopaedia. She had been given cold fomentations but had not been able to bear them. On the second day her period had set in, accompanied by violent pains. (Since her health had been bad, the periods had been very irregular.) At that time she used to suffer continually from constipation.

It was not really possible to regard this state as a purely hysterical one. Although hysterical fever does undoubtedly occur, yet it seemed too arbitrary to put down the fever accompanying this questionable illness to hysteria instead of to some organic cause operative at the time. I was on the point of abandoning the track, when she herself helped me along it by producing her last addendum to the dream: '*she saw herself particularly distinctly going up the stairs.*'

I naturally required a special determinant for this. Dora objected that she would anyhow have had to go upstairs if she had wanted to get to her flat, which was on an upper floor. It was easy to brush aside this objection (which was probably not very seriously intended) by pointing out that if she had been able to travel in her dream from the unknown town to Vienna without making a railway journey she ought also to have been able to leave out a flight of stairs. She then proceeded to relate that after the appendicitis she had not been able to walk properly and had dragged her right foot. This state of things had continued for a long time, and on that account she had been particularly glad to avoid stairs. Even now her foot sometimes dragged. The doctors whom she had consulted at her father's desire had been very much astonished at this most unusual after-effect of an appendicitis, especially as the abdominal pains had not recurred and did not in any way accompany the dragging of the foot.[1]

Here, then, we have a true hysterical symptom. The fever may have been organically determined—perhaps by one of those very frequent attacks of influenza that are not localized in any particular part of the body. Nevertheless it was now established that the neurosis had seized upon this chance event and made use of it for an utterance of its own. Dora had therefore given herself an illness which she had read up about in the encyclopaedia, and she had punished herself for dipping into its pages. But she was forced to recognize that the punishment could not possibly apply to her reading the innocent article in question. It must have been inflicted as the result of a process of displacement, after another occasion of more guilty reading had become associated with this one; and the guilty occasion must lie concealed in her memory behind the contemporaneous innocent one.[2] It might still be possible, perhaps, to discover the nature of the subjects she had read about on that other occasion.

What, then, was the meaning of this condition, of this attempted simulation of a perityphlitis? The remainder of the disorder, the dragging of one leg, was entirely out of keeping with perityphlitis. It must, no doubt, fit in better with the secret and possibly sexual meaning of the clinical picture; and if it were elucidated might in its turn throw light on the meaning which we were in search of. I looked about for a method of approaching the puzzle. Periods of time had been mentioned in the dream; and time is assuredly never a matter of indiffer-

---

[1] We must assume the existence of some somatic connection between the painful abdominal sensations known as 'ovarian neuralgia' and locomotor disturbances in the leg on the same side; and we must suppose that in Dora's case the somatic connection had been given an interpretation of a particularly specialized sort, that is to say, that it had been overlaid with and brought into the service of a particular psychological meaning. The reader is referred to my analogous remarks in connection with the analysis of Dora's symptom of coughing and with the relation between catarrh and loss of appetite [p. 83 f.].

[2] This is quite a typical example of the way in which symptoms arise from exciting causes which appear to be entirely unconnected with sexuality.

ence in any biological event. I therefore asked Dora when this attack of appendicitis had taken place; whether it had been before or after the scene by the lake. Every difficulty was resolved at a single blow by her prompt reply: 'Nine months later.' The period of time is sufficiently characteristic. Her supposed attack of appendicitis had thus enabled the patient with the modest means at her disposal (the pains and the menstrual flow) to realize a phantasy of *childbirth*.[1] Dora was naturally aware of the significance of this period of time, and could not dispute the probability of her having, on the occasion under discussion, read up in the encyclopaedia about pregnancy and childbirth. But what was all this about her dragging her leg? I could now hazard a guess. That is how people walk when they have twisted a foot. So she had made a 'false step': which was true indeed if she could give birth to a child nine months after the scene by the lake. But there was still another requirement upon the fulfilment of which I had to insist. I am convinced that a symptom of this kind can only arise where it has an *infantile* prototype. All my experience hitherto has led me to hold firmly to the view that recollections derived from the impressions of later years do not possess sufficient force to enable them to establish themselves as symptoms. I scarcely dared hope that Dora would provide me with the material that I wanted from her childhood, for the fact is that I am not yet in a position to assert the general validity of this rule, much as I should like to be able to do so. But in this case there came an immediate confirmation of it. Yes, said Dora, once when she was a child she had twisted the same foot; she had slipped on one of the steps as she was going *downstairs*. The foot—and it was actually the same one that she afterwards dragged—had swelled up and had to be bandaged and she had had to lie up for some weeks. This had been a short time before the attack of nervous asthma in her eighth year [p. 21].

The next thing to do was to turn to account our knowledge of the existence of this phantasy: 'If it is true that you were delivered of a child nine months after the scene by the lake, and that you are going about to this very day carrying the

---

[1] I have already indicated [p. 47] that the majority of hysterical symptoms, when they have attained their full pitch of development, represent an imagined situation of sexual life—such as a scene of sexual intercourse, pregnancy, childbirth, confinement, etc.

consequences of your false step with you, then it follows that in your unconscious you must have regretted the upshot of the scene. In your unconscious thoughts, that is to say, you have made an emendation in it. The assumption that underlies your phantasy of childbirth is that on that occasion something took place,[1] that on that occasion you experienced and went through everything that you were in fact obliged to pick up later on from the encyclopaedia. So you see that your love for Herr K. did not come to an end with the scene, but that (as I maintained) it has persisted down to the present day—though it is true that you are unconscious of it.'—And Dora disputed the fact no longer.[2]

[1] The phantasy of defloration [p. 99 f.] is thus found to have an application to Herr K., and we begin to see why this part of the dream contained material taken from the scene by the lake—the refusal, two and a half hours, the wood, the invitation to L——.

[2] I may here add a few supplementary interpretations to those that have already been given: The '*Madonna*' was obviously Dora herself; in the first place because of the 'adorer' who had sent her the pictures [p. 96], in the second place because she had won Herr K.'s love chiefly by the motherliness she had shown towards his children [p. 25], and lastly because she had had a child though she was still a girl (this being a direct allusion to the phantasy of childbirth). Moreover, the notion of the 'Madonna' is a favourite counter-idea in the mind of girls who feel themselves oppressed by imputations of sexual guilt,—which was the case with Dora. A first suspicion of this connection came to me while I was working as a physician at the Psychiatric Clinic of the University. I there came across a case of confusional insanity with hallucinations, in which the attack, which ran a rapid course, turned out to be a reaction to a reproach made against the patient by her *fiancé*.—If the analysis had been continued, Dora's maternal longing for a child would probably have been revealed as an obscure though powerful motive in her behaviour.—The numerous questions which she had been raising latterly seem to have been belated derivatives of questions inspired by the sexual curiosity which she had tried to gratify with the encyclopaedia. The subjects which she read up in it were presumably pregnancy, childbirth, virginity, and so on.—In reproducing the dream Dora had forgotten one of the questions which need to be inserted into the course of the second situation in the dream. This question could only be: 'Does Herr —— live here?' or 'Where does Herr —— live?' There must have been some reason for her having forgotten this apparently innocent question, especially as she need not have brought it into the dream at all. This reason, it seems to me, lay in her surname itself, which also denoted an object and in fact more than one kind of object, and which could therefore be regarded as an 'ambiguous' word. Unluckily I cannot give the name and show how well designed it was to indicate something

The labour of elucidating the second dream had so far occupied two hours. At the end of the second session, when I expressed my satisfaction at the result, Dora replied in a depreciatory tone: 'Why, has anything so very remarkable come out?' These words prepared me for the advent of fresh revelations.

She opened the third session with these words: 'Do you know that I am here for the last time to-day?'—'How can I know, as you have said nothing to me about it?'—'Yes. I made up my mind to put up with it till the New Year.[1] But I shall wait no longer than that to be cured.'—'You know that you are free to stop the treatment at any time. But for to-day we will go on with our work. When did you come to this decision?'—'A fortnight ago, I think.'—'That sounds just like a maidservant or a governess—a fortnight's warning.'—'There was a governess who gave warning with the K.'s, when I was on my visit to them that time at L——, by the lake.'—'Really? You have never told me about her. Tell me.'

'Well, there was a young girl in the house, who was the children's governess; and she behaved in the most extraordinary way to Herr K. She never said good morning to him, never answered his remarks, never handed him anything at table when he asked for it, and in short treated him like thin air. For that matter he was hardly any politer to her. A day or two before the scene by the lake, the girl took me aside and said she had something to tell me. She then told me that Herr K. had made advances to her at a time when his wife was away for several weeks; he had made violent love to her and had implored

'ambiguous' and 'improper'. This interpretation was supported by the discovery of a similar play upon words in another part of the dream, where the material was derived from Dora's recollections of her aunt's death ('they have already gone to the cemetery') and where there was similarly a play upon her aunt's name. These improper words seemed to point to a second and *oral* source of information, since the encyclopaedia would not cover them. I should not have been surprised to hear that this source had been Frau K. herself, Dora's calumniator. [Cf. p. 62.] In that case she would have been the one person whom Dora generously spared, while she pursued the others with an almost malignant vindictiveness. Behind the almost limitless series of displacements which were thus brought to light, it was possible to divine the operation of a single simple factor—Dora's deep-rooted homosexual love for Frau K. [Cf. pages 59 ff. and 120 n.]

[1] It was December 31st.

her to yield to his entreaties, saying that he got nothing from his wife, and so on.'—'Why, those are the very words he used afterwards, when he made his proposal to you and you gave him the slap in his face' [p. 98].—'Yes. She had given way to him, but after a little while he had ceased to care for her, and since then she hated him.'—'And this governess had given warning?'—'No. She meant to give warning. She told me that as soon as she felt she was thrown over she had told her parents what had happened. They were respectable people living in Germany somewhere. Her parents said that she must leave the house instantly; and, as she failed to do so, they wrote to her saying that they would have nothing more to do with her, and that she was never to come home again.'—'And why had she not gone away?'—'She said she meant to wait a little longer, to see if there might not be some change in Herr K. She could not bear living like that any more, she said, and if she saw no change she should give warning and go away.'—'And what became of the girl?'—'I only know that she went away.'—'And she did not have a child as a result of the adventure?'—'No.'

Here, therefore (and quite in accordance with the rules), was a piece of material information coming to light in the middle of the analysis and helping to solve problems which had previously been raised. I was able to say to Dora: 'Now I know your motive for the slap in the face with which you answered Herr K.'s proposal. It was not that you were offended at his suggestions; you were actuated by jealousy and revenge. At the time when the governess was telling you her story you were still able to make use of your gift for putting on one side everything that is not agreeable to your feelings. But at the moment when Herr K. used the words "I get nothing out of my wife"—which were the same words he had used to the governess—fresh emotions were aroused in you and tipped the balance. "Does he dare", you said to yourself, "to treat me like a governess, like a servant?" Wounded pride added to jealousy and to the conscious motives of common sense—it was too much.[1] To prove to you how deeply impressed you were by the governess's story, let me draw your attention to the repeated occasions upon which you

---

[1] It is not a matter of indifference, perhaps, that Dora may have heard her father make the same complaint about his wife, just as I myself did from his own lips [p. 26]. She was perfectly well aware of its meaning.

have identified yourself with her both in your dream and in your conduct. You told your parents what happened—a fact which we have hitherto been unable to account for—just as the governess wrote and told *her* parents. You give me a fortnight's warning, just like a governess. The letter in the dream which gave you leave to go home is the counterpart of the governess's letter from her parents forbidding her to do so.'

'Then why did I not tell my parents at once?'

'How much time did you allow to elapse?'

'The scene took place on the last day of June; I told my mother about it on July 14th.'

'Again a fortnight, then—the time characteristic for a person in service. Now I can answer your question. You understood the poor girl very well. She did not want to go away at once, because she still had hopes, because she expected that Herr K.'s affections would return to her again. So that must have been your motive too. You waited for that length of time so as to see whether he would repeat his proposals; if he had, you would have concluded that he was in earnest, and did not mean to play with you as he had done with the governess.'

'A few days after I had left he sent me a picture post-card.'[1]

'Yes, but when after that nothing more came, you gave free rein to your feelings of revenge. I can even imagine that at that time you were still able to find room for a subsidiary intention, and thought that your accusation might be a means of inducing him to travel to the place where you were living. —'As he actually offered to do at first,' Dora threw in.—'In that way your longing for him would have been appeased'—here she nodded assent, a thing which I had not expected—'and he might have made you the amends you desired.'

'What amends?'

'The fact is, I am beginning to suspect that you took the affair with Herr K. much more seriously than you have been willing to admit so far. Had not the K.'s often talked of getting a divorce?'

'Yes, certainly. At first she did not want to, on account of the children. And now she wants to, but he no longer does.'

'May you not have thought that he wanted to get divorced

---

[1] Here is the point of contact with the engineer [p. 96], who was concealed behind the figure of Dora herself in the first situation in the dream.

from his wife so as to marry you? And that now he no longer
wants to because he has no one to replace her? It is true that
two years ago you were very young. But you told me yourself
that your mother was engaged at seventeen and then waited two
years for her husband. A daughter usually takes her mother's
love-story as her model. So you too wanted to wait for him, and
you took it that he was only waiting till you were grown up
enough to be his wife.[1] I imagine that this was a perfectly serious
plan for the future in your eyes. You have not even got the right
to assert that it was out of the question for Herr K. to have had
any such intention; you have told me enough about him that
points directly towards his having such an intention.[2] Nor does
his behaviour at L—— contradict this view. After all, you did
not let him finish his speech and do not know what he meant to
say to you. Incidentally, the scheme would by no means have
been so impracticable. Your father's relations with Frau K.—
and it was probably only for this reason that you lent them your
support for so long—made it certain that her consent to a
divorce could be obtained; and you can get anything you like
out of your father. Indeed, if your temptation at L—— had had
a different upshot, this would have been the only possible
solution for all the parties concerned. And I think that is why
you regretted the actual event so deeply and emended it in the
phantasy which made its appearance in the shape of the appendicitis. So it must have been a bitter piece of disillusionment for
you when the effect of your charges against Herr K. was not
that he renewed his proposals but that he replied instead with
denials and slanders. You will agree that nothing makes you so
angry as having it thought that you merely fancied the scene by
the lake. [Cf. p. 46.] I know now—and this is what you do not
want to be reminded of—that you *did* fancy that Herr K.'s
proposals were serious, and that he would not leave off until
you had married him.'

Dora had listened to me without any of her usual contradic-

[1] The theme of waiting till the goal is reached occurs in the content
of the first situation in the dream. I recognize in this phantasy of waiting
for a fiancée a portion of the third component of that situation. I have
already alluded [p. 100, *n.* 1] to the existence of this third component.

[2] In particular there was a speech which he had made in presenting
Dora with a letter-case for Christmas in the last year in which they
lived together at B——.

tions. She seemed to be moved; she said good-bye to me very warmly, with the heartiest wishes for the New Year, and—came no more. Her father, who called on me two or three times afterwards, assured me that she would come back again, and said it was easy to see that she was eager for the treatment to continue. But it must be confessed that Dora's father was never entirely straightforward. He had given his support to the treatment so long as he could hope that I should 'talk' Dora out of her belief that there was something more than a friendship between him and Frau K. His interest faded when he observed that it wasnot my intention to bring about that result. I knew Dora would not come back again. Her breaking off so unexpectedly, just when my hopes of a successful termination of the treatment were at their highest, and her thus bringing those hopes to nothing— this was an unmistakable act of vengeance on her part. Her purpose of self-injury also profited by this action. No one who, like me, conjures up the most evil of those half-tamed demons that inhabit the human breast, and seeks to wrestle with them, can expect to come through the struggle unscathed. Might I perhaps have kept the girl under my treatment if I myself had acted a part, if I had exaggerated the importance to me of her staying on, and had shown a warm personal interest in her—a course which, even after allowing for my position as her physician. would have been tantamount to providing her with a substitute for the affection she longed for? I do not know. Since in every case a portion of the factors that are encountered under the form of resistance remains unknown, I have always avoided acting a part, and have contented myself with practising the humbler arts of psychology. In spite of every theoretical interest and of every endeavour to be of assistance as a physician, I keep the fact in mind that there must be some limits set to the extent to which psychological influence may be used, and I respect as one of these limits the patient's own will and understanding.

Nor do I know whether Herr K. would have done any better if it had been revealed to him that the slap Dora gave him by no means signified a final 'No' on her part, but that it expressed the jealousy which had lately been roused in her, while her strongest feelings were still on his side. If he had disregarded that first 'No', and had continued to press his suit with a passion which left room for no doubts, the result might very well have been a triumph of the girl's affection for him over all

her internal difficulties. But I think she might just as well have
been merely provoked into satisfying her craving for revenge
upon him all the more thoroughly. It is never possible to
calculate towards which side the decision will incline in such
a conflict of motives: whether towards the removal of the repression or towards its reinforcement. Incapacity for meeting a
*real* erotic demand is one of the most essential features of a
neurosis. Neurotics are dominated by the opposition between
reality and phantasy. If what they long for the most intensely
in their phantasies is presented to them in reality, they none the
less flee from it; and they abandon themselves to their phantasies the most readily where they need no longer fear to see
them realized. Nevertheless, the barrier erected by repression
can fall before the onslaught of a violent emotional excitement
produced by a real cause; it is possible for a neurosis to be overcome by reality. But we have no general means of calculating
through what person or what event such a cure can be effected.[1]

    [1] I will add a few remarks on the structure of this dream, though
it is not possible to understand it thoroughly enough to allow of a
synthesis being attempted. A prominent piece of the dream is to be seen
in the phantasy of revenge against her father, which stands out like a
façade in front of the rest. (She had gone away from home by her own
choice; her father was ill, and then dead. . . . Then she went home; all
the others were already at the cemetery. She went to her room, not the
least sadly, and calmly began reading the encyclopaedia.) This part of
the material also contained two allusions to her other act of revenge,
which she had actually carried out, when she let her parents discover
a farewell letter from her. (The letter—from her mother, in the dream—
and the mention of the funeral of the aunt who had always been her
model.)—Behind this phantasy lie concealed her thoughts of revenge
against Herr K., for which she found an outlet in her behaviour to me.
(The maidservant, the invitation, the wood, the two and a half hours
[in editions before 1924 'two hours']—all these came from material connected with the events at L——.) Her recollection of the governess, and
of the latter's exchange of letters with her parents, is related, no less than
her farewell letter, to the letter in the dream allowing her to come home.
Her refusal to let herself be accompanied and her decision to go alone
may perhaps be translated into these words: 'Since you have treated
me like a servant, I shall take no more notice of you, I shall go my
own way by myself, and not marry.'—Screened by these thoughts of
revenge, glimpses can be caught in other places of material derived from
tender phantasies based upon the love for Herr K. which still persisted
unconsciously in Dora. ('I would have waited for you till I could be
your wife'—defloration—childbirth.)—Finally, we can see the action
of the fourth and most deeply buried group of thoughts—those relating

to her love for Frau K.—in the fact that the phantasy of defloration is represented from the man's point of view (her identification of herself with her admirer who lived abroad) and in the fact that in two places there are the clearest allusions to ambiguous speeches ('Does Herr —— live here?') and to that source of her sexual knowledge which had not been oral (the encyclopaedia).—Cruel and sadistic tendencies find satisfaction in this dream.

# IV

# POSTSCRIPT

IT is true that I have introduced this paper as a fragment of an analysis; but the reader will have discovered that it is incomplete to a far greater degree than its title might have led him to expect. It is therefore only proper that I should attempt to give a reason for the omissions—which are by no means accidental.

A number of the results of the analysis have been omitted, because at the time when work was broken off they had either not been established with sufficient certainty or they required further study before any general statement could be made about them. At other points, where it seemed to be permissible, I have indicated the direction along which some particular solution would probably have been found to lie. I have in this paper left entirely out of account the technique, which does not at all follow as a matter of course, but by whose means alone the pure metal of valuable unconscious thoughts can be extracted from the raw material of the patient's associations. This brings with it the disadvantage of the reader being given no opportunity of testing the correctness of my procedure in the course of this exposition of the case. I found it quite impracticable, however, to deal simultaneously with the technique of analysis and with the internal structure of a case of hysteria: I could scarcely have accomplished such a task, and if I had, the result would have been almost unreadable. The technique of analysis demands an entirely separate exposition, which would have to be illustrated by numerous examples chosen from a very great variety of cases and which would not have to take the results obtained in each particular case into account. Nor have I attempted in this paper to substantiate the psychological postulates which will be seen to underlie my descriptions of mental phenomena. A cursory attempt to do so would have effected nothing; an exhaustive one would have been a volume in itself. I can only assure the reader that I approached the study of the phenomena revealed by observation of the psychoneuroses without being pledged to any particular psychological system, and that I then proceeded to adjust my views until they seemed adapted for giving an account of the collection of facts which had been observed. I take no pride in having avoided speculation; the material for my hypotheses was collected by the most extensive and laborious series of observations. The decidedness of my attitude on the subject of the unconscious is perhaps specially likely to cause offence, for I handle unconscious ideas, unconscious trains of thought, and unconscious impulses as though they were no less valid and unimpeachable psychological data than conscious ones. But of this I am certain—that any one who sets out to investigate the same region of phenomena and employs the same method will find himself compelled to take up the same position, however much philosophers may expostulate.

Some of my medical colleagues have looked upon my theory of hysteria as a purely psychological one, and have for that reason pronounced it *ipso facto* incapable of solving a pathological problem. They may perhaps discover from this paper that their objection was based upon their having unjustifiably transferred what is a characteristic of the technique on to the theory itself. It is the therapeutic technique alone that is purely psychological; the theory does not by any means fail to point out that neuroses have an organic basis—though it is true that it does not look for that basis in any pathological anatomical changes, and provisionally substitutes the conception of organic functions for the chemical changes which we should expect to find but which we are at present unable to apprehend. No one, probably, will be inclined to deny the sexual function the character of an organic factor, and it is the sexual function that I look upon as the foundation of hysteria and of the psychoneuroses in general. No theory of sexual life will, I suspect, be able to avoid assuming the existence of some definite sexual substances having an excitant action. Indeed, of all the clinical pictures which we meet with in clinical medicine, it is the phenomena of intoxication and abstinence in connection with the use of certain chronic poisons that most closely resemble the genuine psychoneuroses.[1]

But, once again, in the present paper I have not gone fully into all that might be said to-day about 'somatic compliance', about the infantile germs of perversion, about the erotogenic

[1] [Cf. the third of Freud's *Three Essays* (1905*d*), this volume p. 216, and his second paper on sexuality and the aetiology of the neuroses (1906*a*), this volume p. 279.]

zones, and about our predisposition towards bisexuality; I have merely drawn attention to the points at which the analysis comes into contact with these organic bases of the symptoms. More than this could not be done with a single case. And I had the same reasons that I have already mentioned for wishing to avoid a cursory discussion of these factors. There is a rich opportunity here for further works, based upon the study of a large number of analyses.

Nevertheless, in publishing this paper, incomplete though it is, I had two objects in view. In the first place, I wished to supplement my book on the interpretation of dreams by showing how an art, which would otherwise be useless, can be turned to account for the discovery of the hidden and repressed parts of mental life. (Incidentally, in the process of analysing the two dreams dealt with in the paper, the technique of dream-interpretation, which is similar to that of psycho-analysis, has come under consideration.) In the second place, I wished to stimulate interest in a whole group of phenomena of which science is still in complete ignorance to-day because they can only be brought to light by the use of this particular method. No one, I believe, can have had any true conception of the complexity of the psychological events in a case of hysteria—the juxtaposition of the most dissimilar tendencies, the mutual dependence of contrary ideas, the repressions and displacements, and so on. The emphasis laid by Janet upon the '*idée fixe*' which becomes transformed into a symptom amounts to no more than an extremely meagre attempt at schematization.[1] Moreover, it is impossible to avoid the suspicion that, when the ideas attaching to certain excitations are incapable of becoming conscious, those excitations must act upon one another differently, run a different course, and manifest themselves differently from those other excitations which we describe as 'normal' and which have ideas attaching to them of which we become conscious. When once things have been made clear up to this point, no obstacle can remain in the way of an understanding of a therapeutic method which removes neurotic symptoms by transforming ideas of the former kind into normal ones.

I was further anxious to show that sexuality does not simply intervene, like a *deus ex machina*, on one single occasion, at some point in the working of the processes which characterize hysteria,

[1] [See, for instance, Chapter II ('Les idées fixes') of Janet, 1894.]

but that it provides the motive power for every single symptom, and for every single manifestation of a symptom. The symptoms of the disease are nothing else than *the patient's sexual activity*. A single case can never be capable of proving a theorem so general as this one; but I can only repeat over and over again—for I never find it otherwise—that sexuality is the key to the problem of the psychoneuroses and of the neuroses in general. No one who disdains the key will ever be able to unlock the door. I still await news of the investigations which are to make it possible to contradict this theorem or to limit its scope. What I have hitherto heard against it have been expressions of personal dislike or disbelief. To these it is enough to reply in the words of Charcot: 'Ça n'empêche pas d'exister.'[1]

Nor is the case of whose history and treatment I have published a fragment in these pages well calculated to put the value of psycho-analytic therapy in its true light. Not only the brief-ness of the treatment (which hardly lasted three months) but another factor inherent in the nature of the case prevented results being brought about such as are attainable in other instances, where the improvement will be admitted by the patient and his relatives and will approximate more or less closely to a complete recovery. Satisfactory results of this kind are reached when the symptoms are maintained solely by the internal conflict between the impulses concerned with sexuality. In such cases the patient's condition will be seen improving in proportion as he is helped towards a solution of his mental problems by the translation of pathogenic into normal material. The course of events is very different when the symptoms have become enlisted in the service of external motives, as had happened with Dora during the two preceding years. It is sur-prising, and might easily be misleading, to find that the patient's condition shows no noticeable alteration even though consider-able progress has been made with the work of analysis. But in reality things are not as bad as they seem. It is true that the symptoms do not disappear while the work is proceeding; but they disappear a little while later, when the relations between patient and physician have been dissolved. The postponement of recovery or improvement is really only caused by the physician's own person.

[1] [One of Freud's favourite quotations; see his obituary of Charcot (1893*f*).]

I must go back a little, in order to make the matter intelligible. It may be safely said that during psycho-analytic treatment the formation of new symptoms is invariably stopped. But the productive powers of the neurosis are by no means extinguished; they are occupied in the creation of a special class of mental structures, for the most part unconscious, to which the name of '*transferences*' may be given.

What are transferences? They are new editions or facsimiles of the impulses and phantasies which are aroused and made conscious during the progress of the analysis; but they have this peculiarity, which is characteristic for their species, that they replace some earlier person by the person of the physician. To put it another way: a whole series of psychological experiences are revived, not as belonging to the past, but as applying to the person of the physician at the present moment. Some of these transferences have a content which differs from that of their model in no respect whatever except for the substitution. These then—to keep to the same metaphor—are merely new impressions or reprints. Others are more ingeniously constructed; their content has been subjected to a moderating influence—to *sublimation*, as I call it—and they may even become conscious, by cleverly taking advantage of some real peculiarity in the physician's person or circumstances and attaching themselves to that. These, then, will no longer be new impressions, but revised editions.

If the theory of analytic technique is gone into, it becomes evident that transference is an inevitable necessity. Practical experience, at all events, shows conclusively that there is no means of avoiding it, and that this latest creation of the disease must be combated like all the earlier ones. This happens, however, to be by far the hardest part of the whole task. It is easy to learn how to interpret dreams, to extract from the patient's associations his unconscious thoughts and memories, and to practise similar explanatory arts: for these the patient himself will always provide the text. Transference is the one thing the presence of which has to be detected almost without assistance and with only the slightest clues to go upon, while at the same time the risk of making arbitrary inferences has to be avoided. Nevertheless, transference cannot be evaded, since use is made of it in setting up all the obstacles that make the material inaccessible to treatment, and since it is only after the transference has been resolved that a patient arrives at a sense of conviction of the validity of the connections which have been constructed during the analysis.

Some people may feel inclined to look upon it as a serious objection to a method which is in any case troublesome enough that it itself should multiply the labours of the physician by creating a new species of pathological mental products. They may even be tempted to infer from the existence of transferences that the patient will be injured by analytic treatment. Both these suppositions would be mistaken. The physician's labours are not multiplied by transference; it need make no difference to him whether he has to overcome any particular impulse of the patient's in connection with himself or with some one else. Nor does the treatment force upon the patient, in the shape of transference, any new task which he would not otherwise have performed. It is true that neuroses may be cured in institutions from which psycho-analytic treatment is excluded, that hysteria may be said to be cured not by the method but by the physician, and that there is usually a sort of blind dependence and a permanent bond between a patient and the physician who has removed his symptoms by hypnotic suggestion; but the scientific explanation of all these facts is to be found in the existence of 'transferences' such as are regularly directed by patients on to their physicians. Psycho-analytic treatment does not *create* transferences, it merely brings them to light, like so many other hidden psychical factors. The only difference is this —that spontaneously a patient will only call up affectionate and friendly transferences to help towards his recovery; if they cannot be called up, he feels the physician is 'antipathetic' to him, and breaks away from him as fast as possible and without having been influenced by him. In psycho-analysis, on the other hand, since the play of motives is different, all the patient's tendencies, including hostile ones, are aroused; they are then turned to account for the purposes of the analysis by being made conscious, and in this way the transference is constantly being destroyed. Transference, which seems ordained to be the greatest obstacle to psycho-analysis, becomes its most powerful ally, if its presence can be detected each time and explained to the patient.[1]

[1] [*Footnote added* 1923:] A continuation of these remarks upon transference is contained in my technical paper on 'transference-love' (Freud,

I have been obliged to speak of transference, for it is only by means of this factor that I can elucidate the peculiarities of Dora's analysis. Its great merit, namely, the unusual clarity which makes it seem so suitable as a first introductory publication, is closely bound up with its great defect, which led to its being broken off prematurely. I did not succeed in mastering the transference in good time. Owing to the readiness with which Dora put one part of the pathogenic material at my disposal during the treatment, I neglected the precaution of looking out for the first signs of transference, which was being prepared in connection with another part of the same material —a part of which I was in ignorance. At the beginning it was clear that I was replacing her father in her imagination, which was not unlikely, in view of the difference between our ages. She was even constantly comparing me with him consciously, and kept anxiously trying to make sure whether I was being quite straightforward with her, for her father 'always preferred secrecy and roundabout ways'. But when the first dream came, in which she gave herself the warning that she had better leave my treatment just as she had formerly left Herr K.'s house, I ought to have listened to the warning myself. 'Now,' I ought to have said to her, 'it is from Herr K. that you have made a transference on to me. Have you noticed anything that leads you to suspect me of evil intentions similar (whether openly or in some sublimated form) to Herr K.'s? Or have you been struck by anything about me or got to know anything about me which has caught your fancy, as happened previously with Herr K.?' Her attention would then have been turned to some detail in our relations, or in my person or circumstances, behind which there lay concealed something analogous but immeasurably more important concerning Herr K. And when this transference had been cleared up, the analysis would have obtained

1915a) [and in the earlier and more theoretical paper on 'The Dynamics of Transference' (1912b).—Freud had already discussed transference at some length in the last section but one of his chapter on 'The Psychotherapy of Hysteria' in *Studies on Hysteria* (Breuer and Freud, 1895). But the present passage is the first one in which he indicates the importance of transference as a factor in the therapeutic process of psycho-analysis. The term 'transference' ('*Übertragung*'), which made its first appearance in *Studies on Hysteria*, was used in a slightly different and more generalized sense in some passages in *The Interpretation of Dreams*, 1900a (e.g. in Section C of Chapter VII, Standard Ed., 5, 562 ff.)].

access to new memories, dealing, probably, with actual events. But I was deaf to this first note of warning, thinking I had ample time before me, since no further stages of transference developed and the material for the analysis had not yet run dry. In this way the transference took me unawares, and, because of the unknown quantity in me which reminded Dora of Herr K., she took her revenge on me as she wanted to take her revenge on him, and deserted me as she believed herself to have been deceived and deserted by him. Thus she *acted out* an essential part of her recollections and phantasies instead of reproducing it in the treatment.[1] What this unknown quantity was I naturally cannot tell. I suspect that it had to do with money, or with jealousy of another patient who had kept up relations with my family after her recovery. When it is possible to work transferences into the analysis at an early stage, the course of the analysis is retarded and obscured, but its existence is better guaranteed against sudden and overwhelming resistances.

In Dora's second dream there are several clear allusions to transference. At the time she was telling me the dream I was still unaware (and did not learn until two days later) that we had only *two hours* more work before us. This was the same length of time which she had spent in front of the Sistine Madonna [p. 96], and which (by making a correction and putting 'two hours' instead of 'two and a half hours') she had taken as the length of the walk which she had not [2] made round the lake [p. 99]. The striving and waiting in the dream, which related to the young man in Germany, and had their origin in her waiting till Herr K. could marry her, had been expressed in the transference a few days before. The treatment, she had thought, was too long for her; she would never have the patience to wait so long. And yet in the first few weeks she had had discernment enough to listen without making any such objections when I informed her that her complete recovery would require perhaps a year. Her refusing in the dream to be accompanied, and preferring to go alone, also originated from her visit to the gallery at Dresden, and I was myself to experience them on the appointed day. What they meant was, no

---

[1] [This important topic was later discussed in another of Freud's technical papers (1914g).]

[2] [In the German editions from 1909 to 1921 this 'not' was accidentally omitted.]

boubt: 'Men are all so detestable that I would rather not marry. This is my revenge.' [1]

If cruel impulses and revengeful motives, which have already been used in the patient's ordinary life for maintaining her symptoms, become transferred on to the physician during treatment, before he has had time to detach them from himself by tracing them back to their sources, then it is not to be wondered at if the patient's condition is unaffected by his therapeutic efforts. For how could the patient take a more effective revenge than by demonstrating upon her own person the helplessness and incapacity of the physician? Nevertheless, I am not inclined to put too low a value on the therapeutic results even of such a fragmentary treatment as Dora's.

It was not until fifteen months after the case was over and this paper composed that I had news of my patient's condition and the effects of my treatment. On a date which is not a matter of complete indifference, on the first of April (times and dates, as we know, were never without significance for her), Dora came to see me again: to finish her story and to ask for help once more. One glance at her face, however, was enough to tell

[1] The longer the interval of time that separates me from the end of this analysis, the more probable it seems to me that the fault in my technique lay in this omission: I failed to discover in time and to inform the patient that her homosexual (gynaecophilic) love for Frau K. was the strongest unconscious current in her mental life. I ought to have guessed that the main source of her knowledge of sexual matters could have been no one but Frau K.—the very person who later on charged her with being interested in those same subjects. Her knowing all about such things and, at the same time, her always pretending not to know where her knowledge came from was really too remarkable. [Cf. p. 31.] I ought to have attacked this riddle and looked for the motive of such an extraordinary piece of repression. If I had done this, the second dream would have given me my answer. The remorseless craving for revenge expressed in that dream was suited as nothing else was to conceal the current of feeling that ran contrary to it—the magnanimity with which she forgave the treachery of the friend she loved and concealed from every one the fact that it was this friend who had herself revealed to her the knowledge which had later been the ground of the accusations against her. Before I had learnt the importance of the homosexual current of feeling in psychoneurotics, I was often brought to a standstill in the treatment of my cases or found myself in complete perplexity.

me that she was not in earnest over her request. For four or five
weeks after stopping the treatment she had been 'all in a
muddle', as she said. A great improvement had then set in; her
attacks had become less frequent and her spirits had risen. In
the May of that year one of the K.'s two children (it had always
been delicate) had died. She took the opportunity of their loss
to pay them a visit of condolence, and they received her as
though nothing had happened in the last three years. She made
it up with them, she took her revenge on them, and she brought
her own business to a satisfactory conclusion. To the wife she
said: 'I know you have an affair with my father'; and the other
did not deny it. From the husband she drew an admission of the
scene by the lake which he had disputed, and brought the news
of her vindication home to her father. Since then she had not
resumed her relations with the family.

After this she had gone on quite well till the middle of
October, when she had had another attack of aphonia which
had lasted for six weeks. I was surprised at this news, and, on
my asking her whether there had been any exciting cause, she
told me that the attack had followed upon a violent fright. She
had seen some one run over by a carriage. Finally she came out
with the fact that the accident had occurred to no less a person
than Herr K. himself. She had come across him in the street one
day; they had met in a place where there was a great deal of
traffic; he had stopped in front of her as though in bewilderment, and in his abstraction he had allowed himself to be
knocked down by a carriage.[1] She had been able to convince
herself, however, that he escaped without serious injury. She still
felt some slight emotion if she heard any one speak of her father's
affair with Frau K., but otherwise she had no further concern
with the matter. She was absorbed in her work, and had no
thoughts of marrying.

She went on to tell me that she had come for help on account
of a right-sided facial neuralgia, from which she was now suffering day and night. 'How long has it been going on?' 'Exactly a
fortnight.'[2] I could not help smiling; for I was able to show her

[1] We have here an interesting contribution to the problem of indirect
attempts at suicide, which I have discussed in my *Psychopathology of
Everyday Life* [1901b, Chapter VIII].
[2] For the significance of this period of time and its relation to the
theme of revenge, see the analysis of the second dream [p. 105 ff.].

that exactly a fortnight earlier she had read a piece of news that concerned me in the newspaper. (This was in 1902.)[1] And this she confirmed.

Her alleged facial neuralgia was thus a self-punishment—remorse at having once given Herr K. a box on the ear, and at having transferred her feelings of revenge on to me. I do not know what kind of help she wanted from me, but I promised to forgive her for having deprived me of the satisfaction of affording her a far more radical cure for her troubles.

Years have again gone by since her visit. In the meantime the girl has married, and indeed—unless all the signs mislead me—she has married the young man who came into her associations at the beginning of the analysis of the second dream.[2] Just as the first dream represented her turning away from the man she loved to her father—that is to say, her flight from life into disease—so the second dream announced that she was about to tear herself free from her father and had been reclaimed once more by the realities of life.

[1] [No doubt the news was of Freud's appointment to a Professorship in March of that year.]

[2] [P. 96.—In the editions of 1909, 1912 and 1921 the following footnote appeared at this point: 'This, as I afterwards learnt, was a mistaken notion.']

# THREE ESSAYS ON
# THE THEORY OF SEXUALITY
## (1905)

# EDITOR'S NOTE

## DREI ABHANDLUNGEN ZUR SEXUALTHEORIE

*(a)* GERMAN EDITIONS:

1905  Leipzig and Vienna: Deuticke. Pp. ii + 83.
1910  2nd ed. Leipzig and Vienna: Deuticke. Pp. iii + 87. (With additions.)
1915  3rd ed. Leipzig and Vienna: Deuticke. Pp. vi + 101. (With additions.)
1920  4th ed. Leipzig and Vienna: Deuticke. Pp. viii + 104. (With additions.)
1922  5th ed. Leipzig and Vienna: Deuticke. Pp. viii + 104. (Unchanged.)
1924  *G.S.*, **5**, 3–119. (With additions.)
1925  6th ed. Leipzig and Vienna: Deuticke. Pp. 120. (= *G.S.* **5**.)
1942  *G.W.*, **5**, 29–145. (Unchanged.)

*(b)* ENGLISH TRANSLATIONS:

*Three Contributions to the Sexual Theory*

1910  New York: Journal of Nerv. and Ment. Dis. Publ. Co. (Monograph Series No. 7). Pp. x + 91. (Tr. A. A. Brill; Introd. J. J. Putnam.)

*Three Contributions to the Theory of Sex*

1916  2nd ed. of above. Pp. xi + 117. (With additions.)
1918  3rd ed. Pp. xii + 117.
1930  4th ed. Pp. xiv + 104. (Revised.)
1938  *Basic Writings*, 553–629. (Reprint of above.)

*Three Essays on the Theory of Sexuality*

1949  London: Imago Publishing Co. Pp. 133. (Tr. James Strachey.)

The present translation is a corrected and expanded version of the one published in 1949.

Freud's *Three Essays on the Theory of Sexuality* stand, there can be no doubt, beside his *Interpretation of Dreams* as his most momentous and original contributions to human knowledge. Nevertheless, in the form in which we usually read these essays, it is difficult to estimate the precise nature of their impact when they were first published. For they were submitted by their author, in the course of a succession of editions over a period of twenty years, to more modifications and additions than any other of his writings, with the exception of, perhaps, *The Interpretation of Dreams* itself.[1] The present edition differs in an important respect from all previous editions, whether in German or English. Though it is based on the German sixth edition of 1925, the last published in Freud's lifetime, it indicates, with dates, every alteration of substance that has been introduced into the work since its first issue. Wherever material has been dropped or greatly modified in later editions, the cancelled passage or earlier version is given in a footnote. This will enable the reader to arrive at a clearer notion of what these essays were like in their original shape.

It will probably come as a surprise to learn, for instance, that the entire sections on the sexual theories of children and on the pregenital organizations of the libido (both in the second essay) were only added in 1915, ten years after the book was first published. The same year, too, brought the addition of the section on the libido theory to the third essay. Less surprisingly, the advances of biochemistry made it necessary (in 1920) to rewrite the paragraph on the chemical basis of sexuality. Here, indeed, the surprise works the other way. For the original version of this paragraph, here printed in a footnote, shows Freud's remarkable foresight in this connection and how little modification was required in his views (p. 216).

But in spite of the considerable additions made to the book after its first appearance, its essence was already there in 1905 and can, indeed, be traced back to still earlier dates. The whole history of Freud's concern with the subject can now, thanks to the publication of the Fliess correspondence (1950a), be followed in detail; but here it will be enough to indicate its outlines. Clinical observations of the importance of sexual factors in the

---

[1] Freud himself commented at some length on this circumstance, and the possible inconsistencies it might have introduced into the text, in the first paragraph of his paper on the 'phallic phase' (1923e).

causation, first, of anxiety neurosis and neurasthenia, and later, of the psychoneuroses, were what first led Freud into a general investigation of the subject of sexuality. His first approaches, during the early nineties, were from the physiological and chemical standpoints. A hypothesis on neuro-physiological lines, for instance, of the processes of sexual excitation and discharge will be found in Section III of his first paper on anxiety neurosis (1895*b*); and a remarkable diagram illustrating this hypothesis occurs in Draft G in the Fliess letters at about the same date but had been mentioned a year earlier (in Draft D). Freud's insistence on the chemical basis of sexuality goes back at least as far as this. (It, too, is alluded to in Draft D, probably dating to the spring of 1894.) In this case Freud believed that he owed much to suggestions from Fliess, as is shown in, among other places, his associations to the famous dream of Irma's injection in the summer of 1895 (*The Interpretation of Dreams*, Chapter II). He was also indebted to Fliess for hints on the kindred subject of bisexuality (p. 143, footnote), which he mentioned in a letter of December 6, 1896 (Letter 52) and later came to regard as a 'decisive factor' (p. 220), though his ultimate opinion on the operation of that factor brought him into disagreement with Fliess. It was in this same letter at the end of 1896 (Freud, 1950*a*, Letter 52) that we find the first mention of erotogenic zones (liable to stimulation in childhood but later suppressed) and their connections with perversions. And, again, at the beginning of the same year (Draft K, of January 1, 1896)—and here we can see indications of a more psychological approach—a discussion appears of the repressive forces, disgust, shame and morality.

But though so many elements of Freud's theory of sexuality were already present in his mind by 1896, its keystone was still to be discovered. There had from the very first been a suspicion that the causative factors of hysteria went back to childhood; the fact is alluded to in the opening paragraphs of the Breuer and Freud 'Preliminary Communication' of 1893. By 1895 (see, for instance, Part II of the 'Project', printed as an appendix to the Fliess letters) Freud had a complete explanation of hysteria based on the traumatic effects of sexual seduction in early childhood. But during all these years before 1897 infantile sexuality was regarded as no more than a dormant factor, only liable to be brought into the open, with disastrous results, by the intervention of an adult. An apparent exception to this might, it is true, be supposed to follow from the contrast drawn by Freud between the causation of hysteria and obsessional neurosis: the former, he maintained, could be traced to *passive* sexual experiences in childhood, but the latter to *active* ones. But Freud makes it quite plain in his second paper on the 'Neuro-Psychoses of Defence' (1896*b*), in which this distinction is drawn, that the active experiences at the bottom of obsessional neurosis are invariably *preceded* by passive ones—so that once again the stirring-up of infantile sexuality was ultimately due to external interference. It was not until the summer of 1897 that Freud found himself obliged to abandon his seduction theory. He announced the event in a letter to Fliess of September 21 (Letter 69),[1] and his almost simultaneous discovery of the Oedipus complex in his self-analysis (Letters 70 and 71 of October 3 and 15) led inevitably to the realization that sexual impulses operated normally in the youngest children without any need for outside stimulation. With this realization Freud's sexual theory was in fact completed.

It took some years, however, for him to become entirely reconciled to his own discovery. In a passage, for instance, in his paper on 'Sexuality in the Aetiology of the Neuroses' (1898*a*) he blows hot and cold on it. On the one hand he says that children are 'capable of every psychical sexual function and of many somatic ones' and that it is wrong to suppose that their sexual life begins only at puberty. But on the other hand he declares that 'the organization and evolution of the human species seek to avoid any considerable sexual activity in childhood', that the sexual motive forces in human beings should be stored up and only released at puberty and that this explains why sexual experiences in childhood are bound to be pathogenic. It is, he goes on, the *after-effects* produced by such experiences in maturity that are important, owing to the development of the somatic and psychical sexual apparatus that has taken place in the meantime. Even in the first edition of *The Interpretation of Dreams* (1900*a*), there is a curious passage towards the end

[1] His abandonment of the seduction theory was first publicly announced in a brief passage and footnote in the present work (p. 190) and soon afterwards at greater length in his second paper on 'The Part Played by Sexuality in the Aetiology of the Neuroses' (1906*a*; this volume p. 274 ff.). He later described his own reactions to the event in his 'History of the Psycho-Analytic Movement' (1914*d*) and in his *Autobiographical Study* (1925*d*).

of Chapter III (Standard Ed., **4**, 130), in which Freud remarks that 'we think highly of the happiness of childhood because it is still innocent of sexual desires'. (A corrective footnote was added to this passage in 1911.) This was no doubt a relic from an early draft of the book, for elsewhere (e.g. in his discussion of the Oedipus complex in Chapter V) he writes quite unambiguously of the existence of sexual wishes even in normal children. And it is evident that by the time he drew up his case history of 'Dora' (at the beginning of 1901) the main lines of his theory of sexuality were firmly laid down. (See above, p. 5.)

Even so, however, he was in no hurry to publish his results. When *The Interpretation of Dreams* was finished and on the point of appearing, on October 11, 1899 (Letter 121), he wrote to Fliess: 'A theory of sexuality might well be the dream book's immediate successor'; and three months later, on January 26, 1900 (Letter 128): 'I am putting together material for the theory of sexuality and waiting till some spark can set what I have collected ablaze.' But the spark was a long time in coming. Apart from the little essay *On Dreams* and *The Psychopathology of Everyday Life*, both of which appeared before the autumn of 1901, Freud published nothing of importance for another five years.

Then, suddenly, in 1905 he brought out three major works: his book on *Jokes*, his *Three Essays* and his case history of 'Dora'. It is certain that the last-named of these had for the most part been written many years earlier (see p. 3 ff.); but the order of actual publication must remain uncertain. A footnote to the passage in the case history already quoted (p. 51*n.*) speaks of the *Three Essays* as having been 'published this year'; similarly a footnote on p. 211 of the *Three Essays* (first edition) speaks of the book on *Jokes* as having 'appeared in 1905'; whereas a footnote in the second section of Chapter III of the book on *Jokes* refers to the *Three Essays* as 'appearing simultaneously'. It may therefore be provisionally assumed that the works were published in the order in which they are mentioned at the beginning of this paragraph.

In the German editions the sections are numbered only in the first essay; and indeed before 1924 they were numbered only half-way through the first essay. For convenience of reference, the numbering of the sections has here been extended to the second and third essays.

# PREFACE TO THE SECOND EDITION [1]

THE author is under no illusion as to the deficiencies and obscurities of this little work. Nevertheless he has resisted the temptation of introducing into it the results of the researches of the last five years, since this would have destroyed its unity and documentary character. He is, therefore, reprinting the original text with only slight alterations, and has contented himself with adding a few footnotes which are distinguished from the older ones by an asterisk.[2] It is, moreover, his earnest wish that the book may age rapidly—that what was once new in it may become generally accepted, and that what is imperfect in it may be replaced by something better.

VIENNA, *December* 1909

# PREFACE TO THE THIRD EDITION

I HAVE now been watching for more than ten years the effects produced by this work and the reception accorded to it; and I take the opportunity offered by the publication of its third edition to preface it with a few remarks intended to prevent misunderstandings and expectations that cannot be fulfilled. It must above all be emphasized that the exposition to be found in the following pages is based entirely upon everyday medical observation, to which the findings of psycho-analytic research should lend additional depth and scientific significance. It is impossible that these *Three Essays on the Theory of Sexuality* should contain anything but what psycho-analysis makes it necessary to assume or possible to establish. It is, therefore, out of the question that they could ever be extended into a complete 'theory of sexuality', and it is natural that there should be a number of important problems of sexual life with which they do not deal at all. But the reader should not conclude from his that the branches of this large subject which have been thu passed over are unknown to the author or have been neglectedby him as of small importance.

[1] [This preface was omitted from 1920 onwards.]
[2] [The distinction was dropped in all subsequent editions.]

The fact that this book is based upon the psycho-analytic observations which led to its composition is shown, however, not only in the choice of the topics dealt with, but also in their arrangement. Throughout the entire work the various factors are placed in a particular order of precedence: preference is given to the accidental factors, while disposition is left in the background, and more weight is attached to ontogenesis than to phylogenesis. For it is the accidental factors that play the principal part in analysis: they are almost entirely subject to its influence. The dispositional ones only come to light after them, as something stirred into activity by experience: adequate consideration of them would lead far beyond the sphere of psychoanalysis.

The relation between ontogenesis and phylogenesis is a similar one. Ontogenesis may be regarded as a recapitulation of phylogenesis, in so far as the latter has not been modified by more recent experience. The phylogenetic disposition can be seen at work behind the ontogenetic process. But disposition is ultimately the precipitate of earlier experience of the species to which the more recent experience of the individual, as the sum of the accidental factors, is super-added.

I must, however, emphasize that the present work is characterized not only by being completely based upon psycho-analytic research, but also by being deliberately independent of the findings of biology. I have carefully avoided introducing any preconceptions, whether derived from general sexual biology or from that of particular animal species, into this study—a study which is concerned with the sexual functions of human beings and which is made possible through the technique of psycho-analysis. Indeed, my aim has rather been to discover how far psychological investigation can throw light upon the biology of the sexual life of man. It was legitimate for me to indicate points of contact and agreement which came to light during my investigation, but there was no need for me to be diverted from my course if the psycho-analytic method led in a number of important respects to opinions and findings which differed largely from those based on biological considerations.

In this third edition I have introduced a considerable amount of fresh matter, but have not indicated it in any special way, as I did in the previous edition. Progress in our field of scientific work is at present less rapid; nevertheless it was essential to make a certain number of additions to this volume if it was to be kept in touch with recent psycho-analytic literature.[1]

VIENNA, *October* 1914

[1] [The following footnote appeared at this point in 1915 only:] In 1910, after the publication of the second edition, an English translation by A. A. Brill was published in New York; and in 1911 a Russian one by N. Ossipow in Moscow. [Translations also appeared during Freud's lifetime in Hungarian (1915), Italian (1921), Spanish (1922), French (1923), Polish (1924), Czech (1926) and Japanese (1931).]

# PREFACE TO THE FOURTH EDITION

Now that the flood-waters of war have subsided, it is satisfactory to be able to record the fact that interest in psycho-analytic research remains unimpaired in the world at large. But the different parts of the theory have not all had the same history. The purely psychological theses and findings of psycho-analysis on the unconscious, repression, conflict as a cause of illness, the advantage accruing from illness, the mechanisms of the formation of symptoms, etc., have come to enjoy increasing recognition and have won notice even from those who are in general opposed to our views. That part of the theory, however, which lies on the frontiers of biology and the foundations of which are contained in this little work is still faced with undiminished contradiction. It has even led some who for a time took a very active interest in psycho-analysis to abandon it and to adopt fresh views which were intended to restrict once more the part played by the factor of sexuality in normal and pathological mental life.

Nevertheless I cannot bring myself to accept the idea that this part of psycho-analytic theory can be very much more distant than the rest from the reality which it is its business to discover. My recollections, as well as a constant re-examination of the material, assure me that this part of the theory is based upon equally careful and impartial observation. There is, moreover, no difficulty in finding an explanation of this discrepancy in the general acceptance of my views. In the first place, the beginnings of human sexual life which are here described can only be confirmed by investigators who have enough patience and technical skill to trace back an analysis to the first years of a patient's childhood. And there is often no possibility of doing this, since medical treatment demands that an illness should, at least in appearance, be dealt with more rapidly. None, however, but physicians who practise psycho-analysis can have any access whatever to this sphere of knowledge or any possibility of forming a judgement that is uninfluenced by their own dislikes and prejudices. If mankind had been able to learn from a direct observation of children, these three essays could have remained unwritten.

133

It must also be remembered, however, that some of what this book contains—its insistence on the importance of sexuality in all human achievements and the attempt that it makes at enlarging the concept of sexuality—has from the first provided the strongest motives for the resistance against psycho-analysis. People have gone so far in their search for high-sounding catch-words as to talk of the 'pan-sexualism' of psycho-analysis and to raise the senseless charge against it of explaining 'everything' by sex. We might be astonished at this, if we ourselves could forget the way in which emotional factors make people confused and forgetful. For it is some time since Arthur Schopenhauer, the philosopher, showed mankind the extent to which their activities are determined by sexual impulses—in the ordinary sense of the word. It should surely have been impossible for a whole world of readers to banish such a startling piece of information so completely from their minds. And as for the 'stretching' of the concept of sexuality which has been necessitated by the analysis of children and what are called perverts, anyone who looks down with contempt upon psycho-analysis from a superior vantage-point should remember how closely the enlarged sexuality of psycho-analysis coincides with the Eros of the divine Plato. (Cf. Nachmansohn, 1915.)

VIENNA, *May* 1920

# THREE ESSAYS ON
# THE THEORY OF SEXUALITY

## I

## THE SEXUAL ABERRATIONS [1]

THE fact of the existence of sexual needs in human beings and animals is expressed in biology by the assumption of a 'sexual instinct', on the analogy of the instinct of nutrition, that is of hunger. Everyday language possesses no counterpart to the word 'hunger', but science makes use of the word 'libido' for that purpose. [2]

Popular opinion has quite definite ideas about the nature and characteristics of this sexual instinct. It is generally understood to be absent in childhood, to set in at the time of puberty in connection with the process of coming to maturity and to be revealed in the manifestations of an irresistible attraction exercised by one sex upon the other; while its aim is presumed to be sexual union, or at all events actions leading in that direction. We have every reason to believe, however, that these views give a very false picture of the true situation. If we look into them more closely we shall find that they contain a number of errors, inaccuracies and hasty conclusions.

I shall at this point introduce two technical terms. Let us call the person from whom sexual attraction proceeds the *sexual*

---

[1] The information contained in this first essay is derived from the well-known writings of Krafft-Ebing, Moll, Moebius, Havelock Ellis, Schrenck-Notzing, Löwenfeld, Eulenburg, Bloch and Hirschfeld, and from the *Jahrbuch für sexuelle Zwischenstufen*, published under the direction of the last-named author. Since full bibliographies of the remaining literature of the subject will be found in the works of these writers, I have been able to spare myself the necessity for giving detailed references. [*Added* 1910:] The data obtained from the psycho-analytic investigation of inverts are based upon material supplied to me by I. Sadger and upon my own findings.

[2] [*Footnote added* 1910:] The only appropriate word in the German language, '*Lust*', is unfortunately ambiguous, and is used to denote the experience both of a need and of a gratification. [Unlike the English 'lust' it can mean either 'desire' or 'pleasure'. See footnote page 212.]

*object* and the act towards which the instinct tends the *sexual aim*. Scientifically sifted observation, then, shows that numerous deviations occur in respect of both of these—the sexual object and the sexual aim. The relation between these deviations and what is assumed to be normal requires thorough investigation.

## (1) DEVIATIONS IN RESPECT OF THE SEXUAL OBJECT

The popular view of the sexual instinct is beautifully reflected in the poetic fable which tells how the original human beings were cut up into two halves—man and woman—and how these are always striving to unite again in love.[1] It comes as a great surprise therefore to learn that there are men whose sexual object is a man and not a woman, and women whose sexual object is a woman and not a man. People of this kind are described as having 'contrary sexual feelings', or better, as being 'inverts', and the fact is described as 'inversion'. The number of such people is very considerable, though there are difficulties in establishing it precisely.[2]

### (A) INVERSION

BEHAVIOUR OF INVERTS    Such people vary greatly in their behaviour in several respects.

(*a*) They may be *absolute* inverts. In that case their sexual objects are exclusively of their own sex. Persons of the opposite sex are never the object of their sexual desire, but leave them cold, or even arouse sexual aversion in them. As a consequence of this aversion, they are incapable, if they are men, of carrying out the sexual act, or else they derive no enjoyment from it.

(*b*) They may be *amphigenic* inverts, that is psychosexual hermaphrodites. In that case their sexual objects may equally well be of their own or of the opposite sex. This kind of inversion thus lacks the characteristic of exclusiveness.

[1] [This is no doubt an allusion to the theory expounded by Aristophanes in Plato's *Symposium*. Freud recurred to this much later, at the end of Chapter VI of *Beyond the Pleasure Principle* (1920g).]

[2] On these difficulties and on the attempts which have been made to arrive at the proportional number of inverts, see Hirschfeld (1904).

(c) They may be *contingent* inverts. In that case, under certain external conditions—of which inaccessibility of any normal sexual object and imitation are the chief—they are capable of taking as their sexual object someone of their own sex and of deriving satisfaction from sexual intercourse with him.

Again, inverts vary in their views as to the peculiarity of their sexual instinct. Some of them accept their inversion as something in the natural course of things, just as a normal person accepts the direction of *his* libido, and insist energetically that inversion is as legitimate as the normal attitude; others rebel against their inversion and feel it as a pathological compulsion.[1]

Other variations occur which relate to questions of time. The trait of inversion may either date back to the very beginning, as far back as the subject's memory reaches, or it may not have become noticeable till some particular time before or after puberty.[2] It may either persist throughout life, or it may go into temporary abeyance, or again it may constitute an episode on the way to a normal development. It may even make its first appearance late in life after a long period of normal sexual activity. A periodic oscillation between a normal and an inverted sexual object has also sometimes been observed. Those cases are of particular interest in which the libido changes over to an inverted sexual object after a distressing experience with a normal one.

As a rule these different kinds of variations are found side by side independently of one another. It is, however, safe to assume that the most extreme form of inversion will have been present from a very early age and that the person concerned will feel at one with his peculiarity.

Many authorities would be unwilling to class together all

[1] The fact of a person struggling in this way against a compulsion towards inversion may perhaps determine the possibility of his being influenced by suggestion [*added* 1910:] or psycho-analysis.

[2] Many writers have insisted with justice that the dates assigned by inverts themselves for the appearance of their tendency to inversion are untrustworthy, since they may have repressed the evidence of their heterosexual feelings from their memory. [*Added* 1910:] These suspicions have been confirmed by psycho-analysis in those cases of inversion to which it has had access; it has produced decisive alterations in their anamnesis by filling in their infantile amnesia.—[In the first edition (1905) the place of this last sentence was taken by the following one: 'A decision on this point could be arrived at only by a psycho-analytic investigation of inverts.']

the various cases which I have enumerated and would prefer to lay stress upon their differences rather than their resemblances, in accordance with their own preferred view of inversion. Nevertheless, though the distinctions cannot be disputed, it is impossible to overlook the existence of numerous intermediate examples of every type, so that we are driven to conclude that we are dealing with a connected series.

NATURE OF    The earliest assessments regarded inversion as
INVERSION    an innate indication of nervous degeneracy. This
corresponded to the fact that medical observers first came across it in persons suffering, or appearing to suffer, from nervous diseases. This characterization of inversion involves two suppositions, which must be considered separately: that it is innate and that it is degenerate.

DEGENERACY    The attribution of degeneracy in this connection is open to the objections which can be raised against the indiscriminate use of the word in general. It has become the fashion to regard any symptom which is not obviously due to trauma or infection as a sign of degeneracy. Magnan's classification of degenerates is indeed of such a kind as not to exclude the possibility of the concept of degeneracy being applied to a nervous system whose general functioning is excellent. This being so, it may well be asked whether an attribution of 'degeneracy' is of any value or adds anything to our knowledge. It seems wiser only to speak of it where

(1) several serious deviations from the normal are found together, and

(2) the capacity for efficient functioning and survival seem to be severely impaired.[1]

Several facts go to show that in this legitimate sense of the word inverts cannot be regarded as degenerate:

(1) Inversion is found in people who exhibit no other serious deviations from the normal.

[1] Moebius (1900) confirms the view that we should be chary in making a diagnosis of degeneracy and that it has very little practical value: 'If we survey the wide field of degeneracy upon which some glimpses of revealing light have been thrown in these pages, it will at once be clear that there is small value in ever making a diagnosis of degeneracy.'

(2) It is similarly found in people whose efficiency is un-impaired, and who are indeed distinguished by specially high intellectual development and ethical culture.[1]

(3) If we disregard the patients we come across in our medical practice, and cast our eyes round a wider horizon, we shall come in two directions upon facts which make it impossible to regard inversion as a sign of degeneracy:

(a) Account must be taken of the fact that inversion was a frequent phenomenon—one might almost say an institution charged with important functions—among the peoples of anti-quity at the height of their civilization.

(b) It is remarkably widespread among many savage and primitive races, whereas the concept of degeneracy is usually restricted to states of high civilization (cf. Bloch); and, even amongst the civilized peoples of Europe, climate and race exercise the most powerful influence on the prevalence of inversion and upon the attitude adopted towards it.[2]

INNATE           As may be supposed, innateness is only attri-
CHARACTER     buted to the first, most extreme, class of inverts,
              and the evidence for it rests upon assurances given
by them that at no time in their lives has their sexual instinct shown any sign of taking another course. The very existence of the two other classes, and especially the third [the 'contingent' inverts], is difficult to reconcile with the hypothesis of the in-nateness of inversion. This explains why those who support this view tend to separate out the group of absolute inverts from all the rest, thus abandoning any attempt at giving an account of inversion which shall have universal application. In the view of these authorities inversion is innate in one group of cases, while in others it may have come about in other ways.

The reverse of this view is represented by the alternative one that inversion is an acquired character of the sexual

[1] It must be allowed that the spokesmen of 'Uranism' are justified in asserting that some of the most prominent men in all recorded history were inverts and perhaps even absolute inverts.

[2] The pathological approach to the study of inversion has been dis-placed by the anthropological. The merit for bringing about this change is due to Bloch (1902–3), who has also laid stress on the occur-rence of inversion among the civilizations of antiquity.

instinct. This second view is based on the following considerations:

(1) In the case of many inverts, even absolute ones, it is possible to show that very early in their lives a sexual impression occurred which left a permanent after-effect in the shape of a tendency to homosexuality.

(2) In the case of many others, it is possible to point to external influences in their lives, whether of a favourable or inhibiting character, which have led sooner or later to a fixation of their inversion. (Such influences are exclusive relations with persons of their own sex, comradeship in war, detention in prison, the dangers of heterosexual intercourse, celibacy, sexual weakness, etc.)

(3) Inversion can be removed by hypnotic suggestion, which would be astonishing in an innate characteristic.

In view of these considerations it is even possible to doubt the very existence of such a thing as innate inversion. It can be argued (cf. Havelock Ellis [1915]) that, if the cases of allegedly innate inversion were more closely examined, some experience of their early childhood would probably come to light which had a determining effect upon the direction taken by their libido. This experience would simply have passed out of the subject's conscious recollection, but could be recalled to his memory under appropriate influence. In the opinion of these writers inversion can only be described as a frequent variation of the sexual instinct, which can be determined by a number of external circumstances in the subject's life.

The apparent certainty of this conclusion is, however, completely countered by the reflection that many people are subjected to the same sexual influences (e.g. to seduction or mutual masturbation, which may occur in early youth) without becoming inverted or without remaining so permanently. We are therefore forced to a suspicion that the choice between 'innate' and 'acquired' is not an exclusive one or that it does not cover all the issues involved in inversion.

EXPLANATION          The nature of inversion is explained neither
OF INVERSION        by the hypothesis that it is innate nor by the
                    alternative hypothesis that it is acquired. In the
former case we must ask in what respect it is innate, unless we are to accept the crude explanation that everyone is born with

his sexual instinct attached to a particular sexual object. In the latter case it may be questioned whether the various accidental influences would be sufficient to explain the acquisition of inversion without the co-operation of something in the subject himself. As we have already shown, the existence of this last factor is not to be denied.

BISEXUALITY    A fresh contradiction of popular views is involved in the considerations put forward by Lydston [1889], Kiernan [1888] and Chevalier [1893] in an endeavour to account for the possibility of sexual inversion. It is popularly believed that a human being is either a man or a woman. Science, however, knows of cases in which the sexual characters are obscured, and in which it is consequently difficult to determine the sex. This arises in the first instance in the field of anatomy. The genitals of the individuals concerned combine male and female characteristics. (This condition is known as hermaphroditism.) In rare cases both kinds of sexual apparatus are found side by side fully developed (true hermaphroditism); but far more frequently both sets of organs are found in an atrophied condition.[1]

The importance of these abnormalities lies in the unexpected fact that they facilitate our understanding of normal development. For it appears that a certain degree of anatomical hermaphroditism occurs normally. In every normal male or female individual, traces are found of the apparatus of the opposite sex. These either persist without function as rudimentary organs or become modified and take on other functions.

These long-familiar facts of anatomy lead us to suppose that an originally bisexual physical disposition has, in the course of evolution, become modified into a unisexual one, leaving behind only a few traces of the sex that has become atrophied.

It was tempting to extend this hypothesis to the mental sphere and to explain inversion in all its varieties as the expression of a psychical hermaphroditism. All that was required further in order to settle the question was that inversion should be regularly accompanied by the mental and somatic signs of hermaphroditism.

[1] For the most recent descriptions of somatic hermaphroditism, see Taruffi (1903), and numerous papers by Neugebauer in various volumes of the *Jahrbuch für sexuelle Zwischenstufen*.

But this expectation was disappointed. It is impossible to demonstrate so close a connection between the hypothetical psychical hermaphroditism and the established anatomical one. A general lowering of the sexual instinct and a slight anatomical atrophy of the organs is found frequently in inverts (cf. Havelock Ellis, 1915). Frequently, but by no means regularly or even usually. The truth must therefore be recognized that inversion and somatic hermaphroditism are on the whole independent of each other.

A great deal of importance, too, has been attached to what are called the secondary and tertiary sexual characters and to the great frequency of the occurrence of those of the opposite sex in inverts (cf. Havelock Ellis, 1915). Much of this, again, is correct; but it should never be forgotten that in general the secondary and tertiary sexual characters of one sex occur very frequently in the opposite one. They are indications of hermaphroditism, but are not attended by any change of sexual object in the direction of inversion.

Psychical hermaphroditism would gain substance if the inversion of the sexual object were at least accompanied by a parallel change-over of the subject's other mental qualities, instincts and character traits into those marking the opposite sex. But it is only in inverted women that character-inversion of this kind can be looked for with any regularity. In men the most complete mental masculinity can be combined with inversion. If the belief in psychical hermaphroditism is to be persisted in, it will be necessary to add that its manifestations in various spheres show only slight signs of being mutually determined. Moreover the same is true of somatic hermaphroditism: according to Halban (1903),[1] occurrences of individual atrophied organs and of secondary sexual characters are to a considerable extent independent of one another.

The theory of bisexuality has been expressed in its crudest form by a spokesman of the male inverts: 'a feminine brain in a masculine body'. But we are ignorant of what characterizes a feminine brain. There is neither need nor justification for replacing the psychological problem by the anatomical one. Krafft-Ebing's attempted explanation seems to be more exactly framed than that of Ulrichs but does not differ from it in essentials. According to Krafft-Ebing (1895, 5), every indi-

[1] His paper includes a bibliography of the subject.

vidual's bisexual disposition endows him with masculine and feminine brain centres as well as with somatic organs of sex; these centres develop only at puberty, for the most part under the influence of the sex-gland, which is independent of them in the original disposition. But what has just been said of masculine and feminine brains applies equally to masculine and feminine 'centres'; and incidentally we have not even any grounds for assuming that certain areas of the brain ('centres') are set aside for the functions of sex, as is the case, for instance, with those of speech.[1]

Nevertheless, two things emerge from these discussions. In the first place, a bisexual disposition is somehow concerned in

---

[1] It appears (from a bibliography given in the sixth volume of the *Jahrbuch für sexuelle Zwischenstufen*) that E. Gley was the first writer to suggest bisexuality as an explanation of inversion. As long ago as in January, 1884, he published a paper, 'Les aberrations de l'instinct sexuel', in the *Revue Philosophique*. It is, moreover, noteworthy that the majority of authors who derive inversion from bisexuality bring forward that factor not only in the case of inverts, but also for all those who have grown up to be normal, and that, as a logical consequence, they regard inversion as the result of a disturbance in development. Chevalier (1893) already writes in this sense. Krafft-Ebing (1895, 10) remarks that there are a great number of observations 'which prove at least the virtual persistence of this second centre (that of the subordinated sex)'. A Dr. Arduin (1900) asserts that 'there are masculine and feminine elements in every human being (cf. Hirschfeld, 1899); but one set of these—according to the sex of the person in question—is incomparably more strongly developed than the other, so far as heterosexual individuals are concerned. . . .' Herman (1903) is convinced that 'masculine elements and characteristics are present in every woman and feminine ones in every man', etc. [*Added* 1910:] Fliess (1906) subsequently claimed the idea of bisexuality (in the sense of *duality of sex*) as his own. [*Added* 1924:] In lay circles the hypothesis of human bisexuality is regarded as being due to O. Weininger, the philosopher, who died at an early age, and who made the idea the basis of a somewhat unbalanced book (1903). The particulars which I have enumerated above will be sufficient to show how little justification there is for the claim.

[Freud's own realization of the importance of bisexuality owed much to Fliess (cf. p. 220 *n.*), and his forgetfulness of this fact on one occasion provided him with an example in his *Psychopathology of Everyday Life*, 1901*b*, Chapter VII (11). He did not, however, accept Fliess's view that bisexuality provided the explanation of repression. See Freud's discussion of this in 'A Child is Being Beaten' (1919*e*, half-way through Section VI). The whole question is gone into in detail by Kris in Section IV of his introduction to the Fliess correspondence (Freud, 1950*a*).]

inversion, though we do not know in what that disposition consists, beyond anatomical structure. And secondly, we have to deal with disturbances that affect the sexual instinct in the course of its development.

SEXUAL OBJECT     The theory of psychical hermaphroditism
OF INVERTS        presupposes that the sexual object of an invert
                  is the opposite of that of a normal person. An
inverted man, it holds, is like a woman in being subject to the
charm that proceeds from masculine attributes both physical
and mental: he feels he is a woman in search of a man.

But however well this applies to quite a number of inverts, it is, nevertheless, far from revealing a universal characteristic of inversion. There can be no doubt that a large proportion of male inverts retain the mental quality of masculinity, that they possess relatively few of the secondary characters of the opposite sex and that what they look for in their sexual object are in fact feminine mental traits. If this were not so, how would it be possible to explain the fact that male prostitutes who offer themselves to inverts—to-day just as they did in ancient times— imitate women in all the externals of their clothing and behaviour? Such imitation would otherwise inevitably clash with the ideal of the inverts. It is clear that in Greece, where the most masculine men were numbered among the inverts, what excited a man's love was not the *masculine* character of a boy, but his physical resemblance to a woman as well as his feminine mental qualities—his shyness, his modesty and his need for instruction and assistance. As soon as the boy became a man he ceased to be a sexual object for men and himself, perhaps, became a lover of boys. In this instance, therefore, as in many others, the sexual object is not someone of the same sex but someone who combines the characters of both sexes; there is, as it were, a compromise between an impulse that seeks for a man and one that seeks for a woman, while it remains a paramount condition that the object's body (i.e. genitals) shall be masculine. Thus the sexual object is a kind of reflection of the subject's own bisexual nature.[1]

[1] [This last sentence was added in 1915.—*Footnote added* 1910:] It is true that psycho-analysis has not yet produced a complete explanation of the origin of inversion; nevertheless, it has discovered the psychical mechanism of its development, and has made essential contributions to

The position in the case of women is less ambiguous; for among them the active inverts exhibit masculine characteristics, both physical and mental, with peculiar frequency and look for femininity in their sexual objects—though here again a closer knowledge of the facts might reveal greater variety.

SEXUAL AIM OF INVERTS    The important fact to bear in mind is that no one single aim can be laid down as applying in cases of inversion. Among men, intercourse *per anum* by no means coincides with inversion; masturbation is quite as frequently their exclusive aim, and it is even true that

the statement of the problems involved. In all the cases we have examined we have established the fact that the future inverts, in the earliest years of their childhood, pass through a phase of very intense but short-lived fixation to a woman (usually their mother), and that, after leaving this behind, they identify themselves with a woman and take *themselves* as their sexual object. That is to say, they proceed from a narcissistic basis, and look for a young man who resembles themselves and whom *they* may love as their mother loved *them*. Moreover, we have frequently found that alleged inverts have been by no means insusceptible to the charms of women, but have continually transposed the excitation aroused by women on to a male object. They have thus repeated all through their lives the mechanism by which their inversion arose. Their compulsive longing for men has turned out to be determined by their ceaseless flight from women.

[At this point the footnote proceeded as follows in the 1910 edition only: 'It must, however, be borne in mind that hitherto only a single type of invert has been submitted to psycho-analysis—persons whose sexual activity is in general stunted and the residue of which is manifested as inversion. The problem of inversion is a highly complex one and includes very various types of sexual activity and development. A strict conceptual distinction should be drawn between different cases of inversion according to whether the sexual character of the *object* or that of the *subject* has been inverted.']

[*Added* 1915:] Psycho-analytic research is most decidedly opposed to any attempt at separating off homosexuals from the rest of mankind as a group of a special character. By studying sexual excitations other than those that are manifestly displayed, it has found that all human beings are capable of making a homosexual object-choice and have in fact made one in their unconscious. Indeed, libidinal attachments to persons of the same sex play no less a part as factors in normal mental life, and a greater part as a motive force for illness, than do similar attachments to the opposite sex. On the contrary, psycho-analysis considers that a choice of an object independently of its sex—freedom to range equally over male and female objects—as it is found in childhood, in primitive states of society and early periods of history, is the original basis from restrictions of sexual aim—to the point of its being limited to simple outpourings of emotion—are commoner among them than among heterosexual lovers. Among women, too, the sexual aims of inverts are various: there seems to be a special preference for contact with the mucous membrane of the mouth.

CONCLUSION    It will be seen that we are not in a position to base a satisfactory explanation of the origin of inversion upon the material at present before us. Nevertheless our investigation has put us in possession of a piece of knowledge

which, as a result of restriction in one direction or the other, both the normal and the inverted types develop. Thus from the point of view of psycho-analysis the exclusive sexual interest felt by men for women is also a problem that needs elucidating and is not a self-evident fact based upon an attraction that is ultimately of a chemical nature. A person's final sexual attitude is not decided until after puberty and is the result of a number of factors, not all of which are yet known; some are of a constitutional nature but others are accidental. No doubt a few of these factors may happen to carry so much weight that they influence the result in their sense. But in general the multiplicity of determining factors is reflected in the variety of manifest sexual attitudes in which they find their issue in mankind. In inverted types, a predominance of archaic constitutions and primitive psychical mechanisms is regularly to be found. Their most essential characteristics seem to be a coming into operation of narcissistic object-choice and a retention of the erotic significance of the anal zone. There is nothing to be gained, however, by separating the most extreme types of inversion from the rest on the basis of constitutional peculiarities of that kind. What we find as an apparently sufficient explanation of these types can be equally shown to be present, though less strongly, in the constitution of transitional types and of those whose manifest attitude is normal. The differences in the end-products may be of a qualitative nature, but analysis shows that the differences between their determinants are only quantitative. Among the accidental factors that influence object-choice we have found that frustration (in the form of an early deterrence, by fear, from sexual activity) deserves attention, and we have observed that the presence of both parents plays an important part. The absence of a strong father in childhood not infrequently favours the occurrence of inversion. Finally, it may be insisted that the concept of inversion in respect of the sexual object should be sharply distinguished from that of the occurrence in the subject of a mixture of sexual characters. In the relation between these two factors, too, a certain degree of reciprocal independence is unmistakably present.

[*Added* 1920:] Ferenczi (1914) has brought forward a number of interesting points on the subject of inversion. He rightly protests that, because they have in common the symptom of inversion, a large number

which may turn out to be of greater importance to us than the
solution of that problem. It has been brought to our notice that
we have been in the habit of regarding the connection between
the sexual instinct and the sexual object as more intimate than

of conditions, which are very different from one another and which
are of unequal importance both in organic and psychical respects, have
been thrown together under the name of 'homosexuality' (or, to follow
him in giving it a better name, 'homo-erotism'). He insists that a sharp
distinction should at least be made between two types: 'subject homo-
erotics', who feel and behave like women, and 'object homo-erotics',
who are completely masculine and who have merely exchanged a
female for a male object. The first of these two types he recognizes as
true 'sexual intermediates' in Hirschfeld's sense of the word; the second
he describes, less happily, as obsessional neurotics. According to him,
it is only in the case of object homo-erotics that there is any question of
their struggling against their inclination to inversion or of the possibility
of their being influenced psychologically. While granting the existence
of these two types, we may add that there are many people in whom a
certain quantity of subject homo-erotism is found in combination with
a proportion of object homo-erotism.

During the last few years work carried out by biologists, notably by
Steinach, has thrown a strong light on the organic determinants of
homo-erotism and of sexual characters in general. By carrying out experimental castration and subsequently grafting the sex-glands of the
opposite sex, it was possible in the case of various species of mammals
to transform a male into a female and vice versa. The transformation
affected more or less completely both the somatic sexual characters and
the psychosexual attitude (that is, both subject and object erotism). It
appeared that the vehicle of the force which thus acted as a sex-determin-
ant was not the part of the sex-gland which forms the sex-cells but
what is known as its interstitial tissue (the 'puberty-gland'). In one case
this transformation of sex was actually effected in a man who had lost
his testes owing to tuberculosis. In his sexual life he behaved in a
feminine manner, as a passive homosexual, and exhibited very clearly-
marked feminine sexual characters of a secondary kind (e.g. in regard
to growth of hair and beard and deposits of fat on the breasts and hips).
After an undescended testis from another male patient had been
grafted into him, he began to behave in a masculine manner and to
direct his libido towards women in a normal way. Simultaneously his
somatic feminine characters disappeared. (Lipschütz, 1919, 356–7.)

It would be unjustifiable to assert that these interesting experiments
put the theory of inversion on a new basis, and it would be hasty to
expect them to offer a universal means of 'curing' homosexuality. Fliess
has rightly insisted that these experimental findings do not invalidate
the theory of the general bisexual disposition of the higher animals. On
the contrary, it seems to me probable that further research of a similar
kind will produce a direct confirmation of this presumption of bisexuality.

it in fact is. Experience of the cases that are considered abnormal has shown us that in them the sexual instinct and the sexual object are merely soldered together—a fact which we have been in danger of overlooking in consequence of the uniformity of the normal picture, where the object appears to form part and parcel of the instinct. We are thus warned to loosen the bond that exists in our thoughts between instinct and object. It seems probable that the sexual instinct is in the first instance independent of its object; nor is its origin likely to be due to its object's attractions.

### (B) SEXUALLY IMMATURE PERSONS AND ANIMALS AS SEXUAL OBJECTS

People whose sexual objects belong to the normally inappropriate sex—that is, inverts—strike the observer as a collection of individuals who may be quite sound in other respects. On the other hand, cases in which sexually immature persons (children) are chosen as sexual objects are instantly judged as sporadic aberrations. It is only exceptionally that children are the exclusive sexual objects in such a case. They usually come to play that part when someone who is cowardly or has become impotent adopts them as a substitute, or when an urgent instinct (one which will not allow of postponement) cannot at the moment get possession of any more appropriate object. Nevertheless, a light is thrown on the nature of the sexual instinct by the fact that it permits of so much variation in its objects and such a cheapening of them—which hunger, with its far more energetic retention of its objects, would only permit in the most extreme instances. A similar consideration applies to sexual intercourse with animals, which is by no means rare, especially among country people, and in which sexual attraction seems to override the barriers of species.

One would be glad on aesthetic grounds to be able to ascribe these and other severe aberrations of the sexual instinct to insanity; but that cannot be done. Experience shows that disturbances of the sexual instinct among the insane do not differ from those that occur among the healthy and in whole races or occupations. Thus the sexual abuse of children is found with uncanny frequency among school teachers and child attendants, simply because they have the best opportunity for it. The insane merely exhibit any such aberration to an intensified degree; or, what is particularly significant, it may become exclusive and replace normal sexual satisfaction entirely.

The very remarkable relation which thus holds between sexual variations and the descending scale from health to insanity gives us plenty of material for thought. I am inclined to believe that it may be explained by the fact that the impulses of sexual life are among those which, even normally, are the least controlled by the higher activities of the mind. In my experience anyone who is in any way, whether socially or ethically, abnormal mentally is invariably abnormal also in his sexual life. But many people are abnormal in their sexual life who in every other respect approximate to the average, and have, along with the rest, passed through the process of human cultural development, in which sexuality remains the weak spot.

The most general conclusion that follows from all these discussions seems, however, to be this. Under a great number of conditions and in surprisingly numerous individuals, the nature and importance of the sexual object recedes into the background. What is essential and constant in the sexual instinct is something else.[1]

## (2) DEVIATIONS IN RESPECT OF THE SEXUAL AIM

The normal sexual aim is regarded as being the union of the genitals in the act known as copulation, which leads to a release of the sexual tension and a temporary extinction of the sexual instinct—a satisfaction analogous to the sating of hunger. But even in the most normal sexual process we may detect rudiments which, if they had developed, would have led to the deviations described as 'perversions'. For there are certain intermediate relations to the sexual object, such as touching and looking at it, which lie on the road towards copulation and are recognized as being preliminary sexual aims. On the one hand these

[1] [*Footnote added* 1910:] The most striking distinction between the erotic life of antiquity and our own no doubt lies in the fact that the ancients laid the stress upon the instinct itself, whereas we emphasize its object. The ancients glorified the instinct and were prepared on its account to honour even an inferior object; while we despise the instinctual activity in itself, and find excuses for it only in the merits of the object.

activities are themselves accompanied by pleasure, and on the other hand they intensify the excitation, which should persist until the final sexual aim is attained. Moreover, the kiss, one particular contact of this kind, between the mucous membrane of the lips of the two people concerned, is held in high sexual esteem among many nations (including the most highly civilized ones), in spite of the fact that the parts of the body involved do not form part of the sexual apparatus but constitute the entrance to the digestive tract. Here, then, are factors which provide a point of contact between the perversions and normal sexual life and which can also serve as a basis for their classification. Perversions are sexual activities which either (*a*) extend, in an anatomical sense, beyond the regions of the body that are designed for sexual union, or (*b*) linger over the intermediate relations to the sexual object which should normally be traversed rapidly on the path towards the final sexual aim.

## (A) ANATOMICAL EXTENSIONS

OVERVALUATION OF THE SEXUAL OBJECT  It is only in the rarest instances that the psychical valuation that is set on the sexual object, as being the goal of the sexual instinct, stops short at its genitals. The appreciation extends to the whole body of the sexual object and tends to involve every sensation derived from it. The same overvaluation spreads over into the psychological sphere: the subject becomes, as it were, intellectually infatuated (that is, his powers of judgement are weakened) by the mental achievements and perfections of the sexual object and he submits to the latter's judgements with credulity. Thus the credulity of love becomes an important, if not the most fundamental, source of *authority*.[1]

This sexual overvaluation is something that cannot be easily reconciled with a restriction of the sexual aim to union of the

---

[1] In this connection I cannot help recalling the credulous submissiveness shown by a hypnotized subject towards his hypnotist. This leads me to suspect that the essence of hypnosis lies in an unconscious fixation of the subject's libido to the figure of the hypnotist, through the medium of the masochistic components of the sexual instinct. [*Added* 1910:] Ferenczi (1909) has brought this characteristic of suggestibility into relation with the 'parental complex'.—[The relation of the subject to the hypnotist was discussed by Freud much later, in Chapter VIII of his *Group Psychology* (1921c). See also below, p. 294 ff.]

actual genitals and it helps to turn activities connected with other parts of the body into sexual aims.[1]

The significance of the factor of sexual overvaluation can be best studied in men, for their erotic life alone has become accessible to research. That of women—partly owing to the stunting effect of civilized conditions and partly owing to their conventional secretiveness and insincerity—is still veiled in an impenetrable obscurity.[2]

SEXUAL USE OF THE MUCOUS MEMBRANE OF THE LIPS AND MOUTH
The use of the mouth as a sexual organ is regarded as a perversion if the lips (or tongue) of one person are brought into contact with the genitals of another, but not if the mucous membranes of the lips of both of them come together. This exception is the point of contact with what is normal. Those who condemn the other practices (which have no doubt been common among mankind from primaeval times) as being perversions, are giving way to an unmistakable feeling of *disgust*, which protects them from accepting sexual aims of the kind. The limits of such disgust are, however, often purely conventional: a man who will kiss a pretty girl's lips passionately, may perhaps be disgusted at the idea of

[1] [In the editions earlier than 1920 this paragraph ended with the further sentence: 'The emergence of these extremely various anatomical extensions clearly implies a need for variation, and this has been described by Hoche as "craving for stimulation".' The first two sentences of the footnote which follows were added in 1915, before which date it had begun with the sentence: 'Further consideration leads me to conclude that I. Bloch has over-estimated the theoretical importance of the factor of craving for stimulation.' The whole footnote and the paragraph in the text above were recast in their present form in 1920:] It must be pointed out, however, that sexual overvaluation is not developed in the case of *every* mechanism of object-choice. We shall become acquainted later on with another and more direct explanation of the sexual role assumed by the other parts of the body. The factor of 'craving for stimulation' has been put forward by Hoche and Bloch as an explanation of the extension of sexual interest to parts of the body other than the genitals; but it does not seem to me to deserve such an important place. The various channels along which the libido passes are related to each other from the very first like inter-communicating pipes, and we must take the phenomenon of collateral flow into account. [See p. 170.]

[2] [*Footnote added* 1920:] In typical cases women fail to exhibit any sexual overvaluation towards men; but they scarcely ever fail to do so towards their own children.

using her tooth-brush, though there are no grounds for supposing that his own oral cavity, for which he feels no disgust, is
any cleaner than the girl's. Here, then, our attention is drawn
to the factor of disgust, which interferes with the libidinal overvaluation of the sexual object but can in turn be overridden by
libido. Disgust seems to be one of the forces which have led to a
restriction of the sexual aim. These forces do not as a rule extend
to the genitals themselves. But there is no doubt that the genitals
of the opposite sex can in themselves be an object of disgust and
that such an attitude is one of the characteristics of all hysterics,
and especially of hysterical women. The sexual instinct in its
strength enjoys overriding this disgust. (See below [p. 156 f.].)

SEXUAL USE OF THE      Where the anus is concerned it be-
ANAL ORIFICE           comes still clearer that it is disgust which
                       stamps that sexual aim as a perversion.
I hope, however, I shall not be accused of partisanship when
I assert that people who try to account for this disgust by saying
that the organ in question serves the function of excretion and
comes in contact with excrement—a thing which is disgusting
in itself—are not much more to the point than hysterical girls
who account for their disgust at the male genital by saying that
it serves to void urine.

The playing of a sexual part by the mucous membrane of the
anus is by no means limited to intercourse between men: preference for it is in no way characteristic of inverted feeling. On the
contrary, it seems that *paedicatio* with a male owes its origin to
an analogy with a similar act performed with a woman; while
mutual masturbation is the sexual aim most often found in
intercourse between inverts.

SIGNIFICANCE       The extension of sexual interest to other re-
OF OTHER           gions of the body, with all its variations, offers
REGIONS OF         us nothing that is new in principle; it adds
THE BODY           nothing to our knowledge of the sexual instinct,
                   which merely proclaims its intention in this way
of getting possession of the sexual object in every possible
direction. But these anatomical extensions inform us that, besides sexual overvaluation, there is a second factor at work
which is strange to popular knowledge. Certain regions of the
body, such as the mucous membrane of the mouth and anus,

which are constantly appearing in these practices, seem, as it were, to be claiming that they should themselves be regarded and treated as genitals. We shall learn later that this claim is justified by the history of the development of the sexual instinct and that it is fulfilled in the symptomatology of certain pathological states.

UNSUITABLE SUB-
STITUTES FOR THE
SEXUAL OBJECT—
FETISHISM

There are some cases which are quite specially remarkable—those in which the normal sexual object is replaced by another which bears some relation to it, but is entirely unsuited to serve the normal sexual aim. From the point of view of classification, we should no doubt have done better to have mentioned this highly interesting group of aberrations of the sexual instinct among the deviations in respect of the sexual *object*. But we have postponed their mention till we could become acquainted with the factor of sexual overvaluation, on which these phenomena, being connected with an abandonment of the sexual aim, are dependent.

What is substituted for the sexual object is some part of the body (such as the foot or hair) which is in general very inappropriate for sexual purposes, or some inanimate object which bears an assignable relation to the person whom it replaces and preferably to that person's sexuality (e.g. a piece of clothing or underlinen). Such substitutes are with some justice likened to the fetishes in which savages believe that their gods are embodied.

A transition to those cases of fetishism in which the sexual aim, whether normal or perverse, is entirely abandoned is afforded by other cases in which the sexual object is required to fulfil a fetishistic condition—such as the possession of some particular hair-colouring or clothing, or even some bodily defect— if the sexual aim is to be attained. No other variation of the sexual instinct that borders on the pathological can lay so much claim to our interest as this one, such is the peculiarity of the phenomena to which it gives rise. Some degree of diminution in the urge towards the normal sexual aim (an executive weakness of the sexual apparatus) seems to be a necessary precondition in every case.[1] The point of contact with the normal

[1] [*Footnote added* 1915:] This weakness would represent the *constitutional* precondition. Psycho-analysis has found that the phenomenon can also

is provided by the psychologically essential overvaluation of the sexual object, which inevitably extends to everything that is associated with it. A certain degree of fetishism is thus habitually present in normal love, especially in those stages of it in which the normal sexual aim seems unattainable or its fulfilment prevented:

> Schaff' mir ein Halstuch von ihrer Brust,
> Ein Strumpfband meiner Liebeslust![1]

The situation only becomes pathological when the longing for the fetish passes beyond the point of being merely a necessary condition attached to the sexual object and actually *takes the place* of the normal aim, and, further, when the fetish becomes detached from a particular individual and becomes the *sole* sexual object. These are, indeed, the general conditions under which mere variations of the sexual instinct pass over into pathological aberrations.

Binet (1888) was the first to maintain (what has since been confirmed by a quantity of evidence) that the choice of a fetish is an after-effect of some sexual impression, received as a rule in early childhood. (This may be brought into line with the proverbial durability of first loves: *on revient toujours à ses premiers amours*.) This derivation is particularly obvious in cases where there is merely a fetishistic condition attached to the sexual object. We shall come across the importance of early sexual impressions again in another connection [p. 242].[2]

be *accidentally* determined, by the occurrence of an early deterrence from sexual activity owing to fear, which may divert the subject from the normal sexual aim and encourage him to seek a substitute for it.

[1] [Get me a kerchief from her breast,
A garter that her knee has pressed.
    Goethe, *Faust*, Part I, Scene 7. (*Trans.* Bayard Taylor.)]

[2] [*Footnote added* 1920:] Deeper-going psycho-analytic research has raised a just criticism of Binet's assertion. All the observations dealing with this point have recorded a first meeting with the fetish at which it already aroused sexual interest without there being anything in the accompanying circumstances to explain the fact. Moreover, all of these 'early' sexual impressions relate to a time after the age of five or six, whereas psycho-analysis makes it doubtful whether fresh pathological fixations can occur so late as this. The true explanation is that behind the first recollection of the fetish's appearance there lies a submerged and forgotten phase of sexual development. The fetish, like a 'screen-memory', represents this phase and is thus a remnant and precipitate of it. The fact that this early infantile phase turns in the direction of

In other cases the replacement of the object by a fetish is determined by a symbolic connection of thought, of which the person concerned is usually not conscious. It is not always possible to trace the course of these connections with certainty. (The foot, for instance, is an age-old sexual symbol which occurs even in mythology;[1] no doubt the part played by fur as a fetish owes its origin to an association with the hair of the *mons Veneris*.) None the less even symbolism such as this is not always unrelated to sexual experiences in childhood.[2]

### (b) Fixations of Preliminary Sexual Aims

APPEARANCE      Every external or internal factor that hinders
OF NEW AIMS    or postpones the attainment of the normal
               sexual aim (such as impotence, the high price
of the sexual object or the danger of the sexual act) will

fetishism, as well as the choice of the fetish itself, are constitutionally determined.

[1] [*Footnote added* 1910:] The shoe or slipper is a corresponding symbol of the *female* genitals.

[2] [*Footnote added* 1910:] Psycho-analysis has cleared up one of the remaining gaps in our understanding of fetishism. It has shown the importance, as regards the choice of a fetish, of a coprophilic pleasure in smelling which has disappeared owing to repression. Both the feet and the hair are objects with a strong smell which have been exalted into fetishes after the olfactory sensation has become unpleasurable and been abandoned. Accordingly, in the perversion that corresponds to foot-fetishism, it is only dirty and evil-smelling feet that become sexual objects. Another factor that helps towards explaining the fetishistic preference for the foot is to be found among the sexual theories of children (see below p. 195): the foot represents a woman's penis, the absence of which is deeply felt. [*Added* 1915:] In a number of cases of foot-fetishism it has been possible to show that the scopophilic instinct, seeking to reach its object (originally the genitals) from underneath, was brought to a halt in its pathway by prohibition and repression. For that reason it became attached to a fetish in the form of a foot or shoe, the female genitals (in accordance with the expectations of childhood) being imagined as male ones.—[The importance of the repression of pleasure in smell had been indicated by Freud in two letters to Fliess of January 11 and November 14, 1897 (Freud, 1950a, Letters 55 and 75). He returned to the subject at the end of his analysis of the 'Rat Man' (Freud, 1909d), and discussed it at considerable length in two long footnotes to Chapter IV of *Civilization and its Discontents* (1930a). The topic of fetishism was further considered in Freud's paper on that subject (1927e) and again still later in a posthumously published fragment on the splitting of the ego (1940e [1938]) and at the end of Chapter VIII of his *Outline of Psycho-Analysis* (1940a [1938]).]

evidently lend support to the tendency to linger over the preparatory activities and to turn them into new sexual aims that can take the place of the normal one. Attentive examination always shows that even what seem to be the strangest of these new aims are already hinted at in the normal sexual process.

TOUCHING AND        A certain amount of touching is indis-
LOOKING             pensable (at all events among human beings)
                    before the normal sexual aim can be attained.
And everyone knows what a source of pleasure on the one hand and what an influx of fresh excitation on the other is afforded by tactile sensations of the skin of the sexual object. So that lingering over the stage of touching can scarcely be counted a perversion, provided that in the long run the sexual act is carried further.

The same holds true of seeing—an activity that is ultimately derived from touching. Visual impressions remain the most frequent pathway along which libidinal excitation is aroused; indeed, natural selection counts upon the accessibility of this pathway—if such a teleological form of statement is permissible [1]—when it encourages the development of beauty in the sexual object. The progressive concealment of the body which goes along with civilization keeps sexual curiosity awake. This curiosity seeks to complete the sexual object by revealing its hidden parts. It can, however, be diverted ('sublimated') in the direction of art, if its interest can be shifted away from the genitals on to the shape of the body as a whole.[2] It is usual for most normal people to linger to some extent over the inter-

[1] [The words in this parenthesis were added in 1915. Cf. footnote 2, p. 184.]

[2] [This seems to be Freud's first published use of the term 'sublimate', though it occurs as early as May 2, 1897, in the Fliess correspondence (Freud, 1950a, Letter 61). It also appears in the 'Dora' case history, 1905e, actually published later than the present work (this volume, pp. 50 and 116) though drafted in 1901. The concept is further discussed below on p. 178.—*Footnote added* 1915:] There is to my mind no doubt that the concept of 'beautiful' has its roots in sexual excitation and that its original meaning was 'sexually stimulating'. [There is an allusion in the original to the fact that the German word '*Reiz*' is commonly used both as the technical term for 'stimulus' and, in ordinary language, as an equivalent to the English 'charm' or 'attraction'.] This is related to the fact that we never regard the genitals themselves, which produce the strongest sexual excitation, as really 'beautiful'.

mediate sexual aim of a looking that has a sexual tinge to it; indeed, this offers them a possibility of directing some proportion of their libido on to higher artistic aims. On the other hand, this pleasure in looking [scopophilia] becomes a perversion (*a*) if it is restricted exclusively to the genitals, or (*b*) if it is connected with the overriding of disgust (as in the case of *voyeurs* or people who look on at excretory functions), or (*c*) if, instead of being *preparatory* to the normal sexual aim, it supplants it. This last is markedly true of exhibitionists, who, if I may trust the findings of several analyses,[1] exhibit their own genitals in order to obtain a reciprocal view of the genitals of the other person.[2]

In the perversions which are directed towards looking and being looked at, we come across a very remarkable characteristic with which we shall be still more intensely concerned in the aberration that we shall consider next: in these perversions the sexual aim occurs in two forms, an *active* and a *passive* one.

The force which opposes scopophilia, but which may be overridden by it (in a manner parallel to what we have previously seen in the case of disgust), is *shame*.

SADISM AND        The most common and the most significant of
MASOCHISM       all the perversions—the desire to inflict pain
                upon the sexual object, and its reverse—received
from Krafft-Ebing the names of 'sadism' and 'masochism' for its active and passive forms respectively. Other writers [e.g. Schrenck-Notzing (1899)] have preferred the narrower term 'algolagnia'. This emphasizes the pleasure in *pain*, the cruelty; whereas the names chosen by Krafft-Ebing bring into prominence the pleasure in any form of humiliation or subjection.

As regards active algolagnia, sadism, the roots are easy to detect in the normal. The sexuality of most male human beings contains an element of *aggressiveness*—a desire to subjugate; the

---

[1] [In the editions before 1924 this read 'of a single analysis'.]

[2] [*Footnote added* 1920:] Under analysis, these perversions—and indeed most others—reveal a surprising variety of motives and determinants. The compulsion to exhibit, for instance, is also closely dependent on the castration complex: it is a means of constantly insisting upon the integrity of the subject's own (male) genitals and it reiterates his infantile satisfaction at the absence of a penis in those of women. [Cf. p. 195.]

biological significance of it seems to lie in the need for overcoming the resistance of the sexual object by means other than
the process of wooing. Thus sadism would correspond to an
aggressive component of the sexual instinct which has become
independent and exaggerated and, by displacement, has
usurped the leading position.[1]

In ordinary speech the connotation of sadism oscillates
between, on the one hand, cases merely characterized by an
active or violent attitude to the sexual object, and, on the other
hand, cases in which satisfaction is entirely conditional on the
humiliation and maltreatment of the object. Strictly speaking,
it is only this last extreme instance which deserves to be described as a perversion.

Similarly, the term masochism comprises any passive attitude
towards sexual life and the sexual object, the extreme instance
of which appears to be that in which satisfaction is conditional
upon suffering physical or mental pain at the hands of the
sexual object. Masochism, in the form of a perversion, seems to
be further removed from the normal sexual aim than its counterpart; it may be doubted at first whether it can ever occur as a
primary phenomenon or whether, on the contrary, it may not
invariably arise from a transformation of sadism.[2] It can often
be shown that masochism is nothing more than an extension of
sadism turned round upon the subject's own self, which thus,
to begin with, takes the place of the sexual object. Clinical
analysis of extreme cases of masochistic perversion show that a
great number of factors (such as the castration complex and the
sense of guilt) have combined to exaggerate and fixate the
original passive sexual attitude.

[1] [In the editions of 1905 and 1910 the following two sentences
appeared in the text at this point: 'One at least of the roots of masochism
can be inferred with equal certainty. It arises from sexual overvaluation
as a necessary psychical consequence of the choice of a sexual object.'
From 1915 onwards these sentences were omitted and the next two
paragraphs were inserted in their place.]

[2] [*Footnote added* 1924:] My opinion of masochism has been to a large
extent altered by later reflection, based upon certain hypotheses as to
the structure of the apparatus of the mind and the classes of instincts
operating in it. I have been led to distinguish a primary or *erotogenic*
masochism, out of which two later forms, *feminine* and *moral* masochism,
have developed. Sadism which cannot find employment in actual life is
turned round upon the subject's own self and so produces a *secondary*
masochism, which is superadded to the primary kind. (Cf. Freud, 1924*c*.)

Pain, which is overridden in such cases, thus falls into line with disgust and shame as a force that stands in opposition and resistance to the libido.[1]

Sadism and masochism occupy a special position among the perversions, since the contrast between activity and passivity which lies behind them is among the universal characteristics of sexual life.

The history of human civilization shows beyond any doubt that there is an intimate connection between cruelty and the sexual instinct; but nothing has been done towards explaining the connection, apart from laying emphasis on the aggressive factor in the libido. According to some authorities this aggressive element of the sexual instinct is in reality a relic of cannibalistic desires—that is, it is a contribution derived from the apparatus for obtaining mastery, which is concerned with the satisfaction of the other and, ontogenetically, the older of the great instinctual needs.[2] It has also been maintained that every pain contains in itself the possibility of a feeling of pleasure. All that need be said is that no satisfactory explanation of this perversion has been put forward and that it seems possible that a number of mental impulses are combined in it to produce a single resultant.[3]

But the most remarkable feature of this perversion is that its active and passive forms are habitually found to occur together in the same individual. A person who feels pleasure in producing pain in someone else in a sexual relationship is also capable of enjoying as pleasure any pain which he may himself derive from sexual relations. A sadist is always at the same time a masochist, although the active or the passive aspect of the perversion may be the more strongly developed in him and may represent his predominant sexual activity.[4]

[1] [This short paragraph was in the first edition (1905), but the last two, as well as the next one, were only added in 1915.]

[2] [*Footnote added* 1915:] Cf. my remarks below [p. 198] on the pregenital phases of sexual development, which confirm this view.

[3] [*Footnote added* 1924:] The enquiry mentioned above [in footnote 2 on p. 158] has led me to assign a peculiar position, based upon the origin of the instincts, to the pair of opposites constituted by sadism and masochism, and to place them outside the class of the remaining 'perversions'.

[4] Instead of multiplying the evidence for this statement, I will quote a passage from Havelock Ellis (1913, 119): 'The investigation of histories

160 THREE ESSAYS ON SEXUALITY

We find, then, that certain among the impulses to perversion occur regularly as pairs of opposites; and this, taken in conjunction with material which will be brought forward later, has a high theoretical significance.[1] It is, moreover, a suggestive fact that the existence of the pair of opposites formed by sadism and masochism cannot be attributed merely to the element of aggressiveness. We should rather be inclined to connect the simultaneous presence of these opposites with the opposing masculinity and femininity which are combined in bisexuality— a contrast which often has to be replaced in psycho-analysis by that between activity and passivity.[2]

### (3) THE PERVERSIONS IN GENERAL

VARIATION      It is natural that medical men, who first
AND DISEASE  studied perversions in outstanding examples and
                       under special conditions, should have been inclined to regard them, like inversion, as indications of degeneracy or disease. Nevertheless, it is even easier to dispose of that view in this case than in that of inversion. Everyday experience has shown that most of these extensions, or at any rate the less severe of them, are constituents which are rarely absent from the sexual life of healthy people, and are judged by them no differently from other intimate events. If circumstances favour such an occurrence, normal people too can substitute a perversion of this kind for the normal sexual aim for quite a time, or can find place for the one alongside the other. No healthy person, it appears, can fail to make some addition that might be called perverse to the normal sexual aim; and the universality of this finding is in itself enough to show how inappropriate it is to use the word perversion as a term of reproach. In the sphere of sexual life we are brought up against

of sadism and masochism, even those given by Krafft-Ebing (as indeed Colin Scott and Féré have already pointed out), constantly reveals traces of both groups of phenomena in the same individual.'

[1] [Footnote added 1915:] Cf. my discussion of 'ambivalence' below [p. 199].

[2] [The last clause did not occur in the 1905 or 1910 editions. In 1915 the following clause was added: 'a contrast whose significance is reduced in psycho-analysis to that between activity and passivity.' This was replaced in 1924 by the words now appearing in the text.]

peculiar and, indeed, insoluble difficulties as soon as we try to draw a sharp line to distinguish mere variations within the range of what is physiological from pathological symptoms.

Nevertheless, in some of these perversions the quality of the new sexual aim is of a kind to demand special examination. Certain of them are so far removed from the normal in their content that we cannot avoid pronouncing them 'pathological'. This is especially so where (as, for instance, in cases of licking excrement or of intercourse with dead bodies) the sexual instinct goes to astonishing lengths in successfully overriding the resistances of shame, disgust, horror or pain. But even in such cases we should not be too ready to assume that people who act in this way will necessarily turn out to be insane or subject to grave abnormalities of other kinds. Here again we cannot escape from the fact that people whose behaviour is in other respects normal can, under the domination of the most unruly of all the instincts, put themselves in the category of sick persons in the single sphere of sexual life. On the other hand, manifest abnormality in the other relations of life can invariably be shown to have a background of abnormal sexual conduct.

In the majority of instances the pathological character in a perversion is found to lie not in the *content* of the new sexual aim but in its relation to the normal. If a perversion, instead of appearing merely *alongside* the normal sexual aim and object, and only when circumstances are unfavourable to *them* and favourable to *it*—if, instead of this, it ousts them completely and takes their place in *all* circumstances—if, in short, a perversion has the characteristics of exclusiveness and fixation—then we shall usually be justified in regarding it as a pathological symptom.

THE MENTAL FACTOR IN THE PERVERSIONS      It is perhaps in connection precisely with the most repulsive perversions that the mental factor must be regarded as playing its largest part in the transformation of the sexual instinct. It is impossible to deny that in their case a piece of mental work has been performed which, in spite of its horrifying result, is the equivalent of an idealization of the instinct. The omnipotence of love is perhaps never more strongly proved than in such of its aberrations as these. The highest and the lowest are always closest to each other in the sphere of sexuality: 'vom Himmel durch die Welt zur Hölle.' [1]

TWO
CONCLUSIONS

Our study of the perversions has shown us that the sexual instinct has to struggle against certain mental forces which act as resistances, and of which shame and disgust are the most prominent. It is permissible to suppose that these forces play a part in restraining that instinct within the limits that are regarded as normal; and if they develop in the individual before the sexual instinct has reached its full strength, it is no doubt they that will determine the course of its development.[2]

In the second place we have found that some of the perversions which we have examined are only made intelligible if we assume the convergence of several motive forces. If such perversions admit of analysis, that is, if they can be taken to pieces, then they must be of a composite nature. This gives us a hint that perhaps the sexual instinct itself may be no simple thing, but put together from components which have come apart again in the perversions. If this is so, the clinical observation of these abnormalities will have drawn our attention to amalgamations which have been lost to view in the uniform behaviour of normal people.[3]

[1] ['From Heaven, across the world, to Hell.'
Goethe, *Faust*, Prelude in the Theatre. (*Trans.* Bayard Taylor.)
In a letter to Fliess of January 3, 1897 (Freud 1950a, Letter 54), Freud suggests the use of this same quotation as the motto for a chapter on 'Sexuality' in a projected volume. This letter was written at a time when he was beginning to turn his attention to the perversions. His first reference to them in the Fliess correspondence dates from January 1, 1896 (Draft K).]

[2] [*Footnote added* 1915:] On the other hand, these forces which act like dams upon sexual development—disgust, shame and morality—must also be regarded as historical precipitates of the external inhibitions to which the sexual instinct has been subjected during the psychogenesis of the human race. We can observe the way in which, in the development of individuals, they arise at the appropriate moment, as though spontaneously, when upbringing and external influence give the signal.

[3] [*Footnote added* 1920:] As regards the origin of the perversions, I will add a word in anticipation of what is to come. There is reason to suppose that, just as in the case of fetishism, abortive beginnings of normal sexual development occur before the perversions become fixated. Analytic investigation has already been able to show in a few cases that perversions are a residue of development towards the Oedipus complex and that

## (4) THE SEXUAL INSTINCT IN NEUROTICS

PSYCHO-ANALYSIS    An important addition to our knowledge of the sexual instinct in certain people who at least approximate to the normal can be obtained from a source which can only be reached in one particular way. There is only one means of obtaining exhaustive information that will not be misleading about the sexual life of the persons known as 'psychoneurotics'—sufferers from hysteria, from obsessional neurosis, from what is wrongly described as neurasthenia, and, undoubtedly, from dementia praecox and paranoia was well.[1] They must be subjected to psycho-analytic investigation, which is employed in the therapeutic procedure introduced by Josef Breuer and myself in 1893 and known at that time as 'catharsis'.

I must first explain—as I have already done in other writings—that all my experience shows that these psychoneuroses are based on sexual instinctual forces. By this I do not merely mean that the energy of the sexual instinct makes a contribution to the forces that maintain the pathological manifestations (the symptoms). I mean expressly to assert that that contribution is the most important and only constant source of energy of the neurosis and that in consequence the sexual life of the persons in question is expressed—whether exclusively or principally or only partly—in these symptoms. As I have put it elsewhere [1905e, Postscript; this volume, p. 115], the symptoms constitute the sexual activity of the patient. The evidence for this assertion is derived from the ever-increasing number of psycho-analyses of hysterical and other neurotics which I have carried out during the last 25 years [2] and of whose findings I have given (and shall continue to give) a detailed account in other publications.[3]

after the repression of that complex the components of the sexual instinct which are strongest in the disposition of the individual concerned emerge once more.

[1] [Before 1915 the words 'probably paranoia' take the place of the last eight words of this sentence.]

[2] [In 1905 '10 years', the figure being increased with each edition up to and including 1920.]

[3] [*Footnote added* 1920:] It implies no qualification of the above assertion, but rather an amplification of it, if I restate it as follows: neurotic symptoms are based on the one hand on the demands of the libidinal instincts and on the other hand on those made by the ego by way of reaction to them.

The removal of the symptoms of hysterical patients by psycho-analysis proceeds on the supposition that those symptoms are substitutes—transcriptions as it were—for a number of emotionally cathected mental processes, wishes and desires, which, by the operation of a special psychical procedure (repression), have been prevented from obtaining discharge in psychical activity that is admissible to consciousness. These mental processes, therefore, being held back in a state of unconsciousness, strive to obtain an expression that shall be appropriate to their emotional importance—to obtain discharge; and in the case of hysteria they find such an expression (by means of the process of 'conversion') in somatic phenomena, that is, in hysterical symptoms. By systematically turning these symptoms back (with the help of a special technique) into emotionally cathected ideas—ideas that will now have become conscious—it is possible to obtain the most accurate knowledge of the nature and origin of these formerly unconscious psychical structures.

FINDINGS OF PSYCHO-ANALYSIS    In this manner the fact has emerged that symptoms represent a substitute for impulses the source of whose strength is derived from the sexual instinct. What we know about the nature of hysterics before they fall ill—and they may be regarded as typical of all psychoneurotics—and about the occasions which precipitate their falling ill, is in complete harmony with this view. The character of hysterics shows a degree of sexual repression in excess of the normal quantity, an intensification of resistance against the sexual instinct (which we have already met with in the form of shame, disgust and morality), and what seems like an instinctive aversion on their part to any intellectual consideration of sexual problems. As a result of this, in especially marked cases, the patients remain in complete ignorance of sexual matters right into the period of sexual maturity.[1]

On a cursory view, this trait, which is so characteristic of hysteria, is not uncommonly screened by the existence of a second constitutional character present in hysteria, namely the

---

[1] Breuer [in the second paragraph of the first case history, Breuer and Freud, 1895] writes of the patient in connection with whom he first adopted the cathartic method: 'The factor of sexuality was astonishingly undeveloped in her.'

predominant development of the sexual instinct. Psycho-analysis, however, can invariably bring the first of these factors to light and clear up the enigmatic contradiction which hysteria presents, by revealing the pair of opposites by which it is characterized—exaggerated sexual craving and excessive aversion to sexuality.

In the case of anyone who is predisposed to hysteria, the onset of his illness is precipitated when, either as a result of his own progressive maturity or of the external circumstances of his life, he finds himself faced by the demands of a real sexual situation. Between the pressure of the instinct and his antagonism to sexuality, illness offers him a way of escape. It does not solve his conflict, but seeks to evade it by transforming his libidinal impulses into symptoms.[1] The exception is only an *apparent* one when a hysteric—a male patient it may be—falls ill as a result of some trivial emotion, some conflict which does not centre around any sexual interest. In such cases psycho-analysis is regularly able to show that the illness has been made possible by the sexual component of the conflict, which has prevented the mental processes from reaching a normal issue.

NEUROSIS AND        There is no doubt that a large part of the
PERVERSION          opposition to these views of mine is due to the
                    fact that sexuality, to which I trace back psycho-neurotic symptoms, is regarded as though it coincided with the normal sexual instinct. But psycho-analytic teaching goes further than this. It shows that it is by no means only at the cost of the so-called *normal* sexual instinct that these symptoms originate —at any rate such is not exclusively or mainly the case; they also give expression (by conversion) to instincts which would be described as *perverse* in the widest sense of the word if they could be expressed directly in phantasy and action without being diverted from consciousness. Thus symptoms are formed in part at the cost of *abnormal* sexuality; *neuroses are, so to say, the negative of perversions.*[2]

[1] [This theme was elaborated by Freud in his paper on the different types of onset of neurosis (1912*c*).]

[2] [This idea had been expressed by Freud in precisely these terms in a letter to Fliess of January 24, 1897 (Freud, 1950*a*, Letter 57). But it had already been implied in the letters of December 6, 1896, and January 11, 1897 (Letters 52 and 55). It will also be found in the case history of 'Dora' (this volume, p. 50).] The contents of the clearly conscious

The sexual instinct of psychoneurotics exhibits all the aberrations which we have studied as variations of normal, and as manifestations of abnormal, sexual life.

(a) The unconscious mental life of all neurotics (without exception) shows inverted impulses, fixation of their libido upon persons of their own sex. It would be impossible without deep discussion to give any adequate appreciation of the importance of this factor in determining the form taken by the symptoms of the illness. I can only insist that an unconscious tendency to inversion is never absent and is of particular value in throwing light upon hysteria in men.[1]

(b) It is possible to trace in the unconscious of psychoneurotics tendencies to every kind of anatomical extension of sexual activity and to show that those tendencies are factors in the formation of symptoms. Among them we find occurring with particular frequency those in which the mucous membrane of the mouth and anus are assigned the role of genitals.

(c) An especially prominent part is played as factors in the formation of symptoms in psychoneuroses by the component instincts,[2] which emerge for the most part as pairs of opposites and which we have met with as introducing new sexual aims—the scopophilic instinct and exhibitionism and the active and passive forms of the instinct for cruelty. The contribution made by the last of these is essential to the understanding of the fact that symptoms involve *suffering*, and it almost invariably dominates a part of the patient's social behaviour. It is also through the

phantasies of perverts (which in favourable circumstances can be transformed into manifest behaviour), of the delusional fears of paranoics (which are projected in a hostile sense on to other people) and of the unconscious phantasies of hysterics (which psycho-analysis reveals behind their symptoms)—all of these coincide with one another even down to their details.

[1] Psychoneuroses are also very often associated with *manifest* inversion. In such cases the heterosexual current of feeling has undergone complete suppression. It is only fair to say that my attention was first drawn to the necessary universality of the tendency to inversion in psychoneurotics by Wilhelm Fliess of Berlin, after I had discussed its presence in individual cases.—[*Added* 1920:] This fact, which has not been sufficiently appreciated, cannot fail to have a decisive influence on any theory of homosexuality.

[2] [The term 'component instinct' here makes its first appearance in Freud's published works, though the *concept* has already been introduced above on p. 162.]

medium of this connection between libido and cruelty that the transformation of love into hate takes place, the transformation of affectionate into hostile impulses, which is characteristic of a great number of cases of neurosis, and indeed, it would seem, of paranoia in general.

The interest of these findings is still further increased by certain special facts.[1]

(a) Whenever we find in the unconscious an instinct of this sort which is capable of being paired off with an opposite one, this second instinct will regularly be found in operation as well. Every active perversion is thus accompanied by its passive counterpart: anyone who is an exhibitionist in his unconscious is at the same time a *voyeur*; in anyone who suffers from the consequences of repressed sadistic impulses there is sure to be another determinant of his symptoms which has its source in masochistic inclinations. The complete agreement which is here shown with what we have found to exist in the corresponding 'positive' perversions is most remarkable, though in the actual symptoms one or other of the opposing tendencies plays the predominant part.

(β) In any fairly marked case of psychoneurosis it is unusual for only a single one of these perverse instincts to be developed. We usually find a considerable number and as a rule traces of them all. The degree of development of each particular instinct is, however, independent of that of the others. Here, too, the study of the 'positive' perversions provides an exact counterpart.

## (5) COMPONENT INSTINCTS AND EROTOGENIC ZONES [2]

If we put together what we have learned from our investigation of positive and negative perversions, it seems plausible to

[1] [In the editions before 1920 *three* such 'special facts' were enumerated. The first, which was subsequently omitted, ran as follows: 'Among the unconscious trains of thought found in neuroses there is nothing corresponding to a tendency to fetishism—a circumstance which throws light on the psychological peculiarity of this well-understood perversion.']

[2] [This appears to be the first published occurrence of the term 'erotogenic zone'. Freud had already used it in a letter to Fliess on December 6, 1896 (Freud, 1950a, Letter 52). It also occurs in a passage (this volume p. 52) in Section I of the case history of 'Dora' (1905e),

trace them back to a number of 'component instincts', which, however, are not of a primary nature, but are susceptible to further analysis.[1] By an 'instinct' is provisionally to be understood the psychical representative of an endosomatic, continuously flowing source of stimulation, as contrasted with a 'stimulus', which is set up by *single* excitations coming from *without*. The concept of instinct is thus one of those lying on the frontier between the mental and the physical. The simplest and likeliest assumption as to the nature of instincts would seem to be that in itself an instinct is without quality, and, so far as mental life is concerned, is only to be regarded as a measure of the demand made upon the mind for work. What distinguishes the instincts from one another and endows them with specific qualities is their relation to their somatic sources and to their aims. The source of an instinct is a process of excitation occurring in an organ and the immediate aim of the instinct lies in the removal of this organic stimulus.[2]

There is a further provisional assumption that we cannot escape in the theory of the instincts. It is to the effect that excitations of two kinds arise from the somatic organs, based upon differences of a chemical nature. One of these kinds of excitation we describe as being specifically sexual, and we speak of the organ concerned as the 'erotogenic zone' of the sexual component instinct arising from it.[3]

presumably written in 1901. It was evidently constructed on the analogy of the term 'hysterogenic zone' which was already in common use.]

[1] [The passage from this point till the end of the paragraph dates from 1915. In the first two editions (1905 and 1910) the following sentences appeared instead: 'We can distinguish in them [the component instincts] (in addition to an 'instinct' which is not itself sexual and which has its source in motor impulses) a contribution from an organ capable of receiving stimuli (e.g. the skin, the mucous membrane or a sense organ). An organ of this kind will be described in this connection as an "erotogenic zone"—as being the organ whose excitation lends the instinct a sexual character.'—The revised version dates from the period of Freud's paper on 'Instincts and their Vicissitudes' (1915c), where the whole topic is examined at length.]

[2] [*Footnote added* 1924:] The theory of the instincts is the most important but at the same time the least complete portion of psychoanalytic theory. I have made further contributions to it in my later works *Beyond the Pleasure Principle* (1920g) and *The Ego and the Id* (1923b).

[3] [*Footnote added* 1915:] It is not easy in the present place to justify these assumptions, derived as they are from the study of a particular

The part played by the erotogenic zones is immediately obvious in the case of those perversions which assign a sexual significance to the oral and anal orifices. These behave in every respect like a portion of the sexual apparatus. In hysteria these parts of the body and the neighbouring tracts of mucous membrane become the seat of new sensations and of changes in innervation—indeed, of processes that can be compared to erection [1]—in just the same way as do the actual genitalia under the excitations of the normal sexual processes.

The significance of the erotogenic zones as apparatuses subordinate to the genitals and as substitutes for them is, among all the psychoneuroses, most clearly to be seen in hysteria; but this does not imply that that significance is any the less in the other forms of illness. It is only that in them it is less recognizable, because in their case (obsessional neurosis and paranoia) the formation of the symptoms takes place in regions of the mental apparatus which are more remote from the particular centres concerned with somatic control. In obsessional neurosis what is more striking is the significance of those impulses which create new sexual aims and seem independent of erotogenic zones. Nevertheless, in scopophilia and exhibitionism the eye corresponds to an erotogenic zone; while in the case of those components of the sexual instinct which involve pain and cruelty the same role is assumed by the skin—the skin, which in particular parts of the body has become differentiated into sense organs or modified into mucous membrane, and is thus the erotogenic zone *par excellence*.[2]

class of neurotic illness. But on the other hand, if I omitted all mention of them, it would be impossible to say anything of substance about the instincts.

[1] [The phrase in parenthesis was added in 1920.]

[2] We are reminded at this point of Moll's analysis of the sexual instinct into an instinct of 'contrectation' and an instinct of 'detumescence'. Contrectation represents a need for contact with the skin. [The instinct of detumescence was described by Moll (1898) as an impulse for the spasmodic relief of tension of the sexual organs, and the instinct of contrectation as an impulse to come into contact with another person. He believed that the latter impulse arose later than the first in the individual's development. (See also below, p. 180, *n.* 2.)—The following additional sentence appeared at the end of this footnote in 1905 and 1910, but was afterwards omitted: 'Strohmayer has very rightly inferred from a case under his observation that obsessive self-reproaches originate from suppressed sadistic impulses.']

170     THREE ESSAYS ON SEXUALITY

## (6) REASONS FOR THE APPARENT PREPONDERANCE OF PERVERSE SEXUALITY IN THE PSYCHONEUROSES

The preceding discussion may perhaps have placed the sexuality of psychoneurotics in a false light. It may have given the impression that, owing to their disposition, psychoneurotics approximate closely to perverts in their sexual behaviour and are proportionately remote from normal people. It may indeed very well be that the constitutional disposition of these patients (apart from their exaggerated degree of sexual repression and the excessive intensity of their sexual instinct) includes an unusual tendency to perversion, using that word in its widest sense. Nevertheless, investigation of comparatively slight cases shows that this last assumption is not absolutely necessary, or at least that in forming a judgement on these pathological developments there is a factor to be considered which weighs in the other direction. Most psychoneurotics only fall ill after the age of puberty as a result of the demands made upon them by normal sexual life. (It is most particularly against the latter that repression is directed.) Or else illnesses of this kind set in later, when the libido fails to obtain satisfaction along normal lines. In both these cases the libido behaves like a stream whose main bed has become blocked. It proceeds to fill up collateral channels which may hitherto have been empty. Thus, in the same way, what appears to be the strong tendency (though, it is true, a negative one) of psychoneurotics to perversion may be collaterally determined, and must, in any case, be collaterally intensified. The fact is that we must put sexual repression as an internal factor alongside such external factors as limitation of freedom, inaccessibility of a normal sexual object, the dangers of the normal sexual act, etc., which bring about perversions in persons who might perhaps otherwise have remained normal.

In this respect different cases of neurosis may behave differently: in one case the preponderating factor may be the innate strength of the tendency to perversion, in another it may be the collateral increase of that tendency owing to the libido being forced away from a normal sexual aim and sexual object. It would be wrong to represent as opposition what is in fact a co-operative relation. Neurosis will always produce its greatest effects when constitution and experience work together in the same direction. Where the constitution is a marked one it will perhaps not require the support of actual experiences; while a great shock in real life will perhaps bring about a neurosis even in an average constitution. (Incidentally, this view of the relative aetiological importance of what is innate and what is accidentally experienced applies equally in other fields.)

If we prefer to suppose, nevertheless, that a particularly strongly developed tendency to perversion is among the characteristics of psychoneurotic constitutions, we have before us the prospect of being able to distinguish a number of such constitutions according to the innate preponderance of one or the other of the erotogenic zones or of one or the other of the component instincts. The question whether a special relation holds between the perverse disposition and the particular form of illness adopted, has, like so much else in this field, not yet been investigated.

### (7) INTIMATION OF THE INFANTILE CHARACTER OF SEXUALITY

By demonstrating the part played by perverse impulses in the formation of symptoms in the psychoneuroses, we have quite remarkably increased the number of people who might be regarded as perverts. It is not only that neurotics in themselves constitute a very numerous class, but it must also be considered that an unbroken chain bridges the gap between the neuroses in all their manifestations and normality. After all, Moebius could say with justice that we are all to some extent hysterics. Thus the extraordinarily wide dissemination of the perversions forces us to suppose that the disposition to perversions is itself of no great rarity but must form a part of what passes as the normal constitution.

It is, as we have seen, debatable whether the perversions go back to innate determinants or arise, as Binet assumed was the case with fetishism [p. 154], owing to chance experiences. The conclusion now presents itself to us that there is indeed something innate lying behind the perversions but that it is something innate in *everyone*, though as a disposition it may vary in its intensity and may be increased by the influences of actual life. What is in question are the innate constitutional roots of the sexual instinct. In one class of cases (the perversions) these roots may grow into the actual vehicles of sexual activity; in others they may be submitted to an insufficient suppression (repression) and thus be able in a roundabout way to attract a considerable proportion of sexual energy to themselves as symptoms; while in the most favourable cases, which lie between these two extremes, they may by means of effective restriction and other kinds of modification bring about what is known as normal sexual life.

We have, however, a further reflection to make. This postulated constitution, containing the germs of all the perversions, will only be demonstrable in *children*, even though in them it is only with modest degrees of intensity that any of the instincts can emerge. A formula begins to take shape which lays it down that the sexuality of neurotics has remained in, or been brought back to, an infantile state. Thus our interest turns to the sexual life of children, and we will now proceed to trace the play of influences which govern the evolution of infantile sexuality till its outcome in perversion, neurosis or normal sexual life.

# INFANTILE SEXUALITY

NEGLECT OF          One feature of the popular view of the sexual
THE INFANTILE     instinct is that it is absent in childhood and
FACTOR              only awakens in the period of life described as
puberty. This, however, is not merely a simple
error but one that has had grave consequences, for it is mainly
to this idea that we owe our present ignorance of the fundamental conditions of sexual life. A thorough study of the sexual
manifestations of childhood would probably reveal the essential
characters of the sexual instinct and would show us the course
of its development and the way in which it is put together from
various sources.

It is noticeable that writers who concern themselves with
explaining the characteristics and reactions of the adult have
devoted much more attention to the primaeval period which is
comprised in the life of the individual's ancestors—have, that
is, ascribed much more influence to heredity—than to the other
primaeval period, which falls within the lifetime of the individual
himself—that is, to childhood. One would surely have supposed
that the influence of this latter period would be easier to understand and could claim to be considered before that of heredity.[1]
It is true that in the literature of the subject one occasionally
comes across remarks upon precocious sexual activity in small
children—upon erections, masturbation and even activities resembling coitus. But these are always quoted only as exceptional
events, as oddities or as horrifying instances of precocious
depravity. So far as I know, not a single author has clearly
recognized the regular existence of a sexual instinct in childhood; and in the writings that have become so numerous on
the development of children, the chapter on 'Sexual Development' is as a rule omitted.[2]

[1] [*Footnote added* 1915:] Nor is it possible to estimate correctly the
part played by heredity until the part played by childhood has been
assessed.

[2] The assertion made in the text has since struck me myself as being
so bold that I have undertaken the task of testing its validity by looking
through the literature once more. The outcome of this is that I have

INFANTILE    The reason for this strange neglect is to be sought,
AMNESIA     I think, partly in considerations of propriety, which
            the authors obey as a result of their own upbring-
ing, and partly in a psychological phenomenon which has itself
hitherto eluded explanation. What I have in mind is the peculiar
amnesia which, in the case of most people, though by no means
all, hides the earliest beginnings of their childhood up to their
sixth or eighth year. Hitherto it has not occurred to us to feel
any astonishment at the fact of this amnesia, though we might
have had good grounds for doing so. For we learn from other
people that during these years, of which at a later date we retain
nothing in our memory but a few unintelligible and fragmentary
recollections, we reacted in a lively manner to impressions, that
we were capable of expressing pain and joy in a human fashion,
that we gave evidence of love, jealousy and other passionate
feelings by which we were strongly moved at the time, and even
that we gave utterance to remarks which were regarded by
adults as good evidence of our possessing insight and the be-

allowed my statement to stand unaltered. The scientific examination of
both the physical and mental phenomena of sexuality in childhood is
still in its earliest beginnings. One writer, Bell (1902, 327), remarks:
'I know of no scientist who has given a careful analysis of the emotion
as it is seen in the adolescent.' Somatic sexual manifestations from the
period before puberty have only attracted attention in connection with
phenomena of degeneracy and as indications of degeneracy. In none of
the accounts which I have read of the psychology of this priod of life
is a chapter to be found on the erotic life of children; and this applies
to the well-known works of Preyer [1882], Baldwin (1898), Pérez (1886),
Strümpell (1899), Groos (1904), Heller (1904), Sully (1895) and others.
We can obtain the clearest impression of the state of things in this field
to-day from the periodical *Die Kinderfehler* from 1896 onwards. Nevertheless the conviction is borne in upon us that the existence of love in
childhood stands in no need of discovery. Pérez (1886, 272 ff.) argues
in favour of its existence. Groos (1899, 326) mentions as a generally
recognized fact that 'some children are already accessible to sexual
impulses at a very early age and feel an urge to have contact with the
opposite sex'. The earliest instance of the appearance of 'sex-love'
recorded by Bell (1902, 330) concerns a child in the middle of his third
year. On this point compare further Havelock Ellis (1913, Appendix B).
    [*Added* 1910:] This judgement upon the literature of infantile sexuality
need no longer be maintained since the appearance of Stanley Hall's
exhaustive work (1904). No such modification is necessitated by Moll's
recent book (1909). See, on the other hand, Bleuler (1908). [*Added* 1915:]
Since this was written, a book by Hug-Hellmuth (1913) has taken the
neglected sexual factor fully into account.

ginnings of a capacity for judgement. And of all this we, when we are grown up, have no knowledge of our own! Why should our memory lag so far behind the other activities of our minds? We have, on the contrary, good reason to believe that there is no period at which the capacity for receiving and reproducing impressions is greater than precisely during the years of childhood.[1]

On the other hand we must assume, or we can convince ourselves by a psychological examination of other people, that the very same impressions that we have forgotten have none the less left the deepest traces on our minds and have had a determining effect upon the whole of our later development. There can, therefore, be no question of any real abolition of the impressions of childhood, but rather of an amnesia similar to that which neurotics exhibit for later events, and of which the essence consists in a simple witholding of these impressions from consciousness, viz., in their repression. But what are the forces which bring about this repression of the impressions of childhood? Whoever could solve this riddle would, I think, have explained *hysterical* amnesia as well.

Meanwhile we must not fail to observe that the existence of infantile amnesia provides a new point of comparison between the mental states of children and psychoneurotics. We have already [p. 172] come across another such point in the formula to which we were led, to the effect that the sexuality of psychoneurotics has remained at, or been carried back to, an infantile stage. Can it be, after all, that infantile amnesia, too, is to be brought into relation with the sexual impulses of childhood?

Moreover, the connection between infantile and hysterical amnesia is more than a mere play upon words. Hysterical amnesia, which occurs at the bidding of repression, is only explicable by the fact that the subject is already in possession of a store of memory-traces which have been withdrawn from conscious disposal, and which are now, by an associative link, attracting to themselves the material which the forces of repression are engaged in repelling from consciousness.[2] It may be

[1] I have attempted to solve one of the problems connected with the earliest memories of childhood in a paper on 'Screen Memories' (1899a). [*Added* 1924:] See also Chapter IV of my *Psychopathology of Everyday Life* (1901b).

[2] [*Footnote added* 1915:] The mechanism of repression cannot be understood unless account is taken of *both* of these two concurrent

said that without infantile amnesia there would be no hysterical amnesia.

I believe, then, that infantile amnesia, which turns everyone's childhood into something like a prehistoric epoch and conceals from him the beginnings of his own sexual life, is responsible for the fact that in general no importance is attached to childhood in the development of sexual life. The gaps in our knowledge which have arisen in this way cannot be bridged by a single observer. As long ago as in the year 1896[1] I insisted on the significance of the years of childhood in the origin of certain important phenomena connected with sexual life, and since then I have never ceased to emphasize the part played in sexuality by the infantile factor.

## [1] THE PERIOD OF SEXUAL LATENCY IN CHILDHOOD AND ITS INTERRUPTIONS

The remarkably frequent reports of what are described as irregular and exceptional sexual impulses in childhood, as well as the uncovering in neurotics of what have hitherto been unconscious memories of childhood, allow us to sketch out the sexual occurrences of that period in some such way as this.[2]

There seems no doubt that germs of sexual impulses are already present in the new-born child and that these continue to develop for a time, but are then overtaken by a progressive process of suppression; this in turn is itself interrupted by periodical advances in sexual development or may be held up by individual peculiarities. Nothing is known for certain concerning the regularity and periodicity of this oscillating course of development. It seems, however, that the sexual life of

processes. They may be compared with the manner in which tourists are conducted to the top of the Great Pyramid of Giza by being pushed from one direction and pulled from the other. [Cf. Freud's paper on 'Repression' (1915d).]

[1] [E.g. in the last paragraph of Section I of his paper on the aetiology of hysteria (1896c).]

[2] We are able to make use of the second of these two sources of material since we are justified in expecting that the early years of children who are later to become neurotic are not likely in this respect to differ *essentially* from those of children who are to grow up into normal adults, [*added* 1915:] but only in the intensity and clarity of the phenomena involved.

children usually emerges in a form accessible to observation
round about the third or fourth year of life.[1]

SEXUAL          It is during this period of total or only partial
INHIBITIONS    latency that are built up the mental forces which
               are later to impede the course of the sexual instinct
and, like dams, restrict its flow—disgust, feelings of shame and
the claims of aesthetic and moral ideals. One gets an impression
from civilized children that the construction of these dams is a
product of education, and no doubt education has much to do
with it. But in reality this development is organically determined
and fixed by heredity, and it can occasionally occur without any

[1] There is a possible anatomical analogy to what I believe to be the
course of development of the infantile sexual function in Bayer's discovery (1902) that the internal sexual organs (i.e. the uterus) are as a
rule larger in new-born children than in older ones. It is not certain,
however, what view we should take of this involution that occurs after
birth (which has been shown by Halban to apply also to other portions
of the genital apparatus). According to Halban (1904) the process of
involution comes to an end after a few weeks of extra-uterine life.
[*Added* 1920:] Those authorities who regard the interstitial portion of
the sex-gland as the organ that determines sex have on their side been
led by anatomical researches to speak of infantile sexuality and a period
of sexual latency. I quote a passage from Lipschütz's book (1919, 168),
which I mentioned on p. 144 *n.*: 'We shall be doing more justice to the
facts if we say that the maturation of the sexual characters which is
accomplished at puberty is only due to a great acceleration which
occurs at that time of processes which began much earlier—in my view
as early as during intra-uterine life.' 'What has hitherto been described
in a summary way as puberty is probably only a second major phase of
puberty which sets in about the middle of the second decade of life . . .
Childhood, from birth until the beginning of this second major phase,
might be described as "the intermediate phase of puberty" ' (ibid., 170).
Attention was drawn to this coincidence between anatomical findings
and psychological observation in a review [of Lipschütz's book] by
Ferenczi (1920). The agreement is marred only by the fact that the
'first peak' in the development of the sexual organ occurs during the
early intra-uterine period, whereas the early efflorescence of infantile
sexual life must be ascribed to the third and fourth years of life. There
is, of course, no need to expect that anatomical growth and psychical
development must be exactly simultaneous. The researches in question
were made on the sex-glands of human beings. Since a period of latency
in the psychological sense does not occur in animals, it would be very
interesting to know whether the anatomical findings which have led
these writers to assume the occurrence of two peaks in sexual development are also demonstrable in the higher animals.

help at all from education. Education will not be trespassing beyond its appropriate domain if it limits itself to following the lines which have already been laid down organically and to impressing them somewhat more clearly and deeply.

REACTION-FORMATION AND SUBLIMATION     What is it that goes to the making of these constructions which are so important for the growth of a civilized and normal individual? They probably emerge at the cost of the infantile sexual impulses themselves. Thus the activity of those impulses does not cease even during this period of latency, though their energy is diverted, wholly or in great part, from their sexual use and directed to other ends. Historians of civilization appear to be at one in assuming that powerful components are acquired for every kind of cultural achievement by this diversion of sexual instinctual forces from sexual aims and their direction to new ones—a process which deserves the name of 'sublimation'. To this we would add, accordingly, that the same process plays a part in the development of the individual and we would place its beginning in the period of sexual latency of childhood.[1]

It is possible further to form some idea of the mechanism of this process of sublimation. On the one hand, it would seem, the sexual impulses cannot be utilized during these years of childhood, since the reproductive functions have been deferred —a fact which constitutes the main feature of the period of latency. On the other hand, these impulses would seem in themselves to be perverse—that is, to arise from erotogenic zones and to derive their activity from instincts which, in view of the direction of the subject's development, can only arouse unpleasurable feelings. They consequently evoke opposing mental forces (reacting impulses) which, in order to suppress this unpleasure effectively, build up the mental dams that I have already mentioned—disgust, shame and morality.[2]

[1] Once again, it is from Fliess that I have borrowed the term 'period of sexual latency'.

[2] [*Footnote added* 1915:] In the case which I am here discussing, the sublimation of sexual instinctual forces takes place along the path of reaction-formation. But in general it is possible to distinguish the concepts of sublimation and reaction-formation from each other as two different processes. Sublimation can also take place by other and simpler

INTERRUPTIONS OF        We must not deceive ourselves as to the
THE LATENCY            hypothetical nature and insufficient clarity
PERIOD                 of our knowledge concerning the processes
                       of the infantile period of latency or defer-
ment; but we shall be on firmer ground in pointing out that
such an application of infantile sexuality represents an educa-
tional ideal from which individual development usually diverges
at some point and often to a considerable degree. From time to
time a fragmentary manifestation of sexuality which has evaded
sublimation may break through; or some sexual activity may
persist through the whole duration of the latency period until
the sexual instinct emerges with greater intensity at puberty. In
so far as educators pay any attention at all to infantile sexuality,
they behave exactly as though they shared our views as to the
construction of the moral defensive forces at the cost of sexuality,
and as though they knew that sexual activity makes a child
ineducable: for they stigmatize every sexual manifestation by
children as a 'vice', without being able to do much against it.
We, on the other hand, have every reason for turning our
attention to these phenomena which are so much dreaded by
education, for we may expect them to help us to discover the
original configuration of the sexual instincts.

## [2] THE MANIFESTATIONS OF INFANTILE SEXUALITY

THUMB-SUCKING          For reasons which will appear later, I shall
                       take thumb-sucking (or sensual sucking) as a
sample of the sexual manifestations of childhood. (An excellent study of this subject has been made by the Hungarian
paediatrician, Lindner, 1879.)[1]

Thumb-sucking appears already in early infancy and may
continue into maturity, or even persist all through life. It consists in the rhythmic repetition of a sucking contact by the

mechanisms. [Further theoretical discussions of sublimation will be
found in Section III of Freud's paper on narcissism (1914c) and at
several points in *The Ego and the Id* (1923b, Chapters III, IV and V).]
    [1] [There seems to be no nursery word in English equivalent to the
German '*lutschen*' and '*ludeln*', used by Freud alongside '*wonnesaugen*'
('sensual sucking'). Conrad in *Struwwelpeter* was a '*Lutscher*'; but, as will
be seen from the context, 'suck-a-thumbs' and 'thumb-sucking' have in
fact too narrow a connotation for the present purpose.]

mouth (or lips). There is no question of the purpose of this procedure being the taking of nourishment. A portion of the lip itself, the tongue, or any other part of the skin within reach—even the big toe—may be taken as the object upon which this sucking is carried out. In this connection a grasping-instinct may appear and may manifest itself as a simultaneous rhythmic tugging at the lobes of the ears or a catching hold of some part of another person (as a rule the ear) for the same purpose. Sensual sucking involves a complete absorption of the attention and leads either to sleep or even to a motor reaction in the nature of an orgasm.[1] It is not infrequently combined with rubbing some sensitive part of the body such as the breast or the external genitalia. Many children proceed by this path from sucking to masturbation.

Lindner himself [2] clearly recognized the sexual nature of this activity and emphasized it without qualification. In the nursery, sucking is often classed along with the other kinds of sexual 'naughtiness' of children. This view has been most energetically repudiated by numbers of paediatricians and nerve-specialists, though this is no doubt partly due to a confusion between 'sexual' and 'genital'. Their objection raises a difficult question and one which cannot be evaded: what is the general characteristic which enables us to recognize the sexual manifestations of children? The concatenation of phenomena into which we have been given an insight by psycho-analytic investigation justifies us, in my opinion, in regarding thumb-sucking as a sexual mani-

---

[1] Thus we find at this early stage, what holds good all through life, that sexual satisfaction is the best soporific. Most cases of nervous insomnia can be traced back to lack of sexual satisfaction. It is well known that unscrupulous nurses put crying children to sleep by stroking their genitals. [Cf. p. 98, *n*. 1.]

[2] [This paragraph was added in 1915. In its place the following paragraph appears in the editions of 1905 and 1910 only: 'No observer has felt any doubt as to the sexual nature of this activity. Nevertheless, the best theories formed by adults in regard to this example of the sexual behaviour of children leave us in the lurch. Consider Moll's [1898] analysis of the sexual instinct into an instinct of detumescence and an instinct of contrectation. [See above p. 169, *n*. 2.] The first of these factors cannot be concerned in our present instance, and the second one can only be recognized with difficulty, since, according to Moll, it emerges later than the instinct of detumescence and is directed towards other people.'—In 1910 the following footnote was attached to the first sentence of this cancelled paragraph: 'With the exception of Moll (1909).']

festation and in choosing it for our study of the essential features of infantile sexual activity.[1]

AUTO-EROTISM    We are in duty bound to make a thorough examination of this example. It must be insisted that the most striking feature of this sexual activity is that the instinct is not directed towards other people, but obtains satisfaction from the subject's own body. It is 'auto-erotic', to call it by a happily chosen term introduced by Havelock Ellis (1910).[2]

Furthermore, it is clear that the behaviour of a child who indulges in thumb-sucking is determined by a search for some pleasure which has already been experienced and is now remembered. In the simplest case he proceeds to find this satisfaction by sucking rhythmically at some part of the skin or mucous membrane. It is also easy to guess the occasions on which the child had his first experiences of the pleasure which he is now striving to renew. It was the child's first and most vital activity, his sucking at his mother's breast, or at substitutes for it, that must have familiarized him with this pleasure. The child's lips, in our view, behave like an erotogenic zone, and no doubt stimulation by the warm flow of milk is the cause of the pleasurable sensation. The satisfaction of the erotogenic zone is associated, in the first instance, with the satisfaction of the need for

[1] [*Footnote added* 1920:] In 1919, a Dr. Galant published, under the title of 'Das Lutscherli', the confession of a grown-up girl who had never given up this infantile sexual activity and who represents the satisfaction to be gained from sucking as something completely analogous to sexual satisfaction, particularly when this is obtained from a lover's kiss: 'Not every kiss is equal to a "*Lutscherli*"—no, no, not by any means! It is impossible to describe what a lovely feeling goes through your whole body when you suck; you are right away from this world. You are absolutely satisfied, and happy beyond desire. It is a wonderful feeling; you long for nothing but peace—uninterrupted peace. It is just unspeakably lovely: you feel no pain and no sorrow, and ah! you are carried into another world.'

[2] [*Footnote added* 1920:] Havelock Ellis, it is true, uses the word 'auto-erotic' in a somewhat different sense, to describe an excitation which is not provoked from outside but arises internally. What psychoanalysis regards as the essential point is not the genesis of the excitation, but the question of its relation to an object.—[In all editions before 1920 this footnote read as follows: 'Havelock Ellis, however, has spoilt the meaning of the term he invented by including the whole of hysteria and all the manifestations of masturbation among the phenomena of autoerotism.']

nourishment. To begin with, sexual activity attaches itself to functions serving the purpose of self-preservation and does not become independent of them until later.[1] No one who has seen a baby sinking back satiated from the breast and falling asleep with flushed cheeks and a blissful smile can escape the reflection that this picture persists as a prototype of the expression of sexual satisfaction in later life. The need for repeating the sexual satisfaction now becomes detached from the need for taking nourishment—a separation which becomes inevitable when the teeth appear and food is no longer taken in only by sucking, but is also chewed up. The child does not make use of an extraneous body for his sucking, but prefers a part of his own skin because it is more convenient, because it makes him independent of the external world, which he is not yet able to control, and because in that way he provides himself, as it were, with a second erotogenic zone, though one of an inferior kind. The inferiority of this second region is among the reasons why at a later date he seeks the corresponding part—the lips—of another person. ('It's a pity I can't kiss myself', he seems to be saying.)

It is not every child who sucks in this way. It may be assumed that those children do so in whom there is a constitutional intensification of the erotogenic significance of the labial region. If that significance persists, these same children when they are grown up will become epicures in kissing, will be inclined to perverse kissing, or, if males, will have a powerful motive for drinking and smoking. If, however, repression ensues, they will feel disgust at food and will produce hysterical vomiting. The repression extends to the nutritional instinct owing to the dual purpose served by the labial zone. Many[2] of my women patients who suffer from disturbances of eating, *globus hystericus*, constriction of the throat and vomiting, have indulged energetically in sucking during their childhood.

Our study of thumb-sucking or sensual sucking has already given us the three essential characterisitics of an infantile sexual manifestation. At its origin it attaches itself to one of the vital somatic functions;[3] it has as yet no sexual object, and is thus auto-erotic; and its sexual aim is dominated by an erotogenic

---

[1] [This sentence was added in 1915. Cf. Section II of Freud's paper on narcissism (1914c).]    [2] [In the first edition only this reads 'all'.]
[3] [This clause was added in 1915; and in the earlier editions the word 'three' in the last sentence is replaced by 'two'.]

zone. It is to be anticipated that these characteristics will be found to apply equally to most of the other activities of the infantile sexual instincts.

## [3] THE SEXUAL AIM OF INFANTILE SEXUALITY

CHARACTERISTICS      The example of thumb-sucking shows us
OF EROTOGENIC        still more about what constitutes an eroto-
ZONES                genic zone. It is a part of the skin or mucous
                     membrane in which stimuli of a certain sort
evoke a feeling of pleasure possessing a particular quality. There can be no doubt that the stimuli which produce the pleasure are governed by special conditions, though we do not know what those are. A rhythmic character must play a part among them and the analogy of tickling is forced upon our notice. It seems less certain whether the character of the pleasurable feeling evoked by the stimulus should be described as a 'specific' one—a 'specific' quality in which the sexual factor would precisely lie. Psychology is still so much in the dark in questions of pleasure and unpleasure that the most cautious assumption is the one most to be recommended. We may later come upon reasons which seem to support the idea that the pleasurable feeling does in fact possess a specific quality.

The character of erotogenicity can be attached to some parts of the body in a particularly marked way. There are predestined erotogenic zones, as is shown by the example of sucking. The same example, however, also shows us that any other part of the skin or mucous membrane can take over the functions of an erotogenic zone, and must therefore have some aptitude in that direction. Thus the quality of the stimulus has more to do with producing the pleasurable feeling than has the nature of the part of the body concerned. A child who is indulging in sensual sucking searches about his body and chooses some part of it to suck—a part which is afterwards preferred by him from force of habit; if he happens to hit upon one of the predestined regions (such as the nipples or genitals) no doubt it retains the preference. A precisely analogous tendency to displacement is also found in the symptomatology of hysteria. In that neurosis repression affects most of all the actual genital zones and these transmit their susceptibility to stimulation to other erotogenic zones (normally neglected in adult life), which then behave exactly like genitals. But besides this, precisely as in the case of sucking, any other part of the body can acquire the same susceptibility to stimulation as is possessed by the genitals and can become an erotogenic zone. Erotogenic and hysterogenic zones show the same characteristics.[1]

THE INFANTILE     The sexual aim of the infantile instinct con-
SEXUAL AIM     sists in obtaining satisfaction by means of an
               appropriate stimulation of the erotogenic zone
which has been selected in one way or another. This satisfaction must have been previously experienced in order to have left behind a need for its repetition; and we may expect that Nature will have made safe provisions so that this experience of satisfaction shall not be left to chance.[2] We have already learnt what the contrivance is that fulfils this purpose in the case of the labial zone: it is the simultaneous connection which links this part of the body with the taking in of food. We shall come across other, similar contrivances as sources of sexuality. The state of being in need of a repetition of the satisfaction reveals itself in two ways: by a peculiar feeling of tension, possessing, rather, the character of unpleasure, and by a sensation of itching or stimulation which is centrally conditioned and projected on to the peripheral erotogenic zone. We can therefore formulate a sexual aim in another way: it consists in replacing the projected sensation of stimulation in the erotogenic zone by an external stimulus which removes that sensation by producing a feeling of satisfaction. This external stimulus will usually consist in some kind of manipulation that is analogous to the sucking.[3]

[1] [*Footnote added* 1915:] After further reflection and after taking other observations into account, I have been led to ascribe the quality of erotogenicity to all parts of the body and to all the internal organs. Cf. also in this connection what is said below on narcissism [p. 217 f.]. [In the 1910 edition only, the following footnote appeared at this point: 'The biological problems relating to the hypothesis of erotogenic zones have been discussed by Alfred Adler (1907).']

[2] [*Footnote added* 1920:] In biological discussions it is scarcely possible to avoid a teleological way of thinking, even though one is aware that in any particular instance one is not secure against error. [Cf. footnote 1, p. 156.]

[3] [This account of the way in which a particular sexual desire becomes established on the basis of an 'experience of satisfaction' is only a special application of Freud's general theory of the mechanism of wishes, as explained in Section C of Chapter VII of *The Interpretation of Dreams*

The fact that the need can also be evoked peripherally, by a real modification of the erotogenic zone, is in complete harmony with our physiological knowledge. This strikes us as somewhat strange only because, in order to remove one stimulus, it seems necessary to adduce a second one at the same spot.

## [4] MASTURBATORY SEXUAL MANIFESTATIONS [1]

It must come as a great relief to find that, when once we have understood the nature of the instinct arising from a single one of the erotogenic zones, we shall have very little more to learn of the sexual activity of children. The clearest distinctions as between one zone and another concern the nature of the contrivance necessary for satisfying the instinct; in the case of the labial zone it consisted of sucking, and this has to be replaced by other muscular actions according to the position and nature of the other zones.

ACTIVITY OF THE ANAL ZONE     Like the labial zone, the anal zone is well suited by its position to act as a medium through which sexuality may attach itself to other somatic functions. It is to be presumed that the erotogenic significance of this part of the body is very great from the first. We learn with some astonishment from psycho-analysis of the transmutations normally undergone by the sexual excitations arising from this zone and of the frequency with which it retains a considerable amount of susceptibility to genital stimulation throughout life.[2] The intestinal disturbances which are so common in childhood see to it that the zone shall not

(1900a, Standard Ed., 5, 565 f.). This theory had already been sketched out by him in his posthumously published 'Project for a Scientific Psychology' (Freud, 1950a, Appendix, Part I, Section 16). In both these passages the example chosen as an illustration is in fact that of an infant at the breast. The whole topic links up with Freud's views on 'reality-testing', as discussed, for instance, in his paper on 'Negation' (1925h).]

[1] Cf. the very copious literature on the subject of masturbation, which for the most part, however, is at sea upon the main issues, e.g. Rohleder (1899). [Added 1915:] See also the report of the discussion on the subject in the Vienna Psycho-Analytical Society (Diskussionen, 1912)—[and especially Freud's own contributions to it (1912f)].

[2] [Footnote added 1910:] Cf. my papers on 'Character and Anal Erotism' (1908b) [added 1920:] and 'On Transformations of Instinct as Exemplified in Anal Erotism' (1917c).

lack intense excitations. Intestinal catarrhs at the tenderest age make children 'nervy', as people say, and in cases of later neurotic illness they have a determining influence on the symptoms in which the neurosis is expressed, and they put at its disposal the whole range of intestinal disturbances. If we bear in mind the erotogenic significance of the outlet of the intestinal canal, which persists, at all events in a modified form, we shall not be inclined to scoff at the influence of haemorrhoids, to which old-fashioned medicine used to attach so much importance in explaining neurotic conditions.

Children who are making use of the susceptibility to erotogenic stimulation of the anal zone betray themselves by holding back their stool till its accumulation brings about violent muscular contractions and, as it passes through the anus, is able to produce powerful stimulation of the mucous membrane. In so doing it must no doubt cause not only painful but also highly pleasurable sensations. One of the clearest signs of subsequent eccentricity or nervousness is to be seen when a baby obstinately refuses to empty his bowels when he is put on the pot—that is, when his nurse wants him to—and holds back that function till he himself chooses to exercise it. He is naturally not concerned with dirtying the bed, he is only anxious not to miss the subsidiary pleasure attached to defaecating. Educators are once more right when they describe children who keep the process back as 'naughty'.

The contents of the bowels,[1] which act as a stimulating mass upon a sexually sensitive portion of mucous membrane, behave like forerunners of another organ, which is destined to come into action after the phase of childhood. But they have other important meanings for the infant. They are clearly treated as a part of the infant's own body and represent his first 'gift': by producing them he can express his active compliance with his environment and, by witholding them, his disobedience. From being a 'gift' they later come to acquire the meaning of 'baby'—for babies, according to one of the sexual theories of children [see below, p. 196], are acquired by eating and are born through the bowels.

The retention of the faecal mass, which is thus carried out intentionally by the child to begin with, in order to serve, as it

[1] [This paragraph was added in 1915. Its contents were expanded in one of the papers (1917c) mentioned in the last footnote.]

were, as a masturbatory stimulus upon the anal zone or to be employed in his relation to the people looking after him, is also one of the roots of the constipation which is so common among neuropaths. Further, the whole significance of the anal zone is reflected in the fact that few neurotics are to be found without their special scatological practices, ceremonies, and so on, which they carefully keep secret.[1]

Actual masturbatory stimulation of the anal zone by means of the finger, provoked by a centrally determined or peripherally maintained sensation of itching, is by no means rare among older children.

ACTIVITY OF THE GENITAL ZONES    Among the erotogenic zones that form part of the child's body there is one which certainly does not play the opening part, and which cannot be the vehicle of the oldest sexual impulses, but which is destined to great things in the future. In both male and female children it is brought into connection with micturition (in the glans and clitoris) and in the former is enclosed in a pouch of mucous membrane, so that there can be no lack of stimulation of it by secretions which may give an early start to sexual excitation. The sexual activities of this erotogenic zone, which forms part of the sexual organs proper, are the beginning of what is later to become 'normal' sexual life. The anatomical situation of this region, the secretions in which it is bathed, the washing and rubbing to which it is subjected in the course of a child's toilet, as well as accidental stimulation (such as the

[1] [*Footnote added* 1920:] Lou Andreas-Salomé (1916), in a paper which has given us a very much deeper understanding of the significance of anal erotism, has shown how the history of the first prohibition which a child comes across—the prohibition against getting pleasure from anal activity and its products—has a decisive effect on his whole development. This must be the first occasion on which the infant has a glimpse of an environment hostile to his instinctual impulses, on which he learns to separate his own entity from this alien one and on which he carries out the first 'repression' of his possibilities for pleasure. From that time on, what is 'anal' remains the symbol of everything that is to be repudiated and excluded from life. The clear-cut distinction between anal and genital processes which is later insisted upon is contradicted by the close anatomical and functional analogies and relations which hold between them. The genital apparatus remains the neighbour of the cloaca, and actually [to quote Lou Andreas-Salomé] 'in the case of women is only taken from it on lease'.

movement of intestinal worms in the case of girls), make it inevitable that the pleasurable feeling which this part of the body is capable of producing should be noticed by children even during their earliest infancy, and should give rise to a need for its repetition. If we consider this whole range of contrivances and bear in mind that both making a mess and measures for keeping clean are bound to operate in much the same way, it is scarcely possible to avoid the conclusion that the foundations for the future primacy over sexual activity exercised by this erotogenic zone are established by early infantile masturbation, which scarcely a single individual escapes.[1] The action which disposes of the stimulus and brings about satisfaction consists in a rubbing movement with the hand or in the application of pressure (no doubt on the lines of a preexisting reflex) either from the hand or by bringing the thighs together. This last method is by far the more common in the case of girls. The preference for the hand which is shown by boys is already evidence of the important contribution which the instinct for mastery is destined to make to masculine sexual activity.[2]

It will be in the interests of clarity[3] if I say at once that three

---

[1] [In the editions of 1905 and 1910 the last part of this sentence read: 'it is difficult to overlook Nature's purpose of establishing the future primacy over sexual activity exercised by this erotogenic zone by means of early infantile masturbation, which scarcely a single individual escapes.' The teleological nature of this argument in favour of the universality of infantile masturbation was sharply criticized by Rudolf Reitler in the course of the discussions on that topic in the Vienna Psycho-Analytical Society in 1912 (*Diskussionen*, 1912, 92 f.). In his own contribution to the discussion (ibid., 134; = Freud, 1912*f*), Freud agreed that the phrasing he had used was unfortunate, and undertook to alter it in later reprints. The present version of the sentence was accordingly substituted in 1915.

[2] [*Footnote added* 1915:] Unusual techniques in carrying out masturbation in later years seem to point to the influence of a prohibition against masturbation which has been overcome.

[3] [This paragraph was added in 1915. In the edition of that year there were also added the title of the next paragraph and the parenthesis 'as a rule before the fourth year' in its second sentence. Moreover, in the first sentence of the same paragraph the words 'after a short time' were substituted for the words 'at the onset of the latency period' which had appeared in 1905 and 1910. Finally, in those first two editions, the *following* paragraph began with the words 'During the years of childhood (it has not yet been possible to generalize as to the chronology)

phases of infantile masturbation are to be distinguished. The first of these belongs to early infancy, and the second to the brief efflorescence of sexual activity about the fourth year of life; only the third phase corresponds to pubertal masturbation, which is often the only kind taken into account.

SECOND PHASE     The masturbation of early infancy seems to
OF INFANTILE     disappear after a short time; but it may persist
MASTURBATION     uninterruptedly until puberty, and this would
                 constitute the first great deviation from the
course of development laid down for civilized men. At some point of childhood after early infancy, as a rule before the fourth year, the sexual instinct belonging to the genital zone usually revives and persists again for a time until it is once more suppressed, or it may continue without interruption. This second phase of infantile sexual activity may assume a variety of different forms which can only be determined by a precise analysis of individual cases. But all its details leave behind the deepest (unconscious) impressions in the subject's memory, determine the development of his character, if he is to remain healthy, and the symptomatology of his neurosis, if he is to fall ill after puberty.[1] In the latter case we find that this sexual period has been forgotten and that the conscious memories that bear witness to it have been displaced. (I have already mentioned that I am also inclined to relate normal infantile amnesia to this infantile sexual activity.) Psycho-analytic investigation enables us to make what has been forgotten conscious and thus do away with a compulsion that arises from the unconscious psychical material.

the sexual excitation of early infancy returns . . .' The motive for all these changes made in 1915 was evidently to distinguish more sharply between the second and first phases of infantile sexual activity and to assign a more precise date—'about the fourth year'—to the second phase.]

[1] [*Footnote added* 1915:] The problem of why the sense of guilt of neurotics is, as Bleuler [1913] recently recognized, regularly attached to the memory of some masturbatory activity, usually at puberty, still awaits an exhaustive analytic explanation. [*Added* 1920:] The most general and most important factor concerned must no doubt be that masturbation represents the executive agency of the whole of infantile sexuality and is, therefore, able to take over the sense of guilt attaching to it.

RETURN OF            During the years of childhood with which
EARLY INFANTILE      I am now dealing, the sexual excitation of
MASTURBATION         early infancy returns, either as a centrally
                     determined tickling stimulus which seeks
satisfaction in masturbation, or as a process in the nature of
a nocturnal emission which, like the nocturnal emissions of
adult years, achieves satisfaction without the help of any action
by the subject. The latter case is the more frequent with
girls and in the second half of childhood; its determinants
are not entirely intelligible and often, though not invariably, it
seems to be conditioned by a period of earlier *active* masturbation. The symptoms of these sexual manifestations are scanty;
they are mostly displayed on behalf of the still undeveloped
sexual apparatus by the *urinary* apparatus, which thus acts, as it
were, as the former's trustee. Most of the so-called bladder disorders of this period are sexual disturbances: nocturnal enuresis,
unless it represents an epileptic fit, corresponds to a nocturnal
emission.

The reappearance of sexual activity is determined by internal
causes and external contingencies, both of which can be guessed
in cases of neurotic illness from the form taken by their symptoms and can be discovered with certainty by psycho-analytic
investigation. I shall have to speak presently of the internal
causes; great and lasting importance attaches at this period to
the accidental *external* contingencies. In the foreground we find
the effects of seduction, which treats a child as a sexual object
prematurely and teaches him, in highly emotional circumstances, how to obtain satisfaction from his genital zones, a
satisfaction which he is then usually obliged to repeat again
and again by masturbation. An influence of this kind may
originate either from adults or from other children. I cannot
admit that in my paper on 'The Aetiology of Hysteria' (1896c)
I exaggerated the frequency or importance of that influence,
though I did not then know that persons who remain normal
may have had the same experiences in their childhood, and
though I consequently overrated the importance of seduction in
comparison with the factors of sexual constitution and development.[1] Obviously seduction is not required in order to arouse

---

[1] [See Freud's detailed discussion of this in his second paper on the
part played by sexuality in the neuroses (1906a: this volume, p. 274).]
Havelock Ellis [1913, Appendix B] has published a number of auto-

a child's sexual life; that can also come about spontaneously from internal causes.

POLYMORPHOUSLY PERVERSE DISPOSITION It is an instructive fact that under the influence of seduction children can become polymorphously perverse, and can be led into all possible kinds of sexual irregularities. This shows that an aptitude for them is innately present in their disposition. There is consequently little resistance towards carrying them out, since the mental dams against sexual excesses—shame, disgust and morality—have either not yet been constructed at all or are only in course of construction, according to the age of the child. In this respect children behave in the same kind of way as an average uncultivated woman in whom the same polymorphously perverse disposition persists. Under ordinary conditions she may remain normal sexually, but if she is led on by a clever seducer she will find every sort of perversion to her taste, and will retain them as part of her own sexual activities. Prostitutes exploit the same polymorphous, that is, infantile, disposition for the purposes of their profession; and, considering the immense number of women who are prostitutes or who must be supposed to have an aptitude for prostitution without becoming engaged in it, it becomes impossible not to recognize that this same disposition to perversions of every kind is a general and fundamental human characteristic.

COMPONENT INSTINCTS Moreover, the effects of seduction do not help to reveal the early history of the sexual instinct; they rather confuse our view of it by presenting children prematurely with a sexual object for which the infantile sexual instinct at first shows no need. It must, however, be admitted that infantile sexual life, in spite of the preponderating

biographical narratives written by people who remained predominantly normal in later life and describing the first sexual impulses of their childhood and the occasions which gave rise to them. These reports naturally suffer from the fact that they omit the prehistoric period of the writers' sexual lives, which is veiled by infantile amnesia and which can only be filled in by psycho-analysis in the case of an individual who has developed a neurosis. In more than one respect, nevertheless, the statements are valuable, and similar narratives were what led me to make the modification in my aetiological hypotheses which I have mentioned in the text.

dominance of erotogenic zones, exhibits components which from the very first involve other people as sexual objects. Such are the instincts of scopophilia, exhibitionism and cruelty, which appear in a sense independently of erotogenic zones; these instincts do not enter into intimate relations with genital[1] life until later, but are already to be observed in childhood as independent impulses, distinct in the first instance from erotogenic sexual activity. Small children are essentially without shame, and at some periods of their earliest years show an unmistakable satisfaction in exposing their bodies, with especial emphasis on the sexual parts. The counterpart of this supposedly perverse inclination, curiosity to see other people's genitals, probably does not become manifest until somewhat later in childhood, when the obstacle set up by a sense of shame has already reached a certain degree of development.[2] Under the influence of seduction the scopophilic perversion can attain great importance in the sexual life of a child. But my researches into the early years of normal people, as well as of neurotic patients, force me to the conclusion that scopophilia can also appear in children as a spontaneous manifestation. Small children whose attention has once been drawn—as a rule by masturbation—to their own genitals usually take the further step without help from outside and develop a lively interest in the genitals of their playmates. Since opportunities for satisfying curiosity of this kind usually occur only in the course of satisfying the two kinds of need for excretion, children of this kind turn into *voyeurs*, eager spectators of the processes of micturition and defaecation. When repression of these inclinations sets in, the desire to see other people's genitals (whether of their own or the opposite sex) persists as a tormenting compulsion, which in some cases of neurosis later affords the strongest motive force for the formation of symptoms.

The cruel component of the sexual instinct develops in childhood even more independently of the sexual activities that are attached to erotogenic zones. Cruelty in general comes easily

---

[1] ['Sexual' in 1905 and 1910.]

[2] [In the first (1905) edition this sentence read: 'The counterpart . . . does not join in until later in childhood, when. . . .' In 1910 the word 'probably' was inserted; in 1915 'join in' was replaced by 'become manifest'; and in 1920 'somewhat' was inserted before 'later'.—The subject of exhibitionism in young children had been discussed at some length by Freud in his *Interpretation of Dreams*, Chapter V, Section D (α) (Standard Ed., **4**, 224 f.).]

to the childish nature, since the obstacle that brings the instinct for mastery to a halt at another person's pain—namely a capacity for pity—is developed relatively late. The fundamental psychological analysis of this instinct has, as we know, not yet been satisfactorily achieved. It may be assumed that the impulse of cruelty arises from the instinct for mastery and appears at a period of sexual life at which the genitals have not yet taken over their later role. It then dominates a phase of sexual life which we shall later describe as a pregenital organization.[1] Children who distinguish themselves by special cruelty towards animals and playmates usually give rise to a just suspicion of an intense and precocious sexual activity arising from erotogenic zones; and, though all the sexual instincts may display simultaneous precocity, *erotogenic* sexual activity seems, nevertheless, to be the primary one. The absence of the barrier of pity brings with it a danger that the connection between the cruel and the erotogenic instincts, thus established in childhood, may prove unbreakable in later life. Ever since Jean Jacques Rousseau's *Confessions*, it has been well known to all educationalists that the painful stimulation of the skin of the buttocks is one of the erotogenic roots of the *passive* instinct of cruelty (masochism). The conclusion has rightly been drawn by them that corporal punishment, which is usually applied to this part of the body, should not be inflicted upon any children whose libido is liable to be forced into collateral channels by the later demands of cultural education.[2]

[1] [The last two sentences were given their present form in 1915. In 1905 and 1910 they read as follows: 'It may be assumed that the impulses of cruelty arise from sources which are in fact independent of sexuality, but may become united with it at an early stage owing to an anastomosis [cross-connection] near their points of origin. Observation teaches us, however, that sexual development and the development of the instinct of scopophilia and cruelty are subject to mutual influences which limit this presumed independence of the two sets of instincts.']

[2] [*Footnote added* 1910:] When the account which I have given above of infantile sexuality was first published in 1905, it was founded for the most part on the results of psycho-analytic research upon adults. At that time it was impossible to make full use of direct observation on children: only isolated hints and some valuable pieces of confirmation came from that source. Since then it has become possible to gain direct insight into infantile psycho-sexuality by the analysis of some cases of neurotic illness during the early years of childhood. It is gratifying to be able to report that direct observation has fully confirmed the conclusions

## [5] THE SEXUAL RESEARCHES OF CHILDHOOD [1]

THE INSTINCT          At about the same time as the sexual life
FOR KNOWLEDGE    of children reaches its first peak, between
                              the ages of three and five, they also begin to
show signs of the activity which may be ascribed to the instinct
for knowledge or research. This instinct cannot be counted
among the elementary instinctual components, nor can it be
classed as exclusively belonging to sexuality. Its activity corresponds on the one hand to a sublimated manner of obtaining
mastery, while on the other hand it makes use of the energy of
scopophilia. Its relations to sexual life, however, are of particular
importance, since we have learnt from psycho-analysis that the
instinct for knowledge in children is attracted unexpectedly
early and intensively to sexual problems and is in fact possibly
first aroused by them.

THE RIDDLE OF        It is not by theoretical interests but by
THE SPHINX            practical ones that activities of research are
                              set going in children. The threat to the bases
of a child's existence offered by the discovery or the suspicion

arrived at by psycho-analysis—which is incidentally good evidence of
the trustworthiness of that method of research. In addition to this, the
'Analysis of a Phobia in a Five-Year-Old Boy' (1909*b*) has taught us
much that is new for which we have not been prepared by psycho-
analysis: for instance, the fact that sexual symbolism—the representation of what is sexual by non-sexual objects and relations—extends back
into the first years of possession of the power of speech. I was further
made aware of a defect in the account I have given in the text, which,
in the interests of lucidity, describes the conceptual distinction between
the two phases of auto-erotism and object-love as though it were also a
separation in time. But the analyses that I have just mentioned, as well
as the findings of Bell quoted on p. 173, *n.* 2, above, show that children
between the ages of three and five are capable of very clear object-
choice, accompanied by strong affects.—[In 1910 only, this footnote
continued as follows: 'Another addition to our knowledge of infantile
sexual life which has not yet been mentioned in the text relates to the
sexual researches of children, to the theories to which children are led
by them (cf. my paper on the subject, 1908*c*), to the important bearing
of these theories upon later neuroses, to the outcome of these infantile
researches and to their relation to the development of children's intellectual powers.']

  [1] [The whole of this section on the sexual researches of children first
appeared in 1915.]

of the arrival of a new baby and the fear that he may, as a result of it, cease to be cared for and loved, make him thoughtful and clear-sighted. And this history of the instinct's origin is in line with the fact that the first problem with which it deals is not the question of the distinction between the sexes but the riddle of where babies come from.[1] (This, in a distorted form which can easily be rectified, is the same riddle that was propounded by the Theban Sphinx.) On the contrary, the existence of two sexes does not to begin with arouse any difficulties or doubts in children. It is self-evident to a male child that a genital like his own is to be attributed to everyone he knows, and he cannot make its absence tally with his picture of these other people.

CASTRATION COMPLEX AND PENIS ENVY   This conviction is energetically maintained by boys, is obstinately defended against the contradictions which soon result from observation, and is only abandoned after severe internal struggles (the castration complex). The substitutes for this penis which they feel is missing in women play a great part in determining the form taken by many perversions.[2]

The assumption that all human beings have the same (male) form of genital is the first of the many remarkable and momentous sexual theories of children. It is of little use to a child that the science of biology justifies his prejudice and has been obliged to recognize the female clitoris as a true substitute for the penis.

Little girls do not resort to denial of this kind when they see that boys' genitals are formed differently from their own. They are ready to recognize them immediately and are overcome by envy for the penis—an envy culminating in the wish, which is so important in its consequences, to be boys themselves.

[1] [In a later work, Freud (1925*j*) corrected this statement, saying that it is not true of girls, and not always true of boys.]

[2] [*Footnote added* 1920:] We are justified in speaking of a castration complex in women as well. Both male and female children form a theory that women no less than men originally had a penis, but that they have lost it by castration. The conviction which is finally reached by males that women have no penis often leads them to an enduringly low opinion of the other sex.

THEORIES      Many people can remember clearly what an
OF BIRTH      intense interest they took during the prepubertal
              period in the question of where babies come from.
The anatomical answers to the question were at the time very
various: babies come out of the breast, or are cut out of the
body, or the navel opens to let them through.[1] Outside analysis,
there are very seldom memories of any similar researches having
been carried out in the *early* years of childhood. These earlier
researches fell a victim to repression long since, but all their
findings were of a uniform nature: people get babies by eating
some particular thing (as they do in fairy tales) and babies are
born through the bowel like a discharge of faeces. These infantile
theories remind us of conditions that exist in the animal king-
dom—and especially of the cloaca in types of animals lower
than mammals.

SADISTIC VIEW     If children at this early age witness sexual
OF SEXUAL         intercourse between adults—for which an op-
INTERCOURSE       portunity is provided by the conviction of
                  grown-up people that small children cannot
understand anything sexual—they inevitably regard the sexual
act as a sort of ill-treatment or act of subjugation: they view
it, that is, in a sadistic sense. Psycho-analysis also shows us that
an impression of this kind in early childhood contributes a great
deal towards a predisposition to a subsequent sadistic displacement of the sexual aim. Furthermore, children are much concerned with the problem of what sexual intercourse—or, as
they put it, being married—consists in: and they usually seek
a solution of the mystery in some common activity concerned
with the function of micturition or defaecation.

TYPICAL FAILURE       We can say in general of the sexual
OF INFANTILE          theories of children that they are reflec-
SEXUAL RESEARCHES     tions of their own sexual constitution,
                      and that in spite of their grotesque errors
the theories show more understanding of sexual processes than
one would have given their creators credit for. Children also

---

[1] [*Footnote added* 1924:] In these later years of childhood there is a
great wealth of sexual theories, of which only a few examples are given
in the text.

perceive the alterations that take place in their mother owing to pregnancy and are able to interpret them correctly. The fable of the stork is often told to an audience that receives it with deep, though mostly silent, mistrust. There are, however, two elements that remain undiscovered by the sexual researches of children: the fertilizing role of semen and the existence of the female sexual orifice—the same elements, incidentally, in which the infantile organization is itself undeveloped. It therefore follows that the efforts of the childish investigator are habitually fruitless, and end in a renunciation which not infrequently leaves behind it a permanent injury to the instinct for knowledge. The sexual researches of these early years of childhood are always carried out in solitude. They constitute a first step towards taking an independent attitude in the world, and imply a high degree of alienation of the child from the people in his environment who formerly enjoyed his complete confidence.

## [6] THE PHASES OF DEVELOPMENT OF THE SEXUAL ORGANIZATION [1]

The characteristics of infantile sexual life which we have hitherto emphasized are the facts that it is essentially auto-erotic (i.e. that it finds its object in the infant's own body) and that its individual component instincts are upon the whole disconnected and independent of one another in their search for pleasure. The final outcome of sexual development lies in what is known as the normal sexual life of the adult, in which the pursuit of pleasure comes under the sway of the reproductive function and in which the component instincts, under the primacy of a single erotogenic zone, form a firm organization directed towards a sexual aim attached to some extraneous sexual object.

PREGENITAL          The study, with the help of psycho-analysis,
ORGANIZATIONS    of the inhibitions and disturbances of this pro-
                          cess of development enables us to recognize
abortive beginnings and preliminary stages of a firm organization of the component instincts such as this—preliminary stages

[1] [The whole of this section, too, first appeared in 1915. The concept of a 'pregenital organization' of sexual life seems to have been first

which themselves constitute a sexual régime of a sort. These phases of sexual organization are normally passed through smoothly, without giving more than a hint of their existence. It is only in pathological cases that they become active and recognizable to superficial observation.

We shall give the name of 'pregenital' to organizations of sexual life in which the genital zones have not yet taken over their predominant part. We have hitherto identified two such organizations, which almost seem as though they were harking back to early animal forms of life.

The first of these is the oral or, as it might be called, cannibalistic pregenital sexual organization. Here sexual activity has not yet been separated from the ingestion of food; nor are opposite currents within the activity differentiated. The *object* of both activities is the same; the sexual *aim* consists in the incorporation of the object—the prototype of a process which, in the form of identification, is later to play such an important psychological part. A relic of this constructed phase of organization, which is forced upon our notice by pathology, may be seen in thumb-sucking, in which the sexual activity, detached from the nutritive activity, has substituted for the extraneous object one situated in the subject's own body.[1]

A second pregenital phase is that of the sadistic-anal organization. Here the opposition between two currents, which runs through all sexual life, is already developed: they cannot yet, however, be described as 'masculine' and 'feminine', but only as 'active' and 'passive'. The *activity* is put into operation by the instinct for mastery through the agency of the somatic musculature; the organ which, more than any other, represents the *passive* sexual aim is the erotogenic mucous membrane of the anus. Both of these currents have objects, which, however, are not identical. Alongside these, other component instincts operate in an auto-erotic manner. In this phase, therefore, sexual

introduced by Freud in his paper on 'The Predisposition to Obsessional Neurosis' (1913*i*), which, however, deals only with the sadistic-anal organization. The oral organization was apparently recognized as such for the first time in the present passage.]

[1] [*Footnote added* 1920:] For remnants of this phase in adult neurotics, cf. Abraham (1916). [*Added* 1924:] In another, later work (1924) the same writer has divided both this oral phase, and also the later sadistic-anal one, into two sub-divisions, which are characterized by differing attitudes towards the object.

polarity and an extraneous object are already observable. But organization and subordination to the reproductive function are still absent.[1]

AMBIVALENCE This form of sexual organization can persist throughout life and can permanently attract a large portion of sexual activity to itself. The predominance in it of sadism and the cloacal part played by the anal zone give it a quite peculiarly archaic colouring. It is further characterized by the fact that in it the opposing pairs of instincts are developed to an approximately equal extent, a state of affairs described by Bleuler's happily chosen term 'ambivalence'.

The assumption of the existence of pregenital organizations of sexual life is based on the analysis of the neuroses, and without a knowledge of them can scarcely be appreciated. Further analytic investigation may be expected to provide us with far more information on the structure and development of the normal sexual function.

In order to complete our picture of infantile sexual life, we must also suppose that the choice of an object, such as we have shown to be characteristic of the pubertal phase of development, has already frequently or habitually been effected during the years of childhood: that is to say, the whole of the sexual currents have become directed towards a single person in relation to whom they seek to achieve their aims. This then is the closest approximation possible in childhood to the final form taken by sexual life after puberty. The only difference lies in the fact that in childhood the combination of the component instincts and their subordination under the primacy of the genitals have been effected only very incompletely or not at all. Thus the establishment of that primacy in the service of reproduction is the last phase through which the organization of sexuality passes.[2]

---

[1] [*Footnote added* 1924:] Abraham, in the paper last quoted (1924), points out that the anus is developed from the embryonic blastopore—a fact which seems like a biological prototype of psychosexual development.

[2] [*Footnote added* 1924:] At a later date (1923), I myself modified this account by inserting a third phase in the development of childhood, subsequent to the two pregenital organizations. This phase, which already deserves to be described as genital, presents a sexual object and some degree of convergence of the sexual impulses upon that object; but it

DIPHASIC CHOICE          It may be regarded as typical of the choice
OF OBJECT                of an object that the process is diphasic, that
                         is, that it occurs in two waves. The first of
these begins between the ages of two [1] and five, and is brought to
a halt or to a retreat by the latency period; it is characterized
by the infantile nature of the sexual aims. The second wave sets
in with puberty and determines the final outcome of sexual life.

Although the diphasic nature of object-choice comes down in
essentials to no more than the operation of the latency period,
it is of the highest importance in regard to disturbances of that
final outcome. The resultants of infantile object-choice are
carried over into the later period. They either persist as such
or are revived at the actual time of puberty. But as a consequence of the repression which has developed between the
two phases they prove unutilizable. Their sexual aims have become mitigated and they now represent what may be described
as the 'affectionate current' of sexual life. Only psycho-analytic
investigation can show that behind this affection, admiration
and respect there lie concealed the old sexual longings of the
infantile component instincts which have now become unserviceable. The object-choice of the pubertal period is obliged
to dispense with the objects of childhood and to start afresh as a
'sensual current'. Should these two currents fail to converge,
the result is often that one of the ideals of sexual life, the focusing
of all desires upon a single object, will be unattainable.

## [7] THE SOURCES OF INFANTILE SEXUALITY

Our efforts to trace the origins of the sexual instinct have
shown us so far that sexual excitation arises (*a*) as a reproduction
of a satisfaction experienced in connection with other organic
processes, (*b*) through appropriate peripheral stimulation of
erotogenic zones and (*c*) as an expression of certain 'instincts'

is differentiated from the final organization of sexual maturity in one
essential respect. For it knows only one kind of genital: the male one.
For that reason I have named it the 'phallic' stage of organization. (Freud,
1923*e*.) According to Abraham [1924], it has a biological prototype in
the embryo's undifferentiated genital disposition, which is the same for
both sexes.

    [1] [In 1915 this figure was 'three'; it was altered to 'two' in 1920. Cf.
also the end of the footnote on p. 222.]

(such as the scopophilic instinct and the instinct of cruelty) of which the origin is not yet completely intelligible. Psychoanalytic investigation, reaching back into childhood from a later time, and contemporary observation of children combine to indicate to us still other regularly active sources of sexual excitation. The direct observation of children has the disadvantage of working upon data which are easily misunderstandable; psycho-analysis is made difficult by the fact that it can only reach its data, as well as its conclusions, after long détours. But by co-operation the two methods can attain a satisfactory degree of certainty in their findings.

We have already discovered in examining the erotogenic zones that these regions of the skin merely show a special intensification of a kind of susceptibility to stimulus which is possessed in a certain degree by the whole cutaneous surface. We shall therefore not be surprised to find that very definite erotogenic effects are to be ascribed to certain kinds of general stimulation of the skin. Among these we may especially mention thermal stimuli, whose importance may help us to understand the therapeutic effects of warm baths.

MECHANICAL     At this point we must also mention the pro-
EXCITATIONS    duction of sexual excitation by rhythmic mech-
               anical agitation of the body. Stimuli of this kind
operate in three different ways: on the sensory apparatus of the vestibular nerves, on the skin, and on the deeper parts (e.g. the muscles and articular structures). The existence of these pleasurable sensations—and it is worth emphasizing the fact that in this connection the concepts of 'sexual excitation' and 'satisfaction' can to a great extent be used without distinction, a circumstance which we must later endeavour to explain [p. 212] —the existence, then, of these pleasurable sensations, caused by forms of mechanical agitation of the body, is confirmed by the fact that children are so fond of games of passive movement, such as swinging and being thrown up into the air, and insist on such games being incessantly repeated.[1] It is well known

[1] Some people can remember that in swinging they felt the impact of moving air upon their genitals as an immediate sexual pleasure. [A specific instance of this is quoted in a footnote to a passage in *The Interpretation of Dreams* (1900a, near the end of Chapter V) in which this whole topic is discussed (Standard Ed., **4**, 272).]

that rocking is habitually used to induce sleep in restless children. The shaking produced by driving in carriages and later by railway-travel exercises such a fascinating effect upon older children that every boy, at any rate, has at one time or other in his life wanted to be an engine driver or a coachman. It is a puzzling fact that boys take such an extraordinarily intense interest in things connected with railways, and, at the age at which the production of phantasies is most active (shortly before puberty), use those things as the nucleus of a symbolism that is peculiarly sexual. A compulsive link of this kind between railway-travel and sexuality is clearly derived from the pleasurable character of the sensations of movement. In the event of repression, which turns so many childish preferences into their opposite, these same individuals, when they are adolescents or adults, will react to rocking or swinging with a feeling of nausea, will be terribly exhausted by a railway journey, or will be subject to attacks of anxiety on the journey and will protect themselves against a repetition of the painful experience by a dread of railway-travel.

Here again we must mention the fact, which is not yet understood, that the combination of fright and mechanical agitation produces the severe, hysteriform, traumatic neurosis. It may at least be assumed that these influences, which, when they are of small intensity, become sources of sexual excitation, lead to a profound disorder in the sexual mechanism or chemistry[1] if they operate with exaggerated force.

MUSCULAR ACTIVITY        We are all familiar with the fact that children feel a need for a large amount of active muscular exercise and derive extraordinary pleasure from satisfying it. Whether this pleasure has any connection with sexuality, whether it itself comprises sexual satisfaction or whether it can become the occasion of sexual excitation—all of this is open to critical questioning, which may indeed also be directed against the view maintained in the previous paragraphs that the pleasure derived from sensations of *passive* movement is of a sexual nature or may produce sexual excitation. It is, however, a fact that a number of people report that they experienced the first signs of excitement in their genitals while they were romping or wrestling with playmates—a situation in

[1] [The last two words were added in 1924.]

which, apart from general muscular exertion, there is a large amount of contact with the skin of the opponent. An inclination to physical struggles with some one particular person, just as in later years an inclination to *verbal* disputes,[1] is a convincing sign that object-choice has fallen on him. One of the roots of the sadistic instinct would seem to lie in the encouragement of sexual excitation by muscular activity. In many people the infantile connection between romping and sexual excitation is among the determinants of the direction subsequently taken by their sexual instinct.[2]

AFFECTIVE PROCESSES  The further sources of sexual excitation in children are open to less doubt. It is easy to establish, whether by contemporary observation or by subsequent research, that all comparatively intense affective processes, including even terrifying ones, trench upon sexuality—a fact which may incidentally help to explain the pathogenic effect of emotions of that kind. In schoolchildren dread of going in for an examination or tension over a difficult piece of work can be important not only in affecting the child's relations at school but also in bringing about an irruption of sexual manifestations. For quite often in such circumstances a stimulus may be felt which urges the child to touch his genitals, or something may take place akin to a nocturnal emission with all its bewildering consequences. The behaviour of children at school, which confronts a teacher with plenty of puzzles, deserves in general to be brought into relation with their budding sexuality. The sexually exciting effect of many emotions which are in themselves unpleasurable, such as feelings of apprehension, fright or horror, persists in a great number of people throughout their adult life. There is no doubt that this is the explanation of why so many people seek opportunities for sensations of this kind, subject to the proviso that the seriousness of the unpleasurable feeling is damped down by certain qualifying facts, such

---

[1] 'Was sich liebt, das neckt sich.' [Lovers' quarrels are proverbial.]

[2] [*Footnote added* 1910:] The analysis of cases of neurotic abasia and agoraphobia removes all doubt as to the sexual nature of pleasure in movement. Modern education, as we know, makes great use of games in order to divert young people from sexual activity. It would be more correct to say that in these young people it replaces sexual enjoyment by pleasure in movement—and forces sexual activity back to one of its auto-erotic components.

as its occurring in an imaginary world, in a book or in a play.

If we assume that a similar erotogenic effect attaches even to intensely painful feelings, especially when the pain is toned down or kept at a distance by some accompanying condition, we should here have one of the main roots of the masochistic-sadistic instinct, into whose numerous complexities we are very gradually gaining some insight.[1]

INTELLECTUAL     Finally, it is an unmistakable fact that con-
WORK           centration of the attention upon an intellectual
               task and intellectual strain in general produce
a concomitant sexual excitation in many young people as well as adults. This is no doubt the only justifiable basis for what is in other respects the questionable practice of ascribing nervous disorders to intellectual 'overwork'.[2]


If we now cast our eyes over the tentative suggestions which I have made as to the sources of infantile sexual excitation, though I have not described them completely nor enumerated them fully, the following conclusions emerge with more or less certainty. It seems that the fullest provisions are made for setting in motion the process of sexual excitation—a process the nature of which has, it must be confessed, become highly obscure to us. The setting in motion of this process is first and foremost provided for in a more or less direct fashion by the excitations of the sensory surfaces—the skin and the sense organs—and, most directly of all, by the operation of stimuli on certain areas known as erotogenic zones. The decisive element in these sources of sexual excitation is no doubt the *quality* of the stimuli, though the factor of intensity, in the case of pain, is not a matter of complete indifference. But apart from these sources there are present in the organism contrivances which bring it about that in the case of a great number of internal processes sexual excitation arises as a concomitant effect, as soon as the intensity

---

[1] [*Footnote added* 1924:] I am here referring to what is known as 'erotogenic' masochism. [See footnote 2, p. 158.]

[2] [Some earlier remarks by Freud on this subject will be found in the middle of his first paper on 'Sexuality in the Aetiology of the Neuroses' (1898a), and some later ones in a footnote to Section III of 'Analysis Terminable and Interminable' (1937c).]

of those processes passes beyond certain quantitative limits. What we have called the component instincts of sexuality are either derived directly from these internal sources or are composed of elements both from those sources and from the erotogenic zones. It may well be that nothing of considerable importance can occur in the organism without contributing some component to the excitation of the sexual instinct.

It does not seem to me possible at present to state these general conclusions with any greater clarity or certainty. For this I think two factors are responsible: first, the novelty of the whole method of approach to the subject, and secondly, the fact that the whole nature of sexual excitation is completely unknown to us. Nevertheless I am tempted to make two observations which promise to open out wide future prospects:

VARIETIES OF SEXUAL CONSTITUTION  (a) Just as we saw previously [p. 171] that it was possible to derive a multiplicity of innate sexual constitutions from variety in the development of the erotogenic zones, so we can now make a similar attempt by including the *indirect* sources of sexual excitation. It may be assumed that, although contributions are made from these sources in the case of everyone, they are not in all cases of equal strength, and that further help towards the differentiation of sexual constitutions may be found in the varying development of the individual sources of sexual excitation.[1]

PATHWAYS OF MUTUAL INFLUENCE  (b) If we now drop the figurative expression that we have so long adopted in speaking of the 'sources' of sexual excitation, we are led to the suspicion that all the connecting pathways that lead from other functions to sexuality must also be traversable in the reverse direction. If, for instance, the common possession of the labial zone by the two functions is the reason why sexual satisfaction arises during the taking of nourishment, then the

[1] [*Footnote added* 1920:] An inevitable consequence of these considerations is that we must regard each individual as possessing an oral erotism, an anal erotism, a urethral erotism, etc., and that the existence of mental complexes corresponding to these implies no judgement of abnormality or neurosis. The differences separating the normal from the abnormal can lie only in the relative strength of the individual components of the sexual instinct and in the use to which they are put in the course of development.

same factor also enables us to understand why there should be disorders of nutrition if the erotogenic functions of the common zone are disturbed. Or again, if we know that concentration of attention may give rise to sexual excitation, it seems plausible to assume that by making use of the same path, but in a contrary direction, the condition of sexual excitation may influence the possibility of directing the attention. A good portion of the symptomatology of the neuroses, which I have traced to disturbances of the sexual processes, is expressed in disturbances of other, non-sexual, somatic functions; and this circumstance, which has hitherto been unintelligible, becomes less puzzling if it is only the counterpart of the influences which bring about the production of sexual excitation.

The same pathways, however, along which sexual disturbances trench upon the other somatic functions must also perform another important function in normal health. They must serve as paths for the attraction of sexual instinctual forces to aims that are other than sexual, that is to say, for the sublimation of sexuality. But we must end with a confession that very little is as yet known with certainty of these pathways, though they certainly exist and can probably be traversed in both directions.

# THE TRANSFORMATIONS OF PUBERTY

WITH the arrival of puberty, changes set in which are destined to give infantile sexual life its final, normal shape. The sexual instinct has hitherto been predominantly auto-erotic; it now finds a sexual object. Its activity has hitherto been derived from a number of separate instincts and erotogenic zones, which, independently of one another, have pursued a certain sort of pleasure as their sole sexual aim. Now, however, a new sexual aim appears, and all the component instincts combine to attain it, while the erotogenic zones become subordinated to the primacy of the genital zone.[1] Since the new sexual aim assigns very different functions to the two sexes, their sexual development now diverges greatly. That of males is the more straightforward and the more understandable, while that of females actually enters upon a kind of involution. A normal sexual life is only assured by an exact convergence of the affectionate current and the sensual current both being directed towards the sexual object and sexual aim. (The former, the affectionate current, comprises what remains over of the infantile efflorescence of sexuality.)[2] It is like the completion of a tunnel which has been driven through a hill from both directions.

The new sexual aim in men consists in the discharge of the sexual products. The earlier one, the attainment of pleasure, is by no means alien to it; on the contrary, the highest degree of pleasure is attached to this final act of the sexual process. The sexual instinct is now subordinated to the reproductive function; it becomes, so to say, altruistic. If this transformation is to succeed, the original dispositions and all the other characteristics of the instincts must be taken into account in the process. Just as on any other occasion on which the organism should by

---

[1] [*Footnote added* 1915:] The schematic picture which I have given in the text aims at emphasizing differences. I have already shown on p. 199 the extent to which infantile sexuality, owing to its choice of object and to the development of the phallic phase, approximates to the final sexual organization. [See also below, p. 222].

[2] [This sentence was added in 1920.]

rights make new combinations and adjustments leading to complicated mechanisms, here too there are possibilities of pathological disorders if these new arrangements are not carried out. Every pathological disorder of sexual life is rightly to be regarded as an inhibition in development.

## [1] THE PRIMACY OF THE GENITAL ZONES AND FORE-PLEASURE

The starting-point and the final aim of the process which I have described are clearly visible. The intermediate steps are still in many ways obscure to us. We shall have to leave more than one of them as an unsolved riddle.

The most striking of the processes at puberty has been picked upon as constituting its essence: the manifest growth of the external genitalia. (The latency period of childhood is, on the other hand, characterized by a relative cessation of their growth.) In the meantime the development of the internal genitalia has advanced far enough for them to be able to discharge the sexual products or, as the case may be, to bring about the formation of a new living organism. Thus a highly complicated apparatus has been made ready and awaits the moment of being put into operation.

This apparatus is to be set in motion by stimuli, and observation shows us that stimuli can impinge on it from three directions: from the external world by means of the excitation of the erotogenic zones with which we are already familiar, from the organic interior by ways which we have still to explore, and from mental life, which is itself a storehouse for external impressions and a receiving-post for internal excitations. All three kinds of stimuli produce the same effect, namely a condition described as 'sexual excitement', which shows itself by two sorts of indication, mental and somatic. The mental indications consist in a peculiar feeling of tension of an extremely compelling character; and among the numerous somatic ones are first and foremost a number of changes in the genitals, which have the obvious sense of being preparations for the sexual act—the erection of the male organ and the lubrication of the vagina.

SEXUAL      The fact that sexual excitement possesses the char-
TENSION    acter of tension raises a problem the solution of which
           is no less difficult than it would be important in help-
ing us to understand the sexual processes. In spite of all the
differences of opinion that reign on the subject among psychologists, I must insist that a feeling of tension necessarily involves
unpleasure. What seems to me decisive is the fact that a feeling
of this kind is accompanied by an impulsion to make a change
in the psychological situation, that it operates in an urgent way
which is wholly alien to the nature of the feeling of pleasure. If,
however, the tension of sexual excitement is counted as an unpleasurable feeling, we are at once brought up against the fact
that it is also undoubtedly felt as pleasurable. In every case in
which tension is produced by sexual processes it is accompanied
by pleasure; even in the preparatory changes in the genitals a
feeling of satisfaction of some kind is plainly to be observed.
How, then, are this unpleasurable tension and this feeling of
pleasure to be reconciled?

Everything relating to the problem of pleasure and unpleasure touches upon one of the sorest spots of present-day
psychology. It will be my aim to learn as much as possible from
the circumstances of the instance with which we are at present
dealing, but I shall avoid any approach to the problem as a
whole.[1]

Let us begin by casting a glance at the way in which the
erotogenic zones fit themselves into the new arrangement. They
have to play an important part in introducing sexual excitation.
The eye is perhaps the zone most remote from the sexual object,
but it is the one which, in the situation of wooing an object, is
liable to be the most frequently stimulated by the particular
quality of excitation whose cause, when it occurs in a sexual
object, we describe as beauty. (For the same reason the merits
of a sexual object are described as 'attractions'.)[2] This stimulation is on the one hand already accompanied by pleasure, while
on the other hand it leads to an increase of sexual excitement
or produces it if it is not yet present. If the excitation now
spreads to another erotogenic zone—to the hand, for instance,

---

[1] [*Footnote added* 1924:] I have made an attempt at solving this problem
in the first part of my paper on 'The Economic Problem of Masochism'
(1924c).

[2] [See footnote 2, p. 156.]

through tactile sensations—the effect is the same: a feeling of pleasure on the one side, which is quickly intensified by pleasure arising from the preparatory changes [in the genitals], and on the other side an increase of sexual tension, which soon passes over into the most obvious unpleasure if it cannot be met by a further accession of pleasure. Another instance will perhaps make this even clearer. If an erotogenic zone in a person who is not sexually excited (e.g. the skin of a woman's breast) is stimulated by touch, the contact produces a pleasurable feeling; but it is at the same time better calculated than anything to arouse a sexual excitation that demands an increase of pleasure. The problem is how it can come about that an experience of pleasure can give rise to a need for greater pleasure.

THE MECHANISM OF FORE-PLEASURE    The part played in this by the erotogenic zones, however, is clear. What is true of one of them is true of all. They are all used to provide a certain amount of pleasure by being stimulated in the way appropriate to them. This pleasure then leads to an increase in tension which in its turn is responsible for producing the necessary motor energy for the conclusion of the sexual act. The penultimate stage of that act is once again the appropriate stimulation of an erotogenic zone (the genital zone itself, in the glans penis) by the appropriate object (the mucous membrane of the vagina); and from the pleasure yielded by this excitation the motor energy is obtained, this time by a reflex path, which brings about the discharge of the sexual substances. This last pleasure is the highest in intensity, and its mechanism differs from that of the earlier pleasure. It is brought about entirely by discharge: it is wholly a pleasure of satisfaction and with it the tension of the libido is for the time being extinguished.

This distinction between the one kind of pleasure due to the excitation of erotogenic zones and the other kind due to the discharge of the sexual substances deserves, I think, to be made more concrete by a difference in nomenclature. The former may be suitably described as 'fore-pleasure' in contrast to the 'end-pleasure' or pleasure of satisfaction derived from the sexual act. Fore-pleasure is thus the same pleasure that has already been produced, although on a smaller scale, by the infantile sexual instinct; end-pleasure is something new and is thus probably conditioned by circumstances that do not arise till puberty. The formula for the new function of the erotogenic zones runs therefore: they are used to make possible, through the medium of the fore-pleasure which can be derived from them (as it was during infantile life), the production of the greater pleasure of satisfaction.

I was able recently to throw light upon another instance, in a quite different department of mental life, of a slight feeling of pleasure similarly making possible the attainment of a greater resultant pleasure, and thus operating as an 'incentive bonus'. In the same connection I was also able to go more deeply into the nature of pleasure.[1]

DANGERS OF        The connection between fore-pleasure and
FORE-PLEASURE   infantile sexual life is, however, made clearer
                by the pathogenic part which it can come to
play. The attainment of the normal sexual aim can clearly be endangered by the mechanism in which fore-pleasure is involved. This danger arises if at any point in the preparatory sexual processes the fore-pleasure turns out to be too great and the element of tension too small. The motive for proceeding further with the sexual process then disappears, the whole path is cut short, and the preparatory act in question takes the place of the normal sexual aim. Experience has shown that the precondition for this damaging event is that the erotogenic zone concerned or the corresponding component instinct shall already during childhood have contributed an unusual amount of pleasure. If further factors then come into play, tending to bring about a fixation, a compulsion may easily arise in later life which resists the incorporation of this particular fore-pleasure into a new context. Such is in fact the mechanism of many perversions, which consist in a lingering over the preparatory acts of the sexual process.

This failure of the function of the sexual mechanism owing to fore-pleasure is best avoided if the primacy of the genitals too

[1] See my volume on *Jokes and their Relation to the Unconscious* which appeared in 1905 [near the end of Chapter IV]. The 'fore-pleasure' attained by the technique of joking is used in order to liberate a greater pleasure derived from the removal of internal inhibitions. [In a later paper, on creative writing (1908*e*), Freud attributed a similar mechanism to aesthetic pleasure.]

is adumbrated in childhood; and indeed things seem actually arranged to bring this about in the second half of childhood (from the age of eight to puberty). During these years the genital zones already behave in much the same way as in maturity; they become the seat of sensations of excitation and of preparatory changes whenever any pleasure is felt from the satisfaction of other erotogenic zones, though this result is still without a purpose—that is to say, contributes nothing to a continuation of the sexual process. Already in childhood, therefore, alongside of the pleasure of satisfaction there is a certain amount of sexual tension, although it is less constant and less in quantity. We can now understand why, in discussing the sources of sexuality, we were equally justified in saying of a given process that it was sexually satisfying or sexually exciting. [See p. 201.] It will be noticed that in the course of our enquiry we began by exaggerating the distinction between infantile and mature sexual life, and that we are now setting this right. Not only the deviations from normal sexual life but its normal form as well are determined by the infantile manifestations of sexuality.

## [2] THE PROBLEM OF SEXUAL EXCITATION

We remain in complete ignorance both of the origin and of the nature of the sexual tension which arises simultaneously with the pleasure when erotogenic zones are satisfied.[1] The most obvious explanation, that this tension arises in some way out of the pleasure itself, is not only extremely improbable in itself but becomes untenable when we consider that in connection with the greatest pleasure of all, that which accompanies the discharge of the sexual products, no tension is produced, but on the contrary all tension is removed. Thus pleasure and sexual tension can only be connected in an indirect manner.

[1] It is a highly instructive fact that the German language in its use of the word '*Lust*' takes into account the part played by the preparatory sexual excitations which, as has been explained above, simultaneously produce an element of satisfaction and a contribution to sexual tension. '*Lust*' has two meanings, and is used to describe the sensation of sexual tension ('*Ich habe Lust*' = 'I should like to', 'I feel an impulse to') as well as the feeling of satisfaction. [Cf. footnote 2, p. 135.]

PART PLAYED        Apart from the fact that normally it is only
BY THE SEXUAL    the discharge of the sexual substances that
SUBSTANCES        brings sexual excitation to an end, there are
                          other points of contact between sexual ten-
sion and the sexual products. In the case of a man living a
continent life, the sexual apparatus, at varying intervals, which,
however, are not ungoverned by rules, discharges the sexual
substances during the night, to the accompaniment of a pleasurable feeling and in the course of a dream which hallucinates
a sexual act. And in regard to this process (nocturnal emission)
it is difficult to avoid the conclusion that the sexual tension,
which succeeds in making use of the short cut of hallucination as
a substitute for the act itself, is a function of the accumulation
of semen in the vesicles containing the sexual products. Our
experience in connection with the exhaustibility of the sexual
mechanism argues in the same sense. If the store of semen is
exhausted, not only is it impossible to carry out the sexual act,
but the susceptibility of the erotogenic zones to stimulus ceases,
and their appropriate excitation no longer gives rise to any
pleasure. We thus learn incidentally that a certain degree
of sexual tension is required even for the excitability of the
erotogenic zones.

This would seem to lead to what is, if I am not mistaken, the
fairly wide-spread hypothesis that the accumulation of the
sexual substances creates and maintains sexual tension; the
pressure of these products upon the walls of the vesicles containing them might be supposed to act as a stimulus upon a
spinal centre, the condition of which would be perceived by
higher centres and would then give rise in consciousness to the
familiar sensation of tension. If the excitation of the erotogenic
zones increases sexual tension, this could only come about on
the supposition that the zones in question are in an anatomical
connection that has already been laid down with these centres,
that they increase the tonus of the excitation in them, and, if
the sexual tension is sufficient, set the sexual act in motion or,
if it is insufficient, stimulate the production of the sexual substances.[1]

The weakness of this theory, which we find accepted, for
instance, in Krafft-Ebing's account of the sexual processes, lies

[1] [This hypothesis had been discussed by Freud earlier: in Section
III of his first paper on anxiety neurosis (1895*b*).]

in the fact that, having been designed to account for the sexual activity of adult males, it takes too little account of three sets of conditions which it should also be able to explain. These are the conditions in children, in females and in castrated males. In none of these three cases can there be any question of an accumulation of sexual products in the same sense as in males, and this makes a smooth application of the theory difficult. Nevertheless it may at once be admitted that it is possible to find means by which the theory may be made to cover these cases as well. In any case we are warned not to lay more weight on the factor of the accumulation of the sexual products than it is able to bear.

IMPORTANCE OF THE INTERNAL SEXUAL ORGANS    Observations on castrated males seem to show that sexual excitation can occur to a considerable degree independently of the production of the sexual substances. The operation of castration occasionally fails to bring about a limitation of libido, although such limitation, which provides the motive for the operation, is the usual outcome. Moreover, it has long been known that diseases which abolish the production of the masculine sex-cells leave the patient, though he is now sterile, with his libido and potency undamaged.[1] It is therefore by no means as astonishing as Rieger [1900] represents it to be that the loss of the masculine sex-glands in an adult may have no further effect upon his mental behaviour.[2] It is true that if castration is performed at a tender age, before puberty, it approximates in its effect to the aim of obliterating the sexual characters; but here too it is possible that what is in question is, besides the actual loss of the sex-glands, an inhibition (connected with that loss) in the development of other factors.

[1] [This sentence was added in 1920.]

[2] [The following sentence occurs at this point in editions before 1920, when it was omitted: 'For the sex-glands do not constitute sexuality, and the observations on castrated males merely confirm what had been shown long before by removal of the ovaries—namely that it is impossible to obliterate the sexual characters by removing the sex-glands.' Before 1920, too, the second half of the next sentence began: 'but it seems that what is in question here is not the actual loss of the sex-glands but an inhibition . . .']

CHEMICAL     Experiments in the removal of the sex-glands
THEORY       (testes and ovaries) of animals, and in the grafting
             into vertebrates of sex-glands from other individuals
of the opposite sex,[1] have at last thrown a partial light on the
origin of sexual excitation, and have at the same time still
further reduced the significance of a possible accumulation of
cellular sexual products. It has become experimentally possible
(E. Steinach) to transform a male into a female, and conversely
a female into a male. In this process the psychosexual behaviour
of the animal alters in accordance with the somatic sexual
characters and simultaneously with them. It seems, however,
that this sex-determining influence is not an attribute of that
part of the sex-glands which gives rise to the specific sex-cells
(spermatozoa and ovum) but of their interstitial tissue, upon
which special emphasis is laid by being described in the literature as the 'puberty-gland'. It is quite possible that further
investigation will show that this puberty-gland has normally a
hermaphrodite disposition. If this were so, the theory of the
bisexuality of the higher animals would be given anatomical
foundation. It is already probable that the puberty-gland is not
the only organ concerned with the production of sexual excitation and sexual characters. In any case, what we already know
of the part played by the thyroid gland in sexuality fits in with
this new biological discovery. It seems probable, then, that
special chemical substances are produced in the interstitial portion of the sex-glands; these are then taken up in the blood
stream and cause particular parts of the central nervous
system to be charged with sexual tension. (We are already
familiar with the fact that other toxic substances, introduced
into the body from outside, can bring about a similar transformation of a toxic condition into a stimulus acting on a
particular organ.) The question of how sexual excitation arises
from the stimulation of erotogenic zones, when the central apparatus has been previously charged, and the question of what
interplay arises in the course of these sexual processes between
the effects of purely toxic stimuli and of physiological ones—
none of this can be treated, even hypothetically, in the present
state of our knowledge. It must suffice us to hold firmly to what
is essential in this view of the sexual processes: the assumption

[1] Cf. Lipschütz's work (1919), referred to on p. 144 *n*.

that substances of a peculiar kind arise from the sexual metabolism.[1] For this apparently arbitrary supposition is supported
by a fact which has received little attention but deserves the
closest consideration. The neuroses, which can be derived only
from disturbances of sexual life, show the greatest clinical similarity to the phenomena of intoxication and abstinence that
arise from the habitual use of toxic, pleasure-producing substances (alkaloids).

[1] [The whole of this paragraph as far as this point dates in its present
form from 1920. In the first edition (1905) and the two subsequent ones
the following passage appears in its place: 'The truth is that we can
give no information on the nature of sexual excitation, especially since
(having found that the importance of the sex-glands in this respect has
been over-estimated) we are in the dark as to the organ or organs to
which sexuality is attached. After the surprising discoveries of the important part played by the thyroid gland in sexuality, it is reasonable
to suspect that we are still ignorant of the essential factors of sexuality.
Anyone who feels the need of a provisional hypothesis to fill this wide
gap in our knowledge may well take as his starting-point the powerful
substances which have been found to be present in the thyroid gland and
may proceed along some such lines as the following. It may be supposed
that, as a result of an appropriate stimulation of erotogenic zones, or in
other circumstances that are accompanied by an onset of sexual excitation, some substance that is disseminated generally throughout the
organism becomes decomposed and the products of its decomposition
give rise to a specific stimulus which acts on the reproductive organs
or upon a spinal centre related to them. (We are already familiar with
the fact that other toxic substances, introduced into the body from
outside, can bring about a similar transformation of a toxic condition
into a stimulus acting on a particular organ.) The question of what
interplay arises in the course of the sexual processes between the effects
of purely toxic stimuli and of physiological ones cannot be treated, even
hypothetically, in the present state of our knowledge. I may add that I
attach no importance to this particular hypothesis and should be ready
to abandon it at once in favour of another, provided that its fundamental nature remained unchanged—that is, the emphasis which it lays
upon sexual chemistry.'—It is worth remarking how small a modification was made necessary in Freud's hypothesis by the discovery of
the sex-hormones, which, indeed, he had anticipated not merely in
1905 but at least as early as in 1896, as may be seen from his two letters
to Fliess, of March 1 and April 2 of that year (Freud, 1950a, Letters 42
and 44). He further insisted upon the importance of the chemical factor
in his second paper on the part played by sexuality in the neuroses,
published at about the same time as the first edition of the *Three Essays*
(1906a, this volume p. 279.]

## [3] THE LIBIDO THEORY [1]

The conceptual scaffolding which we have set up to help us in dealing with the psychical manifestations of sexual life tallies well with these hypotheses as to the chemical basis of sexual excitation. We have defined the concept of libido as a quantitatively variable force which could serve as a measure of processes and transformations occurring in the field of sexual excitation. We distinguish this libido in respect of its special origin from the energy which must be supposed to underlie mental processes in general, and we thus also attribute a *qualitative* character to it. In thus distinguishing between libidinal and other forms of psychical energy we are giving expression to the presumption that the sexual processes occurring in the organism are distinguished from the nutritive processes by a special chemistry. The analysis of the perversions and psychoneuroses has shown us that this sexual excitation is derived not from the so-called sexual parts alone, but from all the bodily organs. We thus reach the idea of a quantity of libido, to the mental representation of which we give the name of 'ego-libido', and whose production, increase or diminution, distribution and displacement should afford us possibilities for explaining the psychosexual phenomena observed.

This ego-libido is, however, only conveniently accessible to analytic study when it has been put to the use of cathecting sexual objects, that is, when it has become object-libido. We can then perceive it concentrating upon objects,[2] becoming fixed upon them or abandoning them, moving from one object to another and, from these situations, directing the subject's sexual activity, which leads to the satisfaction, that is, to the partial and temporary extinction, of the libido. The psychoanalysis of what are termed transference neuroses (hysteria and obsessional neurosis) affords us a clear insight at this point.

We can follow the object-libido through still further vicissitudes. When it is withdrawn from objects, it is held in suspense

---

[1] [This whole section, except for its last paragraph, dates from 1915. It is largely based on Freud's paper on narcissism (1914c).]

[2] [It is scarcely necessary to explain that here as elsewhere, in speaking of the libido concentrating on 'objects', withdrawing from 'objects', etc., Freud has in mind the mental presentations (*Vorstellungen*) of objects and not, of course, objects in the external world.]

in peculiar conditions of tension and is finally drawn back into the ego, so that it becomes ego-libido once again. In contrast to object-libido, we also describe ego-libido as 'narcissistic' libido. From the vantage-point of psycho-analysis we can look across a frontier, which we may not pass, at the activities of narcissistic libido, and may form some idea of the relation between it and object-libido.[1] Narcissistic or ego-libido seems to be the great reservoir from which the object-cathexes are sent out and into which they are withdrawn once more; the narcissistic libidinal cathexis of the ego is the original state of things, realized in earliest childhood, and is merely covered by the later extrusions of libido, but in essentials persists behind them.

It should be the task of a libido theory of neurotic and psychotic disorders to express all the observed phenomena and inferred processes in terms of the economics of the libido. It is easy to guess that the vicissitudes of the ego-libido will have the major part to play in this connection, especially when it is a question of explaining the deeper psychotic disturbances. We are then faced by the difficulty that our method of research, psycho-analysis, for the moment affords us assured information only on the transformations that take place in the object-libido,[2] but is unable to make any immediate distinction between the ego-libido and the other forms of energy operating in the ego.[3]

For the present, therefore,[4] no further development of the libido theory is possible, except upon speculative lines. It would, however, be sacrificing all that we have gained hitherto from psycho-analytic observation, if we were to follow the example of C. G. Jung and water down the meaning of the concept of libido itself by equating it with psychical instinctual force in general. The distinguishing of the sexual instinctual impulses from the rest and the consequent restriction of the concept of libido to the former receives strong support from the assumption

[1] [*Footnote added* 1924:] Since neuroses other than the transference neuroses have become to a greater extent accessible to psycho-analysis, this limitation has lost its earlier validity.

[2] [*Footnote added* 1924:] See the previous footnote.

[3] [*Footnote added* 1915:] Cf. my paper on narcissism (1914*c*). [*Added* 1920:] The term 'narcissism' was not introduced, as I erroneously stated in that paper, by Näcke, but by Havelock Ellis. [Ellis himself subsequently (1928) discussed this point in detail and considered that the honours should be divided.]

[4] [This paragraph was added in 1920.]

which I have already discussed that there is a special chemistry of the sexual function.

## [4] THE DIFFERENTIATION BETWEEN MEN AND WOMEN

As we all know, it is not until puberty that the sharp distinction is established between the masculine and feminine characters. From that time on, this contrast has a more decisive influence than any other upon the shaping of human life. It is true that the masculine and feminine dispositions are already easily recognizable in childhood. The development of the inhibitions of sexuality (shame, disgust, pity, etc.) takes place in little girls earlier and in the face of less resistance than in boys; the tendency to sexual repression seems in general to be greater; and, where the component instincts of sexuality appear, they prefer the passive form. The auto-erotic activity of the erotogenic zones is, however, the same in both sexes, and owing to this uniformity there is no possibility of a distinction between the two sexes such as arises after puberty. So far as the auto-erotic and masturbatory manifestations of sexuality are concerned, we might lay it down that the sexuality of little girls is of a wholly masculine character. Indeed, if we were able to give a more definite connotation to the concepts of 'masculine' and 'feminine', it would even be possible to maintain that libido is invariably and necessarily of a masculine nature, whether it occurs in men or in women and irrespectively of whether its object is a man or a woman.[1]

[1] [Before 1924 the words from 'libido' to the end of the sentence were printed in spaced type.—*Footnote added* 1915:] It is essential to understand clearly that the concepts of 'masculine' and 'feminine', whose meaning seems so unambiguous to ordinary people, are among the most confused that occur in science. It is possible to distinguish at least three uses. 'Masculine' and 'feminine' are used sometimes in the sense of activity and passivity, sometimes in a biological, and sometimes, again, in a sociological sense. The first of these three meanings is the essential one and the most serviceable in psycho-analysis. When, for instance, libido was described in the text above as being 'masculine', the word was being used in this sense, for an instinct is always active even when it has a passive aim in view. The second, or biological, meaning of 'masculine' and 'feminine' is the one whose applicability can be determined most easily. Here 'masculine' and 'feminine' are characterized by the presence of spermatozoa or ova respectively and by the

Since I have become acquainted [1] with the notion of bisexuality I have regarded it as the decisive factor, and without taking bisexuality into account I think it would scarcely be possible to arrive at an understanding of the sexual manifestations that are actually to be observed in men and women.

LEADING ZONES IN MEN AND WOMEN    Apart from this I have only the following to add. The leading erotogenic zone in female children is located at the clitoris, and is thus homologous to the masculine genital zone of the glans penis. All my experience concerning masturbation in little girls has related to the clitoris and not to the regions of the external genitalia that are important in later sexual functioning. I am even doubtful whether a female child can be led by the influence of seduction to anything other than clitoridal masturbation. If such a thing occurs, it is quite exceptional. The spontaneous discharges of sexual excitement which occur so often precisely in little girls are expressed in spasms of the clitoris. Frequent erections of that organ make it possible for girls to form a correct judgement, even without any instruction, of the sexual manifestations of the other sex: they merely transfer on to boys the sensations derived from their own sexual processes.

If we are to understand how a little girl turns into a woman, we must follow the further vicissitudes of this excitability of the clitoris. Puberty, which brings about so great an accession of libido in boys, is marked in girls by a fresh wave of *repression*, in which it is precisely clitoridal sexuality that is affected. What is

functions proceeding from them. Activity and its concomitant phenomena (more powerful muscular development, aggressiveness, greater intensity of libido) are as a rule linked with biological masculinity; but they are not necessarily so, for there are animal species in which these qualities are on the contrary assigned to the female. The third, or sociological, meaning receives its connotation from the observation of actually existing masculine and feminine individuals. Such observation shows that in human beings pure masculinity or femininity is not to be found either in a psychological or a biological sense. Every individual on the contrary displays a mixture of the character-traits belonging to his own and to the opposite sex; and he shows a combination of activity and passivity whether or not these last character-traits tally with his biological ones. [A later discussion of this point will be found in a footnote at the end of Chapter IV of *Civilization and its Discontents* (1930*a*).]

[1] [In 1905 only: 'through Wilhelm Fliess'. Cf. end of footnote, p. 143.]

thus overtaken by repression is a piece of masculine sexuality. The intensification of the brake upon sexuality brought about by pubertal repression in women serves as a stimulus to the libido in men and causes an increase of its activity. Along with this heightening of libido there is also an increase of sexual over-valuation which only emerges in full force in relation to a woman who holds herself back and who denies her sexuality. When at last the sexual act is permitted and the clitoris itself becomes excited, it still retains a function: the task, namely, of transmitting the excitation to the adjacent female sexual parts, just as—to use a simile—pine shavings can be kindled in order to set a log of harder wood on fire. Before this transference can be effected, a certain interval of time must often elapse, during which the young woman is anaesthetic. This anaesthesia may become permanent if the clitoridal zone refuses to abandon its excitability, an event for which the way is prepared precisely by an extensive activity of that zone in childhood. Anaesthesia in women, as is well known, is often only apparent and local. They are anaesthetic at the vaginal orifice but are by no means incapable of excitement originating in the clitoris or even in other zones. Alongside these erotogenic determinants of anaes-thesia must also be set the psychical determinants, which equally arise from repression.

When erotogenic susceptibility to stimulation has been suc-cessfully transferred by a woman from the clitoris to the vaginal orifice, it implies that she has adopted a new leading zone for the purposes of her later sexual activity. A man, on the other hand, retains his leading zone unchanged from childhood. The fact that women change their leading erotogenic zone in this way, together with the wave of repression at puberty, which, as it were, puts aside their childish masculinity, are the chief determinants of the greater proneness of women to neurosis and especially to hysteria. These determinants, therefore, are intim-ately related to the essence of femininity.[1]

[1] [The course of development of sexuality in women was further examined by Freud more particularly on four later occasions: in his case history of a homosexual woman (1920a), in his discussion of the conse-quences of the anatomical distinction between the sexes (1925j), in his paper on female sexuality (1931b), and in Lecture XXXIII of his *New Introductory Lectures* (1933a).

## [5] THE FINDING OF AN OBJECT

The processes at puberty thus establish the primacy of the genital zones; and, in a man, the penis, which has now become capable of erection, presses forward insistently towards the new sexual aim—penetration into a cavity in the body which excites his genital zone. Simultaneously on the psychical side the process of finding an object, for which preparations have been made from earliest childhood, is completed. At a time at which the first beginnings of sexual satisfaction are still linked with the taking of nourishment, the sexual instinct has a sexual object outside the infant's own body in the shape of his mother's breast. It is only later that the instinct loses that object, just at the time, perhaps, when the child is able to form a total idea of the person to whom the organ that is giving him satisfaction belongs. As a rule the sexual instinct then becomes auto-erotic, and not until the period of latency has been passed through is the original relation restored. There are thus good reasons why a child sucking at his mother's breast has become the prototype of every relation of love. The finding of an object is in fact a refinding of it.[1]

THE SEXUAL OBJECT DURING EARLY INFANCY    But even after sexual activity has become detached from the taking of nourishment, an important part of this first and most significant of all sexual relations is left over, which helps to prepare for the choice of an object and thus to restore the happiness that has been lost. All through the period of latency children learn to feel for other people who help them in their helplessness and satisfy their needs a love which is on the model of, and a continuation of, their relation as sucklings

---

[1] [*Footnote added* 1915:] Psycho-analysis informs us that there are two methods of finding an object. The first, described in the text, is the 'anaclitic' or 'attachment' one, based on attachment to early infantile prototypes. The second is the narcissistic one, which seeks for the subject's own ego and finds it again in other people. This latter method is of particularly great importance in cases where the outcome is a pathological one, but it is not relevant to the present context. [The point is elaborated in the later part of Section II of Freud's paper on narcissism (1914c).—The paragraph in the text above, written in 1905, does not appear to harmonize with the remarks on the subject on pp. 200 and 234, written in 1915 and 1920 respectively.]

to their nursing mother. There may perhaps be an inclination to dispute the possibility of identifying a child's affection and esteem for those who look after him with sexual love. I think, however, that a closer psychological examination may make it possible to establish this identity beyond any doubt. A child's intercourse with anyone responsible for his care affords him an unending source of sexual excitation and satisfaction from his erotogenic zones. This is especially so since the person in charge of him, who, after all, is as a rule his mother, herself regards him with feelings that are derived from her own sexual life: she strokes him, kisses him, rocks him and quite clearly treats him as a substitute for a complete sexual object.[1] A mother would probably be horrified if she were made aware that all her marks of affection were rousing her child's sexual instinct and preparing for its later intensity. She regards what she does as asexual, 'pure' love, since, after all, she carefully avoids applying more excitations to the child's genitals than are unavoidable in nursery care. As we know, however, the sexual instinct is not aroused only by direct excitation of the genital zone. What we call affection will unfailingly show its effects one day on the genital zones as well. Moreover, if the mother understood more of the high importance of the part played by instincts in mental life as a whole—in all its ethical and psychical achievements—she would spare herself any self-reproaches even after her enlightenment. She is only fulfilling her task in teaching the child to love. After all, he is meant to grow up into a strong and capable person with vigorous sexual needs and to accomplish during his life all the things that human beings are urged to do by their instincts. It is true that an excess of parental affection does harm by causing precocious sexual maturity and also because, by spoiling the child, it makes him incapable in later life of temporarily doing without love or of being content with a smaller amount of it. One of the clearest indications that a child will later become neurotic is to be seen in an insatiable demand for his parents' affection. And on the other hand neuropathic parents, who are inclined as a rule to display excessive affection, are precisely those who are most likely by their caresses to arouse the child's disposition to neurotic illness.

[1] Anyone who considers this 'sacrilegious' may be recommended to read Havelock Ellis's views [1913, 18] on the relation between mother and child, which agree almost completely with mine.

Incidentally, this example shows that there are ways more direct than inheritance by which neurotic parents can hand their disorder on to their children.

INFANTILE     Children themselves behave from an early age
ANXIETY      as though their dependence on the people looking
             after them were in the nature of sexual love.
Anxiety in children is originally nothing other than an expression of the fact that they are feeling the loss of the person they love. It is for this reason that they are frightened of every stranger. They are afraid in the dark because in the dark they cannot see the person they love; and their fear is soothed if they can take hold of that person's hand in the dark. To attribute to bogeys and blood-curdling stories told by nurses the responsibility for making children timid is to over-estimate their efficacy. The truth is merely that children who are inclined to be timid are affected by stories which would make no impression whatever upon others, and it is only children with a sexual instinct that is excessive or has developed prematurely or has become vociferous owing to too much petting who are inclined to be timid. In this respect a child, by turning his libido into anxiety when he cannot satisfy it, behaves like an adult. On the other hand an adult who has become neurotic owing to his libido being unsatisfied behaves in his anxiety like a child: he begins to be frightened when he is alone, that is to say when he is away from someone of whose love he had felt secure, and he seeks to assuage this fear by the most childish measures.[1]

---

[1] For this explanation of the origin of infantile anxiety I have to thank a three-year-old boy whom I once heard calling out of a dark room: 'Auntie, speak to me! I'm frightened because it's so dark.' His aunt answered him: 'What good would that do? You can't see me.' 'That doesn't matter,' replied the child, 'if anyone speaks, it gets light.' Thus what he was afraid of was not the dark, but the absence of someone he loved; and he could feel sure of being soothed as soon as he had evidence of that person's presence. [*Added* 1920:] One of the most important results of psycho-analytic research is this discovery that neurotic anxiety arises out of libido, that it is the product of a transformation of it, and that it is thus related to it in the same kind of way as vinegar is to wine. A further discussion of this problem will be found in my *Introductory Lectures on Psycho-Analysis* (1916–17), Lecture XXV, though even there, it must be confessed, the question is not finally cleared up. [For Freud's latest views on the subject of anxiety see his *Inhibitions, Symptoms and Anxiety* (1926*d*) and his *New Introductory Lectures* (1933*a*), Chapter XXXII.]

THE BARRIER    We see, therefore, that the parents' affec-
AGAINST INCEST [1] tion for their child may awaken his sexual
            instinct prematurely (i.e. before the somatic
conditions of puberty are present) to such a degree that the
mental excitation breaks through in an unmistakable fashion to
the genital system. If, on the other hand, they are fortunate
enough to avoid this, then their affection can perform its task
of directing the child in his choice of a sexual object when he
reaches maturity. No doubt the simplest course for the child
would be to choose as his sexual objects the same persons
whom, since his childhood, he has loved with what may be
described as damped-down libido.[2] But, by the postponing of
sexual maturation, time has been gained in which the child can
erect, among other restraints on sexuality, the barrier against
incest, and can thus take up into himself the moral precepts
which expressly exclude from his object-choice, as being blood-
relations, the persons whom he has loved in his childhood.
Respect for this barrier is essentially a cultural demand made
by society. Society must defend itself against the danger that
the interests which it needs for the establishment of higher
social units may be swallowed up by the family; and for this
reason, in the case of every individual, but in particular of
adolescent boys, it seeks by all possible means to loosen their
connection with their family—a connection which, in their
childhood, is the only important one.[3]

It is in the world of ideas, however, that the choice of an
object is accomplished at first; and the sexual life of maturing

[1] [This side-heading was omitted, probably by an oversight, from
1924 onwards.]
[2] [Footnote added 1915:] Cf. what has been said on p. 200 about
children's object-choice and the 'affectionate current'.
[3] [Footnote added 1915:] The barrier against incest is probably among
the historical acquisitions of mankind, and, like other moral taboos, has
no doubt already become established in many persons by organic inheritance. (Cf. my Totem and Taboo, 1912–13.) Psycho-analytic investigation shows, however, how intensely the individual struggles with the
temptation to incest during his period of growth and how frequently the
barrier is transgressed in phantasies and even in reality.—[Though this
is its first published appearance, the 'horror of incest' had been discussed by Freud on May 31, 1897 (Draft N in Freud, 1950a)—some
months, that is, before his first revelation of the Oedipus complex.
In that draft too he accounts for it on the ground that incest is
'antisocial'.]

youth is almost entirely restricted to indulging in phantasies, that is, in ideas that are not destined to be carried into effect.[1] In these phantasies the infantile tendencies invariably emerge

[1] [*Footnote added* 1920:] The phantasies of the pubertal period have as their starting-point the infantile sexual researches that were abandoned in childhood. No doubt, too, they are also present before the end of the latency period. They may persist wholly, or to a great extent, unconsciously and for that reason it is often impossible to date them accurately. They are of great importance in the origin of many symptoms, since they precisely constitute preliminary stages of these symptoms and thus lay down the forms in which the repressed libidinal components find satisfaction. In the same way, they are the prototypes of the nocturnal phantasies which become conscious as dreams. Dreams are often nothing more than revivals of pubertal phantasies of this kind under the influence of, and in relation to, some stimulus left over from the waking life of the previous day (the 'day's residues'). [See Chapter VII, Section I, of *The Interpretation of Dreams* (1900a); Standard Ed., **5**, 492 f.] Some among the sexual phantasies of the pubertal period are especially prominent, and are distinguished by their very general occurrence and by being to a great extent independent of individual experience. Such are the adolescent's phantasies of overhearing his parents in sexual intercourse, of having been seduced at an early age by someone he loves and of having been threatened with castration [cf. the discussion of 'primal phantasies' in Lecture XXIII of Freud's *Introductory Lectures* (1916–17)]; such, too, are his phantasies of being in the womb, and even of experiences there, and the so-called 'Family Romance', in which he reacts to the difference between his attitude towards his parents now and in his childhood. The close relations existing between these phantasies and myths has been demonstrated in the case of the last instance by Otto Rank (1909). [Cf. also Freud's own paper on 'Family Romances' (1909c) and his long footnote to Section G of Part I of his case history of the 'Rat Man' (1909d).]

It has justly been said that the Oedipus complex is the nuclear complex of the neuroses, and constitutes the essential part of their content. It represents the peak of infantile sexuality, which, through its after-effects, exercises a decisive influence on the sexuality of adults. Every new arrival on this planet is faced by the task of mastering the Oedipus complex; anyone who fails to do so falls a victim to neurosis. With the progress of psycho-analytic studies the importance of the Oedipus complex has became more and more clearly evident; its recognition has become the shibboleth that distinguishes the adherents of psycho-analysis from its opponents.

[*Added* 1924:] In another work (1924), Rank has traced attachment to the mother back to the prehistoric intra-uterine period and has thus indicated the biological foundation of the Oedipus complex. He differs from what has been said above, by deriving the barrier against incest from the traumatic effect of anxiety at birth. [See Chapter X of *Inhibitions, Symptoms and Anxiety* (1926d).]

once more, but this time with intensified pressure from somatic sources. Among these tendencies the first place is taken with uniform frequency by the child's sexual impulses towards his parents, which are as a rule already differentiated owing to the attraction of the opposite sex—the son being drawn towards his mother and the daughter towards her father.[1] At the same time as these plainly incestuous phantasies are overcome and repudiated, one of the most significant, but also one of the most painful, psychical achievements of the pubertal period is completed: detachment from parental authority, a process that alone makes possible the opposition, which is so important for the progress of civilization, between the new generation and the old. At every stage in the course of development through which all human beings ought by rights to pass, a certain number are held back; so there are some who have never got over their parents' authority and have withdrawn their affection from them either very incompletely or not at all. They are mostly girls, who, to the delight of their parents, have persisted in all their childish love far beyond puberty. It is most instructive to find that it is precisely these girls who in their later marriage lack the capacity to give their husbands what is due to them; they make cold wives and remain sexually anaesthetic. We learn from this that sexual love and what appears to be non-sexual love for parents are fed from the same sources; the latter, that is to say, merely corresponds to an infantile fixation of the libido.

The closer one comes to the deeper disturbances of psychosexual development, the more unmistakably the importance of incestuous object-choice emerges. In psychoneurotics a large portion or the whole of their psychosexual activity in finding an object remains in the unconscious as a result of their repudiation of sexuality. Girls with an exaggerated need for affection and an equally exaggerated horror of the real demands made by sexual life have an irresistible temptation on the one hand to realize the ideal of asexual love in their lives and on the other hand to conceal their libido behind an affection which they can express without self-reproaches, by holding fast throughout their lives to their infantile fondness, revived at

[1] Cf. my remarks in *The Interpretation of Dreams* (1900a), on the inevitability of Fate in the fable of Oedipus [Chapter V, Section D (β); Standard Ed., 4, 260 ff.].

puberty, for their parents or brothers and sisters. Psycho-analysis has no difficulty in showing persons of this kind that they are *in love*, in the everyday sense of the word, with these blood-relations of theirs; for, with the help of their symptoms and other manifestations of their illness, it traces their uncon-scious thoughts and translates them into conscious ones. In cases in which someone who has previously been healthy falls ill after an unhappy experience in love it is also possible to show with certainty that the mechanism of his illness consists in a turning-back of his libido on to those whom he preferred in his infancy.

AFTER-EFFECTS    Even a person who has been fortunate
OF INFANTILE    enough to avoid an incestuous fixation of his
OBJECT-CHOICE    libido does not entirely escape its influence. It
often happens that a young man falls in love seriously for the first time with a mature woman, or a girl with an elderly man in a position of authority; this is clearly an echo of the phase of development that we have been discussing, since these figures are able to re-animate pictures of their mother or father.[1] There can be no doubt that every object-choice what-ever is based, though less closely, on these prototypes. A man, especially, looks for someone who can represent his picture of his mother, as it has dominated his mind from his earliest child-hood; and accordingly, if his mother is still alive, she may well resent this new version of herself and meet her with hostility. In view of the importance of a child's relations to his parents in determining his later choice of a sexual object, it can easily be understood that any disturbance of those relations will produce the gravest effects upon his adult sexual life. Jealousy in a lover is never without an infantile root or at least an infantile rein-forcement. If there are quarrels between the parents or if their marriage is unhappy, the ground will be prepared in their children for the severest predisposition to a disturbance of sexual development or to a neurotic illness.

A child's affection for his parents is no doubt the most im-portant infantile trace which, after being revived at puberty, points the way to his choice of an object; but it is not the only one. Other starting-points with the same early origin enable a

[1] [*Footnote added* 1920:] Cf. my paper 'A Special Type of Choice of Object made by Men' (1910*h*).

man to develop more than one sexual line, based no less upon his childhood, and to lay down very various conditions for his object-choice.[1]

PREVENTION OF    One of the tasks implicit in object-choice is
INVERSION    that it should find its way to the opposite sex.

This, as we know, is not accomplished without a certain amount of fumbling. Often enough the first impulses after puberty go astray, though without any permanent harm resulting. Dessoir [1894] has justly remarked upon the regularity with which adolescent boys and girls form sentimental friendships with others of their own sex. No doubt the strongest force working against a permanent inversion of the sexual object is the attraction which the opposing sexual characters exercise upon one another. Nothing can be said within the framework of the present discussion to throw light upon it.[2] This factor is not in itself, however, sufficient to exclude inversion; there are no doubt a variety of other contributory factors. Chief among these is its authoritative prohibition by society. Where inversion is not regarded as a crime it will be found that it answers fully to the sexual inclinations of no small number of people. It may be presumed, in the next place, that in the case of men a childhood recollection of the affection shown them by their mother and others of the female sex who looked after them when they were children contributes powerfully to directing their choice towards women;[3] on the other hand their early experience of being deterred by their father from sexual activity and their competitive relation with him deflect them from their own sex. Both of these two factors apply equally to girls, whose sexual

[1] [*Footnote added* 1915:] The innumerable peculiarities of the erotic life of human beings as well as the compulsive character of the process of falling in love itself are quite unintelligible except by reference back to childhood and as being residual effects of childhood.

[2] [*Footnote added* 1924:] This is the place at which to draw attention to Ferenczi's *Versuch einer Genitaltheorie* (1924), a work which, though somewhat fanciful, is nevertheless of the greatest interest, and in which the sexual life of the higher animals is traced back to their biological evolution.

[3] [The rest of this sentence and the two following ones date from 1915. In the editions of 1905 and 1910 the following passage takes their place: 'while in the case of girls, who in any case enter a period of repression at puberty, impulses of rivalry play a part in discouraging them from loving members of their own sex.']

activity is particularly subject to the watchful guardianship of their mother. They thus acquire a hostile relation to their own sex which influences their object-choice decisively in what is regarded as the normal direction. The education of boys by male persons (by slaves, in antiquity) seems to encourage homosexuality. The frequency of inversion among the present-day aristocracy is made somewhat more intelligible by their employment of menservants, as well as by the fact that their mothers give less personal care to their children. In the case of some hysterics it is found that the early loss of one of their parents, whether by death, divorce or separation, with the result that the remaining parent absorbs the whole of the child's love, determines the sex of the person who is later to be chosen as a sexual object, and may thus open the way to permanent inversion.

# SUMMARY

THE time has arrived for me to attempt to summarize what I
have said. We started out from the aberrations of the sexual
instinct in respect of its object and of its aim and we were faced
by the question of whether these arise from an innate disposition or are acquired as a result of experiences in life. We
arrived at an answer to this question from an understanding,
derived from psycho-analytic investigation, of the workings of
the sexual instinct in psychoneurotics, a numerous class of
people and one not far removed from the healthy. We found
that in them tendencies to every kind of perversion can be
shown to exist as unconscious forces and betray their presence
as factors leading to the formation of symptoms. It was thus
possible to say that neurosis is, as it were, the negative of perversion. In view of what was now seen to be the wide dissemination of tendencies to perversion we were driven to the conclusion
that a disposition to perversions is an original and universal
disposition of the human sexual instinct and that normal sexual
behaviour is developed out of it as a result of organic changes
and psychical inhibitions occurring in the course of maturation;
we hoped to be able to show the presence of this original disposition in childhood. Among the forces restricting the direction
taken by the sexual instinct we laid emphasis upon shame,
disgust, pity and the structures of morality and authority erected
by society. We were thus led to regard any established aberration from normal sexuality as an instance of developmental
inhibition and infantilism. Though it was necessary to place
in the foreground the importance of the variations in the
original disposition, a co-operative and not an opposing relation
was to be assumed as existing between them and the influences
of actual life. It appeared, on the other hand, that since the
original disposition is necessarily a complex one, the sexual
instinct itself must be something put together from various
factors, and that in the perversions it falls apart, as it were, into
its components. The perversions were thus seen to be on the one
hand inhibitions, and on the other hand dissociations, of normal
development. Both these aspects were brought together in the
supposition that the sexual instinct of adults arises from a

combination of a number of impulses of childhood into a unity, an impulsion with a single aim.

After having explained the preponderance of perverse tendencies in psychoneurotics by recognizing it as a collateral filling of subsidiary channels when the main current of the instinctual stream has been blocked by 'repression',[1] we proceeded to a consideration of sexual life in childhood. We found it a regrettable thing that the existence of the sexual instinct in childhood has been denied and that the sexual manifestations not infrequently to be observed in children have been described as irregularities. It seemed to us on the contrary that children bring germs of sexual activity with them into the world, that they already enjoy sexual satisfaction when they begin to take nourishment and that they persistently seek to repeat the experience in the familiar activity of 'thumb-sucking'. The sexual activity of children, however, does not, it appeared, develop *pari passu* with their other functions, but, after a short period of efflorescence from the ages of two to five,[2] enters upon the so-called period of latency. During that period the production of sexual excitation is not by any means stopped but continues and produces a store of energy which is employed to a great extent for purposes other than sexual—namely, on the one hand in contributing the sexual components to social feelings and on the other hand (through repression and reaction-forming) in building up the subsequently developed barriers against sexuality. On this view, the forces destined to retain the sexual instinct upon certain lines are built up in childhood chiefly at the cost of perverse sexual impulses and with the assistance of education. A certain portion of the infantile sexual impulses would seem to evade these uses and succeed in expressing itself as sexual activity. We next found that sexual excitation in children springs from a multiplicity of forces. Satis-

[1] [*Footnote added* 1915:] This does not apply only to the 'negative' tendencies to perversion which appear in neuroses but equally to the 'positive', properly so-called, perversions. Thus these latter are to be derived not merely from a fixation of infantile tendencies but also from a regression to those tendencies as a result of other channels of the sexual current being blocked. It is for this reason that the positive perversions also are accessible to psycho-analytic therapy.

[2] [The last seven words were first inserted in 1915. In the edition of that year, however, the ages given were 'three to five'. The 'two' was substituted in 1920.]

faction arises first and foremost from the appropriate sensory
excitation of what we have described as erotogenic zones.
It seems probable that any part of the skin and any sense-organ
—probably, indeed, *any* organ[1]—can function as an erotogenic
zone, though there are some particularly marked erotogenic
zones whose excitation would seem to be secured from the very
first by certain organic contrivances. It further appears that
sexual excitation arises as a by-product, as it were, of a large
number of processes that occur in the organism, as soon as they
reach a certain degree of intensity, and most especially of any
relatively powerful emotion, even though it is of a distressing
nature. The excitations from all these sources are not yet combined; but each follows its own separate aim, which is merely
the attainment of a certain sort of pleasure. In childhood, therefore, the sexual instinct is not unified and is at first[2] without an
object, that is, auto-erotic.

The erotogenic zone of the genitals begins to make itself
noticeable, it seems, even during the years of childhood. This
may happen in two ways. Either, like any other erotogenic
zone, it yields satisfaction in response to appropriate sensory
stimulation; or, in a manner which is not quite understandable,
when satisfaction is derived from other sources, a sexual excitation is simultaneously produced which has a special relation to
the genital zone. We were reluctantly obliged to admit that we
could not satisfactorily explain the relation between sexual satisfaction and sexual excitation, or that between the activity of the
genital zone and the activity of the other sources of sexuality.

We found from the study of neurotic disorders[3] that beginnings of an organization of the sexual instinctual components
can be detected in the sexual life of children from its very
beginning. During a first, very early phase, oral erotism occupies
most of the picture. A second of these pregenital organizations
is characterized by the predominance of sadism and anal
erotism. It is not until a third phase has been reached that the
genital zones proper contribute their share in determining sexual
life, and in children this last phase is developed only so far as to
a primacy of the phallus.[4]

---

[1] [This parenthesis was added in 1915.]
[2] [The words 'not unified and is at first' were added in 1920.]
[3] [This and the next two paragraphs were added in 1920.]
[4] [The last clause was added in 1924.]

We were then obliged to recognize, as one of our most surprising findings, that this early efflorescence of infantile sexual life (between the ages of two and five) already gives rise to the choice of an object, with all the wealth of mental activities which such a process involves.[1] Thus, in spite of the lack of synthesis between the different instinctual components and the uncertainty of the sexual aim, the phase of development corresponding to that period must be regarded as an important precursor of the subsequent final sexual organization.

The fact that the onset of sexual development in human beings occurs in two phases, i.e. that the development is interrupted by the period of latency, seemed to call for particular notice. This appears to be one of the necessary conditions of the aptitude of men for developing a higher civilization, but also of their tendency to neurosis. So far as we know, nothing analogous is to be found in man's animal relatives. It would seem that the origin of this peculiarity of man must be looked for in the prehistory of the human species.

It was not possible to say what amount of sexual activity can occur in childhood without being described as abnormal or detrimental to further development. The nature of these sexual manifestations was found to be predominantly masturbatory. Experience further showed that the external influences of seduction are capable of provoking interruptions of the latency period or even its cessation, and that in this connection the sexual instinct of children proves in fact to be polymorphously perverse; it seems, moreover, that any such premature sexual activity diminishes a child's educability.

In spite of the gaps in our knowledge of infantile sexual life, we had to proceed to an attempt at examining the alterations brought about in it by the arrival of puberty. We selected two of these as being the decisive ones: the subordination of all the other sources of sexual excitation under the primacy of the genital zones and the process of finding an object. Both of these are already adumbrated in childhood. The first is accomplished by the mechanism of exploiting fore-pleasure: what were formerly self-contained sexual acts, attended by pleasure and excitation, become acts preparatory to the new sexual aim (the discharge of the sexual products), the attainment of which enormously pleasurable, brings the sexual excitation to an end.

[1] [Cf. the end of the footnote on p. 222.]

In this connection we had to take into account the differentiation of sexuality into masculine and feminine; and we found that in order to become a woman a further stage of repression is necessary, which discards a portion of infantile masculinity and prepares the woman for changing her leading genital zone. As regards object-choice, we found that it is given its direction by the childhood hints (revived at puberty) of the child's sexual inclination towards his parents and others in charge of him, but that it is diverted away from them, on to other people who resemble them, owing to the barrier against incest which has meanwhile been erected. Finally it must be added that during the transition period of puberty the processes of somatic and of psychical development continue for a time side by side independently, until the irruption of an intense mental erotic impulse, leading to the innervation of the genitals, brings about the unity of the erotic function which is necessary for normality.

FACTORS
INTERFERING
WITH
DEVELOPMENT

Every step on this long path of development can become a point of fixation, every juncture in this involved combination can be an occasion for a dissociation of the sexual instinct, as we have already shown from numerous instances.[1] It remains for us to enumerate the various factors, internal and external, that interfere with development, and to indicate the place in the mechanism on which the disturbance arising from each of them impinges. The factors that we shall enumerate can evidently not be of equal importance, and we must be prepared for difficulties in assigning an appropriate value to each.

CONSTITUTION
AND HEREDITY

First and foremost we must name the innate variety of sexual constitutions, upon which it is probable that the principal weight falls, but which can clearly only be inferred from their later manifestations and even then not always with great certainty. We picture this variety as a preponderance of one or another of the many

[1] [The further problem of a possible relation between the point of fixation and the type of neurosis developed—the problem of the 'choice of neurosis'—is not dealt with in these essays, though it had long been in Freud's thoughts. See, for instance, his letters to Fliess of May 30, 1896, and of December 9, 1899 (Freud, 1950a, Letters 46 and 125). The subject was touched on in a paper almost contemporary with the

sources of sexual excitation, and it is our view that a difference in disposition of this kind is always bound to find expression in the final result, even though that result may not overstep the limits of what is normal. No doubt it is conceivable that there may also be variations in the original disposition of a kind which must necessarily, and without the concurrence of any other factors, lead to the development of an abnormal sexual life. These might be described as 'degenerative' and be regarded as an expression of inherited degeneracy. In this connection I have a remarkable fact to record. In more than half of the severe cases of hysteria, obsessional neurosis, etc., which I have treated psychotherapeutically, I have been able to prove with certainty that the patient's father suffered from syphilis before marriage, whether there was evidence of tabes or general paralysis, or whether the anamnesis indicated in some other way the presence of syphilitic disease. I should like to make it perfectly plain that the children who later became neurotic bore no physical signs of hereditary syphilis, so that it was their abnormal sexual constitution that was to be regarded as the last echo of their syphilitic heritage. Though I am far from wishing to assert that descent from syphilitic parents is an invariable or indispensable aetiological condition of a neuropathic constitution, I am nevertheless of opinion that the coincidence which I have observed is neither accidental nor unimportant.

The hereditary conditions in the case of positive perverts are less well known, for they know how to avoid investigation. Yet there are good reasons to suppose that what is true of the neuroses applies also to the perversions. For it is no rare thing to find perversions and psychoneuroses occurring in the same family, and distributed between the two sexes in such a way that the male members of the family, or one of them, are positive perverts, while the females, true to the tendency of their sex to repression, are negative perverts, that is, hysterics.[1] This is good evidence of the essential connections which we have shown to exist between the two disorders.

present work (1906a, p. 275 of the present volume) and discussed more fully in a later paper on 'The Predisposition to Obsessional Neurosis' (1913i).]

[1] [A detailed family tree of this kind is given in a letter to Fliess of January 11, 1897 (Freud, 1950a, Letter 55).]

FURTHER                On the other hand, it is not possible to adopt
MODIFICATION     the view that the form to be taken by sexual
                 life is unambiguously decided, once and for all,
with the inception of the different components of the sexual constitution. On the contrary, the determining process continues,
and further possibilities arise according to the vicissitudes of the
tributary streams of sexuality springing from their separate
sources. This further modification is clearly what brings the
decisive outcome, and constitutions which might be described
as the same can lead to three different final results:—

[1] If the relation between all the different dispositions—a
relation which we will assume to be abnormal—persists and
grows stronger at maturity, the result can only be a perverse
sexual life. The analysis of abnormal constitutional disposisition
of this kind has not yet been properly taken in hand. But we
already know cases which can easily be explained on such a basis
as this. Writers on the subject, for instance, have asserted [see
p. 142] that the necessary precondition of a whole number of
perverse fixations lies in an innate weakness of the sexual
instinct. In this form the view seems to me untenable. It makes
sense, however, if what is meant is a constitutional weakness of
one particular factor in the sexual instinct, namely the genital
zone—a zone which takes over the function of combining the
separate sexual activities for the purposes of reproduction. For
if the genital zone is weak, this combination, which is required
to take place at puberty, is bound to fail, and the strongest of
the other components of sexuality will continue its activity as
a perversion.[1]

REPRESSION       [2] A different result is brought about if in the
                 course of development some of the components
which are of excessive strength in the disposition are submitted
to the process of repression (which, it must be insisted, is not
equivalent to their being abolished). If this happens, the excitations concerned continue to be generated as before; but they are
prevented by psychical obstruction from attaining their aim and

[1] [*Footnote added* 1915:] In such circumstances one often finds that
at puberty a normal sexual current begins to operate at first, but that,
as a result of its internal weakness, it breaks down in face of the first
external obstacles and is then replaced by regression to the perverse
fixation.

are diverted into numerous other channels till they find their way to expression as symptoms. The outcome may be an approximately normal sexual life—though usually a restricted one —but there is in addition psychoneurotic illness. These particular cases have become familiar to us from the psycho-analytic investigation of neurotics. Their sexual life begins like that of perverts, and a considerable part of their childhood is occupied with perverse sexual activity which occasionally extends far into maturity. A reversal due to repression then occurs, owing to internal causes (usually before puberty, but now and then even long afterwards), and from that time onwards neurosis takes the place of perversion, without the old impulses being extinguished. We are reminded of the proverb 'Junge Hure, alte Betschwester',[1] only that here youth has lasted all too short a time. The fact that perversion can be replaced by neurosis in the life of the same person, like the fact which we have already mentioned that perversion and neurosis can be distributed among different members of the same family, tallies with the view that neurosis is the negative of perversion.

SUBLIMATION    [3] The third alternative result of an abnormal constitutional disposition is made possible by the process of sublimation. This enables excessively strong excitations arising from particular sources of sexuality to find an outlet and use in other fields, so that a not inconsiderable increase in psychical efficiency results from a disposition which in itself is perilous. Here we have one of the origins of artistic activity; and, according to the completeness or incompleteness of the sublimation, a characterological analysis of a highly gifted individual, and in particular of one with an artistic disposition, may reveal a mixture, in every proportion, of efficiency, perversion and neurosis. A sub-species of sublimation is to be found in suppression by reaction-formation, which, as we have seen, begins during a child's period of latency and continues in favourable cases throughout his whole life. What we describe as a person's 'character' is built up to a considerable extent from the material of sexual excitations and is composed of instincts that have been fixed since childhood, of constructions achieved by means of sublimation, and of other constructions, employed for

[1] ['A young whore makes an old nun.']

effectively holding in check perverse impulses which have been recognized as being unutilizable.[1] The multifariously perverse sexual disposition of childhood can accordingly be regarded as the source of a number of our virtues, in so far as through reaction-formation it stimulates their development.[2]

ACCIDENTAL      No other influences on the course of sexual
EXPERIENCES    development can compare in importance with
               releases of sexuality, waves of repression and sub-
limations—the two latter being processes of which the inner causes are quite unknown to us. It might be possible to include repressions and sublimations as a part of the constitutional disposition, by regarding them as manifestations of it in life; and anyone who does so is justified in asserting that the final shape taken by sexual life is principally the outcome of the innate constitution. No one with perception will, however, dispute that an interplay of factors such as this also leaves room for the modifying effects of accidental events experienced in childhood and later. It is not easy [3] to estimate the relative efficacy of the constitutional and accidental factors. In theory one is always inclined to overestimate the former; therapeutic practice emphasizes the importance of the latter. It should, however, on no account be forgotten that the relation between the two is a co-operative and not a mutually exclusive one. The constitutional factor must await experiences before it can make itself felt; the accidental factor must have a constitutional basis in order to come into operation. To cover the majority of cases we can picture what has been described as a 'complemental

[1] [Footnote added 1920:] In the case of some character-traits it has even been possible to trace a connection with particular erotogenic components. Thus, obstinacy, thrift and orderliness arise from an exploitation of anal erotism, while ambition is determined by a strong urethral-erotic disposition. [See Freud, 1908b (last paragraph).]

[2] Emile Zola, a keen observer of human nature, describes in La joie de vivre how a girl, cheerfully and selflessly and without thought of reward, sacrificed to those she loved everything that she possessed or could lay claim to—her money and her hopes. This girl's childhood was dominated by an insatiable thirst for affection, which was transformed into cruelty on an occasion when she found herself slighted in favour of another girl.

[3] [The remainder of this paragraph and the whole of the next one were added in 1915.]

series',[1] in which the diminishing intensity of one factor is balanced by the increasing intensity of the other; there is, however, no reason to deny the existence of extreme cases at the two ends of the series.

We shall be in even closer harmony with psycho-analytic research if we give a place of preference among the accidental factors to the experiences of early childhood. The single aetiological series then falls into two, which may be called the dispositional and the definitive. In the first the constitution and the accidental experiences of childhood interact in the same manner as do the disposition and later traumatic experiences in the second. All the factors that impair sexual development show their effects by bringing about a regression, a return to an earlier phase of development.

Let us now resume our task of enumerating the factors which we have found to exercise an influence on sexual development, whether they are themselves operative forces or merely manifestations of such forces.

PRECOCITY    One such factor is spontaneous sexual precocity, whose presence at least can be demonstrated with certainty in the aetiology of the neuroses though, like other factors, it is not in itself a sufficient cause. It is manifested in the interruption, abbreviation or bringing to an end of the infantile period of latency; and it is a cause of disturbances by occasioning sexual manifestations which, owing on the one hand to the sexual inhibitions being incomplete and on the other hand to the genital system being undeveloped, are bound to be in the nature of perversions. These tendencies to perversion may thereafter either persist as such or, after repressions have set in, become the motive forces of neurotic symptoms. In any case sexual precocity makes more difficult the later control of the sexual instinct by the higher mental agencies which is so desirable, and it increases the impulsive quality which, quite apart from this, characterizes the psychical representations of

---

[1] [In 1915 the term used was 'aetiological series', which was altered to 'complemental series' in 1920. The latter term seems to have been first used by Freud in Lecture XXII of his *Introductory Lectures* (1916–17). The correction of the phrase was not carried out where it occurs again a few lines lower down.]

the instinct. Sexual precocity often runs parallel with premature intellectual development and, linked in this way, is to be found in the childhood history of persons of the greatest eminence and capacity; under such conditions its effects do not seem to be so pathogenic as when it appears in isolation.[1]

TEMPORAL FACTORS     Other factors which, along with precocity, may be classed as temporal also deserve attention. The order in which the various instinctual impulses come into activity seems to be phylogenetically determined; so, too, does the length of time during which they are able to manifest themselves before they succumb to the effects of some freshly emerging instinctual impulse or to some typical repression. Variations, however, seem to occur both in temporal sequence and in duration, and these variations must exercise a determining influence upon the final result. It cannot be a matter of indifference whether a given current makes its appearance earlier or later than a current flowing in the opposite direction, for the effect of a repression cannot be undone. Divergences in the temporal sequence in which the components come together invariably produce a difference in the outcome. On the other hand, instinctual impulses which emerge with special intensity often run a surprisingly short course—as, for instance, the heterosexual attachment of persons who later become manifest homosexuals. There is no justification for the fear that trends which set in with the greatest violence in childhood will permanently dominate the adult character; it is just as likely that they will disappear and make way for an opposite tendency. ('Gestrenge Herren regieren nicht lange.')[2]

We are not in a position to give so much as a hint as to the causes of these temporal disturbances of the process of development. A prospect opens before us at this point upon a whole phalanx of biological and perhaps, too, of historical problems of which we have not even come within striking distance.

[1] [Cf. some remarks on this point in the case history of 'Little Hans' (1909b), near the beginning of the third section of Chapter III.—The paragraph which follows was added in 1915.]
[2] ['Harsh rulers have short reigns.']

PERTINACITY      The importance of all early sexual manifesta-
OF EARLY        tions is increased by a psychical factor of un-
IMPRESSIONS     known origin, which at the moment, it must be
                admitted, can only be brought forward as a pro-
visional psychological concept. I have in mind the fact that,
in order to account for the situation, it is necessary to assume
that these early impressions of sexual life are characterized by
an increased pertinacity or susceptibility to fixation in persons
who are later to become neurotics or perverts. For the same
premature sexual manifestations, when they occur in other persons, fail to make so deep an impression; they do not tend in
a compulsive manner towards repetition nor do they lay down
the path to be taken by the sexual instinct for a whole lifetime.
Part of the explanation of this pertinacity of early impressions
may perhaps lie in another psychical factor which we must not
overlook in the causation of the neuroses, namely the preponderance attaching in mental life to memory-traces in comparison
with recent impressions. This factor is clearly dependent on
intellectual education and increases in proportion to the degree
of individual culture. The savage has been described in contrast
as 'das unglückselige Kind des Augenblickes'.[1] In consequence
of the inverse relation holding between civilization and the free
development of sexuality, of which the consequences can be
followed far into the structure of our existences, the course taken
by the sexual life of a child is just as unimportant for later life
where the cultural or social level is relatively low as it is important where that level is relatively high.

FIXATION      The ground prepared by the psychical factors
              which have just been enumerated affords a favour-
able basis for such stimulations of infantile sexuality as are
experienced accidentally. The latter (first and foremost, seduction by other children or by adults) provide the material which,
with the help of the former, can become fixated as a permanent
disorder. A good proportion of the deviations from normal
sexual life which are later observed both in neurotics and in
perverts are thus established from the very first by the impressions of childhood—a period which is regarded as being devoid

[1] ['The hapless child of the moment.'] Increase in pertinacity may
also possibly be the effect of an especially intense somatic manifestation
of sexuality in early years.

of sexuality. The causation is shared between a compliant con-stitution, precocity, the characteristic of increased pertinacity of early impressions and the chance stimulation of the sexual instinct by extraneous influences.

The unsatisfactory conclusion, however, that emerges from these investigations of the disturbances of sexual life is that we know far too little of the biological processes constituting the essence of sexuality to be able to construct from our fragmentary information a theory adequate to the understanding alike of normal and of pathological conditions.

# APPENDIX

[*References to sexuality are, of course, to be found in a large majority of Freud's writings. The following list comprises those which are more directly concerned with the subject. The date at the beginning of each entry gives the year of publication. Fuller particulars of each work will be found in the bibliography at the end of the present volume.*]

1898a.  'Sexuality in the Aetiology of the Neuroses.'
1905d.  *Three Essays on the Theory of Sexuality.*
1906a.  'My Views on the Part Played by Sexuality in the Aetiology of the Neuroses.'
1907c.  'The Sexual Enlightenment of Children.'
1908b.  'Character and Anal Erotism.'
1908c.  'On the Sexual Theories of Children.'
1908d.  ' "Civilized" Sexual Morality and Modern Nervous Sickness.'
1910a.  *Five Lectures on Psycho-Analysis,* Lecture IV.
1910c.  *Leonardo da Vinci,* Chapter III.
1910h.  'A Special Type of Choice of Object made by Men,
1912d.  'On the Universal Tendency to Debasement in the Sphere of Love.'
1912f.  'Contributions to a Discussion on Masturbation.'
1913i.  'The Disposition to Obsessional Neurosis.'
1913j.  'The Claims of Psycho-Analysis to Scientific Interest'. Part II (C).
1913k.  Preface to Bourke's *Scatalogic Rites of All Nations.*
1914c.  'On Narcissism: an Introduction.'
1916–17.  *Introductory Lectures on Psycho-Analysis,* Lectures XX, XXI, XXII and XXVI.
1917c.  'On the Transformation of Instincts, with Special Reference to Anal Erotism.'
1918a.  'The Taboo of Virginity.'
1919e.  ' "A Child is Being Beaten." '
1920a.  'The Psychogenesis of a Case of Female Homosexuality.'

1922*b*.   'Some Neurotic Mechanisms in Jealousy, Paranoia and Homosexuality', Section C.
1923*a*.   Two Encyclopaedia Articles: (2) 'The Libido Theory.'
1923*e*.   'The Infantile Genital Organization.'
1924*c*.   'The Economic Problem of Masochism.'
1924*d*.   'The Dissolution of the Oedipus Complex.'
1925*j*.   'Some Psychical Consequences of the Anatomical Distinction between the Sexes.'
1927*e*.   'Fetishism.'
1931*a*.   'Libidinal Types.'
1931*b*.   'Female Sexuality.'
1933*a*.   *New Introductory Lectures on Psycho-Analysis*, Lectures XXXII and XXXIII.
1940*a* [1938].   *An Outline of Psycho-Analysis*, Chapters III and VII.
1940*e* [1938].   'Splitting of the Ego in the Process of Defence.'

# FREUD'S
# PSYCHO-ANALYTIC PROCEDURE
## (1904 [1903])

# DIE FREUD'SCHE PSYCHOANALYTISCHE METHODE

(a) GERMAN EDITIONS:

(1903    Probable date of composition.)

1904    In Loewenfeld's *Die psychischen Zwangserscheinungen*, 545–
        551. (Wiesbaden: Bergmann.)

1906    *S.K.S.N.* I, 218–224. (1911, 2nd. ed., 213–219; 1920,
        3rd. ed.; 1922, 4th. ed.)

1924    *Technik und Metapsychol.*, 3–10.

1925    *G.S.*, 6, 3–10.

1942    *G.W.*, 5, 3–10.

(b) ENGLISH TRANSLATION:

              'Freud's Psycho-Analytic Method'

1924    *C.P.*, 1, 264–271. (Tr. J. Bernays.)

The present translation, with a new title, 'Freud's Psycho-Analytic Procedure', is a considerably altered version of the one published in 1924.

Loewenfeld's book on obsessional phenomena, to which this paper was originally contributed, is spoken of by Freud in his case history of the 'Rat Man' (1909*d*, in a footnote at the opening of Part II) as the 'standard text-book' on obsessional neurosis. Loewenfeld explains that he persuaded Freud to make this contribution because his technique had been so greatly modified since it was described in *Studies on Hysteria* (1895*d*). Loewenfeld's preface is dated 'November, 1903'; so that Freud's paper was presumably written earlier in the same year.

# FREUD'S PSYCHO-ANALYTIC PROCEDURE

THE particular psychotherapeutic procedure which Freud practises and describes as 'psycho-analysis' is an outgrowth of what was known as the 'cathartic' method and was discussed by him in collaboration with Josef Breuer in their *Studies on Hysteria* (1895). This cathartic therapy was a discovery of Breuer's, and was first used by him some ten years earlier in the successful treatment of a hysterical woman patient, in the course of which he obtained an insight into the pathogenesis of her symptoms. As the result of a personal suggestion from Breuer, Freud revived this procedure and tested it on a considerable number of patients.

The cathartic method of treatment presupposed that the patient could be hypnotized, and was based on the widening of consciousness that occurs under hypnosis. Its aim was the removal of the pathological symptoms, and it achieved this by inducing the patient to return to the psychical state in which the symptom had appeared for the first time. When this was done, there emerged in the hypnotized patient's mind memories, thoughts and impulses which had previously dropped out of his consciousness; and, as soon as he had related these to the physician, to the accompaniment of intense expressions of emotion, the symptom was overcome and its return prevented. This experience, which could be regularly repeated, was taken by the authors in their joint paper to signify that the symptom takes the place of suppressed processes which have not reached consciousness, that is, that it represents a transformation ('conversion') of these processes. They explained the therapeutic effectiveness of their treatment as due to the discharge of what had previously been, as it were, 'strangulated' affect attaching to the suppressed mental acts ('abreaction'). But in practice the simple schematic outline of the therapeutic operation was almost always complicated by the circumstance that it was not a *single* ('traumatic') impression, but in most cases a *series* of impressions —not easily scanned—which had participated in the creation of the symptom.

The main characteristic of the cathartic method, in contrast to all other methods used in psychotherapy, consists in the fact that its therapeutic efficacy does not lie in a prohibitive suggestion by the physician. The expectation is rather that the symptoms will disappear automatically as soon as the operation, based on certain hypotheses concerning the psychical mechanism, succeeds in diverting the course of mental processes from their previous channel, which found an outlet in the formation of the symptom.

The changes which Freud introduced in Breuer's cathartic method of treatment were at first changes in technique; these, however, led to new findings and have finally necessitated a different though not contradictory conception of the therapeutic process.

The cathartic method had already renounced suggestion; Freud went a step further and gave up hypnosis as well. At the present time he treats his patients as follows. Without exerting any other kind of influence, he invites them to lie down in a comfortable attitude on a sofa, while he himself sits on a chair behind them outside their field of vision. He does not even ask them to close their eyes,[1] and avoids touching them in any way, as well as any other procedure which might be reminiscent of hypnosis. The session thus proceeds like a conversation between two people equally awake, but one of whom is spared every muscular exertion and every distracting sensory impression which might divert his attention from his own mental activity.

Since, as we all know, it depends upon the choice of the patient whether he can be hypnotized or not, no matter what the skill of the physician may be, and since a large number of neurotic patients cannot be hypnotized by any means whatever, it followed that with the abandonment of hypnosis the applicability of the treatment was assured to an unlimited number of patients. On the other hand, the widening of consciousness, which had supplied the physician with precisely the psychical material of memories and images by the help of which the transformation of the symptoms and the liberation of the affects was accomplished, was now missing. Unless a substitute could

[1] [In his account of his procedure given in *The Interpretation of Dreams* (1900*a*, Chapter II; Standard Ed., 4, 101) Freud still recommended that the subject should keep his eyes closed.]

be produced for this missing element, any therapeutic effect was out of the question.

Freud found such a substitute—and a completely satisfactory one—in the 'associations' of his patients; that is, in the involuntary thoughts (most frequently regarded as disturbing elements and therefore ordinarily pushed aside) which so often break across the continuity of a consecutive narrative.

In order to secure these ideas and associations he asks the patient to 'let himself go' in what he says, 'as you would do in a conversation in which you were rambling on quite disconnectedly and at random'. Before he asks them for a detailed account of their case history he insists that they must include in it whatever comes into their heads, even if they think it unimportant or irrelevant or nonsensical; he lays special stress on their not omitting any thought or idea from their story because to relate it would be embarrassing or distressing to them. In the course of collecting this material of otherwise neglected ideas Freud made the observations which became the determining factor of his entire theory. Gaps appear in the patient's memory even while he narrates his case: actual occurrences are forgotten, the chronological order is confused, or causal connections are broken, with unintelligible results. No neurotic case history is without amnesia of some kind or other. If the patient is urged to fill these gaps in his memory by an increased application of attention, it is noticed that all the ideas which occur to him are pushed back by every possible critical expedient, until at last he feels positive discomfort when the memory really returns. From this experience Freud concludes that the amnesias are the result of a process which he calls '*repression*' and the motive for which he finds in feelings of unpleasure. The psychical forces which have brought about this repression can also be detected, according to him, in the '*resistance*' which operates against the recovery of the lost memories.

The factor of resistance has become one of the corner-stones of his theory. The ideas which are normally pushed aside on every sort of excuse—such as those mentioned above—are regarded by him as derivatives of the repressed psychical phenomena (thoughts and impulses), distorted owing to the resistance against their reproduction.

The greater the resistance, the greater is the distortion. The

value of these unintentional thoughts for the purposes of therapeutic technique lies in this relation of theirs to the repressed
psychical material. If one possesses a procedure which makes it
possible to arrive at the repressed material from the associations,
at the distorted material from the distortions, then what was
formerly unconscious in mental life can be made accessible to
consciousness even without hypnosis.

Freud has developed on this basis an art of interpretation
which takes on the task of, as it were, extracting the pure metal
of the repressed thoughts from the ore of the unintentional ideas.
This work of interpretation is applied not only to the patient's
ideas but also to his dreams, which open up the most direct
approach to a knowledge of the unconscious, to his unintentional as well as to his purposeless actions (symptomatic acts)
and to the blunders he makes in everyday life (slips of the
tongue, bungled actions, and so on). The details of this technique of interpretation or translation have not yet been published by Freud. According to indications he has given, they
comprise a number of rules, reached empirically, of how the unconscious material may be reconstructed from the associations,
directions on how to know what it means when the patient's
ideas cease to flow, and experiences of the most important
typical resistances that arise in the course of such treatments. A
bulky volume called *The Interpretation of Dreams*, published by
Freud in 1900, may be regarded as the forerunner of an initia-
tion into his technique.

From these remarks on the technique of the psycho-analytic
method the conclusion might be drawn that its inventor has
given himself needless trouble and has made a mistake in
abandoning the less complicated hypnotic mode of procedure.
However, in the first place, the technique of psycho-analysis is
much easier in practice, when once one has learnt it, than any
description of it would indicate; and, secondly, there is no other
way which leads to the desired goal, so that the hard road is still
the shortest one to travel. The objection to hypnosis is that it
conceals the resistance and for that reason has obstructed the
physician's insight into the play of psychical forces. Hypnosis
does not do away with the resistance but only evades it and
therefore yields only incomplete information and transitory
therapeutic success.

The task which the psycho-analytic method seeks to perform

may be formulated in different ways, which are, however, in their essence equivalent. It may, for instance, be stated thus: the task of the treatment is to remove the amnesias. When all gaps in memory have been filled in, all the enigmatic products of mental life elucidated, the continuance and even a renewal of the morbid condition are made impossible. Or the formula may be expressed in this fashion: all repressions must be undone. The mental condition is then the same as one in which all amnesias have been removed. Another formulation reaches further: the task consists in making the unconscious accessible to consciousness, which is done by overcoming the resistances. But it must be remembered that an ideal condition such as this is not present even in the normal, and further that it is only rarely possible to carry the treatment to a point approaching it. Just as health and sickness are not different from each other in essence but are only separated by a quantitative line of demarcation which can be determined in practice, so the aim of the treatment will never be anything else but the *practical* recovery of the patient, the restoration of his ability to lead an active life and of his capacity for enjoyment. In a treatment which is incomplete or in which success is not perfect, one may at any rate achieve a considerable improvement in the general mental condition, while the symptoms (though now of smaller importance to the patient) may continue to exist without stamping him as a sick man.

The therapeutic procedure remains the same, apart from insignificant modifications, for all the various clinical pictures that may be presented in hysteria, and all forms of obsessional neurosis. This does not imply, however, that it can have an un-limited application. The nature of the psycho-analytic method involves indications and contra-indications with respect to the person to be treated as well as with respect to the clinical picture. Chronic cases of psychoneuroses without any very violent or dangerous symptoms are the most favourable ones for psycho-analysis: thus in the first place every species of obsessional neurosis, obsessive thinking and acting, and cases of hysteria in which phobias and aboulias play the most important part; further, all somatic expressions of hysteria whenever they do not, as in anorexia, require the physician to attend promptly to the speedy removal of symptoms. In acute cases of hysteria it will be necessary to wait for a calmer stage; in all cases where nervous exhaustion dominates the clinical picture a treatment which in itself demands effort, brings only slow improvement and for a time cannot take the persistence of the symptoms into account, will have to be avoided.

Various qualifications are required of anyone who is to be beneficially affected by psycho-analysis. To begin with, he must be capable of a psychically normal condition; during periods of confusion or melancholic depression nothing can be accomplished even in cases of hysteria. Furthermore, a certain measure of natural intelligence and ethical development are to be required of him; if the physician has to deal with a worthless character, he soon loses the interest which makes it possible for him to enter profoundly into the patient's mental life. Deep-rooted malformations of character, traits of an actually degenerate constitution, show themselves during treatment as sources of a resistance that can scarcely be overcome. In this respect the constitution of the patient sets a general limit to the curative effect of psychotherapy. If the patient's age is in the neighbourhood of the fifties the conditions for psycho-analysis become unfavourable. The mass of psychical material is then no longer manageable; the time required for recovery is too long; and the ability to undo psychical processes begins to grow weaker.

In spite of all these limitations, the number of persons suitable for psycho-analytic treatment is extraordinarily large and the extension which has come to our therapeutic powers from this method is, according to Freud, very considerable. Freud requires long periods, six months to three years, for an effective treatment; yet he informs us that up to the present, owing to various circumstances which can easily be guessed, he has for the most part been in a position to try his treatment only on very severe cases: patients have come to him after many years of illness, completely incapacitated for life, and, after being disappointed by all kinds of treatments, have had recourse as a last resort to a method which is novel and has been greeted with many doubts. In cases of less severe illness the duration of the treatment might well be much shorter, and very great advantage in the direction of future prevention might be achieved.

# ON PSYCHOTHERAPY
## (1905 [1904])

# ÜBER PSYCHOTHERAPIE

(a) GERMAN EDITIONS:
(1904   Dec. 12. Delivered as a lecture before the Wiener
          medizinisches Doktorenkollegium.)
1905   *Wien. med. Presse*, Jan. 1, 9–16.
1906   *S.K.S.N.* I, 205–217. (1911, 2nd. ed., 201–212; 1920,
          3rd. ed.; 1922, 4th. ed.)
1924   *Technik und Metapsychol.*, 11–24.
1925   *G.S.*, **6**, 11–24.
1942   *G.W.*, **5**, 13–26.

(b) ENGLISH TRANSLATIONS:
                    'On Psychotherapy'
1909   *S.P.H.*, 175–185. (Tr. A. A. Brill.) (1912, 2nd. ed.; 1920,
          3rd. ed.)
1924   *C.P.*, **1**, 249–263. (Tr. J. Bernays.)

The present translation is a considerably modified version of
the one published in 1924.

# ON PSYCHOTHERAPY

GENTLEMEN,—Some eight years have passed since I had the opportunity, on the invitation of your much regretted chairman, Professor von Reder, of speaking here on the subject of hysteria.[1] Shortly before that occasion I had published, in 1895, in collaboration with Dr. Josef Breuer, the *Studies on Hysteria* in which, on the basis of the new knowledge which we owe to his researches, an attempt was made to introduce a new method of treating the neuroses. I am glad to be able to say that the efforts we made in our *Studies* have met with success; the ideas expressed in them concerning the effects produced by psychical traumas owing to retention of affect, as well as the conception of hysterical symptoms as the results of an excitation transposed from the sphere of the mental to the physical—ideas for which we coined the terms 'abreaction' and 'conversion'—are to-day generally known and understood. There is, at least in German-speaking countries, no presentation of hysteria to-day that does not take them to some extent into account, and we have no colleagues who do not, for a short distance at least, follow the road pointed out by us. And yet, while they were still new, these theorems and this terminology must have sounded not a little strange.

I cannot say the same of the therapeutic procedure which was introduced to our colleagues at the same time as our theory; it is still struggling for recognition. There may be special reasons for this. At that time the technique of the method was as yet undeveloped; it was impossible for me to give medical readers of the book the directions necessary to enable them to carry through the treatment completely. But causes of a general nature have certainly also played a part. To many physicians, even to-day, psychotherapy seems to be a product of modern

[1] [The occasion referred to was a series of three lectures on hysteria given by Freud before the Wiener medizinisches Doktorenkollegium on October 14, 21 and 28, 1895—that is, *nine* years earlier. These were never published by him, though they were reported very fully in the Vienna medical papers (Freud, 1895g). He had lectured on a similar subject, the aetiology of hysteria, a year later (May 2, 1896; 1896c) before the Verein für Psychiatrie und Neurologie, and the 'eight years' in the text above may have been due to a confusion between the two occasions.]

mysticism and, compared with our physico-chemical remedies which are applied on the basis of physiological knowledge, appears positively unscientific and unworthy of the attention of a serious investigator. Allow me, therefore, to defend the cause of psychotherapy before you, and to point out to you what may be described as unjust or mistaken in this condemnation of it.

In the first place, let me remind you that psychotherapy is in no way a modern method of treatment. On the contrary, it is the most ancient form of therapy in medicine. In Loewenfeld's instructive *Lehrbuch der gesamten Psychotherapie* [1897] many of the methods of primitive and ancient medical science are described. The majority of them must be classed under the head of psychotherapy; in order to effect a cure a condition of 'expectation coloured by faith' was induced in sick persons—a condition which answers a similar purpose for us to-day. Even since physicians have come upon other remedies, psychotherapeutic endeavours of one kind or another have never completely disappeared from medicine.[1]

Secondly, let me draw your attention to the fact that we physicians cannot discard psychotherapy, if only because another person intimately concerned in the process of recovery —the patient—has no intention of discarding it. You will know of the increase in knowledge on this subject that we owe to the Nancy school, to Liébeault and Bernheim. A factor dependent on the psychical disposition of the patient contributes, without any intention on our part, to the effect of every therapeutic process initiated by a physician; most frequently it is favourable to recovery, but often it acts as an inhibition. We have learned to use the word 'suggestion' for this phenomenon, and Möbius has taught us that the unreliability which we deplore in so many of our therapeutic measures may be traced back to the disturbing influence of this very powerful factor. All physicians, therefore, yourselves included, are continually practising psychotherapy, even when you have no intention of doing so and are not aware of it; it is a disadvantage, however, to leave the mental factor in your treatment so completely in the patient's

[1] [The contents of this and the next few paragraphs will be found in a much expanded form in Freud's paper on 'Psychical Treatment' (1905*b*, this volume p. 298 ff.), to which the present paper may almost be regarded as a sequel.]

hands. Thus it is impossible to keep a check on it, to administer it in doses or to intensify it. Is it not then a justifiable endeavour on the part of a physician to seek to obtain command of this factor, to use it with a purpose, and to direct and strengthen it? This and nothing else is what scientific psychotherapy proposes.

And, in the third place, Gentlemen, I would remind you of the well-established fact that certain diseases, in particular the psychoneuroses, are far more readily accessible to mental influences than to any other form of medication. It is not a modern dictum but an old saying of physicians that these diseases are not cured by the drug but by the physician, that is, by the personality of the physician, inasmuch as through it he exerts a mental influence. I am well aware that you favour the view which Vischer, the professor of aesthetics, expressed so well in his parody of Faust:

> Ich weiß, das Physikalische
> Wirkt öfters aufs Moralische [1]

But would it not be more to the point to say—and is it not more often the case—moral (that is, mental) means can influence a man's moral side?

There are many ways and means of practising psychotherapy. All that lead to recovery are good. Our usual word of comfort, which we dispense so liberally to our patients—'You'll soon be all right again'—, corresponds to one of these psychotherapeutic methods; but now that we have deeper insight into the neuroses, we are no longer obliged to confine ourselves to the word of comfort. We have developed the technique of hypnotic suggestion, and psychotherapy by mental distraction, by exercise, and by eliciting suitable affects. I despise none of these methods and would use them all in appropriate circumstances. If I have actually come to confine myself to one form of treatment, to the method which Breuer called *cathartic*, but which I myself prefer to call 'analytic', it is because I have allowed myself to be influenced by purely subjective motives. Because of the part I have played in founding this therapy, I feel a personal obligation to devote myself to closer investigation of it and to

[1] [I know that the physical
  Often influences the moral.]
  F. T. Vischer, *Faust: der Tragödie III Teil* (Scene 4).

the development of its technique. And I may say that the analytic method of psychotherapy is the one that penetrates most deeply and carries farthest, the one by means of which the most extensive transformations can be effected in patients. Putting aside for a moment the therapeutic point of view, I may also say of it that it is the most interesting method, the only one which informs us at all about the origin and inter-relation of morbid phenomena. Owing to the insight which we gain into mental illness by this method, it alone should be capable of leading us beyond its own limits and of pointing out the way to other forms of therapeutic influence.

Permit me now to correct a few mistakes that have been made in regard to this cathartic or analytic method of psychotherapy, and to give a few explanations on the subject.

(a) I have observed that this method is very often confused with hypnotic treatment by suggestion; I have noticed this because it happens comparatively often that colleagues who do not ordinarily confide their cases to me send me patients—refractory patients, of course—with a request that I should hypnotize them. Now I have not used hypnosis for therapeutic purposes for some eight years (except for a few special experiments) so that I habitually send back these cases with the recommendation that anyone who relies upon hypnosis may employ it himself. There is, actually, the greatest possible antithesis between suggestive and analytic technique—the same antithesis which, in regard to the fine arts, the great Leonardo da Vinci summed up in the formulas: *per via di porre* and *per via di levare*.[1] Painting, says Leonardo, works *per via di porre*, for it applies a substance—particles of colour—where there was nothing before, on the colourless canvas; sculpture, however, proceeds *per via di levare*, since it takes away from the block of stone all that hides the surface of the statue contained in it. In a similar way, the technique of suggestion aims at proceeding *per via di porre*; it is not concerned with the origin, strength and meaning of the morbid symptoms, but instead, it superimposes something—a suggestion—in the expectation that it will be strong enough to restrain the pathogenic idea from coming to

[1] [A full discussion of this will be found in Richter (1939), 1, 87 ff., where the relevant passages from Leonardo are given in Italian and English.]

expression. Analytic therapy, on the other hand, does not seek to add or to introduce anything new, but to take away something, to bring out something; and to this end concerns itself with the genesis of the morbid symptoms and the psychical context of the pathogenic idea which it seeks to remove. It is by the use of this mode of investigation that analytic therapy has increased our knowledge so notably. I gave up the suggestive technique, and with it hypnosis, so early in my practice because I despaired of making suggestion powerful and enduring enough to effect permanent cures. In every severe case I saw the suggestions which had been applied crumble away again; after which the disease or some substitute for it was back once more. Besides all this I have another reproach to make against this method, namely, that it conceals from us all insight into the play of mental forces; it does not permit us, for example, to recognize the *resistance* with which the patient clings to his disease and thus even fights against his own recovery; yet it is this phenomenon of resistance which alone makes it possible to understand his behaviour in daily life.

(*b*) It seems to me that there is a widespread and erroneous impression among my colleagues that this technique of searching for the origins of an illness and removing its manifestations by that means is an easy one which can be practised off-hand, as it were. I conclude this from the fact that not one of all the people who have shown an interest in my therapy and passed definite judgements upon it has ever asked me how I actually go about it. There can be only one reason for this: that they think there is nothing to enquire about, that the thing is perfectly self-evident. Again, I am now and then astonished to hear that in this or that department of a hospital a young assistant has received an order from his chief to undertake a 'psychoanalysis' of a hysterical patient. I am sure he would not be allowed to examine an extirpated tumour unless he had convinced his chiefs that he was conversant with histological technique. Similarly, reports reach my ears that this or that colleague has arranged appointments with a patient in order to undertake a mental treatment of the case, though I am certain he knows nothing of the technique of any such therapy. His expectation must be therefore that the patient will make him a present of his secrets, or perhaps that he is looking for salvation in some sort of confession or confidence. I should not be surprised if a patient were injured rather than benefited by being treated in such a fashion. For it is not so easy to play upon the instrument of the mind. I am reminded on such occasions of the words of a world-famous neurotic—though it is true that he was never treated by a physician but existed only in a poet's imagination—Hamlet, Prince of Denmark. The King has ordered two courtiers, Rosenkranz and Guildenstern, to follow him, to question him and drag the secret of his depression out of him. He wards them off. Then some recorders are brought on the stage and Hamlet, taking one of them, begs one of his tormentors to play upon it, telling him that it is as easy as lying. The courtier excuses himself, for he knows no touch of the instrument, and when he cannot be persuaded to try it, Hamlet finally breaks out with these words: 'Why, look you now, how unworthy a thing you make of me! You would play upon me; . . . you would pluck out the heart of my mystery; you would sound me from my lowest note to the top of my compass; and there is much music, excellent voice, in this little organ; yet you cannot make it speak. *'Sblood, do you think I am easier to be played on than a pipe? Call me what instrument you will, though you can fret me, you cannot play upon me.'* (Act III, Scene 2.)

(c) From certain of my remarks you will have gathered that there are many characteristics in the analytic method which prevent it from being an ideal form of therapy. *Tuto, cito, jucunde*: investigation and probing do not indicate speedy results, and the resistance I have mentioned would prepare you to expect unpleasantness of various kinds. Psycho-analytic treatment certainly makes great demands upon the patient as well as upon the physician. From the patient it requires perfect sincerity—a sacrifice in itself; it absorbs time and is therefore also costly; for the physician it is no less time-absorbing, and the technique which he must study and practise is fairly laborious. I consider it quite justifiable to resort to more convenient methods of treatment as long as there is any prospect of achieving anything by their means. That, after all, is the only point at issue. If the more difficult and lengthy method accomplishes considerably more than the short and easy one, then, in spite of everything, the use of the former is justified. Only consider, Gentlemen, how much more inconvenient and costly is the Finsen therapy of lupus than the method of cauterizing and scraping previously employed; and yet the use of the former signifies a great advance, for it performs a radical cure. Although I do not wish to carry this comparison to extremes, the psycho-analytic method may claim a similar privilege. Actually, I have been able to elaborate and to test my therapeutic method only on severe, indeed on the severest cases; at first my material consisted entirely of patients who had tried everything else without success, and had spent long years in sanatoria. I have scarcely been able to bring together sufficient material to enable me to say how my method works with those slighter, episodic cases which we see recovering under all kinds of influences and even spontaneously. Psycho-analytic therapy was created through and for the treatment of patients permanently unfit for existence, and its triumph has been that it has made a satisfactorily large number of these permanently *fit* for existence. In the face of such an achievement all the effort expended seems trivial. We cannot conceal from ourselves what, as physicians, we are in the habit of denying to our patients, namely, that a severe neurosis is no less serious for the sufferer than any cachexia or any of the dreaded major diseases.

(*d*) The conditions under which this method is indicated, or contra-indicated, can scarcely be definitely laid down as yet, because of the many practical limitations to which my activities have been subjected. Nevertheless, I will attempt to discuss a few of them here:

(1) One should look beyond the patient's illness and form an estimate of his whole personality; those patients who do not possess a reasonable degree of education and a fairly reliable character should be refused. It must not be forgotten that there are healthy people as well as unhealthy ones who are good for nothing in life, and that there is a temptation to ascribe to their illness everything that incapacitates them, if they show any sign of neurosis. In my opinion a neurosis is by no means a stamp of degeneracy, though it may often enough be found in one person along with the signs of degeneracy. Now analytic psychotherapy is not a process suited to the treatment of neuropathic degeneracy; on the contrary, degeneracy is a barrier to its effectiveness. Nor is the method applicable to people who are not driven to seek treatment by their own sufferings, but

who submit to it only because they are forced to by the authority of relatives. The qualification which is the determining factor of fitness for psycho-analytic treatment—that is, whether the patient is educable—must be discussed further from another standpoint.

(2) To be quite safe, one should limit one's choice of patients to those who possess a normal mental condition, since in the psycho-analytic method this is used as a foothold from which to obtain control of the morbid manifestations. Psychoses, states of confusion and deeply-rooted (I might say toxic) depression are therefore not suitable for psycho-analysis; at least not for the method as it has been practised up to the present. I do not regard it as by any means impossible that by suitable changes in the method we may succeed in overcoming this contra-indication—and so be able to initiate a psychotherapy of the psychoses.

(3) The age of patients has this much importance in determining their fitness for psycho-analytic treatment, that, on the one hand, near or above the age of fifty the elasticity of the mental processes, on which the treatment depends, is as a rule lacking—old people are no longer educable—and, on the other hand, the mass of material to be dealt with would prolong the duration of the treatment indefinitely. In the other direction the age limit can be determined only individually; youthful persons under the age of adolescence are often exceedingly amenable to influence.

(4) Psycho-analysis should not be attempted when the speedy removal of dangerous symptoms is required, as, for example, in a case of hysterical anorexia.

By this time you will have formed an impression that the field of analytic psychotherapy is a very narrow one, since you have in fact heard nothing from me except indications that point against it. There remain, however, cases and types of disease enough on which this therapy may be tested—as, for instance, all chronic forms of hysteria with residual manifestations, the broad field of obsessive conditions, aboulias, and the like.

It is gratifying that precisely the most valuable and most highly developed persons are best suited for this procedure; and one may also safely claim that in cases where analytic psychotherapy has been able to achieve but little, any other therapy would certainly not have been able to effect anything at all.

(*e*) You will no doubt wish to enquire about the possibility of doing harm by undertaking a psycho-analysis. In reply to this I may say that if you are willing to judge impartially, if you will consider this procedure in the same spirit of critical fairness that you show to our other therapeutic methods, you will have to agree with me that no injury to the patient is to be feared when the treatment is conducted with comprehension. Anyone who is accustomed, like the lay public, to blame the treatment for whatever happens during an illness will doubtless judge differently. It is not so very long since the same prejudice was directed against our hydropathic establishments. Many patients who were advised to go into an establishment of that kind hesitated because they had known someone who had entered the place as a nervous invalid and had become insane there. As you may guess, these were cases of early general paralysis that could still in their first stage be sent to a hydropathic establishment; once there, they had run their inevitable course until manifest mental disorder supervened: but the public blamed the water for this disastrous change. When it is a matter of new kinds of therapeutic treatment even physicians are not always free from such errors of judgement. I recall once making an attempt at psychotherapy with a woman who had passed the greater part of her life in a state alternating between mania and melancholia. I took on the case at the close of a period of melancholia and for two weeks things seemed to go smoothly; in the third week we were already at the beginning of the next attack of mania. This was undoubtedly a spontaneous transformation of the clinical picture, since in two weeks analytic psychotherapy cannot accomplish anything. And yet the eminent physician (now deceased) who saw the case with me could not refrain from the remark that psychotherapy was probably to blame for this 'relapse'. I am quite convinced that in other circumstances he would have shown a more critical judgement.

(*f*) Finally, Gentlemen, I must confess that it is hardly fair to take up your attention for so long on the subject of

psycho-analytic therapy without telling you in what this treatment consists and on what it is based. Still, as I am forced to be
brief, I can only hint at this. This therapy, then, is based on the
recognition that unconscious ideas—or better, the unconsciousness of certain mental processes—are the direct cause of the
morbid symptoms. We share this opinion with the French school
(Janet) who, by the way, owing to excessive schematization,
refer the cause of hysterical symptoms to an unconscious *idée
fixe*.[1] Now please do not be afraid that this is going to land us
in the depths of philosophical obscurities. Our unconscious is
not quite the same thing as that of philosophers and, moreover,
the majority of philosophers will hear nothing of 'unconscious
mental processes'. If, however, you will look at the matter from
our point of view, you will understand that the transformation
of this unconscious material in the mind of the patient into conscious material must have the result of correcting his deviation
from normality and of lifting the compulsion to which his mind
has been subjected. For conscious will-power governs only conscious mental processes, and every mental compulsion is rooted
in the unconscious. Nor need you ever fear that the patient will
be harmed by the shock accompanying the introduction of the
unconscious into consciousness, for you can convince yourselves
theoretically that the somatic and emotional effect of an impulse that has become conscious can never be so powerful as
that of an unconscious one. It is only by the application of our
highest mental functions, which are bound up with consciousness, that we can control all our impulses.

There is, however, another angle from which you may seek
to understand the psycho-analytic method. The uncovering and
translating of the unconscious occurs in the face of a continuous *resistance* on the part of the patient. The process of
bringing this unconscious material to light is associated with unpleasure, and because of this the patient rejects it again and
again. It is for you then to interpose in this conflict in the
patient's mental life. If you succeed in persuading him to
accept, by virtue of a better understanding, something that up
to now, in consequence of this automatic regulation by unpleasure, he has rejected (repressed), you will have accomplished something towards his education. For it is education
even to induce someone who dislikes getting up early to do so

[1] [See Janet, 1894, Chapter II.]

all the same. Psycho-analytic treatment may in general be conceived of as such a *re-education in overcoming internal resistances*. Re-education of this kind is, however, in no respect more necessary to nervous patients than in regard to the mental element in their sexual life. For nowhere else have civilization and education done so much harm as in this field, and this is the point, as experience will show you, at which to look for those aetiologies of the neuroses that are amenable to influence; for the other aetiological factor, the constitutional component, consists of something fixed and unalterable. And from this it follows that one important qualification is required of the physician in this work: not only must his own character be irreproachable—'As to morals, that goes without saying', as the hero of Vischer's novel *Auch Einer* was in the habit of declaring —but he must also have overcome in his own mind that mixture of prurience and prudery with which, unfortunately, so many people habitually consider sexual problems.

At this juncture another remark is perhaps not out of place. I know that the emphasis which I lay upon the part played by sexuality in creating the psychoneuroses has become generally known. But I know, too, that qualifications and exact particularization are of little use with the general public; there is very little room in the memory of the multitude; it only retains the bare gist of any thesis and fabricates an extreme version which is easy to remember. It may be, too, that some physicians vaguely apprehend the content of my doctrine to be that I regard sexual privation as the ultimate cause of the neuroses. In the conditions of life in modern society there is certainly no lack of sexual privation. On this basis, would it not be simpler to aim directly at recovery by recommending sexual activity as a therapeutic measure, instead of pursuing the circuitous and laborious path of mental treatment? I know of nothing which could impel me to suppress such an inference if it were justified. The real state of things, however, is otherwise. Sexual need and privation are merely one factor at work in the mechanism of neurosis; if there were no others the result would be dissipation, not disease. The other, no less essential, factor, which is all too readily forgotten, is the neurotic's aversion from sexuality, his incapacity for loving, that feature of the mind which I have called 'repression'. Not until there is a conflict between the two tendencies does nervous illness break out, and therefore to advise sexual activity in the psychoneuroses can only very rarely be described as good advice.

Let me end upon this defensive note. And let us hope that your interest in psychotherapy, when freed from every hostile prejudice, may lend us support in our endeavour to achieve success in treating even severe cases of psychoneurosis.

# MY VIEWS ON THE PART PLAYED
# BY SEXUALITY IN THE
# AETIOLOGY OF THE NEUROSES
## (1906 [1905])

MEINE ANSICHTEN ÜBER DIE ROLLE DER
SEXUALITÄT IN DER ÄTIOLOGIE DER NEUROSEN

(a) GERMAN EDITIONS:

(1905   June. Date of MS.)
 1906   In Loewenfeld's *Sexualleben und Nervenleiden*, 4th. ed.
          (1914, 5th. ed., 313–322).
 1906   *S.K.S.N.*, I, 225–234. (1911, 2nd. ed., 220–229; 1920,
          3rd. ed.; 1922, 4th. ed.)
 1924   *G.S.*, **5**, 123–133.
 1942   *G.W.*, **5**, 149–159.

(b) ENGLISH TRANSLATIONS:
          'My Views on the Rôle of Sexuality in the
              Etiology of the Neuroses'
 1909   *S.P.H.*, 186–193. (Tr. A. A. Brill) (1912, 2nd. ed.; 1920,
          3rd. ed.)
          'My Views on the Part Played by Sexuality
              in the Aetiology of the Neuroses'
 1924   *C.P.*, **1**, 272–283. (Tr. J. Bernays.)

The present translation is a new one by James Strachey.


Earlier editions of this book of Loewenfeld's had included
discussions of Freud's views; but for the 4th edition Loewenfeld
persuaded Freud to write this paper. He agreed to revise it for
the 5th edition, but in fact only made a single trivial alteration.

# MY VIEWS ON THE PART PLAYED BY SEXUALITY IN THE AETIOLOGY OF THE NEUROSES

My theory of the aetiological importance of the sexual factor in the neuroses can best be appreciated, in my opinion, by following the history of its development. For I have no desire whatever to deny that it has gone through a process of evolution and been modified in the course of it. My professional colleagues may find a guarantee in this admission that the theory is nothing other than the product of continuous and ever deeper-going experience. What is born of speculation, on the contrary, may easily spring into existence complete and thereafter remain unchangeable.

Originally my theory related only to the clinical pictures comprised under the term 'neurasthenia', among which I was particularly struck by two, which occasionally appear as pure types and which I described as 'neurasthenia proper' and 'anxiety neurosis'. It had, to be sure, always been a matter of common knowledge that sexual factors *may* play a part in the causation of these forms of illness; but those factors were not regarded as invariably operative, nor was there any idea of giving them precedence over other aetiological influences. I was surprised to begin with at the frequency of gross disturbances in the *vita sexualis* of nervous patients; the more I set about looking for such disturbances—bearing in mind the fact that everyone hides the truth in matters of sex—and the more skilful I became at pursuing my enquiries in the face of a preliminary denial, the more regularly was I able to discover pathogenic factors in sexual life, till little seemed to stand in the way of my assuming their universal occurrence. It was necessary, however, to presuppose from the start that sexual irregularities occurred with similar frequency in our ordinary society under the pressure of social conditions; and a doubt might remain as to the degree of deviation from normal sexual functioning which should be regarded as pathogenic. I was therefore obliged to attach less importance to the invariable evidence of sexual noxae than to a second discovery which seemed to me

271

less ambiguous. It emerged that the form taken by the illness—neurasthenia or anxiety neurosis—bore a constant relation to the nature of the sexual noxa involved. In typical cases of neurasthenia a history of regular masturbation or persistent emissions was found; in anxiety neurosis factors appeared such as *coitus interruptus*, 'unconsummated excitation', and other conditions—in all of which there seemed to be the common element of an insufficient discharge of the libido that had been produced. It was only after this discovery, which was easy to make and could be confirmed as often as one liked, that I had the courage to claim a preferential position for sexual influences in the aetiology of the neuroses. Furthermore, in the mixed forms of neurasthenia and anxiety neurosis which are so common it was possible to trace a combination of the aetiologies which I had assumed for the two pure forms. Moreover, this twofold form assumed by the neurosis seemed to tally with the polar (i.e. the masculine and feminine) character of sexuality.

At the time at which I was attributing to sexuality this important part in the production of the *simple* neuroses,[1] I was still faithful to a purely psychological theory in regard to the *psychoneuroses*—a theory in which the sexual factor was regarded as no more significant than any other emotional source of feeling. On the basis of some observations made by Josef Breuer on a hysterical patient more than ten years earlier, I collaborated with him in a study of the mechanism of the generation of hysterical symptoms, using the method of awakening the patient's memories in a state of hypnosis; and we reached conclusions which enabled us to bridge the gap between Charcot's traumatic hysteria and common non-traumatic hysteria (Breuer and Freud, 1895). We were led to the assumption that hysterical symptoms are the permanent results of psychical traumas, the sum of affect attaching to which has, for particular reasons, been prevented from being worked over consciously and has therefore found an abnormal path into somatic innervation. The terms 'strangulated affect', 'conversion' and 'abreaction' cover the distinctive features of this hypothesis.

But in view of the close connections between the psychoneuroses and the simple neuroses, which go so far, indeed, that

[1] In my [first] paper on anxiety neurosis (1895*b*).

a differential diagnosis is not always easy for inexperienced observers, it could not be long before the knowledge arrived at in the one field was extended to the other. Moreover, apart from this consideration, a deeper investigation of the psychical mechanism of hysterical symptoms led to the same result. For if the psychical traumas from which the hysterical symptoms were derived were pursued further and further by means of the 'cathartic' procedure initiated by Breuer and me, experiences were eventually reached which belonged to the patient's childhood and related to his sexual life. And this was so, even in cases in which the onset of the illness had been brought about by some commonplace emotion of a non-sexual knd. Unless these sexual traumas of childhood were taken into account it was impossible either to elucidate the symptoms (to understand the way in which they were determined) or to prevent their recurrence. In this way the unique significance of sexual experiences in the aetiology of the psychoneuroses seemed to be established beyond a doubt; and this fact remains to this day one of the corner-stones of my theory.

This theory might be expressed by saying that the cause of life-long hysterical neuroses lies in what are in themselves for the most part the trivial sexual experiences of early childhood; and, put in this way, it might no doubt sound strange. But if we take the historical development of the theory into account, and see as its essence the proposition that hysteria is the expression of a particular behaviour of the individual's sexual function and that this behaviour is decisively determined by the first influences and experiences brought to bear in childhood, we shall be a paradox the poorer but the richer by a motive for turning our attention to something of the highest importance (though it has hitherto been grossly neglected)—the after-effects of the impressions of childhood.

I will postpone until later in this paper a more thorough-going discussion of the question whether we are to regard the sexual experiences of childhood as the causes of hysteria (and obsessional neurosis), and I will now return to the form taken by the theory in some of my shorter preliminary publications during the years 1895 and 1896 (Freud, 1896*b* and 1896*c*). By laying stress on the supposed aetiological factors it was possible at that time to draw a contrast between the common neuroses as disorders with a *contemporary* aetiology and psychoneuroses whose aetiology was chiefly to be looked for in the sexual experiences of the remote past. The theory culminated in this thesis: if the *vita sexualis* is normal, there can be no neurosis.

Though even to-day I do not consider these assertions incorrect, it is not to be wondered at that, in the course of ten years of continuous effort at reaching an understanding of these phenomena, I have made a considerable step forward from the views I then held, and now believe that I am in a position, on the basis of deeper experience, to correct the insufficiencies, the displacements and the misunderstandings under which my theory then laboured. At that time my material was still scanty, and it happened by chance to include a disproportionately large number of cases in which sexual seduction by an adult or by older children played the chief part in the history of the patient's childhood. I thus over-estimated the frequency of such events (though in other respects they were not open to doubt). Moreover, I was at that period unable to distinguish with certainty between falsifications made by hysterics in their memories of childhood and traces of real events. Since then I have learned to explain a number of phantasies of seduction as attempts at fending off memories of the subject's *own* sexual activity (infantile masturbation). When this point had been clarified, the 'traumatic' element in the sexual experiences of childhood lost its importance and what was left was the realization that infantile sexual activity (whether spontaneous or provoked) prescribes the direction that will be taken by later sexual life after maturity. The same clarification (which corrected the most important of my early mistakes) also made it necessary to modify my view of the mechanism of hysterical symptoms. They were now no longer to be regarded as direct derivatives of the repressed memories of childhood experiences; but between the symptoms and the childish impressions there were inserted the patient's *phantasies* (or imaginary memories), mostly produced during the years of puberty, which on the one side were built up out of and over the childhood memories and on the other side were transformed directly into the symptoms. It was only after the introduction of this element of hysterical phantasies that the texture of the neurosis and its relation to the patient's life became intelligible; a surprising analogy came to light, too, between these unconscious phantasies of hysterics and the imaginary creations of paranoics which become conscious as delusions.[1]

After I had made this correction, 'infantile sexual traumas' were in a sense replaced by the 'infantilism of sexuality'. A second modification of the original theory lay not far off. Along with the supposed frequency of seduction in childhood, I ceased also to lay exaggerated stress on the *accidental* influencing of sexuality on to which I had sought to thrust the main responsibility for the causation of the illness, though I had not on that account denied the constitutional and hereditary factors. I had even hoped to solve the problem of choice of neurosis (the decision to which form of psychoneurosis the patient is to fall a victim) by reference to the details of the sexual experiences of childhood. I believed at that time—though with reservations—that a passive attitude in these scenes produced a predisposition to hysteria and, on the other hand, an active one a predisposition to obsessional neurosis. Later on I was obliged to abandon this view entirely, even though some facts demand that in some way or other the supposed correlation between passivity and hysteria and between activity and obsessional neurosis shall be maintained.[2] Accidental influences derived from experience having thus receded into the background, the factors of constitution and heredity necessarily gained the upper hand once more; but there was this difference between my views and those prevailing in other quarters, that on my theory

[1] [This passage was Freud's first explicit published intimation of his change of views on the relative importance of traumatic experiences and unconscious phantasies in childhood, apart from a brief allusion in his *Three Essays* (1905*d*; this volume, p. 190). In fact, however, he had become aware of his error many years earlier, for he revealed it in a letter to Fliess on September 21, 1897 (Freud, 1950*a*, Letter 69). The effects on Freud's own mind of the discovery of his mistake are vividly related by him in the first section of his 'History of the Psycho-Analytic Movement' (1914*d*) and in the third section of his 'Autobiographical Study' (1925*d*).]

[2] [This particular solution of the problem of 'choice of neurosis' is most clearly expressed in Freud's second paper on the 'Neuropsychoses of Defence' (1896*b*) and his French paper of the same date (1896*a*). His interest in the general question of choice of neurosis goes back at least to the beginning of the same year (Draft K in Freud, 1950*a*) and he used the term itself in a letter to Fliess of May 30, 1896 (Letter 46). He was to return to the subject a few years later in special reference to obsessional neurosis (1913*i*), and indeed the problem never ceased to occupy his mind.]

the 'sexual constitution' took the place of a 'general neuro-pathic disposition'. In my recently published *Three Essays on the Theory of Sexuality* (1905*d* [this volume p. 125]) I have tried to give a picture of the variegated nature of this sexual constitu-tion as well as of the composite character of the sexual instinct in general and its derivation from contributory sources from different parts of the organism.

As a further corollary to my modified view of 'sexual traumas in childhood', my theory now developed further in a direction which had already been indicated in my publications between 1894 and 1896. At that time, and even before sexuality had been given its rightful place as an aetiological factor, I had maintained that no experience could have a pathogenic effect unless it appeared intolerable to the subject's ego and gave rise to efforts at defence (Freud, 1894*a*). It was to this defence that I traced back the split in the psyche (or, as we said in those days, in consciousness) which occurs in hysteria. If the defence was successful, the intolerable experience with its affective con-sequences was expelled from consciousness and from the ego's memory. In certain circumstances, however, what had been expelled pursued its activities in what was now an unconscious state, and found its way back into consciousness by means of symptoms and the affects attaching to them, so that the illness corresponded to a failure in defence. This view had the merit of entering into the interplay of the psychical forces and of thus bringing the mental processes in hysteria nearer to normal ones, instead of characterizing the neurosis as nothing more than a mysterious disorder insusceptible to further analysis.

Further information now became available relating to people who had remained normal; and this led to the unexpected find-ing that the sexual history of *their* childhood did not necessarily differ in essentials from that of neurotics, and, in particular, that the part played by seduction was the same in both cases. As a consequence, accidental influences receded still further into the background as compared with 'repression' (as I now began to say instead of 'defence').[1] Thus it was no longer a

---

[1] [Actually the term '*Verdrängung*' ('repression') had made its first published appearance as early as in the Breuer and Freud 'Preliminary Communication' (1893). Many years later, in *Inhibitions, Symptoms and Anxiety* (1926*d*; see particularly Chap. XI A(*c*), Freud once more returned to the term '*Abwehr*' ('defence') as denoting a comprehensive concept, of which 'repression' represented only a single form.]

question of what sexual experiences a particular individual had had in his childhood, but rather of his reaction to those experiences—of whether he had reacted to them by 'repression' or not. It could be shown how in the course of development a spontaneous infantile sexual activity was often broken off by an act of repression. Thus a mature neurotic individual was invariably pursued by a certain amount of 'sexual repression' from his childhood; this found expression when he was faced by the demands of real life, and the psycho-analyses of hysterics showed that they fell ill as a result of the conflict between their libido and their sexual repression and that their symptoms were in the nature of compromises between the two mental currents.

I could not further elucidate this part of my theory without a detailed discussion of my views on repression. It will be enough here to refer to my *Three Essays* (1905*d*), in which I have attempted to throw some light—if only a feeble one—on the somatic processes in which the essential nature of sexuality is to be looked for. I have there shown that the constitutional sexual disposition of children is incomparably more variegated than might have been expected, that it deserves to be described as 'polymorphously perverse' and that what is spoken of as the normal behaviour of the sexual function emerges from this disposition after certain of its components have been repressed. By pointing out the infantile elements in sexuality I was able to establish a simple correlation between health, perversion and neurosis. I showed that *normality* is a result of the repression of certain component instincts and constituents of the infantile disposition and of the subordination of the remaining constituents under the primacy of the genital zones in the service of the reproductive function. I showed that *perversions* correspond to disturbances of this coalescence owing to the overpowering and compulsive development of certain of the component instincts, while *neuroses* can be traced back to an excessive repression of the libidinal trends. Since almost all the perverse instincts of the infantile disposition can be recognized as the forces concerned in the formation of symptoms in neuroses, though in a state of repression, I was able to describe neurosis as being the 'negative' of perversion.

I think it is worth emphasizing the fact that, whatever modifications my views on the aetiology of the psychoneuroses have passed through, there are two positions which I have never repudiated or abandoned—the importance of sexuality and of infantilism. Apart from this, accidental influences have been replaced by constitutional factors and 'defence' in the purely psychological sense has been replaced by organic 'sexual repression'. The question may, however, be raised of where convincing evidence is to be found in favour of the alleged aetiological importance of sexual factors in the psychoneuroses, in view of the fact that the onset of these illnesses may be observed in response to the most commonplace emotions or even to somatic precipitating causes, and since I have had to abandon a specific aetiology depending on the particular form of the childhood experiences concerned. To such a question I would reply that the psycho-analytic examination of neurotics is the source from which this disputed conviction of mine is derived. If we make use of that irreplaceable method of research, we discover that *the patient's symptoms constitute his sexual activity* (whether wholly or in part), which arises from the sources of the normal or perverse component instincts of sexuality. Not only is a large part of the symptomatology of hysteria derived directly from expressions of sexual excitement, not only do a number of erotogenic zones attain the significance of genitals during neuroses owing to an intensification of infantile characteristics, but the most complicated symptoms are themselves revealed as representing, by means of 'conversion', phantasies which have a sexual situation as their subject-matter. Anyone who knows how to interpret the language of hysteria will recognize that the neurosis is concerned only with the patient's repressed sexuality. The sexual function must, however, be understood in its true extent, as it is laid down by disposition in infancy. Wherever some commonplace emotion must be included among the determinants of the onset of the illness, analysis invariably shows that it is the sexual component of the traumatic experience—a component that is never lacking—which has produced the pathogenic result.

We have been led on imperceptibly from the question of the causation of the psychoneuroses to the problem of their essential nature. If we are prepared to take into account what has been learnt from psycho-analysis, we can only say that the essence of these illnesses lies in disturbances of the sexual processes, the processes which determine in the organism the formation and utilization of sexual libido. It is scarcely possible to avoid picturing these processes as being in the last resort of a chemical nature; so that in what are termed the 'actual' neuroses [1] we may recognize the *somatic* effects of disturbances of the sexual metabolism, and in the psychoneuroses the *psychical* effects of those disturbances as well. The similarity of the neuroses to the phenomena of intoxication and abstinence after the use of certain alkaloids, as well as to Graves' disease and Addison's disease, is forced upon our notice clinically. And just as these last two illnesses should no longer be described as 'nervous diseases', so also the 'neuroses' proper, in spite of their name, may soon have to be excluded from that category as well.[2]

Accordingly, the aetiology of the neuroses comprises everything which can act in a detrimental manner upon the processes serving the sexual function. In the forefront, then, are to be ranked the noxae which affect the sexual function itself—in so far as these are regarded as injurious by the sexual constitution, varying as it does with different degrees of culture and education. In the next place comes every other kind of noxa and trauma which, by causing general damage to the organism, may lead secondarily to injury to its sexual processes. It should not, however, be forgotten that the aetiological problem in the case of the neuroses is at least as complicated as the causative factors of any other illness. A single pathogenic influence is scarcely ever sufficient; in the large majority of cases a *number* of aetiological factors are required, which support one another and must therefore not be regarded as being in mutual opposition. For this reason a state of neurotic illness cannot be sharply differentiated from health. The onset of the illness is the product of a summation and the necessary total of aetiological determinants can be completed from any direction. To look for the aetiology of the neuroses exclusively in heredity or in the constitution would be just as one-sided as to attribute that aetiology solely to the accidental influences brought to bear upon sexuality in the course of the subject's life—whereas better insight shows that the essence of these illnesses lies solely in a disturbance of the organism's sexual processes.

VIENNA, *June* 1905.

[1] [I.e. those with a contemporary aetiology (neurasthenia and anxiety neurosis).]

[2] [Cf. *Three Essays*, this volume p. 216 and footnote.]

# PSYCHICAL (OR MENTAL)
# TREATMENT
## (1905)

PSYCHISCHE BEHANDLUNG (SEELENBEHANDLUNG)

(a) GERMAN EDITIONS :
1905   In *Die Gesundheit,* ed. R. Kossmann and J. Weiss, **1,**
          368–384. (Stuttgart, Berlin & Leipzig: Union Deut-
          sche Verlagsgesellschaft.)
1942   *G.W.,* **5,** 289–315

(b) ENGLISH TRANSLATION:
          'Psychical (or Mental) Treatment'

The present translation, by James Strachey, now appears for the
first time and, so far as is known, is the first to be published.


*Die Gesundheit* was a collective work on medicine of a semi-
popular character in two volumes with a large number of
collaborators. Freud's contribution formed part of a section
dealing with various methods of treatment. It was never re-
printed during his lifetime.

# PSYCHICAL (OR MENTAL) TREATMENT

'Psyche' is a Greek word which may be translated 'mind' [1] Thus 'psychical treatment' means 'mental treatment'. The term might accordingly be supposed to signify 'treatment of the pathological phenomena of mental life'. This, however, is *not* its meaning. 'Psychical treatment' denotes, rather, treatment taking its start in the mind, treatment (whether of mental or physical disorders) by measures which operate in the first instance and immediately upon the human mind.

Foremost among such measures is the use of words; and words are the essential tool of mental treatment. A layman will no doubt find it hard to understand how pathological disorders of the body and mind can be eliminated by 'mere' words. He will feel that he is being asked to believe in magic. And he will not be so very wrong, for the words which we use in our everyday speech are nothing other than watered-down magic. But we shall have to follow a roundabout path in order to explain how science sets about restoring to words a part at least of their former magical power.

It is only comparatively recently, too, that physicians with a scientific training have learnt to appreciate the value of mental treatment. And we can easily see why this was so when we reflect on the evolution of medicine during the last half-century. After a somewhat unfruitful period during which it was dependent on what was known as 'Natural Philosophy', [2] it came under the happy influence of the natural sciences and has achieved the greatest advances alike as a science and as an art: it has shown that the organism is built up from microscopically small elements (the cells), it has learnt to understand the physics and chemistry of the various vital processes (functions), it has distinguished the visible and observable modifications which are brought about in the bodily organs by different morbid

[1] ['*Seele*'—a word which is in fact nearer to the Greek 'psyche' than is the English 'mind'.]

[2] [This was a school of thought of a pantheistic type, associated chiefly with the name of Schelling, which was predominant in Germany during the first half of the nineteenth century. Cf. Bernfeld, 1944.]

processes, and has discovered, on the other hand, the signs that reveal the operation of deep-lying morbid processes in the living body; moreover it has identified a great number of the micro-organisms which cause illness and, with the help of its newly acquired knowledge, it has reduced to a quite extraordinary degree the dangers arising from severe surgical operations. All of these advances and discoveries were related to the *physical* side of man, and it followed, as a result of an incorrect though easily understandable trend of thought, that physicians came to restrict their interest to the physical side of things and were glad to leave the mental field to be dealt with by the philosophers whom they despised.

Modern medicine, it is true, had reason enough for studying the indisputable connection between the body and the mind; but it never ceased to represent mental events as determined by physical ones and dependent on them. Thus stress was laid on the fact that intellectual functioning was conditional upon the presence of a normally developed and sufficiently nourished brain, that any disease of that organ led to disturbances of intellectual functioning, that the introduction of toxic substances into the circulation could produce certain states of mental illness, or—to descend to more trivial matters—that dreams could be modified by stimuli brought to bear upon a sleeper for experimental purposes.[1]

The relation between body and mind (in animals no less than in human beings) is a reciprocal one; but in earlier times the other side of this relation, the effect of the mind upon the body, found little favour in the eyes of physicians. They seemed to be afraid of granting mental life any independence, for fear of that implying an abandonment of the scientific ground on which they stood.

This one-sided attitude of medicine towards the body has undergone a gradual change in the course of the last decade and a half, a change brought about directly by clinical experience. There are a large number of patients, suffering from affections of greater or less severity, whose disorders and complaints make great demands on the skill of their physicians, but in whom no visible or observable signs of a pathological process

[1] [Cf. *The Interpretation of Dreams* (Freud, 1900a), Chapter I, Section C (1); Standard Ed., 4, 24 ff.]

can be discovered either during their life or after their death, in spite of all the advances in the methods of investigation made by scientific medicine. One group of these patients are distinguished by the copiousness and variety of their symptoms: they are incapable of intellectual work because of headaches or inability to concentrate their attention, their eyes ache when they read, their legs become fatigued when they walk, develop dull pains or go to sleep, their digestion is disturbed by distressing sensations, by eructations or gastric spasms, they cannot defaecate without aperients, they are subject to sleeplessness, and so on. They may suffer from all these disorders simultaneously or in succession, or from only a selection of them; but in every case the illness is evidently the same. Moreover, its signs are often variable and replace one another. A patient who has hitherto been incapacitated by headaches but has had a fairly good digestion may next day enjoy a clear head but may thenceforward be unable to manage most kinds of food. Again, his sufferings may suddenly cease if there is a marked change in the circumstances of his existence. If he is travelling he may feel perfectly well and be able to enjoy the most varied diet without any ill effects, but when he gets home he may once more have to restrict himself to sour milk. In a few cases the disorder—whether it is a pain or a weakness resembling a paralysis—may suddenly pass from one side of the body to the other: it may jump from his right side to the corresponding part of the body on his left side. But in every instance it is to be observed that the symptoms are very clearly influenced by excitement, emotion, worry, etc., and also that they can disappear and give place to perfect health without leaving any traces, even if they have persisted over a long period.

Medical research has at last shown that people of this kind are not to be looked upon as suffering from a disease of the stomach or of the eyes or whatever it may be, but that it must be a question in their case of an illness of the nervous system as a whole. Examination of the brain and nerves of these patients has so far, however, revealed no perceptible changes; and, indeed, some of the features of their symptomatology prohibit any expectation that even more accurate methods of investigation could ever discover changes of a sort that would throw light upon the illness. This condition has been described as 'nervousness' (neurasthenia or hysteria) and has been characterized as a merely 'functional' disorder of the nervous system.[1] Incidentally, an exhaustive examination of the brain (after the patient's death) has been equally without results in the case of many more permanent nervous disorders, as well as in illnesses with exclusively mental symptoms, such as what are known as obsessions and delusional insanity.

Physicians were thus faced by the problem of investigating the nature and origin of the symptoms shown by these nervous or neurotic patients. In the course of this investigation it was found that in some at least of these patients the signs of their illness originate from nothing other than *a change in the action of their minds upon their bodies* and that the immediate cause of their disorder is to be looked for in their minds. What may be the remoter causes of the disturbance which affects their minds is another question, with which we need not now concern ourselves. But medical science was here provided with an opportunity for directing its full attention to what had previously been the neglected side of the mutual relation between body and mind.

It is not until we have studied pathological phenomena that we can get an insight into normal ones. Many things which had long been known of the influence of the mind on the body were only now brought into their true perspective. The commonest, everyday example of the mind's action on the body, and one that is to be observed in everyone, is offered by what is known as the 'expression of the emotions'. A man's states of mind are manifested, almost without exception, in the tensions and relaxations of his facial muscles, in the adaptations of his eyes, in the amount of blood in the vessels of his skin, in the modifications in his vocal apparatus and in the movements of his limbs and in particular of his hands. These concomitant physical changes are for the most part of no advantage to the person concerned; on the contrary, they often stand in his way if he wishes to conceal his mental processes from other people. But they serve these other people as trustworthy indications from which his mental processes can be inferred and in which more confidence can be placed than in any simultaneous verbal expressions that may be made deliberately.[2] If we are able to

[1] See Volume II, Part X, Chapter 4 [of the work, *Die Gesundheit*, in which this paper of Freud's first appeared.]

[2] [Cf. the example in the case of 'Dora' (this volume p. 76).]

submit anyone to a more accurate examination during certain of his mental activities, we come upon further physical
consequences, in the shape of changes in his heart-action,
alterations in the distribution of blood in his body, and
so on.

In certain mental states described as 'affects', the part played
by the body is so obvious and on so large a scale that some
psychologists have even adopted the view that the essence of
these affects consists only in their physical manifestations. It is a
matter of common knowledge that extraordinary changes occur
in the facial expression, in the circulation, in the excretions and
in the state of tension of the voluntary muscles under the influence of fear, of rage, of mental pain and of sexual delight.
What is less well known, though equally well established, is the
occurrence of other physical results of the affects which cannot
be counted as their expression. Persistent affective states of a
distressing or 'depressive' nature (as they are called), such as
sorrow, worry or grief, reduce the state of nourishment of the
whole body, cause the hair to turn white, the fat to disappear
and the walls of the blood-vessels to undergo morbid changes.
On the other hand, under the influence of feelings of joy, of
'happiness', we find that the whole body blossoms out and shows
signs of a renewal of youth. The major affects evidently have a
large bearing on the capacity to resist infectious illness; a good
example of this is to be seen in the medical observation that
there is a far greater liability to contract such diseases as typhus
and dysentery in defeated armies than in victorious ones. The
affects, moreover,—this applies almost exclusively to depressive
affects—are often sufficient in themselves to bring about both
diseases of the nervous system accompanied by manifest anatomical changes and also diseases of other organs. In such
cases it must be assumed that the patient already had a
predisposition, though hitherto an inoperative one, to the
disease in question.

States of illness that are already present can be very considerably influenced by violent affects. Such changes are usually
for the worse; but there is no lack of instances in which a severe
shock or a sudden bereavement brings about a peculiar alteration in the tone of the organism which may have a favourable
influence on some well-established pathological condition or
may even bring it to an end. Finally, there can be no doubt that

the duration of life can be appreciably shortened by depressive affects and that a violent shock, or a deep humiliation or disgrace, may put a sudden end to life. Strange to say, this same result may be found to follow too from the unexpected impact of a great joy.

The affects in the narrower sense are, it is true, characterized by a quite special connection with somatic processes ; but, strictly speaking, all mental states, including those that we usually regard as 'processes of thought', are to some degree 'affective', and not one of them is without its physical manifestations or is incapable of modifying somatic processes. Even when a person is engaged in quietly thinking in a string of 'ideas', there are a constant series of excitations, corresponding to the content of these ideas, which are discharged into the smooth or striated muscles. These excitations can be made apparent if they are appropriately reinforced, and certain striking and, indeed, ostensibly 'supernatural' phenomena can be explained by this means. Thus, what is known as 'thought-reading' [Gedanken erraten] may be explained by small, involuntary muscular movements carried out by the 'medium' in the course of an experiment—when, for instance, he has to make someone discover a hidden object [without giving any ostensible prompting]. The whole phenomenon might more suitably be described as 'thought-betraying' [Gedanken verraten].

The processes of volition and attention are also capable of exercising a profound effect on somatic processes and of playing a large part in promoting or hindering physical illnesses. A famous English physician has reported that he can succeed in producing a great variety of sensations and pains in any part of his body to which he may choose to direct his attention, and the majority of people appear to behave similarly. It is in general true that in forming a judgement of pains (which are usually regarded as physical phenomena) we must bear in mind their unmistakable dependence upon mental determinants. Laymen, who like to sum up mental influences of this kind under the name of 'imagination', are inclined to have little respect for pains that are due to imagination as contrasted with those caused by injury, illness or inflammation. But this is clearly unjust. However pains may be caused—even by imagination—they themselves are no less real and no less violent on that account.

Just as pains are produced or increased by having attention paid to them, so, too, they disappear if attention is diverted from them. This experience can always be employed as a means of soothing children; adult soldiers do not feel the pain of a wound in the feverish heat of battle; martyrs are probably quite impervious to the pain of their tortures in the over-excitement of their religious feeling and in the concentration of all their thoughts upon the heavenly reward that awaits them. It is not so easy to produce evidence of the influence of *volition* on pathological somatic processes; but it is quite possible that a determination to recover or a will to die may have an effect on the outcome even of severe and precarious illnesses.

Our interest is most particularly engaged by the mental state of *expectation*, which puts in motion a number of mental forces that have the greatest influence on the onset and cure of physical diseases. *Fearful* expectation is certainly not without its effect on the result. It would be of importance to know with certainty whether it has as great a bearing as is supposed on falling ill; for instance, whether it is true that during an epidemic those who are afraid of contracting the illness are in the greatest danger. The contrary state of mind, in which expectation is coloured by hope and faith, is an effective force with which we have to reckon, strictly speaking, in *all* our attempts at treatment and cure. We could not otherwise account for the peculiar results which we find produced by medicaments and therapeutic procedures.

The most noticeable effects of this kind of expectation coloured by faith are to be found in the 'miraculous' cures which are brought about even to-day under our own eyes without the help of any medical skill. Miraculous cures properly so-called take place in the case of believers under the influence of adjuncts calculated to intensify religious feelings—that is to say, in places where a miracle-working image is worshipped, or where a holy or divine personage has revealed himself to men and has promised them relief from their sufferings in return for their worship, or where the relics of a saint are preserved as a treasure. Religious faith alone does not seem to find it easy to suppress illness by means of expectation; for as a rule other contrivances as well are brought into play in the case of miraculous cures. The times and seasons at which divine mercy is sought must be specially indicated; the patient must submit to physical toil, to the trials and sacrifices of a pilgrimage, before he can become worthy of this divine mercy.

It would be convenient, but quite wrong, simply to refuse all credence to these miraculous cures and to seek to explain the accounts of them as a combination of pious fraud and inaccurate observation. Though an explanation of this kind may often be justified, it is not enough to enable us to dismiss entirely the fact of miraculous cures. They do really occur and have occurred at every period of history. And they concern not merely illnesses of mental origin—those, that is, which are based on 'imagination' and are therefore likely to be especially affected by the circumstances of a pilgrimage—but also illnesses with an 'organic' basis which had previously resisted all the efforts of physicians.

There is no need, however, to bring forward anything other than mental forces in order to explain miraculous cures. Even under conditions such as these, nothing happens that can be considered as beyond our understanding. Everything proceeds naturally. Indeed, the power of religious faith is reinforced in these cases by a number of eminently human motive forces. The individual's pious belief is intensified by the enthusiasm of the crowd of people in whose midst he makes his way as a rule to the sacred locality. All the mental impulses of an individual can be enormously magnified by group influence such as this. In cases in which someone proceeds to the holy place by himself, the reputation of the place and the respect in which it is held act as substitutes for the influence of the group, so that in fact the power of a group is once more in operation. And there is yet another way in which this influence makes itself felt. Since it is well known that divine mercy is always shown only to a few of the many who seek it, each of these is eager to be among the chosen few; the ambition that lies hidden in everyone comes to the help of pious faith. Where so many powerful forces converge, we need feel no surprise if the goal is sometimes really reached.

Even those who are without religious faith need not forgo miraculous cures. In their case reputation and group-influence act as a complete substitute for faith. There are always fashionable treatments and fashionable physicians, and these play an especially dominant part in high society, where the most powerful psychological motive forces are the endeavour to excel and to do what the 'best' people do. Fashionable treatments of this kind produce therapeutic results which are outside the scope of their actual power, and the same procedures effect far more in the hands of a fashionable doctor (who, for instance, may have become well-known as an attendant upon some prominent personality) than in those of another physician. Thus there are human as well as divine miracle-workers. Such men, however, who have reached eminence owing to the favour of fashion and of imitation, soon lose their power, as is to be expected from the nature of the forces which give it to them.

An intelligible dissatisfaction with the frequent inadequacy of the help afforded by medical skill, and perhaps, too, an internal rebellion against the duress of scientific thought, which reflects the remorselessness of nature, have in all periods (and in our own once more) imposed a strange condition on the therapeutic powers alike of persons and of procedures. The necessary faith only emerges if the practitioner is not a doctor, if he can boast of having no knowledge of the scientific basis of therapeutics, if the procedure has not been subjected to accurate testing but is recommended by some popular prejudice. Hence it is that we find a swarm of 'nature cures' and 'nature healers', who compete with physicians in the exercise of their profession and of whom we can at least say with some degree of certainty that they do far more harm than good. If this gives us grounds for blaming the patients' faith, we must yet not be so ungrateful as to forget that the same force is constantly at work in support of our own medical efforts. The results of every procedure laid down by the physician and of every treatment that he undertakes are probably composed of two portions. And one of these, which is sometimes greater and sometimes less, but can never be completely disregarded, is determined by the patient's mental attitude. The faith with which he meets the immediate effect of a medical procedure depends on the one hand on the amount of his own desire to be cured, and on the other hand on his confidence that he has taken the right steps in that direction —on his general respect, that is, for medical skill—and, further, on the power which he attributes to his doctor's personality, and even on the purely human liking aroused in him by the doctor. There are some physicians who have a greater capacity than others for winning their patients' confidence; a patient will often feel better the very moment the doctor enters his room.

Physicians have practised mental treatment from the beginning of time, and in early days to a far greater extent even than to-day. If by mental treatment we mean an endeavour to produce such mental states and conditions in the patient as will be the most propitious for his recovery, this kind of medical treatment is historically the oldest. Psychical treatment was almost the only sort at the disposal of the peoples of antiquity, and they invariably reinforced the effects of therapeutic potions and other therapeutic measures by intensive mental treatment. Such familiar procedures as the use of magical formulas and purificatory baths, or the elicitation of oracular dreams by sleeping in the temple precincts, can only have had a curative effect by psychical means. The physician's personality acquired a reputation derived directly from divine power, since in its beginnings the art of healing lay in the hands of priests. So that then as now the physician's personality was one of the chief instruments for bringing the patient into a state of mind favourable for his recovery.

Now, too, we begin to understand the 'magic' of words. Words are the most important media by which one man seeks to bring his influence to bear on another; words are a good method of producing mental changes in the person to whom they are addressed. So that there is no longer anything puzzling in the assertion that the magic of words can remove the symptoms of illness, and especially such as are themselves founded on mental states.

All the mental influences which have proved effective in curing illnesses have something incalculable about them. Affects, concentration of the will, distracting the attention, expectation coloured by faith—all of these forces, which occasionally remove an illness, sometimes fail to do so without there being anything in the character of the illness to account for the different result. What stands in the way of regularity in the therapeutic results achieved is evidently the autocratic nature of the personalities of the subjects, with their variety of mental differences. Since physicians came to realize clearly the important part played in recovery by the patient's state of mind, the idea naturally occurred to them of no longer leaving it to the patient to decide how much mental compliance he should show but of deliberately imposing a propitious state of mind by suitable methods. It is from this attempt that modern mental treatment has taken its start.

Quite a number of different methods of treatment have thus arisen, some of them simple to arrive at and others which could only be reached on the basis of complex hypotheses. It is easy to see, for instance, that the physician, who can no longer command respect as a priest or as the possessor of secret knowledge, should use his personality in such a way as to gain his patient's confidence and, to some degree, his affection. He himself may succeed in doing this with only a limited number of patients, whereas other patients, according to their inclinations and degree of education, will be attracted to other physicians. Such a distribution will serve a useful purpose; but *if the right of a patient to make a free choice of his doctor were suspended, an important precondition for influencing him mentally would be abolished.*

There are many very effective mental procedures which the physician is obliged to renounce. He either has not the power or has not the right to invoke them. This applies in particular to the provocation of strong affects—the most powerful of all the means by which the mind affects the body. The vicissitudes of life often cure illnesses through the experience of great joy, through the satisfaction of needs or the fulfilment of wishes. The physician, who is often impotent outside his profession, cannot compete along these lines. It might be more within his power to employ fear and fright for therapeutic ends; but, except in the case of children, he must have the gravest doubts about the use of such double-edged tools. On the other hand, the physician must rule out any relations with his patient that are bound up with tender feelings, owing to their implications in practical life. Thus from the first his power to bring about mental changes in his patients seems so restricted that mental treatment conducted on a deliberate plan would seem to offer no advantages over the earlier haphazard method.

The physician can seek to direct his patient's volition and attention, and he has good grounds for doing so in the case of various pathological conditions. He may, for instance, persistently oblige a person who believes he is paralysed to carry out the movements of which he professes himself incapable; or he may refuse to fall in with the wishes of an anxious patient who insists on being examined for an illness from which he is quite certainly not suffering. In these instances the physician will be taking the right course, but such isolated cases would scarcely justify us in setting up mental treatment as a special therapeutic procedure. There exists, nevertheless, a queer and unforeseeable method which offers the physician a possibility of exercising a profound, even though transitory, influence on the mental life of his patients and of employing that influence for therapeutic purposes.

It has long been known, though it has only been established beyond all doubt during the last few decades, that it is possible, by certain gentle means, to put people into a quite peculiar mental state very similar to sleep and on that account described as 'hypnosis'. The various means by which hypnosis can be brought about have at first sight little in common. It is possible to hypnotize someone by getting him to stare fixedly at a bright object for some minutes, or by holding a watch to his ear for a similar length of time, or by repeatedly passing the open hands, at a short distance away, over his face and limbs. But the same result can be brought about by describing the onset of the state of hypnosis and its characteristics quietly and firmly to the subject—that is, by 'talking him into' hypnosis. The two procedures may also be combined. We may make the subject sit down, hold a finger in front of his eyes, tell him to gaze at it fixedly and then say to him: 'You're feeling tired. Your eyes are closing; you can't hold them open. Your limbs are heavy; you can't move them any more. You're falling asleep——' and so on. It will be observed that all the procedures have in common a fixing of the attention; in those first mentioned the attention is fatigued by slight and monotonous sensory stimuli. It is not yet satisfactorily explained, however, how it comes about that mere talking produces exactly the same state as the other procedures. Experienced hypnotists assert that by these means a definite hypnotic change can be brought about in some eighty per cent of subjects. There is no way of telling beforehand, however, which subjects are hypnotizable and which are not. Illness is far from being one of the necessary preconditions of hypnosis: normal people are said to be particularly easy to hypnotize, while some neurotics can only be hypnotized with great diffi-

culty and the insane are completely resistant. The hypnotic
state exhibits a great variety of gradations. In its lightest degree
the hypnotic subject is aware only of something like a slight
insensibility, while the most extreme degree, which is marked
by special peculiarities, is known as 'somnambulism', on account of its resemblance to the natural phenomenon of sleep-
walking. But hypnosis is in no sense a sleep like our nocturnal
sleep or like the sleep produced by drugs. Changes occur in it
and mental functions are retained during it which are absent
in normal sleep.

Some of the phenomena of hypnosis (for instance, alterations
in muscular activity) possess a merely scientific interest. But the
most significant indication of hypnosis, and the most important
one from our point of view, lies in the hypnotic subject's attitude
to his hypnotist. While the subject behaves to the rest of the
external world as though he were asleep, that is, as though all
his senses were diverted from it, he is *awake* in his relation to the
person who hypnotized him; he hears and sees him alone, and
him he understands and answers. This phenomenon, which is
described as *rapport* in the case of hypnosis, finds a parallel in
the way in which some people sleep—for instance, a mother
who is nursing her baby.[1] It is so striking that it may well lead
us to an understanding of the relation between the hypnotic
subject and the hypnotist.

But the fact that the subject's universe is, so to say, confined
to the hypnotist is not the whole story. There is the further fact
of the former's *docility* in relation to the latter: he becomes
obedient and credulous—in the case of deep hypnosis, to an
almost unlimited extent. And the manner in which this obedience and credulity are carried out reveals a characteristic of
the hypnotic state, namely that in the hypnotized subject the
influence of the mind over the body is extraordinarily increased. If the hypnotist says 'You can't move your arm', the
arm drops motionless; the subject obviously tries with all his
strength but is unable to move it. If the hypnotist says: 'Your
arm's moving of its own accord, you can't stop it', the arm
moves and the subject is seen making vain efforts to keep it
still. The idea which the hypnotist has given to the subject by
his words has produced in him precisely the mental-physical

[1] [Cf. various remarks on this subject in *The Interpretation of Dreams*
(Freud, 1900a), e.g. in Chapter V, Section C; Standard Ed., 4, 223.]

behaviour corresponding to the idea's content. This implies on
the one hand obedience but on the other an increase in the
physical influence of an idea. Words have once more regained
their magic.

The same thing happens in the domain of sense perceptions.
The hypnotist says: 'You see a snake; you're smelling a rose;
you're listening to the loveliest music', and the hypnotic subject
sees, smells and hears what is required of him by the idea that
he has been given. How do we know that the subject really has
these perceptions? It might be thought that he is only pretending to have them. But after all we have no reason for doubts on
the point; for he behaves exactly as though he had them, he
expresses all the appropriate emotions, and in some circumstances he can even describe his imaginary perceptions and
experiences after the hypnosis is at an end. We then perceive
that he has been seeing and hearing just as we see and hear in
dreams—he has been 'hallucinating'. He was evidently so
credulous in relation to the hypnotist that he was *convinced* that
there must be a snake to be seen when the hypnotist told him
so; and this conviction had such a strong effect on his body
that he really saw the snake—a thing which, incidentally,
can sometimes happen even to people who have not been
hypnotized.

It may be remarked, by the way, that, outside hypnosis and
in real life, credulity such as the subject has in relation to his
hypnotist is shown only by a child towards his beloved parents,
and that an attitude of similar subjection on the part of one
person towards another has only one parallel, though a complete one—namely in certain love-relationships where there is
extreme devotion. A combination of exclusive attachment and
credulous obedience is in general among the characteristics of
love.[1]


Some further points may be mentioned in connection with
the state of hypnosis. The words spoken by the hypnotist which
have the magical results that I have described are known as a
'suggestion' and it has become customary to apply the term as
well where there is merely an intention to produce a similar

[1] [Freud returned to this topic many years later, in Chapter VIII
of his *Group Psychology* (1921*c*).]

effect.[1] Not only do the hypnotic subject's movements and feel-ings obey suggestions, but all his other mental activities; and he does not as a rule take any action on his own initiative. Hypnotic obedience can be employed in making a number of highly remarkable experiments, which afford a deep insight into the workings of the mind and produce in the observer an ineradicable conviction of the unsuspected power of the mind over the body. Just as a hypnotized subject can be obliged to see what is not there, so he can be forbidden to see what *is* there and is seeking to impress itself on his senses—some parti-cular person, for instance. (This is known as a 'negative hallucination'.) The person in question then finds it impossible to attract the subject's attention by any kind of stimulation; he is treated as though he were 'thin air'. Again, a suggestion may be made to the subject to carry out some action a certain length of time after waking from hypnosis ('post-hypnotic suggestion'); the subject keeps to the allotted time and performs the suggested action in the middle of his waking state without being able to give any reason for it. If he is asked why he has done what he has, he will either refer to an obscure impulse which he was unable to resist, or he will invent some half-satisfactory excuse without remembering the real explanation—namely the sug-gestion he has been given.

The state of hypnosis is brought to an end without any difficulty by the hypnotist's authority asserted in the words: 'Wake up!' After the deepest hypnosis there is no recollection of anything that has been experienced during it under the hypnotist's influence. That portion of the subject's mental life remains cut off, as it were, from the rest. Other subjects retain a dream-like memory, and yet others remember everything but report that they have been under an irresistible mental compulsion.

The scientific gain brought to physicians and psychologists by a knowledge of the facts of hypnotism can scarcely be exag-gerated. But in order to gauge the practical importance of the

[1] [In French and English the technical use of the term 'suggestion' was, of course, derived from the everyday use of the word. In German the process was reversed, since '*Suggestion*' was first imported into German in its technical sense and only subsequently acquired a wider meaning.]

new discoveries we must put a physician in place of the
hypnotist and a patient in place of the hypnotic subject.
Hypnosis would then seem pre-ordained to fulfil all the physician's requirements, in so far as he seeks to act towards the
patient as a 'mind-doctor'. Hypnosis endows the physician with
an authority such as was probably never possessed by the priest
or the miracle man, since it concentrates the subject's whole
interest upon the figure of the physician; it does away with the
autocratic power of the patient's mind which, as we have seen,
interferes so capriciously with the influence of the mind over
the body; it automatically produces an increase of the mind's
control over the body, such as is normally to be observed only
as an effect of the most powerful emotions; and, owing to the
possibility of arranging that the instructions given to the patient
during hypnosis shall only become manifest subsequently, in his
normal state—owing, that is, to post-hypnotic suggestion—,
hypnosis enables the physician to use the great power he wields
during hypnosis in order to bring about changes in the patient
in his waking condition. A simple pattern of procedure would
thus seem to emerge for the purposes of mental treatment: the
physician puts the patient into a state of hypnosis, he suggests
to him (according to the particular circumstances) that he is
not ill and that after waking he will not be aware of his symptoms. The physician then wakes the patient up and may feel
confident that the suggestion has done its duty against the illness.
And if a single application of this procedure were not sufficient,
it could be repeated as many times as necessary.

There is only one consideration that might discourage the
physician and the patient from making use of such a promising
therapeutic method: the possibility that the advantages of
hypnotism might be balanced by some damage—if, for instance, it left behind it a permanent disorder or weakness in the
subject's mind. But enough experience has already been gained
to set aside such doubts: single hypnotic treatments are completely harmless and even if they are frequently repeated they
are on the whole without bad effects. Only one point is to be
noticed: if circumstances demand a persistent use of hypnotism,
the patient falls into a habit of hypnosis and dependence on the
physician which cannot be among the purposes of the therapeutic procedure.

Thus hypnotic treatment really implies a great extension of

medical power and consequently an advance in therapy. Every sufferer may be advised to entrust himself to it, so long as it is carried out by an experienced and trustworthy physician. Hypnosis should, however, be used in a manner different from what is usual to-day. As a rule this method of treatment is only embarked upon after every other method has failed and when the patient is already despondent and dejected. He has then to leave his own doctor, who cannot or does not employ hypnotism, and turn to a strange doctor, who as a rule does not or cannot employ anything else. Both practices are disadvantageous to the patient. The family doctor should himself be familiar with hypnotic procedure and he should make use of it from the first, as soon as he judges the illness and the patient appropriate for it. Wherever hypnotism can be employed it should be on a par with other therapeutic procedures and should not be regarded as a last resort or even as a descent from science to quackery. But hypnotism can be employed not only in all nervous conditions and in disorders due to the 'imagination', as well as for breaking morbid habits (such as alcoholism, morphine addiction, or sexual aberrations), but also in many organic diseases, even of an inflammatory nature, in which, though the underlying disorder persists, there is a prospect of relieving the symptoms (such as pains or impediments to movement) which are troubling the patient. The selection of cases for hypnotic treatment must depend entirely on the judgement of the physician.

The time has now come, however, to dissipate the notion that with the expedient of hypnosis a period of easy miracle-working has dawned for the physician. A number of circumstances must be taken into account which are calculated to lower our expectations from hypnotic therapy considerably, and to reduce to their proper proportions the hopes that may have been raised in patients. First and foremost, one of the basic assumptions turns out to be untenable: namely, that hypnosis makes it possible to deprive patients of the interfering autocratic element in their mental behaviour. In fact they retain it, and manifest it even in their attitude to the attempt to hypnotize them. It was stated above that some eighty per cent of people can be hypnotized; but that high figure is only reached by including among the positive cases any that show the slightest sign of being influenced. Really deep hypnoses, with complete tractability, such as are chosen as examples in describing the state, are actually rare or at all events not as frequent as one would wish from the therapeutic point of view. The impression made by this fact can, however, in turn be modified when it is borne in mind that depth of hypnosis and tractability to suggestions do not go *pari passu*; so that one often sees good suggestive results where there is no more than a slight hypnotic insensibility. But even if we consider hypnotic tractability independently, as being the more essential feature of the condition, it has to be admitted that different people show their idiosyncracies by only letting themselves be influenced up to a certain degree of tractability, at which point they come to a halt. Thus different people show a very varying degree of suitability for hypnotic treatment. If it were possible to find a means by which all these various grades of the hypnotic state could be intensified to the point of complete hypnosis, the idiosyncrasies of patients would once more have been eliminated and the ideal of mental treatment would have been attained. But this advance has not yet been made; it still depends far more on the patient than on the physician with what degree of tractability a suggestion will be received—it depends once more, that is, upon the patient's choice.

And there is another, still more important consideration. In describing the very remarkable results of suggestion, people are only too ready to forget that here, as in all mental operations, relative size and strength must be taken into account. If we put a healthy person into deep hypnosis and then tell him to take a bite out of a potato under the impression that it is a pear, or if we tell him that he is meeting one of his acquaintances and must greet him as such, he is likely to prove completely tractable, because the hypnotized subject has no serious reason for resisting the suggestion. But in the case of other instructions—if, for instance, we ask a naturally modest girl to uncover herself or if we ask an honest man to steal some valuable object—we may already find the subject putting up a resistance, which may even go to the length of his refusing to obey the suggestion. This teaches us that even in the best hypnosis suggestion does not exercise unlimited power but only power of a definite strength. The hypnotic subject will make small sacrifices, but, just as though he were awake, he hesitates before making great ones.

If, then, we are dealing with a patient, and urge him by suggestion to give up his illness, we perceive that this means a great
sacrifice to him and not a small one. Here the power of suggestion is contending against the force which created the symptoms
and maintains them, and experience shows that that force is
of quite a different order of strength from hypnotic influence.
The same patient who is perfectly tractable in putting himself
into any dream-situation one may suggest to him (if it is not
actually objectionable) may remain completely recalcitrant
towards a suggestion which denies the reality of, let us say, an
imaginary paralysis. There is the further fact, moreover, that
precisely neurotic patients are for the most part bad hypnotic
subjects, so that the struggle against the powerful forces by
which the illness is rooted in the patient's mind has to be waged
not by a complete hypnotic influence but only by a fragment
of it.

Thus suggestion is not certain as a matter of course of
defeating the illness as soon as hypnosis (even deep hypnosis)
has been achieved. A further battle has to be fought, and its
outcome is very often uncertain. A single hypnotic treatment
will accordingly effect nothing against severe disturbances of
mental origin. If, however, hypnosis is repeated, it loses some of
the miraculous effect which the patient may perhaps have
anticipated. A succession of hypnoses may eventually bring
about by degrees the influence over the illness which was
lacking at first, till in the end a satisfactory result is achieved.
But a hypnotic treatment such as this may be just as tedious and
wearisome as a treatment of any other kind.

There is yet another way in which the relative weakness of
suggestion is betrayed as compared with the illnesses it has to
combat. It is true that suggestion can bring about a cessation
of the symptoms of an illness—but only for a short time. At the
end of this time they return and have to be repelled once again
by renewed hypnosis and suggestion. If this course of events is
repeated often enough, it usually exhausts the patience both of
the patient and the physician and ends in the abandonment of
hypnotic treatment. These, too, are the cases in which the
patient becomes dependent on the physician and a kind of
addiction to hypnosis is established.

It is a good thing for patients to be aware of these weaknesses
in hypnotic therapy and of the possibilities of disappointment in

its use. The curative power of hypnotic suggestion is something real and it needs no exaggerated recommendation. On the other hand, it is not surprising that physicians, to whom hypnotic mental treatment promised so much more than it could give, are indefatigable in their search for other procedures, which would make possible a deeper, or at least a less unpredictable, influence on a patient's mind. It may safely be anticipated that systematic modern mental treatment, which is a quite recent revival of ancient therapeutic methods, will provide physicians with far more powerful weapons for the fight against illness. A deeper insight into the processes of mental life, the beginnings of which are based precisely on hypnotic experience, will point out the ways and means to this end.[1]

[1] [Earlier writings by Freud on the subject of hypnotism and suggestion will be found in the first and third volumes of the *Standard Edition*.]

# PSYCHOPATHIC CHARACTERS
# ON THE STAGE
## (1942 [1905 or 1906])

# PSYCHOPATHISCHE PERSONEN AUF DER BÜHNE

(*a*) GERMAN EDITIONS:

(1905 or 1906    Probable date of composition. Not hitherto,
1953, published in German.)

(*b*) ENGLISH TRANSLATION:

'Psychopathic Characters on the Stage'

1942    *Psychoanal. Quart.*, **11** (4), Oct., 459–464.    (Tr. H. A. Bunker.)

The present translation is a new one by James Strachey.

Dr. Max Graf, in an article in the *Psychoanal. Quart.*, **11**, (1942), 465, relates that this paper was written by Freud in 1904 and presented to him by its author. It was never published by Freud himself. There must be some mistake about this date (the MS. itself is undated), for Hermann Bahr's play, *Die Andere*, which is discussed on p. 310, was first produced (in Munich and Leipzig) at the beginning of November, 1905, and had its first Vienna performance on the 25th of the same month. It was not published in book form till 1906. The probability is, therefore, that the present paper was written late in 1905 or early in 1906. Our thanks are due to Dr. Raymond Gosselin, editor of the *Psychoanalytic Quarterly*, for supplying us with a photostat of Freud's original manuscript. The handwriting is in places difficult to decipher, which accounts for a few divergences between the two English translations.

# PSYCHOPATHIC CHARACTERS
## ON THE STAGE

IF, as has been assumed since the time of Aristotle, the purpose of drama is to arouse 'terror and pity' [1] and so 'to purge the emotions', we can describe that purpose in rather more detail by saying that it is a question of opening up sources of pleasure or enjoyment in our emotional life, just as, in the case of intellectual activity, joking or fun open up similar sources, many of which that activity had made inaccessible. In this connection the prime factor is unquestionably the process of getting rid of one's own emotions by 'blowing off steam'; and the consequent enjoyment corresponds on the one hand to the relief produced by a thorough discharge and on the other hand, no doubt, to an accompanying sexual excitation; for the latter, as we may suppose, appears as a by-product whenever an affect is aroused, and gives people the sense, which they so much desire, of a raising of the potential of their psychical state. Being present as an interested spectator at a spectacle or play [2] does for adults what play does for children, whose hesitant hopes of being able to do what grown-up people do are in that way gratified. The spectator is a person who experiences too little, who feels that he is a 'poor wretch to whom nothing of importance can happen', who has long been obliged to damp down, or rather displace, his ambition to stand in his own person at the hub of world affairs; he longs to feel and to act and to arrange things according to his desires—in short, to be a hero. And the playwright and actor enable him to do this by allowing him *to identify himself* with a hero. They spare him something, too. For the spectator knows quite well that actual heroic conduct such as this would be impossible for him without pains and sufferings and acute fears, which would almost cancel

[1] [The German '*Mitleid*' has the meaning of 'sympathetic suffering'.]
[2] ['*Schauspiel*' is the ordinary German word for a dramatic performance. Freud writes it here with a hyphen '*Schau-spiel*' to bring out the word's two components: '*Schau*', 'spectacle', and '*Spiel*', 'play' or 'game'. Freud returned to this topic in his subsequent paper on creative art and phantasy (1908e) and again, many years later, at the end of Chapter II of *Beyond the Pleasure Principle* (1920g).]

out the enjoyment. He knows, moreover, that he has only *one* life and that he might perhaps perish even in a *single* such struggle against adversity. Accordingly, his enjoyment is based on an illusion; that is to say, his suffering is mitigated by the certainty that, firstly, it is someone other than himself who is acting and suffering on the stage, and, secondly, that after all it is only a game, which can threaten no damage to his personal security. In these circumstances he can allow himself to enjoy being a 'great man', to give way without a qualm to such suppressed impulses as a craving for freedom in religious, political, social and sexual matters, and to 'blow off steam' in every direction in the various grand scenes that form part of the life represented on the stage.

Several other forms of creative writing, however, are equally subject to these same preconditions for enjoyment. Lyric poetry serves the purpose, more than anything, of giving vent to intense feelings of many sorts—just as was at one time the case with dancing. Epic poetry aims chiefly at making it possible to feel the enjoyment of a great heroic character in his hour of triumph. But drama seeks to explore emotional possibilities more deeply and to give an enjoyable shape even to forebodings of misfortune; for this reason it depicts the hero in his struggles, or rather (with masochistic satisfaction) in defeat. This relation to suffering and misfortune might be taken as characteristic of drama, whether, as happens in serious plays, it is only *concern* that is aroused, and afterwards allayed, or whether, as happens in tragedies, the suffering is actually realized. The fact that drama originated out of sacrificial rites (cf. the goat and the scapegoat) in the cult of the gods cannot be unrelated to this meaning of drama.[1] It appeases, as it were, a rising rebellion against the divine regulation of the universe, which is responsible for the existence of suffering. Heroes are first and foremost rebels against God or against something divine; and pleasure is derived, as it seems, from the affliction of a weaker being in the face of divine might—a pleasure due to masochistic satisfaction as well as to direct enjoyment of a character whose greatness is insisted upon in spite of everything. Here we have a mood like that of Prometheus, but alloyed with a paltry readiness to let oneself be soothed for the moment by a temporary satisfaction.

[1] [The subject of the Hero in Greek tragedy was discussed by Freud in his *Totem and Taboo* (1912–13), in Section 7 of the fourth essay].

Suffering of every kind is thus the subject-matter of drama, and from this suffering it promises to give the audience pleasure. Thus we arrive at a first precondition of this form of art: that it should not cause suffering to the audience, that it should know how to compensate, by means of the possible satisfactions involved, for the sympathetic suffering which is aroused. (Modern writers have particularly often failed to obey this rule.) But the suffering represented is soon restricted to *mental* suffering; for no one wants *physical* suffering who knows how quickly all mental enjoyment is brought to an end by the changes in somatic feeling that physical suffering brings about. If we are sick we have one wish only: to be well again and to be quit of our present state. We call for the doctor and medicine, and for the removal of the inhibition on the play of phantasy which has pampered us into deriving enjoyment even from our own sufferings. If a spectator puts himself in the place of someone who is physically ill he finds himself without any capacity for enjoyment or psychical activity. Consequently a person who is physically ill can only figure on the stage as a piece of stage-property and not as a hero, unless, indeed, some peculiar physical aspects of his illness make psychical activity possible —such, for instance, as the sick man's forlorn state in the *Philoctetes* or the hopelessness of the sufferers in the class of plays that centre round consumptives.

People are acquainted with mental suffering principally in connection with the circumstances in which it is acquired; accordingly, dramas dealing with it require some event out of which the illness shall arise and they open with an exposition of this event. It is only an apparent exception that some plays, such as the *Ajax* and the *Philoctetes*, introduce the mental illness as already fully established; for in Greek tragedies, owing to the familiarity of the material, the curtain rises, as one might say, in the middle of the play. It is easy to give an exhaustive account of the preconditions governing an event of the kind that is here in question. It must be an event involving conflict and it must include an effort of will together with resistance. This precondition found its first and grandest fulfilment in a struggle against divinity. I have already said that a tragedy of this kind is one of rebellion, in which the dramatist and the audience take the side of the rebel. The less belief there comes to be in divinity, the more important becomes the *human* regulation of affairs; and it is this which, with increasing insight, comes to be held responsible for suffering. Thus the hero's next struggle is against human society, and here we have the class of *social* tragedies. Yet another fulfilment of the necessary pre-condition is to be found in a struggle between individual men. Such are tragedies of *character*, which exhibit all the excitement of an '*agon*' [ἀγών, conflict], and which are best played out between outstanding characters who have freed themselves from the bond of human institutions—which, in fact, must have *two* heroes. Fusions between these two last classes, with a hero struggling against institutions embodied in powerful characters, are of course admissible without question. Pure tragedies of character lack the rebellious source of enjoyment, but this emerges once again no less forcibly in social dramas (in Ibsen for instance) than it did in the historical plays of the Greek classical tragedians.

Thus *religious* drama, *social* drama and drama of *character* differ essentially in the terrain on which the action that leads to the suffering is fought out. And we can now follow the course of drama on to yet another terrain, where it becomes *psycho-logical* drama. Here the struggle that causes the suffering is fought out in the hero's mind itself—a struggle between different impulses, and one which must have its end in the extinction, not of the hero, but of one of his impulses; it must end, that is to say, in a renunciation. Combinations of any kind between this precondition and the earlier types are, of course, possible; thus institutions, for instance, can themselves be the cause of internal conflicts. And this is where we have tragedies of love; for the suppression of love by social culture, by human conventions, or the struggle between 'love and duty', which is so familiar to us in opera, are the starting-point of almost endless varieties of situations of conflict: just as endless, in fact, as the erotic day-dreams of men.

But the series of possibilities grows wider; and psychological drama turns into psychopathological drama when the source of the suffering in which we take part and from which we are meant to derive pleasure is no longer a conflict between two almost equally conscious impulses but between a conscious impulse and a repressed one. Here the precondition of enjoy-ment is that the spectator should himself be a neurotic, for it is only such people who can derive pleasure instead of simple aversion from the revelation and the more or less conscious recognition of a repressed impulse. In anyone who is *not* neurotic this recognition will meet only with aversion and will call up a readiness to repeat the act of repression which has earlier been successfully brought to bear on the impulse: for in such people a single expenditure of repression has been enough to hold the repressed impulse completely in check. But in neurotics the repression is on the brink of failing; it is unstable and needs a constant renewal of expenditure, and this expenditure is spared if recognition of the impulse is brought about. Thus it is only in neurotics that a struggle can occur of a kind which can be made the subject of a drama; but even in them the dramatist will provoke not merely an *enjoyment* of the liberation but a *resistance* to it as well.

The first of these modern dramas is *Hamlet*.[1] It has as its subject the way in which a man who has so far been normal becomes neurotic owing to the peculiar nature of the task by which he is faced, a man, that is, in whom an impulse that has hitherto been successfully suppressed endeavours to make its way into action. *Hamlet* is distinguished by three characteristics which seem important in connection with our present discussion. (1) The hero is not psychopathic, but only *becomes* psychopathic in the course of the action of the play. (2) The repressed impulse is one of those which are similarly repressed in all of us, and the repression of which is part and parcel of the foundations of our personal evolution. It is this repression which is shaken up by the situation in the play. As a result of these two characteristics it is easy for us to recognize ourselves in the hero: we are susceptible to the same conflict as he is, since 'a person who does not lose his reason under certain conditions can have no reason to lose'.[2] (3) It appears as a necessary precondition of this form of art that the impulse that is struggling into consciousness, however clearly it is recognizable, is never given a definite name; so that in the spectator too the process is carried through with his attention averted, and he is in the grip of his emotions instead of taking stock of what is happening. A certain amount of resistance is no doubt saved in this way, just as, in an analytic treatment, we find derivatives of the repressed material

[1] [Freud's first published discussion of *Hamlet* was in *The Interpretation of Dreams* (Chapter V, Section D (β); Standard Ed., 4, 264 ff).]
[2] [Lessing, *Emilia Galotti*, Act IV, Scene 7.]

reaching consciousness, owing to a lower resistance, while the repressed material itself is unable to do so. After all, the conflict in *Hamlet* is so effectively concealed that it was left to me to unearth it.

It may be in consequence of disregarding these three pre-conditions that so many other psychopathic characters are as unserviceable on the stage as they are in real life. For the victim of a neurosis is someone into whose conflict we can gain no insight if we first meet it in a fully established state. But, *per contra*, if we recognize the conflict, we forget that he is a sick man, just as, if he himself recognizes it, he ceases to be ill. It would seem to be the dramatist's business to induce the same illness in *us*; and this can best be achieved if we are made to follow the development of the illness along with the sufferer. This will be especially necessary where the repression does not already exist in us but has first to be set up; and this represents a step further than *Hamlet* in the use of neurosis on the stage. If we are faced by an unfamiliar and fully established neurosis, we shall be inclined to send for the doctor (just as we do in real life) and pronounce the character inadmissible to the stage.

This last mistake seems to occur in Bahr's *Die Andere*,[1] apart from a second one which is implicit in the problem presented in the play—namely, that it is impossible for us to put ourselves with conviction into the position of believing that one parti-cular person has a prescriptive right to give the girl complete satisfaction. So that her case cannot become ours. Moreover, there remains a third mistake: namely that there is nothing left for us to discover and that our entire resistance is mobilized against this predetermined condition of love which is so un-acceptable to us. Of the three formal preconditions that I have been discussing, the most important seems to be that of the diversion of attention.

In general, it may perhaps be said that the neurotic instab-ility of the public and the dramatist's skill in avoiding resistances and offering fore-pleasures can alone determine the limits set upon the employment of abnormal characters on the stage.

[1] [This play by Hermann Bahr, the Austrian novelist and playwright (1863–1934), was first produced at the end of 1905. Its plot turns upon the dual personality of its heroine, who is unable, in spite of every effort, to escape from an attachment (based on her physical feelings) to a man who has her in his power.—This paragraph was omitted from the 1942 translation.]

# BIBLIOGRAPHY

[Titles of books and periodicals are in italics; titles of papers are in inverted commas. Abbreviations are in accordance with the *World List of Scientific Periodicals* (London, 1952). Further abbreviations used in this volume will be found in the List at the end of this bibliography. Numerals in thick type refer to volumes; ordinary numerals refer to pages. The figures in round brackets at the end of each entry indicate the page or pages of this volume on which the work in question is mentioned. In the case of the Freud entries, the letters attached to the dates of publication are in accordance with the corresponding entries in the complete bibliography of Freud's writings to be included in the last volume of the *Standard Edition*.

For non-technical authors, and for technical authors where no specific work is mentioned, see the *General Index*.]

ABRAHAM, K. (1916) 'Untersuchungen über die früheste prägenital) Entwicklungsstufe der Libido', *Int. Z. Psychoanal.*, **4**, 71. (198 n., [*Trans.:* 'The First Pregenital Stage of the Libido', *Selected Papers* London, 1927, Chap. XII.]

    (1924) *Versuch einer Entwicklungsgeschichte der Libido*, Vienna. (198 n., 199 nn.)
    [*Trans.:* 'A Short Study of the Development of the Libido', *Selected Papers*, London, 1927, Chap. XXVI.]

ADLER, A. (1907) *Studie über Minderwertigkeit von Organen*, Vienna. (184, *n.* 1)

ANDREAS-SALOMÉ, L. (1916) ' "Anal" und "Sexual" ', *Imago*, **4**, 249. (187 n.)

ARDUIN (1900) 'Die Frauenfrage und die sexuellen Zwischenstufen', *Jb. sex. Zwischenst.*, **2**. (143 n.)

BALDWIN, J. M. (1895) *Mental Development in the Child and the Race*, New York. (173, *n.* 2)

BAYER, H. (1902) 'Zur Entwicklungsgeschichte der Gebärmutter', *Dtsch. Arch. klin. Med.*, **73**, 422. (177 n.)

BELL, S. (1902) 'A Preliminary Study of the Emotion of Love between the Sexes', *Amer. J. Psychol.*, **13**, 325. (173, *n.* 2, 193, *n.* 2)

BERNFELD, S. (1944) 'Freud's Earliest Theories and the School of Helmholtz', *Psychoanal. Quart.*, **13**, 341. (283, *n.* 2)

BINET, A. (1888) *Études de psychologie expérimentale: le fétichisme dans l'amour*, Paris. (154, 171)

BLEULER, E. (1908) 'Sexuelle Abnormitäten der Kinder', *Jb. schwez. Ges. Schulgesundh. Pfl.*, **9**, 623. (173, *n.* 2)

    (1913) 'Der Sexualwiderstand', *Jb. psychoanal. psychopath. Forsch.*, **5**, 442. (189 n.)

BLOCH, I. (1902–3) *Beiträge zur Ätiologie der Psychopathia sexualis* (2 vols.), Dresden. (51, *n.* 1, 139, *n.* 2)

BREUER, J., and FREUD, S. (1893) See FREUD, S. (1893a)
    (1895) See FREUD, S. (1895d)
CHEVALIER, J. (1893) *L'inversion sexuelle*, Lyon. (141, 143 n.)
DESSOIR, M. (1894) 'Zur Psychologie der Vita sexualis', *Allg. Z. Psychiat.*,
    **50**, 941. (229)
DISKUSSIONEN DER WIENER PSYCHOANALYTISCHEN VEREINIGUNG (1912)
    II, 'Die Onanie', Wiesbaden. (185, n. 1, 188, n. 1)
ELLIS, HAVELOCK (1910) *Studies in the Psychology of Sex*, Vol. I: *The Evolu-
    tion of Modesty; the Phenomena of Sexual Periodicity; and Auto-erotism*,
    3rd ed., Philadelphia. (1st ed., 'Leipzig' [London], 1899.) (181)
    (1913) *Studies in the Psychology of Sex*, Vol. III: *Analysis of the Sexual
    Impulse; Love and Pain; the Sexual Impulse in Women*, 2nd ed.,
    Philadelphia. (1st ed., Philadelphia, 1903.) (159, n. 4, 173, n. 2,
    190 n., 223 n.)
    (1915) *Studies in the Psychology of Sex*, Vol. II: *Sexual Inversion*, 3rd
    ed., Philadelphia. (1st Engl. ed., London, 1897.) (140, 142)
    (1928) *Studies in the Psychology of Sex*, Vol. VII: *Eonism, etc.*, Phila-
    delphia. (218, n. 3)
FERENCZI, S. (1909) 'Introjektion und Übertragung', *Jb. psychoanal.
    psychopath. Forsch.*, **1**, 422. (150 n.)
    [*Trans.:* 'Introjection and Transference', *Contributions to Psycho-
    Analysis*, Boston, 1916, Chap. II.]
    (1914) 'Zur Nosologie der männlichen Homosexualität (Homoëro-
    tik)', *Int. Z. Psychoanal.*, **2**, 131. (144 n.)
    [*Trans.:* 'The Nosology of Male Homosexuality (Homoerotism)',
    *Contributions to Psycho-Analysis*, Boston, 1916, Chap. XII.]
    (1920) Review of Lipschütz, *Die Pubertätsdrüse*, *Int. Z. Psychoanal.*,
    **6**, 84. (177 n.)
    [*Trans.:* *Int. J. Psycho-Anal.*, **2** (1921), 143.]
    (1924) *Versuch einer Genitaltheorie*, Vienna. (229, n. 2)
    [*Trans.:* *Thalassa, a Theory of Genitality*, New York, 1938.]
FLIESS, W. (1906) *Der Ablauf des Lebens*, Vienna. (143 n.)
FREUD, S. (1893a) With BREUER, J., 'Über den psychischen Mechanis-
    mus hysterischer Phänomene: Vorläufige Mitteilung', *G.S.*, **1**, 7;
    *G.W.*, **1**, 81. (127, 276 n.)
    [*Trans.:* 'On the Psychical Mechanism of Hysterical Phenomena:
    Preliminary Communication', *C.P.*, **1**, 24; *Standard Ed.*, **2**.]
    (1893f) 'Charcot', *G.S.*, **1**, 243; *G.W.*, **1**, 19. (115 n.)
    [*Trans.:* 'Charcot', *C.P.*, **1**, 9; *Standard Ed.*, **3**.]
    (1894a) 'Die Abwehr-Neuropsychosen', *G.S.*, **1**, 290; *G.W.*, **1**, 57.
    (53n., 276)
    [*Trans.:* 'The Neuro-Psychoses of Defence', *C.P.*, **1**, 59; *Standard
    Ed.*, **3**.]
    (1895b) 'Über die Berechtigung, von der Neurasthenie einen bes-
    timmten Symptomenkomplex als "Angstneurose" abzutrennen,'
    *G.S.*, **1**, 306; *G.W.*, **1**, 313. (80 n., 127, 213 n., 272 n.)
    [*Trans.:* 'On the Grounds for Detaching a Particular Syndrome
    from Neurasthenia under the Description "Anxiety Neurosis" ',
    *C.P.*, **1**, 76; *Standard Ed.*, **3**.]

FREUD, S. (cont.)

(1895d) With BREUER, J., *Studien über Hysterie*, Vienna. (*G.S.*, 1; *G.W.*, 1. 75. Omitting Breuer's contributions.) (7 n., 12, 24, 27, n. 1, 31, n. 2, 117 n., 164 n., 248–9, 257, 272)
[*Trans.: Studies on Hysteria, Standard Ed.*, 2. Including Breuer's contributions.]

(1895f) 'Zur Kritik der "Angstneurose" ', *G.S.*, 1, 343; *G.W.*, 1, 355. (81, n. 2)
[*Trans.:* 'A Reply to Criticisms of my Paper on Anxiety Neurosis', *C.P.*, 1, 107; *Standard Ed.*, 3.]

(1895g) 'Über Hysterie', three lectures by Freud abstracted in *Wiener klin. Rundschau*, 9, Nos. 42–4. (257 n.)

(1896a) 'L'hérédité et l'étiologie des Névroses', *G.S.*, 1, 388; *G.W.*, 1, 405. (20 n., 275, n. 2)
[*Trans.:* 'Heredity and the Aetiology of the Neuroses', *C.P.*, 1, 138; *Standard Ed.*, 3.]

(1896b) 'Weitere Bemerkungen über die Abwehr-Neuropsychosen', *G.S.*, 1, 363; *G.W.*, 1, 377. (128, 273, 275, n. 2)
[*Trans.:* 'Further Remarks on the Neuro-Psychoses of Defence', *C.P.*, 1, 155; *Standard Ed.*, 3.]

(1896c) 'Zur Ätiologie der Hysterie', *G.S.*, 1, 404; *G.W.*, 1, 423. (7 n., 27, n. 2, 176, n. 1, 190, 257 n., 273)
[*Trans.:* 'The Aetiology of Hysteria', *C.P.*, 1, 183; *Standard Ed.*, 3.]

(1898a) 'Die Sexualität in der Ätiologie der Neurosen', *G.S.*, 1, 439; *G.W.*, 1, 489. (128, 204, n. 2)
[*Trans.:* 'Sexuality in the Aetiology of the Neuroses', *C.P.*, 1, 220; *Standard Ed.*, 3.]

(1899a) 'Über Deckerinnerungen', *G.S.*, 1, 465; *G.W.*, 1, 529. (175, n. 1)
[*Trans.:* 'Screen Memories', *C.P.*, 5, 47; *Standard Ed.*, 3.]

(1900a) *Die Traumdeutung*, Vienna. (*G.S.*, 2–3; *G.W.*, 2–3.) (4, 10, 11, n. 1, 15, 17, n. 2, 29, n. 1, 56 n., 67, 71 nn., 85–6, 87 n., 88 n., 92 n., 97, n. 2, 100, n. 2, 117 n., 126–9, 184, n. 3, 192, n. 2, 201 n., 226 n., 227 n., 250 n., 252, 284 n., 295 n., 309, n. 1)
[*Trans.: The Interpretation of Dreams*, London and New York, 1955; *Standard Ed.*, 4–5.]

(1901a) *Über den Traum*, Wiesbaden. (*G.S.*, 3, 189; *G.W.*, 2–3, 643.) (129)
[*Trans.: On Dreams*, London, 1951; *Standard Ed.*, 5, 629.]

(1901b) *Zur Psychopathologie des Alltagslebens*, Berlin, 1904. (*G.S.*, 4; *G.W.*, 4.) (3 4, 21, n. 1, 76, n. 2, 121, n. 1, 129, 143 n., 175, n.1)
[*Trans.: The Psychopathology of Everyday Life, Standard Ed.*, 6.]

(1905b) 'Psychische Behandlung (Seelenbehandlung)', *G.W.*, 5, 289. (258 n.)
[*Trans.:* 'Psychical (or Mental) Treatment', *Standard Ed.*, 7, 283.]

(1905c) *Der Witz und seine Beziehung zum Unbewussten*, Vienna. (*G.S.*, 9, 5; *G.W.*, 6.) (129, 211 n.)
[*Trans.: Jokes and their Relation to the Unconscious, Standard Ed.*, 8.]

(1905d) *Drei Abhandlungen zur Sexualtheorie*, Vienna. (*G.S.*, 5, 3;

FREUD, S. (*cont.*)

    *G.W.*, **5**, 29.) (4–5, 50 *n.*, 51, *n.* 1, 52, *n.* 1, 56 *n.*, 74, *n.* 2, 81, *n.* 1, 113 *n.*, 275, *n.* 1, 276–7, 279, *n.* 2)

    [*Trans.: Three Essays on the Theory of Sexuality*, London, 1949; *Standard Ed.*, **7**, 125.]

(1905*e*) 'Bruchstück einer Hysterie-Analyse', *G.S.*, **8**, 3; *G.W.*, **5**, 163. (129, 156, *n.* 2, 163, 165, *n.* 2, 167, *n.* 2, 286, *n.* 2)

    [*Trans.:* 'Fragment of an Analysis of a Case of Hysteria', *C.P.*, **3**, 13; *Standard Ed.*, **7**, 3.]

(1906*a*) 'Meine Ansichten über die Rolle der Sexualität in der Ätiologie der Neurosen', *G.S.*, **5**, 123; *G.W.*, **5**, 149. (113 *n.*, 128 *n.*, 190 *n.*, 216 *n.*, 235 *n.*)

    [*Trans.:* 'My Views on the Part played by Sexuality in the Aetiology of the Neuroses', *C.P.*, **1**, 272; *Standard Ed.*, **7**, 271.]

(1907*c*) 'Zur sexuellen Aufklärung der Kinder', *G.S.*, **5**, 134; *G.W.*, **7**, 19. (Appendix, 244)

    [*Trans.:* 'The Sexual Enlightenment of Children', *C.P.*, **2**, 36; *Standard Ed.*, **9**.]

(1908*b*) 'Charakter und Analerotik', *G.S.*, **5**, 261; *G.W.*, **7**, 203. (185, *n.* 2, 239, *n.* 2)

    [*Trans.:* 'Character and Anal Erotism', *C.P.*, **2**, 45; *Standard Ed.*, **9**.]

(1908*c*) 'Über infantile Sexualtheorien', *G.S.*, **5**, 168; *G.W.*, **7**, 171. (193, *n.* 2)

    [*Trans.:* 'On the Sexual Theories of Children', *C.P.*, **2**, 59; *Standard Ed.*, **9**.]

(1908*d*) 'Die "kulturelle" Sexualmoral und die moderne Nervosität', *G.S.*, **5**, 143; *G.W.*, **7**, 143. (Appendix, 244)

    [*Trans.:* ' "Civilized" Sexual Ethics and Modern Nervous Illness', *C.P.*, **2**, 76; *Standard Ed.*, **9**.]

(1908*e*) 'Der Dichter und das Phantasieren', *G.S.*, **10**, 229; *G.W.*, **7**, 213. (211 *n.*, 305, *n.* 2)

    [*Trans.:* 'Creative Writers and Day-Dreaming', *C.P.*, **4**, 173; *Standard Ed.*, **9**.]

(1909*a*) 'Allgemeines über den hysterischen Anfall', *G.S.*, **5**, 255; *G.W.*, **7**, 235. (43 *n.*)

    [*Trans.:* 'Some General Remarks on Hysterical Attacks', *C.P.*, **2**, 100; *Standard Ed.*, **9**.]

(1909*b*) 'Analyse der Phobie eines fünfjährigen Knaben', *G.S.*, **8**, 129; *G.W.*, **7**, 243. (13 *n.*, 52, *n.* 2, 193, *n.* 2, 241, *n.* 1)

    [*Trans.:* 'Analysis of a Phobia in a Five-Year-Old Boy', *C.P.*, **3**, 149; *Standard Ed.*, **10**.]

(1909*c*) 'Der Familienroman der Neurotiker', *G.S.*, **12**, 367; *G.W.*, **7**, 227. (226 *n.*)

    [*Trans.:* 'Family Romances', *C.P.*, **5**, 74; *Standard Ed.*, **9**.]

(1909*d*) 'Bemerkungen über einen Fall von Zwangsneurose', *G.S.*, **8**, 269; *G.W.*, **7**, 381. (13 *n.*, 17, *n.* 2, 155, *n.* 2, 226 *n.*, 248)

    [*Trans.:* 'Notes on a Case of Obsessional Neurosis', *C.P.*, **3**, 293; *Standard Ed.*, **10**.]

FREUD, S. (*cont.*)

(1910*a*) *Über Psychoanalyse,* Vienna. (*G.S.,* 4, 349; *G.W.,* 8, 3.) (Appendix, 244)
[*Trans.: Five Lectures on Psycho-Analysis, Standard Ed.,* 11.]

(1910*c*) *Eine Kindheitserinnerung des Leonardo da Vinci,* Vienna. (*G.S.,* 9, 371; *G.W.,* 8, 128.) (Appendix, 244)
[*Trans.: Leonardo da Vinci and a Memory of his Childhood, Standard Ed.,* 11.]

(1910*h*) 'Über einen besonderen Typus der Objektwahl beim Manne', *G.S.,* 5, 186; *G.W.,* 8, 66. (228 *n.*)
[*Trans.:* 'A Special Type of Choice of Object made by Men', *C.P.,* 4, 192; *Standard Ed.,* 11.]

(1910*i*) 'Die psychogene Sehstörung in psychoanalytischer Auffassung', *G.S.,* 5, 301; *G.W.,* 8, 94. (40 *n.*)
[*Trans.:* 'The Psycho-Analytic View of Psychogenic Disturbance of Vision', *C.P.,* 2, 105; *Standard Ed.,* 11.]

(1911*c*) 'Psychoanalytische Bemerkungen über einen autobiographisch beschriebenen Fall von Paranoia (Dementia paranoides)', *G.S.,* 8, 355; *G.W.,* 8, 240. (13 *n.*)
[*Trans.:* 'Psycho-Analytic Notes on an Autobiographical Account of a Case of Paranoia (Dementia Paranoides)', *C.P.,* 3, 387; *Standard Ed.,* 12.]

(1911*e*) 'Die Handhabung der Traumdeutung in der Psychoanalyse', *G.S.,* 6, 45; *G.W.,* 8, 350. (11, *n.* 2)
[*Trans.:* 'The Handling of Dream-Interpretation in Psycho-Analysis', *C.P.,* 2, 305; *Standard Ed.,* 12.]

(1912*b*) 'Zur Dynamik der Übertragung', *G.S.,* 6, 53; *G.W.,* 8, 364. (117 *n.*)
[*Trans.:* 'The Dynamics of Transference', *C.P.,* 2, 312; *Standard Ed.,* 12.]

(1912*c*) 'Über neurotische Erkrankungstypen', *G.S.,* 5, 400; *G.W.,* 8, 322. (165, *n.* 1)
[*Trans.:* 'Types of Onset of Neurosis', *C.P.,* 2, 113; *Standard Ed.,* 12.]

(1912*d*) 'Über die allgemeinste Erniedrigung des Liebeslebens', *G.S.,* 5, 198; *G.W.,* 8, 78. (Appendix, 244)
[*Trans.:* 'On the Universal Tendency to Debasement in the Sphere of Love', *C.P.,* 4, 203; *Standard Ed.,* 11.]

(1912*f*) 'Zur Onanie-Diskussion', *G.S.,* 3, 324; *G.W.,* 8, 332. (40 *n.,* 185, *n.* 1, 188, *n.* 2)
[*Trans.:* 'Contributions to a Discussion on Masturbation', *Standard Ed.,* 12.]

(1912–13) *Totem und Tabu,* Vienna, 1913. (*G.S.,* 10; *G.W.,* 9.) (225, *n.* 3, 306 *n.*)
[*Trans.: Totem and Taboo,* London, 1950; *Standard Ed.,* 13.]

(1913*i*) 'Die Disposition zur Zwangsneurose', *G.S.,* 5, 277; *G.W.,* 8, 442. (197 *n.,* 235 *n.,* 275, *n.* 2)
[*Trans.:* 'The Predisposition to Obsessional Neurosis', *C.P.,* 2, 122; *Standard Ed.,* 12.]

FREUD, S. (*cont.*)

(1913*j*) 'Das Interesse an der Psychoanalyse', *G.S.*, **4**, 313; *G.W.*, **8**, 390. (Appendix, 244)
[*Trans.*: 'The Claims of Psycho-Analysis to Scientific Interest', *Standard Ed.*, **13**.]

(1913*k*) 'Geleitwort zu Bourke *Der Unrat in Sitte, Brauch, Glauben und Gewohnheitsrecht der Völker*', Leipzig. (*G.S.*, **11**, 249; *G.W.*, **10**, 453.) (Appendix, 244)
[*Trans.*: 'Preface to Bourke's *Scatalogic Rites of All Nations*', *C.P.*, **5**, 88; *Standard Ed.*, **12**.]

(1914*c*) 'Zur Einführung des Narzissmus', *G.S.*, **6**, 155; *G.W.*, **10**, 138. (178, *n*. 2, 182, *n*. 1, 217, *n*. 1, 218, *n*. 3, 222 *n*.)
[*Trans.*: 'On Narcissism: an Introduction', *C.P.*, **4**, 30; *Standard Ed.*, **14**.]

(1914*d*) 'Zur Geschichte der psychoanalytischen Bewegung', *G.S.*, **4**, 411; *G.W.*, **10**, 44. (5, 27, *n*. 1, 128 *n*., 275, *n*. 1)
[*Trans.*: 'On the History of the Psycho-Analytic Movement', *C.P.*, **1**, 287; *Standard Ed.*, **14**.]

(1914*g*) 'Weitere Ratschläge zur Technik der Psychoanalyse: II. Erinnern, Wiederholen und Durcharbeiten', *G.S.*, **6**, 109; *G.W.*, **10**, 126. (119, *n*. 1)
[*Trans.*: 'Recollecting, Repeating and Working Through (Further Recommendations on the Technique of Psycho-Analysis, II)', *C.P.*, **2**, 366; *Standard Ed.*, **12**.]

(1915*a*) 'Weitere Ratschläge zur Technik der Psychoanalyse: III. Bemerkungen über die Übertragungsliebe', *G.S.*, **6**, 120; *G.W.*, **10**, 306. (117 *n*.)
[*Trans.*: 'Observations on Transference-Love (Further Recommendations on the Technique of Psycho-Analysis, III)', *C.P.*, **2**, 377; *Standard Ed.*, **12**.]

(1915*c*) 'Triebe und Triebschicksale', *G.S.*, **5**, 443; *G.W.*, **10**, 210. (168, *n*. 1)
[*Trans.*: 'Instincts and their Vicissitudes', *C.P.*, **4**, 60; *Standard Ed.*, **14**.]

(1915*d*) 'Die Verdrängung', *G.S.*, **5**, 466; *G.W.*, **10**, 248. (29, *n*. 1, 175, *n*. 2)
[*Trans.*: 'Repression', *C.P.*, **4**, 84; *Standard Ed.*, **14**.]

(1916–17) *Vorlesungen zur Einführung in die Psychoanalyse*, Vienna. (*G.S.*, **7**; *G.W.*, **11**.) (43 *n*., 224 *n*., 226 *n*., 240 *n*.)
[*Trans.*: *Introductory Lectures on Psycho-Analysis*, revised ed., London, 1929; *A General Introduction to Psychoanalysis*, New York, 1935; *Standard Ed.*, **15–16**.]

(1917*c*) 'Über Triebumsetzungen insbesondere der Analerotik', *G.S.*, **5**, 268; *G.W.*, **10**, 402. (185, *n*. 2, 186 *n*.)
[*Trans.*: 'On Transformations of Instinct as Exemplified in Anal Erotism', *C.P.*, **2**, 164; *Standard Ed.*, **17**.]

(1918*a*) 'Das Tabu der Virginität', *G.S.*, **5**, 212; *G.W.*, **12**, 161. (Appendix, 244)
[*Trans.*: 'The Taboo of Virginity', *C.P.*, **4**, 217; *Standard Ed.*, **11**.]

FREUD, S. (cont.)

(1918b) 'Aus der Geschichte einer infantilen Neurose', G.S., 8, 439; G.W., 12, 29. (13 n.)
[Trans.: 'From the History of an Infantile Neurosis', C.P., 3, 473; Standard Ed., 17.]

(1919e) ' "Ein Kind wird geschlagen" ', G.S., 5, 344; G.W., 12, 197. (143 n.)
[Trans.: ' "A Child is Being Beaten" ', C.P., 2, 172; Standard Ed., 17.]

(1920a) 'Über die Psychogenese eines Falles von weiblicher Homosexualität', G.S., 5, 312; G.W., 12, 271. (221 n.)
[Trans.: 'The Psychogenesis of a Case of Female Homosexuality', C.P., 2, 202; Standard Ed., 18.]

(1920g) Jenseits des Lustprinzips, Vienna. (G.S., 6, 191; G.W., 13, 3.) (29, n. 1, 136, n. 1, 168, n. 2, 305, n. 2)
[Trans.: Beyond the Pleasure Principle, London, 1950; Standard Ed., 18.]

(1921c) Massenpsychologie und Ich-Analyse, Vienna. (G.S., 6, 261; G.W., 13, 73.) (150 n., 296 n.)
[Trans.: Group Psychology and the Analysis of the Ego, London, 1922; Standard Ed., 18.]

(1923a [1922]) ' "Psychoanalyse" und "Libido Theorie" ', G.S., 11, 201; G.W., 13, 211. (Appendix, 245)
[Trans.: 'Two Encyclopaedia Articles', C.P., 5, 107; Standard Ed., 18.]

(1923b) Das Ich und das Es, Vienna. (G.S., 6, 353; G.W., 13, 237.) (46 n., 168, n. 2, 178, n. 2)
[Trans.: The Ego and the Id, London, 1927; Standard Ed., 19.]

(1923e) 'Die infantile Genitalorganization', G.S., 5, 232; G.W., 13, 293. (126 n., 199, n. 2)
[Trans.: 'The Infantile Genital Organization of the Libido', C.P., 2, 244; Standard Ed., 19.]

(1924c) 'Das ökonomische Problem des Masochismus', G.S., 5, 374; G.W., 13, 371. (158, n. 2, 209, n. 1)
[Trans.: 'The Economic Problem of Masochism', C.P., 2, 255; Standard Ed., 19.]

(1924d) 'Der Untergang des Ödipuskomplexes', G.S., 5, 423; G.W., 13, 395. (Appendix, 245)
[Trans.: 'The Dissolution of the Oedipus Complex', C.P., 2, 269; Standard Ed., 19.]

(1925d) 'Selbstdarstellung', Vienna, 1934. (G.S., 11, 119; G.W., 14, 33.) (128 n., 275, n. 1)
[Trans.: An Autobiographical Study, London and New York, 1935; Standard Ed., 20.]

(1925h) 'Die Verneinung', G.S., 11, 3; G.W., 14, 11. (57, n. 2, 184, n. 3)
[Trans.: 'Negation', C.P., 5, 181; Standard Ed., 19.]

(1925j) 'Einige psychische Folgen des anatomischen Geschlechtsunterschieds', G.S., 11, 8; G.W., 14, 19. (195, n. 1, 221 n.)

FREUD, S. (*cont.*)
    [*Trans.:* 'Some Psychological Consequences of the Anatomical
    Distinction between the Sexes', *C.P.*, **5**, 186; *Standard Ed.*, **19**.]
    (1926*d*) *Hemmung, Symptom und Angst*, Vienna. (*G.S.*, **11**, 23; *G.W.*,
    **14**, 113.) (29, *n.* 1, 43 *n.*, 80 *n.*, 224 *n.*, 226 *n.*, 276 *n.*)
    [*Trans.: Inhibitions, Symptoms and Anxiety*, London, 1936; *The
    Problem of Anxiety*, New York, 1936; *Standard Ed.*, **20**.]
    (1927*e*) 'Fetischismus', *G.S.*, **11**, 395; *G.W.*, **14**, 311. (155, *n.* 2)
    [*Trans.:* 'Fetishism', *C.P.*, **5**, 198; *Standard Ed.*, **21**.]
    (1930*a*) *Das Unbehagen in der Kultur*, Vienna. (*G.S.*, **12**, 29; *G.W.*,
    **14**, 421.) (32 *n.*, 155, *n.* 2, 219 *n.*)
    [*Trans.: Civilization and its Discontents*, London and New York,
    1930; *Standard Ed.*, **21**.]
    (1931*a*) 'Über libidinöse Typen', *G.S.*, **12**, 115; *G.W.*, **14**, 509.
    (Appendix, 245)
    [*Trans.:* 'Libidinal Types', *C.P.*, **5**, 247; *Standard Ed.*, **21**.]
    (1931*b*) 'Über die weibliche Sexualität', *G.S.*, **12**, 120; *G.W.*, **14**,
    517. (221 *n.*)
    [*Trans.:* 'Female Sexuality', *C.P.*, **5**, 252; *Standard Ed.*, **21**.]
    (1932*a*) 'Zur Gewinnung des Feuers', *G.S.*, **12**, 141; *G.W.*, **16**, 3. (72 *n.*)
    [*Trans.:* 'The Acquisition and Control of Fire', *C.P.*, **5**, 288;
    *Standard Ed.*, **22**.]
    (1933*a*) *Neue Folge der Vorlesungen zur Einführung in die Psychoanalyse*,
    Vienna. (*G.S.*, **12**, 151; *G.W.*, **15**.) (221 *n.*, 224 *n.*)
    [*Trans.: New Introductory Lectures on Psycho-Analysis*, London and
    New York, 1933; *Standard Ed.*, **22**.]
    (1937*c*) 'Die endliche und die unendliche Analyse', *G.W.*, **16**, 59.
    (204, *n.* 2)
    [*Trans.:* 'Analysis Terminable and Interminable', *C.P.*, **5**, 316;
    *Standard Ed.*, **23**.]
    (1937*d*) 'Konstruktionen in der Analyse', *G.W.*, **16**, 43. (57, *n.* 2)
    [*Trans.:* 'Constructions in Analysis', *C.P.*, **5**, 358; *Standard Ed.*, **23**.]
    (1940*a* [1938]) *'Abriss der Psychoanalyse'*, *G.W.*, **17**, 67. (155, *n.* 2)
    [*Trans.: An Outline of Psycho-Analysis*, London and New York,
    1949; *Standard Ed.*, **23**.]
    (1940*e* [1938]) 'Die Ichspaltung im Abwehrvorgang', *G.W.*, **17**,
    59. (155, *n.* 2)
    [*Trans.:* 'Splitting of the Ego in the Process of Defence', *C.P.*, **5**,
    372; *Standard Ed.*, **23**.]
    (1950*a* [1887–1902]) *Aus den Anfängen der Psychoanalyse*, London.
    Includes the 'Entwurf einer Psychologie' (1895). (3–5, 32 *n.*,
    43 *n.*, 55, *n.* 1, 78 *n.*, 126–9, 143 *n.*, 156, *n.* 2, 162, *n.* 1, 165, *n.* 2,
    167, *n.* 2, 184, *n.* 3, 216 *n.*, 225, *n.* 3, 235 *n.*, 236 *n.*, 275 *nn.*)
    [*Trans.: The Origins of Psycho-Analysis*, London and New York,
    1954. (Partly, including 'A Project for a Scientific Psychology',
    in *Standard Ed.*, **1**.)]
GALANT, S. (1919) 'Sexualleben im Säuglings- und Kindesalter',
    *Neurol. Zbl.*, **38**, 652. Reprinted, *Int. Z. Psychoanal.*, **6** (1920), 164.
    (181, *n.* 1)

GLEY, E. (1884) 'Les aberrations de l'instinct sexuel', *Revue philosophique*, **17**, 66. (143 n.)

GRAF, M. (1942) 'Reminiscences of Professor Sigmund Freud', *Psychoanal. Quart.*, **11**, 46c. (304).

GROOS, K. (1899) *Die Spiele der Menschen*, Jena. (173, n. 2)
      (1904) *Das Seelenleben des Kindes*, Berlin. (173, n. 2)

HALBAN, J. (1903) 'Die Entstehung der Geschlechtscharaktere', *Arch. Gynaek.*, **70**, 205. (142)
      (1904) Schwangerschaftsreaktionen der fötalen Organe und ihre puerperale Involution', *Z. Geburtsh. Gynäk.*, **53**, 191. (177 n.)

HALL, G. STANLEY (1940) *Adolescence: its Psychology and its relations to Physiology, Anthropology, Sociology, Sex, Crime, Religion and Education*, 2 vols., New York. (173, n. 2)

HELLER, T. (1904) *Grundriss der Heilpädogogik*, Leipzig. (173, n. 2)

HERMAN, G. (1903) *'Genesis', das Gesetz der Zeugung*, Bd. *c*, *Libido und Mania*, Leipzig. (143 n.)

HIRSCHFELD, M. (1899) 'Die objecktive Diagnose der Homosexualität', *Jb. sex. Zwischenst.*, **1**, 8. (143 n.)
      (1904) 'Statistiche Untersuchungen über den Prozentsatz der Homosexuellen', *Jb. sex. Zwischenst.*, **6**, (136, n. 2)

HUG-HELLMUTH, H. VON (1913) *Aus dem Seelenleben des Kindes*, Vienna. (173, n. 2)
      ]*Trans.: A Study of the Mental Life of the Child*, New York, 1919.]

JAHRBUCH FÜR SEXUELLE ZWISCHENSTUFEN (135, n. 1, 141 n., 143 n.)

JANET, P. (1894) *Etat mental des hystériques*, Paris. (114 n., 266 n.)

KIERNAN, J. G. (1888) *Med. Stand.* (Chicago), Nov. and Dec. (141)

KINDERFEHLER, DIE (173, n. 2)

KOSSMANN, R., and WEISS, J. (1905) *Die Gesundheit*, Stuttgart. (282,   286, n. 1)

KRAFFT-EBING, R. VON (1895) 'Zur Erklärung der conträren Sexualempfindung', *Jb. Psychiat. Neurol.*, **13**, 1. (142, 143 n.)
      (1893) *Psychopathia Sexualis*, 8th ed., Stuttgart. (50)
      [*Trans.: Psychopathia Sexualis*, New York, 1922.]

LINDNER, S. (1879) 'Das Saugen an den Fingern, Lippen, etc., bei den Kindern (Ludeln)', *Jb. Kinderheilk.*, N.F., **14**, 68. (179)

LIPSCHÜTZ, A. (1919) *Die Pubertätsdrüse und ihre Wirkungen*, Bern. (144 n., 177 n., 215 n.)

LOEWENFELD, L. (1897) *Lehrbuch der gesamten Psychotherapie*, Wiesbaden. (258)
      (1904) *Die psychischen Zwangserscheinungen*, Wiesbaden. (248)
      (1906) *Sexualleben und Nervenleiden*, Wiesbaden. (4th edition.) (270)

LYDSTON, G. F. (1889) *Philadelphia Med. Surg. Rep.*, Sept. 7. (141)

MANTEGAZZA, P. (1875) *Fisiologia dell'amore*, 2nd ed., Milan. (26, 62)

MEDICAL CONGRESS (1900) *Thirteenth International Medical Congress*, Paris. (20 n.)

MOEBIUS, P. J. (1900) 'Über Entartung', *Grenzfr. Nerv.-u. Seelenleb.*, **3**. (138 n.)

MOLL, A. (1898) *Untersuchungen über die Libido sexualis*, Bd. I, Berlin. (169, n. 2, 180, n. 2)

MOLL, A. (*cont.*)
   (1909) *Das Sexualleben des Kindes*, Berlin. (173, *n.* 2, 180, *n.* 2)
NACHMANSOHN, M. (1915) 'Freuds Libidotheorie verglichen mit der
    Eroslehre Platos', *Int. Z. Psychoanal.*, **3**, 65. (134)
PÉREZ, B. (1886) *L'enfant de trois à sept ans*, Paris. (173, *n.* 2)
PREYER, W. (1882) *Die Seele des Kindes*, Leipzig. (173, *n.* 2)
RANK, O. (1909) *Der Mythus von der Geburt des Helden*, Vienna (226 *n.*)
    [*Trans.: The Myth of the Birth of the Hero*, New York, 1914.]
   (1924) *Das Trauma der Geburt*, Vienna. (226 *n.*)
    [*Trans.: The Trauma of Birth*, London, 1929.]
RICHTER, J. P. (1939) *The Literary Works of Leonardo da Vinci* (2nd ed.),
    2 vols., Oxford. (260 *n.*)
RIEGER, C. (1900) *Die Castration*, Jena. (214)
ROHLEDER, H. (1899) *Die Masturbation*, Berlin. (185, *n.* 1)
SCHMIDT, R. (1902) *Beiträge zur indischen Erotik*, Leipzig. (9)
STRÜMPELL, L. (1899) *Die pädagogische Pathologie*, Leipzig. (173, *n.* 2)
SULLY, J. (1895) *Studies of Childhood*, London. (173, *n.* 2)
TARUFFI, C. (1903) *Hermaphroditismus und Zeugungsunfähigkeit* (German
    trans. by R. Teuscher), Berlin. (141 *n.*)    .
WEININGER, O. (1903) *Geschlecht und Charakter*, Vienna. (143 *n.*)
    [*Trans.: Sex and Character*, London, 1906.]
WERNICKE, C. (1900) *Grundr iss der Psychiatrie*, Leipzig. (54)

# LIST OF ABBREVIATIONS

| | |
|---|---|
| *G.S.* | = Freud, *Gesammelte Schriften* (12 vols.), Vienna, 1924–34 |
| *G.W.* | = Freud, *Gesammelte Werke* (18 vols.), London, from 1940 |
| *C.P.* | = Freud, *Collected Papers* (5 vols.), London, 1924–50 |
| *Standard Ed.* | = Freud, *Standard Edition* (24 vols.), London, from 1953 |
| *S.K.S.N.* | = *Sammlung kleiner Schriften zur Neurosenlehre* (5 vols.), Vienna, 1906–22 |
| *S.P.H.* | = *Selected Papers on Hysteria and Other Psychoneuroses*, 3rd. ed., New York, 1920 |

# ADDENDA

P. 4, bottom line. *Add after* 'years': We learn from Dr. Ernest Jones's biography of Freud (Volume **2**, p. 286) that the periodical to which the case history was first sent was the *Journal für Psychologie und Neurologie*. Its editor, Brodmann, declined to publish it, apparently on the grounds that it was a breach of discretion.

P. 200, line 25. *Add* Editor's Note: 'The two currents were discussed at length in the second of Freud's "Contributions to the Psychology of Love" (1912*d*).'

P. 207, lines 15–17. *For* 'affectionate current . . . sexual aim' *read:* 'two currents directed towards the sexual object and the sexual aim, the affectionate current and the sensual one', *and add:* Editor's Note: 'The last seven words were added in 1915.'

# GENERAL INDEX

This index includes the names of non-technical authors. It also includes the names of technical authors where no reference is made in the text to specific works. For references to specific technical works, the Bibliography should be consulted.—The compilation of the index was undertaken by Mrs. R. S. Partridge.

Component instincts (*cont.*)—
independent pursuit of pleasure by, 197, 199, 207, 233–4
order of emergence of, 241
repression of, and neurosis, 182, 202, 237, 238
theory of, 5, 277–8
Compulsive behaviour, 30,137, 189, 192, 211
Condensation, 92
*Confessions* of *Rousseau*, 193
Confusional states, 19, 104 *n.*, 254, 264
Consciousness, 15, 17–18, 55, 58–9, 114, 164–5, 175, 189, 228, 249–53, 266, 272, 276
Constipation, 101, 185–7
Constitutional factors (*see* Heredity and experience)
Contrectation, 169 *n.*, 180 *n.*
Conversion, hysterical, 53, 164, 249, 257, 272, 278
Convulsions, hysterical, 23 *n.*
Coprophilia, 155 *n.*, 161
Corporal punishment, 193
*Creusa*, 61
Cruelty (*see also* Sadism), 111 *n.*, 120, 157–60, 166–7, 169, 192–3, 200–1, 239 *n.*
Cultural development, 149, 177–8, 193, 225–7, 234, 242
*Cunnilinctus*, 151
Curiosity (*see also* Infantile sexual researches; Knowledge, instinct for; Scopophilia), 156–7, 192

Dark, children's fear of, 224
Day's residues as dream-sources (*see also* Recent impressions), 86–7, 96, 226 *n.*
Death, dreams of, 94, 97, 100, 110 *n.*
Defaecation (*see also* Faeces), 31, 32 *n.*, 152, 157, 186–7, 192, 196
Defence, 276, 278
Defloration phantasy, 99, 100, 104 *n.*, 110 *n.*
Degeneracy, 50, 138–9, 160, 174 *n.*, 236, 254, 263
Deliria, 23 *n.*
Delusions, 165 *n.*, 274–5, 286
Dementia praecox, 163
Depression (*see also* Melancholia), 24, 26, 30 *n.*, 54 *n.*, 254, 264, 287–8
Detumescence, 169 *n.*, 180 *n.*
Diphasic choice of object, 200

Diphasic onset of sexuality, 234
Disgust
and perversions, 151–2, 157–9,182
as force opposing sexual instinct, 127, 157, 159, 161–2, 164, 177–8, 191, 219, 231
hysterical, 27–31, 74, 84, 87, 90, 92
Displacement, 91–2, 102, 105 *n.*,114, 217
from lower to upper part of body, 29, 30, 83 *n.*, 183–4
Distortion, 251–2
Dora, case of, 3–122, 129, 286 *n.*
Dora's aunt, 19–20, 22, 38, 101, 105 *n.*, 110 *n.*
Dora's brother, 18, 19, 21–2, 51, 54, 64–5, 72, 82 *n.*, 92
Dora's father
character of, 18, 23–4, 34–5, 109, 118
death of (in dream), 94, 97–8, 110 *n.*
health of, 18–19, 20 *n.*, 38, 42, 57, 75, 80, 82, 84
relations with Dora, 18, 20–1, 23, 34, 37–8, 46, 56–8, 62, 80, 83, 86, 88–90, 108, 122
relations with Frau K., 25–6, 32–7, 42, 46–7, 54–8, 60, 62–3, 86, 88, 97–8, 108–9, 121
relations with his wife, 26, 65, 68–70, 79–80, 90–1, 98 *n.*, 106 *n.*
suicidal impulses of, 33
Dora's governess, 36–7, 60–2, 84, 88
Dora's grandmother, 78, 83 *n.*
Dora's mother
character of, 7, 26
relations with Dora, 20, 23, 56, 75–6, 90–1
relations with her husband, 26, 65, 68–70, 79–80, 90–1, 98 *n.*, 106 *n.*
Doubt, 17, 66 *n.*
Drama, 304–10
Dream-instigators
day's residues as, 86–7, 96, 226 *n.*
recent impression as, 71, 89, 92
sensory stimuli as, 284
Dream-interpretation, 10–13, 15, 67–8, 73, 114, 116, 252
Dreams (*see also* Death, dreams of; Forgetting of dreams; Recurrent dreams), 4, 67–8, 87, 89, 213, 226 *n.*, 296